Main Street
Renewal

ALSO BY ROGER L. KEMP

Forms of Local Government:
A Handbook on City, County and Regional Options (1999)

Local Government Election Practices:
A Handbook for Public Officials and Citizens (1999)

Managing America's Cities:
A Handbook for Local Government Productivity (1998)

Economic Development in Local Government:
A Handbook for Public Officials and Citizens (1995)

Strategic Planning for Local Government:
A Handbook for Officials and Citizens (1993)

Privatization: The Provision of Public
Services by the Private Sector (1991)

Main Street Renewal

A Handbook for Citizens and Public Officials

Edited by
Roger L. Kemp

McFarland & Company, Inc., Publishers
Jefferson, North Carolina, and London

The present work is a reprint of the library bound edition of
Main Street Renewal: A Handbook for Citizens and
Public Officials, *first published in 2000 by McFarland.*

LIBRARY OF CONGRESS CATALOGUING-IN-PUBLICATION DATA

Main street renewal : a handbook for citizens and public officials /
  edited by Roger L. Kemp.
      p.   cm.
  Includes bibliographical references and index.

  ISBN 0-7864-2659-4 (softcover : 50# alkaline paper) ∞

  1. Urban renewal—United States.   2. Central business
districts—United States.   3. Economic development.
I. Kemp, Roger L.
HT175.M35   2006
307.3'416'0973—dc21   00-22197

British Library Cataloguing-in-Publication data are available

Cover photograph ©2006 PhotoSpin.

Manufactured in the United States of America

*McFarland & Company, Inc., Publishers
  Box 611, Jefferson, North Carolina 28640
    www.mcfarlandpub.com*

To Jonathon,
may you always reach for the stars

Acknowledgments

Grateful acknowledgment is made to the following organizations and publishers for granting permission to reprint the material contained in this volume.

American Economic Development
  Council
American Planning Association
Community Development Society
Congressional Quarterly, Inc.
Government Finance Officers
  Association
HyettPalma, Inc.
International City/County Management Association
Intertec Publishing Corporation

League of California Cities
Maryland Municipal League
National Center for Small
  Communities
National League of Cities
National Trust for Historic
  Preservation
Small Towns Institute
The Atlantic Monthly Company
Urban Land Institute

Table of Contents

Part IV: The Case Studies

Part V: Conclusion

Preface

America's downtowns, typically located on Main Street in communities throughout America, were once the center of our lives. These downtowns were the places where families congregated on Friday nights, where young people went to the movies on Saturday nights, and where citizens went to church on Sundays. Our main streets, for these reasons, for many generations, served as the showcases of our nation's cities and towns. Conversely, they also served as society's window as to the quality of life in our communities. Through this window, one could see downtown as a gathering place for families, merchants selling goods to match local preferences and values, and professionals offering traditional services to families, merchants, and captains of local industry.

As we enter our civilization's third millennium, the state of our downtowns and the quality of life they provide to citizens has changed drastically over the past few decades. During the past generation, our transportation patterns have been drastically altered. Interstates, highways, and freeways have opened up the suburbs for unprecedented residen-

tial and commercial development. Our family living habits have changed from urban to suburban, from the city to what used to be the country. Our shopping preferences have also changed from patronizing those stores on Main Street to frequenting aggregations of retail stores in shopping malls. As the use of the automobile grew, parking downtown became a problem, while the suburban shopping mall was tailor-made for the automobile, with acres upon acres of readily accessible free parking.

In recent years, particularly the past decade, citizens have demanded that their aging main streets be brought back to life. Our municipal officials have responded to this challenge in a number of different and creative ways. Numerous strategies have evolved in recent years to revitalize our main streets, including the use of economic development incentives. While municipal officials can ensure the public's safety by hiring police officers and fire fighters, and they can rebuild the public infrastructure, other measures are needed to attract merchants and professionals to fill up vacant space on Main Street. Over the

1

past decade, the tools to rebuild our downtowns have evolved from a loose assortment of inducements to the use of many diverse, yet highly focused, incentive programs. In many cases, these incentives can be tailored in such a way as to achieve those goals desired by public officials as they rebuild their main streets.

The first section of this volume includes an introduction into the state of America's small cities, and provides a brief overview of their economic development programs as they relate to revitalizing our main streets. The actual steps required to get started with the downtown renewal process are also briefly examined. Current economic development trends and practices are reviewed based on a national study conducted by the International City/County Management Association. The survey results lend insight into how communities plan their economic development programs, the levels and sources of their funding, the types and number of people assigned to these programs, and to what extent they use performance measurements to determine program results. Since small businesses play such an important role on Main Street, issues facing small businesses are reviewed. This chapter also examines how to tailor assistance and incentive programs to address these issues. The chapters in this section provide the reader with insight into the evolving field of Main Street renewal.

The second section examines how communities should organize and manage their Main Street renewal programs. The results of a national study on how local governments organize for economic development set the stage for a detailed discussion on this topic. The

role of municipal government in the economic development process is examined. The author stresses that public officials at City Hall must be involved in the revitalization of their downtowns. Because of its importance, a chapter is included on precisely how to create partnerships between city government and small businesses. The various participants involved in this process, as well as their roles and responsibilities, are also highlighted. Public officials, prior to initiating a Main Street program, need to conduct a critical self-evaluation of their community to assess their commitment and involvement in this process. The concluding chapter of this section examines ways to manage development and growth, placing emphasis on sustainable community development practices, including preservation strategies.

The two longest sections are devoted to the tools available for Main Street renewal, and the actual case studies showing the successful application of these tools. These tools include, but are certainly not limited to, how a community should assess its development potential, requirements of the Community Reinvestment Act, ways to revitalize our main streets, practices to improve downtown safety, and the use of the Rehabilitation Tax Credit to attract investment. Chapters are also included on how to keep retailers on Main Street, the importance of parking facilities and the proper ways to manage them, how to use rural banks for economic growth, available small business development tools, methods to strengthen downtown businesses, and the use of tax increment financing. Eleven chapters examine the tools available for Main Street renewal. A discussion of these tools, however, would not be complete without showing how they have been successfully applied in our communities across America.

Case studies describe, among other things, how municipalities should evaluate and assess their Main Streets, the initial phase of a longer-range strategic planning process. Other case studies examine how to use plazas and public spaces to attract citizens, how residential streets can be brought back to life, what public officials should learn from the shopping malls, and how to use a community's available infill development potential. Public officials in a few municipalities have even created new Main Streets to foster a "sense of community." Some communities have carefully focused their attention on the use of architecture and building design criteria to attract downtown merchants and shoppers. Others have sought out specific types of retail development and tenants to match the needs of their citizens. One case study even examines how an old Eastern mill town was revitalized. In all, 18 case studies highlight the successful application of the Main Street renewal tools described in the previous section.

The communities examined in this volume are typically small ones, ranging in size from a few thousand citizens in rural locations to over 50,000 in a few cases like Santa Monica, California, and West Palm Beach, Florida. These cities are larger because they are located in highly congested metropolitan areas. Clearly, most of America's cities are not large population centers. The municipalities selected for this volume are typically very small by big city standards, and usually, with few exceptions, include those communities with populations under 25,000. The focus of this work is on ways to revitalize our Main Streets—

that single street that represents the very *essence* of our downtown. Geographically, those communities examined range from the west (California, Colorado, Washington) to the east (Massachusetts, New York, and Ohio), and from the north (North Dakota and Wisconsin) to the south (Florida, Georgia, Louisiana, and Texas), as well as the midwest (Illinois, Indiana, Iowa, and Kansas). In short, the cities and towns examined in this volume represent a healthy mix of small communities in virtually every geographic region of the United States.

The final section of this volume includes a chapter that provokes critical thinking about how local economic development programs are conducted as we enter the 21st century. Also examined are the private pressures brought to bear for incentive programs, and how local government officials can use them judiciously, keeping in mind their goal of serving the public's interest. Next, ten traditional myths about downtown revitalization are highlighted, along with seven secrets of downtown success. A national survey reveals that jobs and economic development scored high on the minds of community leaders across the nation. Slightly over one-half of the survey respondents felt that local public officials should be doing more in the area of municipal economic development. The final chapter stresses the importance of cities and suburbs working together, based on the strong justification that is provided for them to achieve the mutual needs of their local economic region. This study, conducted by the National League of Cities, proves that a positive economic linkage exists between center cities and the towns and communities that surround them. The bottom line is that it is in the best interest for cities and their suburbs to work together to achieve their economic development goals.

A listing of resource organizations for local economic development is provided in the Appendix. This listing categorizes resources into four main areas: general, business attraction, business retention and expansion, and tourism and retirement development. Two Internet resources are also listed. One provides on-line information about rural resources available to communities. The other provides access to the on-line resources provided by the National Center for Small Communities.

A comprehensive annotated bibliography on small city economic development is included. The brief narrative descriptions for each entry provide the reader with quick insight into the essence of each book contained in this selective bibliography.

The use of Main Street assistance and incentive programs has evolved primarily over the past few decades. They are typically applied in a piecemeal and incremental fashion by public officials from community to community, depending upon the unique set of inducements considered by individual municipalities. While federal and state law may limit the types of incentives that can be provided by communities, the need exists to codify the available information concerning those generally acceptable practices of local Main Street programs. This information must be made available to our local elected leaders, our municipal public officials, and, most importantly, to the citizens they represent. Most published works on eco-

nomic development practices deal with large cities and bid deals. This volume, on the other hand, deals with small towns and community-business partnerships. For this reason, this work is important because it is a collection of the best written resources available focusing exclusively on this topic.

I would like to personally thank representatives from the following national professional associations, research organizations, periodicals covering local government, and state municipal associations for providing the resources for this project and granting me permission to reprint the material contained in this volume. Professional associations include the American Economic Development Council, American Planning Association, Community Development Society, Government Finance Officers Association, International City/County Management Association, National Center for Small Communities, National League of Cities, Small Towns Institute, and the Urban Land Institute. Research organizations included the National Trust for Historic Preservation. Periodicals included *Governing*, published by Congressional Quarterly, Inc.; *American City and County*, published by Intertec Publishing Corporation; and *The Atlantic Monthly*, published by The Atlantic Monthly Company. Also, two state municipal associations, the League of California Cities and the Maryland Municipal League, allowed me to reprint articles from their respective journals.

Roger L. Kemp
Meriden, Connecticut
June 2000

PART I
Introduction

CHAPTER 1

The State of Small Cities

Virginia M. Mayer

While the elements of economic development are the same for all areas, the problems and basic characteristics of small towns and large cities differ. Local leaders should note these differences when crafting an economic development strategy for a community.

Charles Bartsch
Northeast-Midwest Institute[1]

It is difficult to define the state of small communities, those with populations of 50,000 or less, because their overall economic and fiscal conditions vary considerably. Some are faring better than others, but all are suffering as a result of the current recession, dramatic reductions in federal and state funding, and increasing burden of federal and state mandates. Declines in certain industrial sectors, including agriculture, energy, mining, timber, and manufacturing, have had devastating effects on some small communities who were economically dependent on them.

The deregulation of banking, transportation, and communications have,

according to some authorities, made the cost of doing business higher for smaller communities. Not only is the cost higher, but small communities don't always have the opportunity to fully operate in the global market. A level playing field is needed to ensure less disparity between small communities and larger cities.

In defining an economic development strategy, it is important to consider several characteristics of small cities and towns:

- More income is in the hands of the elderly.
- Job growth is dominated by the service producing sector.

Reprinted with permission from Small City Economic Development, *1991. Published by the National League of Cities, Washington, D.C.*

7

- The largest share of new jobs comes from small business.
- Most new jobs come from expansion and start-ups.
- Local economies are increasingly linked to international markets.

These characteristics represent both challenges and opportunities. For example, while the shift from manufacturing to a service sector economy presents challenges, more income in the hands of the elderly could result in sources of capital for new business in a small community that has a large elderly population.

Why Economic Development?

Economic development is a process of stimulating new activity—income and jobs. Economic development programs help communities adjust to changing economic times by:

- preserving and stimulating existing businesses;
- helping the community expand and diversify its economic base;
- removing barriers to economic growth; and
- encouraging new business growth in the community.

Local economic development is the term for the process in which local governments engage to stimulate or maintain business activity and employment. The principal goal of local economic development is to develop local employment opportunities in sectors that improve the community using existing human, natural, and institutional resources.[2]

Small city economic development, then, can be defined as the process of local economic development undertaken in a jurisdiction with a population of 50,000 or less and incorporating the special characteristics of small communities defined earlier.

How the Local Economy Works

It is critical that local officials in small communities understand how their local economy works so they can be successful in their efforts to generate jobs and income in their communities.

As a rule, local governments pursue economic development to assure growth in jobs and income for the future. Development strategies and programs aimed at local growth will succeed only if they relate to the factors that create growth. Consequently, it is important to examine the workings of a local economy and the reasons it expands. One way to analyze the local economy is through the flow of dollars and income. After all, the desire for income drives decisions about job growth, local business creation and expansion, capital investment, resource allocation, and production. A community's prosperity depends in large part on the level and distribution of local income.

Three factors set the income level of a community:

- the dollars flowing in from the outside,
- the likelihood that local dollars will be spent or invested locally, and
- the share of that spending that becomes wages, profits or other income for local residents.

The second and third factors determine the circulation of dollars through a local economy and the share of those dollars that will remain in a community as they are spent again and again. All three factors, taken together, show that local income levels depend both on a community's ability to attract outside dollars through its economy as well as spending and income. While this model oversimplifies actual circumstances, it provides a useful guide for exploring issues of local development and growth.[3]

Increasing Economic Activity

Glen Pulver, formerly an agricultural economist at the University of Wisconsin at Madison, proposes five general categories of strategies to increase economic activity in a community:

- Improve the efficiency of existing firms.
- Improve the community's ability to capture existing income.
- Encourage new business formation.
- Attract basic employers.
- Increase funding received from other levels of government.[4]

Each of these broad categories of strategies is worth looking at more closely.

IMPROVE THE EFFICIENCY OF EXISTING FIRMS

Businesses already located in a community are often overlooked by local government leaders, both in terms of assistance and potential opportunities for growth. Local leaders can help small businesses expand and keep local firms from closing or leaving the community by learning about the needs of these firms. Visit with local firms, ask about their future plans, identify assistance needs and work with the local firms to structure assistance programs. You will help your local businesses become more competitive and your local economy stronger.

IMPROVE THE COMMUNITY'S ABILITY TO CAPTURE EXISTING INCOME

Dollars flow in and out of a local economy. It is important to ensure that dollars are spent locally and economic out-flows or "leakages" are limited. Leakages refer to dollars spent in regional shopping centers and out-of-town businesses and wages earned by commuter work forces.

Ways to plug the income leaks in a community include surveying the community to identify holes and developing strategies for retaining income. Strategies may include downtown redevelopment, employee training programs, increased tourism, buy-local programs, and special events.

ENCOURAGE NEW BUSINESS FORMATION

Create a more entrepreneurial environment in your community. Most new jobs are created by local residents and businesses. Identify strategies to nurture startup and new business ventures. Some of those strategies might include forming capital groups to invest private funds locally, provide counseling and intensive education for those interested in forming new businesses, study the new market potential for service and retail businesses, and promote an entrepreneurial attitude within the community.

Six elements of a local environment that nurture entrepreneurial initiatives are:

- **Committed Local Leadership:** Leadership focuses attention on the crucial role of small businesses in the local economy.
- **Pool of Entrepreneurial Talent:** Pool includes successful entrepreneurs, potential entrepreneurs, and a skilled network of business professionals to support new business development.
- **Knowledge About Opportunities:** Identify the information needs of local businesses and potential start-up firms, including market information, new technologies, business practices and resources. Provide access to information.
- **Sources of Innovation:** Universities, technical colleges, and corporations.
- **Access to Capital:** Organize pools of capital locally, perhaps establishing venture capital networks where entrepreneurs can meet potential funding sources.
- **Community Spirit:** Civic pride, local image and attitudes, and the quality of life all contribute to the decision of a local resident to go into business.[5]

ATTRACT BASIC EMPLOYERS

While business recruitment is overrated in terms of its ability to produce income and jobs in most communities, it is a viable development option if it is pursued with some caution. Some communities focus their energies on attracting new basic employers, such as the service industries (including insurance, business services, telecommunications, tourism) and research and development facilities.

INCREASE FUNDING RECEIVED FROM OTHER LEVELS OF GOVERNMENT

Two forms of financial assistance are often discussed as ways to enhance funding in small communities: individual transfer payments (social security, public assistance and pensions) and community-level transfers such as grants, loans and contracts. Individual transfer payments are primarily spent locally on goods and services while grants, loans, and contracts fund work on infrastructure, education, and health programs.

Ways to increase this funding include monitoring government programs, educating the community about programs and resources available, and supporting initiatives that encourage a greater share of resources for the local level.

Challenges for Small Communities

It is in attempting to operate on a level playing field that small cities and towns find the greatest challenges. Some of them include:

- **The economic competitiveness of small communities is diminishing.** Small cities need to help existing businesses grow by improving marketing, management and financial services to existing businesses. Provide the necessary infrastructure and business support services to allow them to grow.
- **Small communities are dependent on too few sources of income.** Strategies to diversify the local economic base by encouraging business start-up are needed, in addition to strategies to capture dollars from outside through such means as tourism and retirees.
- **Small communities are more dependent on volunteer leadership.** Small cities and towns should seek ways to expand the pool of skilled community leaders, build the capacity of existing leaders, improve the support for existing leaders and attract/identify new leadership.

While these represent significant challenges, many small cities and towns have surmounted these challenges. How? The difference is local leadership and the level of community involvement and action.

Getting Started

How do you begin the economic development process in a small city or town? There are six steps which provide a framework for pursuing economic development.

1. **Determine the Role of Local Government in the Economic Development Process.** At the outset of an economic development process, local government must decide what role it wants to play in the process. The local government may want to take full responsibility for the planning and implementation of the community's economic development initiative. In some cases, the local government may have other agencies or organizations such as the Chamber of Commerce or a not-for-profit organization take the lead, with the local government providing financial or technical assistance. Or, a public-private partnership may be established where the local government and the private sector collaborate on the economic development programs.

The type of role is less important than the importance of the local government deciding its role. When deciding its role, the local government should consider the amount of control it desires, its fiscal and staff resources, and the match between the role and the ability to achieve desired goals.

2. **Analyze the Local Economy.** In addition to understanding how the local economy works—the inflow and outflow of dollars—it is important for local leaders to inventory their local business and labor sectors and to conduct a frank assessment of the community's strengths and weaknesses.

Studies have shown there is a significant lack of planning for local economic development in small cities and towns. Small communities need to be able to diagnose their current conditions. Through such an analysis, communities can determine realistic actions to take.

Collect data to determine the

current economic base. This will help target strategies and ultimately will serve as a benchmark for evaluating the results of your efforts. Information on local economic conditions should include an inventory of:

- existing businesses and their products;
- local labor force—age, skills, education levels, employment level, underemployed, underskilled;
- development sites, including business parks, vacant public real estate and the condition of all sites;
- physical conditions of the community, including the current state of infrastructure (infrastructure that is directly tied to business expansion, such as sewers and roads, as well as the infrastructure in downtown, such as sidewalks and parking, could affect investment in the community);
- quality of life, both real assets and perceptions; and
- opportunities or constraints for economic development.

In addition to inventorying local conditions, it is also important to gauge the impact of national phenomena on the community and to take this impact into consideration throughout the economic development process. The shift from a manufacturing to a service economy and the growth in world markets and global competition have affected small communities, some more than others. By incorporating these factors into your analysis, you will have a better context within which to develop a realistic local development strategy.

Local community colleges, universities, and state planning offices may be helpful in collecting information or in structuring a survey form to be used to conduct the research.

In addition to data collection, it is also important to conduct a frank assessment of your community's competitive advantage or entrepreneurial environment. Competitive advantage changes with international, national, state, and local economic and political circumstances, so it is critical to assess the community's competitive advantage regularly.

Ask a series of questions such as: What are the community's strengths and weaknesses? What is the source of economic decline or the source of growth? Who generates jobs locally? Where are the growth sectors in the community? What are potential growth sectors that don't currently exist but could be an outgrowth of current activity? What is the city or town's reason for being?[5]

3. **Identify Key Issues.** Once the community's profile has been developed, it is now possible to define problems to address and opportunities to explore. Issue identification is a continuing process that should be conducted regularly.

The key point for issue identification is to ensure that you are defining the actual issue or problem at hand and not the consequences of another problem. For example, many communities define lack of capital as a problem. But you need to be more specific. You need to define the purposes for which the capital will be used and why you have not been able to obtain the capital in the past.

Begin by defining what you are most proud of in your community. Then identify the issues you think need to be addressed in your community. At this point, goal setting becomes important. Identify the issues you are most likely to target for initial action. Are they in line with your community's overall objectives?

4. **Define Strategies.** Once you've identified the key issues that need to be addressed in your community, you can begin to define strategies to address each of the issues. A strategy is a compilation of individual programs and initiatives. For example, if you identified as an issue the need to encourage new business development, one strategy is to develop a more entrepreneurial environment in your community. You then need to define specific projects or initiatives that will collectively represent your strategy for creating a more entrepreneurial environment and ultimately will result in the creation of new businesses in the city or town.

5. **Define Implementation Plans.** Err on the side of action! Moving the plan from paper to action is often where many communities have trouble. Implementation requires the definition of specific programs or actions needed to achieve a goal. In addition to the actual programs, it is necessary to define resources and responsibilities for each initiative. Start small, with one well-defined problem, one strategy, and a few specific activities.

One way to do this is to use a form. On it you can list resources—people (and their skills, expertise, influence), physical assets (facilities, supplies, equipment), financial assets, and other resources. Then you can use the form to identify the resources you have and the ones you need (and where you will get them).

Fill out one of these resource inventories for each project. If you determine that you don't have the people or perhaps the financial resources necessary for the initiative, and you can't identify how you will get them, you can eliminate this program. This will save time and resources by eliminating programs that aren't feasible as early in the process as possible.

Once you have defined what is needed, it is necessary to define specific tasks. In addition to tasks, list the responsible party, the resources they have or will need and the projected completion date. This will help you keep track of each of your initiatives and keep your community plan active.

6. **Evaluate Your Efforts.** If it is going to sustain your efforts, the community must be able to feel progress if not see it. Economic development is a long-term process. By evaluating your efforts, you can constantly update your strategies and programs based on the results of your efforts. This keeps your economic development process alive and on target, and it helps keep local interest in your activities.

You can measure success in many different ways. Some communities measure success in terms of jobs created, jobs retained, increases in the local tax base, new businesses created and other statistical factors.

Another way to measure success is to conduct an evaluation of each community action. Define each of your objectives for a given period of time (a year, for example, or six months). Describe specifically what was accomplished toward each objective. Define the resources used (financial, work force, physical, etc.) and the people responsible for the effort.

This will enable you to keep a

record of what was accomplished and by whom. It is important to recognize all successes and those who helped make them happen. Because economic development is a long-term investment, you need to celebrate successes along the way to show you are making progress toward your goals. If an objective was not achieved, you can use this opportunity to assess the problems, correct them, and keep progressing toward your desired goal or objective.

Keys to Successful Economic Development

Local economic development is a long-term process, often made more difficult for small communities by the challenges outlined earlier in this chapter. The National Governors' Association's book *A Brighter Future for Rural America* outlined some keys to successful economic development that are applicable to small as well as rural communities.

- **Pro-growth attitude:** Develop unifying goals across the community and involve critical actors.
- **Sustained community effort:** Since there are fewer people to share the burden of activity, divide the tasks and encourage broader involvement.
- **Develop effective organizations and nurture existing organizations:** Assure continuity of efforts by involving a wider age range and including those who are negative.
- **External technical assistance:** Small communities often have a narrow knowledge base and are a greater distance from central sources of information and assistance. Get help when and if you need it.
- **Willingness to take risk:** Both the public and the private sectors need to be willing to take financial and political risks.
- **Comprehensive effort:** Help existing business, encourage start-ups, attract business, and capture dollars.
- **Practical Programs:** Develop practical programs including strong partnerships between government and business and including business visitation, financial, facility and information improvements.[6]

Local Leadership

Small cities and towns typically possess a significant amount of determination, energy and innovative spirit. Community leaders can make the difference between success and failure, particularly in small communities.

Local elected officials play an important role in framing the economic and social agendas for a city or town, often undertaking a delicate balancing act. Community leaders can identify the situation their city or town faces and place it within a larger context—such as the impact of the shifts in agriculture and manufacturing on a small community's economy. In a small community, the elected officials not only set these agendas, but they serve as the visionary, the designer, and the implementor.

While the local leaders of small communities reflect a great deal of energy and enthusiasm that often serve as a catalyst for action, there are inherent limitations within small communities as well. The leadership base is narrow. And the leadership base for economic development is even narrower.

In small communities, the elected officials usually serve on a volunteer basis, holding other professional jobs. Thus their own role must be greater in economic development initiatives than their counterparts in larger communities. They typically lack the full-time professional staff to plan and implement economic development programs.

Community leaders in small cities often find it difficult to identify and retain leaders for economic development because of the limited resource base and the attraction for young leaders to larger areas with stronger economic development climates. Training and capacity building for local leaders in small communities is critical, and it should be part of the community's plan to enhance its overall competitiveness. Because local elected leaders play such an important role in economic development, they need specific economic development training as well.

Local government is in a unique position to create and stimulate economic development. Municipal governments are familiar with the needs, resources, and characteristics of the community; they have access to and can mobilize all aspects of the community; and they can provide access to resources at other levels of government and in the private sector. Most important, local leaders can provide the vision on which all of this activity is based.

Summary

This chapter has looked at ways that small communities have used economic development to strengthen their local economies.

Armed with a broad understanding of the challenges faced by small cities and towns, the impact of the changing nature of world phenomena on small cities, a basic understanding of the workings of their local economy, and an outline of a planning and implementation process within which to undertake change in their communities, local leaders will be ready to select the appropriate economic development strategies for their communities.

Local economic development is both a challenge to be faced and an opportunity to be seized. It is up to the elected local leaders in small communities to define their economic development program and hence, their destiny. If they don't, someone else surely will.

Notes

1. Northeast-Midwest Institute. *Revitalizing Small Town America: State and Federal Initiatives for Economic Development.* Washington, D.C. 1990.

2. Blakely, Edward J. *Planning Local Economic Development: Theory and Practice.* Newbury Park, CA. 1989.

3. National League of Cities. *Economic Development: What Works at the Local Level.* Washington, D.C. 1989.

4. Pulver, Glen C. *Community Economic Development Strategies.* Madison, Wisconsin, University of Wisconsin Extension.

5. Gregerman, Alan S. "Rekindling the Future," *Commentary.* National Council for Urban Economic Development. Washington, D.C., Winter 1991.

6. National Governors' Association. *A Brighter Future for Rural America: Strategies for Communities and States.* Washington, D.C. 1988.

CHAPTER 2

Overview of Local Economic Development

James M. Banovetz, Drew A. Dolan, and John W. Swain

A preoccupation with economic development appears well on its way to replacing baseball as the national pastime of American communities in the twenty-first century. Given the dramatic increase of local interest in job creation, business expansion, and new-income generation, the importance of economic development in the strategic plans of local governments cannot be doubted. As concern over economic development has grown, smaller cities and counties have increased their economic development role, and recent research indicates a continuation of this trend.[1] As competition among communities for prospective business intensifies, the sophistication of economic development programs will also increase.

Both people and jobs are moving farther out, migrating to smaller communities. In his book *Penturbia*, Jack Lessinger describes this move of people and jobs from the suburbs to new and old towns distant from metropolitan areas. As examples of Penturbia, Lessinger points to such places as Whatcom County, Washington (eighty miles north of Seattle); Greene County, New York (one hundred miles north of New York City); and Adams County, Wisconsin (sixty-five miles northwest of Madison). This pattern is also described by G. Scott Thomas in *The Rating Guide to Life in America's Small Cities*, which evaluates the advantages offered to residents and businesses in 219 "micropolitan" areas found across the

Originally published as "Economic Development," Chapter 5 of Managing Small Cities and Counties, *1994. Published by the International City/County Management Association, Washington, D.C. Reprinted with permission of the publisher.*

United States. Communities such as San Luis Obispo, California; Corvallis, Oregon; Fredericksburg, Virginia; Wenatchee, Washington; Hattiesburg, Mississippi; and Ames, Iowa, rank high on Thomas's list of leading small places.[2] These communities are finding increased success in attracting new business operations while maintaining a high quality of life for residents.

A 1991 study by the National League of Cities (NLC), entitled *Small City Economic Development: Roads to Success*, examined economic development in cities with populations of 50,000 or less. The study found that small-town economic development programs are growing in number and sophistication and that smaller communities are doing what they can for themselves to shore up and expand their economic base. A 1991 American Economic Development Council (AEDC) study, as well as the NLC report, suggests that the economic development concerns of smaller communities are becoming increasingly similar to those of this nation's largest central cities.[3]

These concerns are developing particularly in larger urban areas such as Greater Cleveland, Ohio, where several smaller suburban communities are experiencing increased poverty, higher unemployment rates, and decreased tax revenues, prompting inner-ring suburbs such as Euclid, Garfield Heights, Brook Park, and others to mount new economic development programs aimed at restoring the economic health of their communities.

Many counties and smaller cities across the country face problems caused by major plant closings and other economic disruptions. For example, during the late 1970s and early 1980s, communities in Eastern Ohio, such as Martins Ferry, Bellaire, and Steubenville, were shaken by the closing of several major steel, chemical, and coal mining operations. Many smaller New England communities suffered major job and tax-base losses with the relocation of older textile mills. Petersburg, Virginia, an older Southern tobacco town, endured extreme losses when its major employer, Brown and Williamson, shut its doors in 1982.

However, the new wave of economic activism by smaller communities has been sparked by opportunities as well as problems. Communities with established economic bases are likely to experience pressures of both growth and decline in the future, as the supply of jobs expands and contracts in response to changes in the economy. Elected officials, economic developers, and planners must adopt more comprehensive approaches to economic development that enable the community to anticipate these phenomena and adjust to future changes.

Many local governments serving smaller cities and counties are faced with severe budget problems stemming from declining tax revenues, reduced intergovernmental support, and a slow national economy. This trend means that, as local governments prepare economic development programs, they must look increasingly at how economic development activities both add to and draw upon the local tax base.

Most definitions of economic development cite job creation, business expansion, new-income generation, and tax-base expansion as expected outcomes of local economic development efforts. Cities and counties seek these benefits in exchange for assisting businesses with facility expansion and location services. ICMA's 1989 survey of local government economic development activities indicates how commonplace this exchange of benefits is.[4] However, local governments' expectations have become more refined over time as communities target higher-quality jobs and business enterprises that are more compatible with community goals, values, and resources. Moreover, communities now seek to build more diverse, stable local economies that more fully support the local population. This chapter discusses these refinements and reviews trends shaping the present and future roles of economic development in counties and smaller cities.

An Integrated Approach to Economic Development

The central issue for local governments has shifted from the general decision of whether to get involved in economic development to much more specific choices about what goals to pursue and what programs and strategies to adopt to bring the greatest success in job and wealth creation. This shift indicates that city and county officials are beginning to view economic development as a more integral aspect of the community's overall strategy for community advancement. The AEDC study mentioned earlier confirms this direction and suggests that local practitioners and policymakers are adopting new, more integrated strategies designed to better link overall community well-being with economic development goals.

STRATEGIC PLANNING IN SMALL COMMUNITIES

Strategic planning and community consensus-building techniques are being employed by large and small communities alike in an attempt to get community, business, and government leaders involved. In short, strategic planning means a more systematic approach to economic development that recognizes the importance of internal (local) and external (regional, national, global) factors in the economic development process. As part of the strategic planning process, a community identifies critical issues and problems that might have an impact on the community and assesses its strengths, weaknesses, opportunities, and threats in relation to the critical issues. The process thus enriches the "information environment" in which a community's public and private sector stakeholders make decisions about how to use its resources to support job development, generate income, and increase tax collections. Better information contributes to better decision making.

Numerous smaller communities have prepared strategic economic development plans in recent years. For example, Mentor, Ohio (45,000), prepared a strategic economic development plan in 1986-1987 following the closing of three major industrial plants, which eliminated more than 3,000 well-paid jobs from the local economic base. Mentor, like many other smaller communities attracted to strategic planning, saw the need to take account of external issues in its analysis of future development options. The strategic planning process enabled the community to gain a broader prospective of its economic environment.

A 1990 survey of communities in the states of Montana, North Dakota, South Dakota, and Wyoming indicated that seventy-two of the ninety-eight communities surveyed (74 percent) used strategic planning to guide their development activities. The vast majority of the surveyed communities were very small in size.[5] Beulah, North Dakota, and Hutchinson, Kansas, represent two good examples of smaller communities combining strategic planning and consensus-building techniques to produce implementable city economic plans. Both communities allowed diverse groups to participate in the planning process.

Most cities included in ICMA's 1989 survey stated that business retention and expansion and business attraction were the top two priorities being pursued through their economic development programs. Downtown development, small business development, and economic base diversification were other top priorities identified in the survey. Strategic planning can help the city or county to develop effective responses to all of these issues.

TARGETING

As an element of strategic planning, targeting can help smaller communities identify those industries and jobs that best match community resources, goals, and values. This matching process serves to increase the long-term success of local economic development efforts. Because many companies focus on the larger regional area when making a decision to locate, it may be worthwhile for smaller communities to work with utility companies and other regional economic development groups in conducting target industry studies. For example, Utah Power and Light Company, which serves a wide range of smaller communities in Utah, conducts for them target industry studies based on different regions of the state. Local communities are actively involved in the implementation of study results and in working with prospective employers to evaluate the advantages of their communities.

Precise targeting of development opportunities is a common characteristic of economic development programs. A 1991 nationwide survey of almost 500 economic development organizations conducted by Growth Strategies Organization in Reston, Virginia, found that 92 percent targeted their business prospects.[6] Targeting is indicative of greater selectivity in the type of growth being encouraged by communities, a sign of the increasing sophistication of local programs.

Attracting and Retaining Business

Communities that develop a strategic economic development plan often identify as major goals the attraction of new business and the retention and expansion of existing business. After briefly introducing these topics, this section describes some of the activities that local governments in small communities may undertake in their efforts to attract and retain business. These activities include promoting downtown, small business, and workforce development; formulating and implementing a policy on economic development incentives; and marketing.

BUSINESS ATTRACTION

Many smaller communities have been successful in their efforts to attract new business operations. Such efforts have become increasingly important because companies are more mobile than ever, according to leading site location consultants such as PHH Fantus; CRS Sirrine; and Moran, Stahl, and Boyer. Business attraction efforts are becoming better integrated with other community economic development efforts, greatly improving their effectiveness.

Back-office relocations head the current list of hot recruitment targets for many smaller communities. Smaller communities are competing for the back-office operations—the routine clerical and administrative functions—of large manufacturing and service corporations, which in many cases have fled high-cost centers such as New York City and Los Angeles and relocated to small cities and counties. Citibank recently relocated its credit card processing operations from New York City to Sioux City, South Dakota. Scranton, Pennsylvania, has attracted back-office operations from Metropolitan Life Insurance, U.S. Fidelity and Guaranty, Warner Communications, and other large corporations.

Competition for manufacturing plants remains very keen, as states and communities work to improve their advantages and increase their attractiveness. Smaller communities are growing in popularity as locations for a wide range of manufacturing and service industries because of such factors as the lower cost of doing business, relative absence of the social and economic problems facing big cities, and availability of high-quality land resources. Small towns such as Bentonville, Arkansas;

Orrville, Ohio; Freeport, Maine; and Park City, Utah, have been put on the map by attracting and developing the corporate headquarters of major companies such as Wal-Mart, J.M. Smucker, L.L. Bean, and Mrs. Fields Cookies.[7] And smaller cities and counties are no strangers to the large Japanese auto manufacturers and their suppliers, who have chosen places such as Marysville, Ohio; Georgetown, Kentucky; and Smyrna, Tennessee, as locations for new manufacturing operations.

EXISTING BUSINESS RETENTION AND EXPANSION

A community's success in attracting new employers depends to a great degree on how successfully the community has taken care of existing businesses, and increased attention is now being given to the needs of those businesses. This added attention is reflected in new and improved services in areas such as workforce development, site location assistance, infrastructure improvements to accommodate existing industry growth, reducing local business operating costs, and streamlining government regulations related to local business operations.

However, smaller communities should not overlook the benefits to be gained in using outside resource groups such as the state government, colleges and universities, and regional planning organizations to organize and undertake retention and expansion activities.

Working with Utility Companies. Utility companies are valuable allies to local governments in conducting effective business retention and expansion programs. Telephone companies such as New Jersey Bell, Illinois Bell, and

Michigan Bell play an important role in helping smaller communities within their service areas to survey and assist existing businesses. A 1991 survey by GTE Telephone Operations indicates that business retention is a growing concern to the thousands of smaller communities the company serves across the nation.[8]

Working with state governments. Similarly, states can play an important role in this area, as evidenced by the role played by the Minnesota Department of Trade and Economic Development in the Minnesota Business Retention and Expansion Program. Almost ninety Minnesota communities currently participate in the program, relying upon it to help them retain existing companies. The Ohio Cooperative Extension Service has helped more than fifty smaller Ohio cities and counties to organize effective ongoing business retention and expansion programs. Most of these communities are located in rural or non-metropolitan locations, but some are suburbs of larger metropolitan areas.

Most communities strive for a healthy balance of residential, commercial, and industrial development. Toward this end, specific areas within the community are often targeted for development.

Downtown development. Downtown areas are the focal point for development of various types of retail and office space in many smaller communities. Key priorities in downtown development include retail business retention and attraction; street and building beautification and revitalization; consumer attraction; image building; security enhancement; promotion of tourism; and other actions that contribute to downtown viability.

Downtown business in many smaller communities is significantly affected by the development of regional shopping malls and other activities that draw shoppers away from the central business district. Often the only strategy that works in these cases is to re-establish the downtown area as a multi-use center providing for tourism, specialized retail shopping, government and local business offices, and other activities. This approach requires comprehensive planning by local government and private development groups.

Community-wide planning. Effective community-wide strategic planning helps city and county officials coordinate downtown development efforts with neighborhood and industrial development activities. Five smaller cities (Cranford, New Jersey; Longmont, Colorado; Morris, Minnesota; Roswell, Georgia; and Wharton, Texas) were identified as examples of successful and innovative downtown development efforts in the NLC's 1991 study on small city economic development.[9] The common denominator in all cases was a strategic and comprehensive approach to solving downtown development problems such as consumer attraction, street and storefront beautification, and crime reduction. This broader approach addresses both the internal, or local, factors (such as crime reduction) and the external factors (such as competition from regional shopping malls) that shape development prospects in downtown areas.

SMALL BUSINESS DEVELOPMENT

Most local economies are dominated by smaller businesses. A variety of programs have been created to strengthen the competitiveness of smaller companies and increase their contribution to local economic development. Business incubators, small business development centers, local entrepreneurial training programs, community-based seed and venture capital pools, and other resources have been created by local and state economic development organizations to assist smaller companies and entrepreneurs. Many of these programs are realistic possibilities for smaller communities to consider.

Business incubators are facilities used by many communities across the country. Originally these facilities offered low-cost commercial space for new firms; now they provide a variety of managerial and technical support to fledgling businesses. Many incubators have been started in older industrial facilities that have been rehabilitated to accommodate smaller companies.

Many other communities are developing new programs focused on helping smaller companies increase international exports, apply new technology to increase productivity and enhance product quality, and increase access to existing capital markets for both investment and working capital.

Targeting high-growth and technology-based smaller companies is becoming more common as an economic diversification strategy. *Inc.* 500 companies, which include some of the fastest growing companies in the country, are a regular target for prospect development efforts. Strategies to develop and attract smaller companies with direct links to the existing local economic base are becoming more common. These efforts focus on encouraging smaller companies that are suppliers or customers of exist-

ing local companies and industries to develop new facilities and jobs within the area.

WORKFORCE DEVELOPMENT

The quality of the local workforce is an increasingly important factor in business investment and location decisions. The issue is equally important to existing and new industries in evaluating the advantages of a community. To compete for new business opportunities, smaller communities must demonstrate that the local labor market can meet the future growth needs of business.

Working with education institutions. Local schools, colleges, and universities often need assistance from local governments in planning improvements to their education and training programs that focus on the local labor force. Local government economic development offices, because of their regular contact with business and industry, can provide educational institutions with useful advice on how to plan more effective training programs that meet the needs of local employers and residents. Several communities have used local community colleges extensively to address area labor needs. Reports by the National Council for Urban Economic Development and the Midwest Research Institute identify both urban and rural models for successfully drawing upon community colleges as economic development resources.[10]

Working with the private sector. Where private industry councils (PICs) have been formed to provide job-training services to area residents and employers, these programs should be integrated and coordinated with local economic development programs and other training resources such as those found at community colleges and vocational schools. Adams County, Colorado, is a very good example of how employment and training programs can be better linked to local economic development efforts. The Adams County Employment Center and the Adams County Economic Development Corporation coordinate their efforts to help existing industry and attract new companies to this suburban county near Denver by jointly identifying types of jobs to be developed in the future. Their efforts include promoting employment opportunities for recipients of public assistance.

Training and resource inventory. Local job-training programs, high-quality schools, college- and university-based training facilities, and other resources should be the first priority for communities preparing for future economic development. An inventory of nearby training programs and resources can be very useful to corporate human resource managers. The Greater Cleveland Growth Association, serving a seven-county area in Northeast Ohio, prepares such an inventory for use by its members and other businesses interested in training opportunities in the region. The inventory includes training resources found in several smaller communities in the area.

Workforce information. Accurate and current information about the local labor force should be included in marketing materials designed for business investors. These materials should include data on skill availability, wage levels and benefits, commuting patterns, and sources of new labor in order to allow corporate site selectors and their consultants to evaluate the area as a business location. An annual employer survey is a useful approach to collecting these data. Data collecting is another area in which utility groups can be helpful to communities. Illinois Power, for example, has developed a standardized survey to help communities in its service area collect employer data on a regular basis.

State employment service bureaus, like the Ohio Bureau of Employment Services, are important labor-market information sources for smaller communities preparing labor profiles of their areas. The Economic Development Program at Cleveland State University has been working with state officials to expand the availability and use of industry and employment data from Ohio's employment security agency files. A research database and network of statewide researchers are being formed to make this information available to local governments and other groups concerned with economic development and employment generation.

ECONOMIC DEVELOPMENT INCENTIVES

Communities and states across the country have used various public sector financing and tax incentives to encourage job creation and economic development, and many local government officials now face a "catch–22" situation in which they are criticized whether they use these tools or not. The incentive issue remains a difficult one as local government officials attempt to prepare their cities and counties for future job creation and business expansion.

Many businesses see these incentives as important to expansion and site location decisions, especially in economically distressed areas that may pose greater than average risks to successful operations. Economic developers and elected officials often believe that in order to be competitive in recruiting business they must offer incentives. Others, however, do not believe that public funds should be used to increase the profits earned by private parties, such as business owners and stockholders. Regardless of the position taken, it is essential that businesses know beforehand a community's policies on these matters. It will save much confusion and misunderstanding in the long run.

Perhaps local officials would find it helpful to think of the incentive issue in the larger context of the community's development goals. How can public and private sector investments be best used to finance development? It is important to think beyond the individual project level when setting policies on local economic development finance. At the same time, the policies established should have a positive impact on individual projects.

Impact of incentives. Academic and professional journals have been flooded with articles in recent years criticizing economic developers, planners, and elected officials for using incentives.[11] Other researchers raise concerns that incentives are unnecessary and waste taxpayers' money; they do not work the way they were intended; and they give to those firms receiving them an unfair advantage over those that do not. These are common issues that local officials must be prepared to deal with.

Although some studies have produced accurate and useful analyses of the impact of incentive programs, others are biased and fail to grasp ade-

quately the overall context in which development occurs. One of the most useful analyses of government develop-financing programs is a book by Timothy J. Bartik entitled *Who Benefits from State and Local Economic Development Programs?* Unlike many earlier researchers, Bartik finds that these programs produce a measurable benefit to local economies by redistributing jobs to high-unemployment areas and improving business productivity. His findings suggest that (1) state and local policies affect local growth; (2) local growth has long-term effects on the labor market; (3) faster growth helps educationally disadvantaged workers; and (4) state and local economic development is not a zero-sum game.[12]

Tax abatement. Although many earlier incentive programs—such as the federal Urban Development Action Grant Program (UDAG), Industrial Revenue Bonds (IRBs), and many state grant and loan programs—have disappeared, the use of locally approved tax abatement has grown significantly in states where abatements are legal. Tax abatement is a procedure used by local government to freeze real property taxes at a pre-development level for a period ranging from five to fifteen years. The community chooses to forgo collection of the additional tax revenues produced by the new investment in order to gain the advantages of new economic development. The advantage to the developer is a reduction in initial and ongoing operating costs, which improves the investment's profitability. After the abatement period, property taxes are assessed at the prevailing rate.

Critics claim that these abatements rob local school districts had local governments of the property tax revenues required to balance their diminishing budgets. Economic developers and elected officials using tax abatement contend that the tax revenues forgone through the abatement are more than recovered through the income and tax stream created by the investment.

A growing concern raised by critics is the use of tax abatement by economically healthy communities, especially suburbs, to encourage the relocation to their community of a plant or office from the central city or a neighboring suburb. They maintain that abatements should be used only in economically distressed areas that need additional help to develop new business and jobs. Those offering abatements maintain that the move is good for the company from a competitive standpoint and also good for the community from a job and tax standpoint.

Tax increment financing. As an alternative to tax abatement, some communities have used tax increment financing (TIF) to assist developers with initial development costs. The two are quite different in their impact on the developer and the community, and TIF is finding increased use. Basically, the technique uses the increase in property taxes from the development to help fund certain development costs such as infrastructure. These taxes are placed in a special fund, which is used to retire bonds issued to finance qualified site development costs. Tax increment financing is available to communities in twenty-four states.

State restrictions. State and local government officials in several states are re-examining the policies guiding the use of public financial and tax incentives. Newer approaches seek to limit the use of these programs to projects that clearly alleviate distress in the community and also provide an equitable return on the community's investment in terms of future jobs and taxes. Some groups are pushing for the outright elimination of these programs by state legislatures or the federal government. For the most part, these actions are seen as unrealistic. If taken, they could place a state or community at a serious competitive disadvantage for future business expansions.

MARKETING

Downtown development, infrastructure improvements, support for small businesses, education of the workforce, and economic incentives are all necessary parts of any program to attract and retain business, but marketing is also essential. The local economic development effort must include a comprehensive strategy to promote the community as an attractive location for business. After a realistic assessment has been made of the community's assets and liabilities, local government officials should devise a plan to present the community as a potential site for appropriate businesses and industry. A 1989 economic development marketing study completed by Cleveland State University for AEDC found that public-private partnerships play a key role in this area. Innovative marketing programs were identified in smaller cities such as Gadsden, Alabama; Savannah, Georgia; Spartanburg, South Carolina; and Joliet, Illinois.[13]

Regional Approaches and Strategies

As communities increase their efforts to attract and retain business, the competition for economic opportunities grows. Communities have thus become aware that the characteristics of different localities and the benefits they offer (for example, an attractive physical environment, a skilled workforce, a good educational system, and economic development incentives) have a major impact on a company's decision concerning where to set up or expand a business. Community officials are also more aware of the interdependence of places: what happens in one area has an impact on others. A plant opening or closing in one city can help or hurt the economic base of a neighboring community, especially within specific regions, where related firms and industries may cluster, or where a business operation in one community draws a significant part of its workforce from nearby communities.

This growing realization of the interdependence of places has led to a trend toward a regional approach to economic development. Smaller cities and counties sharing the same economic region have much in common with one another. These common interests and resources are good reasons for communities to cooperate with one another in increasing economic opportunities. The trend toward regionalism is reflected in an array of new economic development programs and policies. Growth management planning, cooperative approaches to regional development marketing, tax-base sharing, coordinated regional infrastructure planning, and other strategies are receiving greater attention from smaller cities and counties.[14]

REGIONAL DEVELOPMENT

A number of state governments are encouraging regional cooperation by communities. Ohio recently opened twelve regional economic development offices across the state that help local officials receive state assistance with development projects. Each of Ohio's eighty-eight counties has prepared and submitted plans outlining its top development priorities. Many relate to local infrastructure and environmental cleanup needs. The Ohio regional offices are intended to expedite state assistance and serve as catalysts for regional cooperation. The offices report significant progress toward both goals.

Other states, including Illinois, Virginia, New York, and Indiana, have also implemented strategies for regional economic development. Illinois's Corridors of Opportunity Program provides a geographic and industrial focus for economic development across the state. The industry-targeting component of the program focuses on high-technology, automotive, agribusiness, service-sector, and tourist industries in various regions. The Southern Illinois Corridor, composed of a twenty-county area in the southern part of the state, is heavily focused on development of tourism but also encourages growth in industries such as production of secondary wood products and poultry farming. Most of the corridors encourage smaller communities to join forces in marketing for job creation and business investment.

Virginia established regional planning and development districts in the 1960s. These regions encourage intercommunity cooperation in setting broader priorities related to economic development. A recent report by the Joint Legislative Audit and Review Committee of the Virginia General Assembly found that these districts have reduced the fragmentation of economic development efforts by localities and contributed to more efficient and effective use of limited resources. Predominantly smaller cities and counties are served by these districts.

TAX-BASE SHARING

Interest in regional tax-base sharing arrangements is growing in several states. Although many political and management problems hamper the use of these approaches, several communities are using them or considering their use. For example, the city of Bloomington, the town of Normal, and McLean County, Illinois, developed a plan for sharing costs and tax revenues in connection with a plan that brought a major new automobile assembly plant to the community. Generally, tax-base sharing describes a situation in which two or more local governments share the tax revenues generated by future economic growth. As a policy initiative, this strategy aims to reduce disparities and competition among local governments, encourage long-range development planning, stabilize local tax revenues, and enhance the capacity of local government to meet future service and infrastructure needs.

The Minnesota Fiscal Disparities Program, created in 1971, was the first known program for local tax-base sharing. More recent programs have been created in Wisconsin, Michigan, and other states. Under Ohio law, cities can enter into a contract to establish a joint economic development zone and share the costs and tax revenues resulting from development within the zone. Several cities are now exploring the use of such zones. Sub-state programs have been created in Louisville–Jefferson County,

Kentucky; Hackensack, New Jersey; and selected other places.

Public-Private Partnerships

Public-private partnerships are playing a much larger role in an increasing number of counties and smaller cities. In these partnerships, public and private sector resources come together to promote the development of existing industry and to attract new business. Nearly 30 percent of all communities responding to ICMA's survey had partnerships in place. Another 25 percent of respondents reported that private business groups such as chambers of commerce had taken the lead in their community.[15]

Local government is a key actor in these partnerships. It plays several roles in the local economic development process, such as helping businesses to expand and develop through site location assistance, infrastructure improvements, and various economic incentives and ensuring that development projects are consistent with laws, regulations, and community values.

The form (or organization) of a public-private partnership should always follow function (tasks and goals). Too many communities select an organizational form before defining the job to be done. As a result, many self-inflicted problems arise that limit success. A very common problem is that the organization excludes certain key stakeholder groups from the economic development process. The right people—including representatives of government agencies, businesses, community groups, and the educational establishment—must be involved to get the job done right.

Globalization

As the trend toward globalization brings countries closer together, foreign business investment in the United States has grown, and a significant number of international companies make investments each year in smaller communities. Overall, British and Canadian companies have made the largest number of these investments; however, Japanese companies have had the highest increase in the rate of new investments in recent years. States like Ohio, Indiana, Kentucky, and Michigan have experienced rapid growth in this area, particularly in the automotive sector; hundreds of Japanese auto manufacturers and their suppliers have located in these states.

The majority of investments have occurred in smaller cities and counties.[16] Some of them, such as Madisonville, Kentucky (16,800) have aggressively promoted themselves as locations for foreign business. Madisonville has implemented an attraction program aimed at specific industry targets, zeroing in on Dutch and Canadian companies. The program has been highly effective. Two Canadian firms have located in the community since 1990, and in 1993 the city hosted a Dutch-American golf tournament to attract Dutch business leaders, twenty of whom attended and learned about the advantages the city has to offer for future investment.

More communities and states are helping local companies to increase their share of the global marketplace. Export development programs are common in state development agencies and large metropolitan development organizations. Although smaller communities tend not to operate their own export promotion programs because of the lack of economy of scale, development officials in these communities are working with state and regional groups to offer trade development services to interested businesses. Because these services help existing companies to increase their market, they can be considered tools for the retention and expansion of existing business.

Growth Management

Although most small communities still rank economic development and growth among their goals, many realize that unchecked economic development can have negative as well as beneficial effects. Possible negative effects are overcrowding, environmental and aesthetic degradation, increased demand for services, and overburdened infrastructure. For many smaller communities, therefore, the concern has shifted from encouraging growth to managing growth.

The greatest growth pressure comes from housing, retail, and office development. Communities in California, Florida, and the Northern Virginia area experienced extreme development pressure in the 1980s, causing them to become more selective about what type of growth to encourage. States such as Colorado and Oregon have long maintained tight control over development for environmental and aesthetic reasons. Interest in growth management is growing in many other states as well, and not just in those growing most rapidly. Common objectives are to alleviate congestion and crowding caused by high density; to reduce or avoid environmental degradation; and to provide equitable ways to finance infrastructure improvements required by new development projects.

The range of growth management techniques includes tighter enforcement of environmental regulations; development transfer rights; restrictive covenants; subdivision regulations; exactions; various tax and free systems, including development impact fees; large-lot zoning; conservation zoning; and development moratoriums. The use of these techniques should be defined by the community's overall development plan or strategy. Smaller communities may find it beneficial to examine the experience of communities already using these growth control strategies, such as Fairfax and Loudoun counties in Virginia; Dade and Orange counties in Florida; Prince George's and Montgomery counties in Maryland; and the city of Petaluma, California.

Growth management is also a concern in "new" communities such as Reston, Virginia, and Columbia, Maryland. A recent Urban Land Institute study examined the experiences of fifty-eight new communities across the country. The study found master planning, coupled with various other techniques, to be a common strategy for managing growth in these communities.[17]

Conclusion

It is difficult to offer general advice applicable to the thousands of counties and smaller cities found across the country. Nevertheless, these communities may want to consider the following observations.

America's smaller communities are prime candidates for future growth. This is evident from past and current patterns of commercial and industrial development. Moreover, many of these localities already recognize their potential and are working hard to achieve it. The rich and diverse array of programs and strategies identified by the studies reviewed in this chapter suggest that economic developers, planners, and elected officials serving these communities are open to experimentation and innovation.

Several authors, including David Osborne and Ted Gaebler, have written about the need to reinvent government and make government units more entrepreneurial.[18] Already, many established and emerging smaller communities around the country reflect an entrepreneurial spirit not unlike that of the entrepreneurs who are building America's fastest-growing and most exciting businesses, and the widespread use of public-private partnerships to achieve local government goals is one obvious manifestation of that spirit. Hard work lies ahead for communities that follow this path, but initial developments are encouraging. For example, more communities are devising and implementing strategic plans to guide their economic development efforts. More communities are concerned about the creation of higher-quality jobs that offer residents a respectable living standard. Finally, many communities are focusing increased attention on helping existing businesses to become more competitive through workforce development, improvements in current technologies, and expanded opportunities for international sales. If these preliminary efforts hold true, the new, more entrepreneurial approach to government will have a positive impact on these communities' economies.

Those individuals guiding economic development efforts in smaller communities are more professional and strategic in their approach than earlier generations of economic development practitioners working in the public sector. This improvement is due at least in part to the efforts of national associations such as ICMA, the National Council for Urban Economic Development, AEDA, and others that provide valuable opportunities for local practitioners to increase their knowledge and sharpen their skills.

Current indications point to a greater reliance on regional approaches to economic development, which will call upon counties and smaller communities to work more closely with their neighbors to improve local resources and develop new opportunities. New regional development programs, like the one launched by the Ohio governor's office and department of development, offer the promise of more intergovernmental cooperation in economic development. Increased cooperation is especially important in light of shrinking budget support for infrastructure and educational improvements.

Counties and smaller cities must strike a balance between promoting and managing growth in the future. Although this need is especially evident in fast-growth areas, it will be more necessary in slower-growth environments as well. New environmental regulations addressing issues such as wetlands, solid waste disposal, and other problems will represent new challenges for local governments concerned about achieving economic growth in an environmentally conscious time. Limited funds for development-related infrastructure will contribute to more growth management as well.

Smaller community economic development programs must address issues associated with both economic growth and decline in the future. Even growing communities must be ready for possible plant and office closings that dislocate workers and reduce the local tax base. A slower national economy and the impact of broader social, economic, political, and technological events can introduce new pressures for local economic change.

Competition for economic development opportunities is expected to remain keen in the future. Smaller communities fared reasonably well in this competition in the past decade. Future competition will require even better-focused strategies that link community resources and development opportunities. The key in the future will be to sustain growth and achieve long-term community stability. This challenge goes beyond simply keeping existing employers and attracting a sufficient number of new ones. It requires that economic development activities be more closely coordinated with other community priorities such as education, quality of life, and environmental management.

In general, smaller communities have much to be encouraged about in considering their future economic health; nevertheless, hard work lies ahead.

Afterword

Economic development may not replace baseball as the national pastime, but it surely has become the biggest game in town for the governments of small cities and counties. In fact, Kane County, Illinois, used economic development techniques creatively when it purchased a minor league baseball team in a successful effort to make residents aware of the county as a community. Kane County's efforts also demonstrated the importance and value of strategic planning, not only for economic development, but more important, for community development.

The communities that ultimately win at the economic development game will be those that employ strategic planning and economic development as tools to achieve a predetermined set of community goals. When thus employed, economic development contributes to the task of building a better community, and development of the total community is, after all, the ultimate purpose of any economic development activity.

Notes

1. See Cheryl Farr, "Encouraging Local Economic Development: The State of the Practice," in *Municipal Year Book 1990* (Washington, DC: ICMA); Donald Haider, "Place Wars: New Realities of the 1990's," *Economic Development Quarterly* (May 1992); John P. Pelissero and David Fasenfest, "A Typology of Suburban Economic Development Policy Orientations," *Economic Development Quarterly* (November 1989); *Small City Economic Development: Roads to Success* (Washington, DC: National League of Cities, 1991); and Harry Black, *Achieving Economic Development Success: Tools That Work* (Washington, DC: ICMA, 1991).

2. See Jack Lessinger, *Penturbia* (Seattle, WA: SocioEconomics, 1991) and G. Scott Thomas, *The Rating Guide to Life in America's Small Cities* (Buffalo, NY: Prometheus, 1990).

3. See American Economic Development Council, *Economic Development Tomorrow: A Report from the Profession* (Chicago: 1991).

4. See Cheryl Farr, "Encouraging Local Economic Development."

5. See Michael Fladeland, "Strategic Planning in Communities in North Central States," *Economic Development Review* (Summer 1991)

6. See Ross M. Boyle, "Summary of 1991 GSO Survey Responses on Targeting Practices of Local Economic Development Organizations" (Reston, VA: Growth Strategies Organization, 1992).

7. See David A. Heenan, *The New Corporate Frontier: The Big Move to Small Town, USA* (New York: McGraw-Hill, 1991).

8. See Nancy Williams, "Community Agenda for the 1990's: A Corporate View," *Economic Development Review* 9 (Summer 1991).

9. See *Small City Economic Development* (Washington, DC: National League of Cities, 1991).

10. See CUED, *Community Colleges: An Economic Development Resource* (Washington, DC: December 1989) and Midwest Research Institute, *A Portfolio of Community College Initiatives in Rural Economic Development* (Kansas City, MO: April 1989).

11. Many articles on this topic have appeared in the last two or three years in *Economic Development Quarterly*.

12. See Timothy J. Bartik, *Who Benefits from State and Local Economic Development Programs?* (Kalamazoo, MI: W.E. Upjohn Institute for Employment Research, 1991).

13. In 1989, the Economic Development Program at Cleveland State University conducted a national study of how cities and urban areas marketed themselves for economic development. The findings were published in a monograph by the American Economic Development Council entitled *Marketing Cities in the 1980's and Beyond: New Patterns, New Pressures, and New Promises* (Chicago: 1989).

14. See David A. Heenan, *The New Corporate Frontier*.

15. See Cheryl Farr, "Encouraging Local Economic Development."

16. See Donald T. Iannone, "Policy Implications of Foreign Business Recruitment as an Economic Development Strategy: The Case of Japanese Automotive Investment in the United States," *Economic Development Review* 6 (Fall 1988).

17. See *Developing Successful New Communities* (Washington, DC: Urban Land Institute, 1991).

18. See David Osborne and Ted Gaebler, *Reinventing Government: How the Entrepreneurial Spirit Is Transforming the Public Sector* (New York: Addison-Wesley, 1992).

CHAPTER 3

Trends and Practices in Local Economic Development

Adam J. Prager, Philip Benowitz, and *Robert Schein*

Local economic development has made considerable strides over the last few decades. Whereas formal, professional efforts to influence local economic direction and growth were once primarily the domain of states and major cities, today economic development programs can be found in virtually every level of government and throughout the private sector.

Although certain economic development programs around the country have evolved in a systematic fashion, the majority in United States have developed in response to economic change. As a result, two commonalities can be found among most programs, regardless of their sophistication or geographic orientation. First, economic development programs are considerably more reactive than proactive. They tend to respond to the shifts in local or regional economies and attempt to alter or enhance economic trends. Second, economic development professionals today are more in tune with the needs of the end-user, or target audience, than in the past.

At one time economic development programs were dedicated primarily to the attraction of industry, with little thought given to industry retention or expansion. Furthermore, government-dominated programs emphasized the resources and location advantages that

Originally published as "Local Economic Development: Trends and Prospects," Chapter 3 of Municipal Year Book, *1995. Published by the International City/County Management Association, Washington, D.C. Reprinted with permission of the publisher.*

they could readily offer rather than those of most importance to their target audiences. The work of today's economic development professionals is rapidly becoming market driven, with programs and delivery mechanisms implemented that are responsive to the demands and desires of the business community.

Economic development today offers much more of a continuum of services than previously, with the provision of services carrying over after the local business investment has been made. Responsive stand-alone programs dedicated solely to existing industry are relatively rare today at the local level; however, they are evolving faster than any other facet of the economic development profession. Additionally, with considerable private sector influence, economic development programs have become more flexible and customer-driven than in the past, offering services that are requested rather than merely those readily available or easily accessible.

ICMA conducted an economic development survey to understand better the level of commitment and focus of local government economic development programs. This chapter uses the survey results to describe economic development funding, staffing, and participation levels; program planning and direction; and use of performance measures. It provides insight into economic development program variations by community size and geographic location within the United States.

Survey Methodology

In 1994, ICMA conducted a mail survey on local government economic development. In May 1994, the survey questionnaire was sent to all cities and counties with populations 2,500 and over and to those cities and counties under 2,500 that are recognized by ICMA as providing for an appointed position of professional management. In July 1994, a second mailing was sent to those local governments that did not respond to the first mailing. Of the 7,135 cities surveyed, 20% responded; 12% of the 3,108 counties responded.

Approximately 80% of more than 1,700 survey respondents are from municipalities; the rest are from counties. Approximately half the local governments responding have populations between 5,000 and 25,000, which reflects the overall survey universe. Only 7% of the respondents are from communities with populations over 100,000, which also mirrors the survey universe.

All geographic divisions throughout the United States are well represented by the survey respondents, with the greatest representation from communities in the North Central and South Atlantic divisions. Central cities account for 10% of total respondents, with suburban and independent locations accounting for 46% and 44%, respectively.

Economic Overview

Successful development strategies are contingent upon a strong grasp of the current economic climate as well as on an ability to anticipate future changes and trends. For example, the decision to invest funds in a campaign to promote tourism must be predicated upon certain assumptions about future spending patterns by population segments in different markets. The long-term outlook is an essential part of any examination of economic development policies at the local level. The way local governments understand present conditions and anticipate future trends provides insight into the rationale behind many economic development policies. Three important elements in those policies are the commitment of a locality to a particular industry or sector of the economy, the economic outlook of the locality, and particularly relevant national trends or policies that may have an impact on the economy of a locality.

PRIMARY ECONOMIC BASE

Survey respondents were asked to identify the economic base of their local government over the last five years and to predict the economic base for the next five years. Residential and manufacturing economic foundations have supported the economy for 24% and 23% of the respondents, respectively, followed by combined retail/service economies (18%). The survey results suggest that many local areas believe that agriculture will no longer occupy a position of prominence in their communities. Over the last five years, this sector has been the primary economic base for 17% of survey respondents. However, only 12% of the communities in the survey indicate that agriculture will retain this position during the next five years.

These trends are also reflected across population groups. With only one or two negligible exceptions, fewer cities and counties of all sizes anticipate that either manufacturing or agriculture will be the core of their economic base during the next five years. Similarly, almost all population groups show an increase in the number of localities where either the tourism/hospitality or the retail/service sector is expected to be the main source of economic activity over the next five years. It is anticipated that the decline in the agricultural base will be felt nationwide because the percentage of jurisdictions listing agriculture as the main sector of their economy dropped in all population groups and geographic divisions.

Several developments are worth noting. Among cities and counties with populations from 100,000 to 500,000, the prominence of manufacturing is expected to decline dramatically. Whereas 30% of those localities indicate that manufacturing was their primary economic base over the last five years, only 18% predict that the sector will have such a status during the next five years. Meanwhile, 49% of these local governments expect that retail/service will be their top industry in the next five years, up from 35% during the previous period.

The survey suggests that the retail/service and tourism/hospitality sectors will see increased activity as more and more jurisdictions rely upon them to be growth engines for their economies. The retail/service segment is expected to be the largest portion of the economy for 21% of localities in the next five years, up from 18% over the previous period. Tourism/hospitality will be the top industry in the economies of 8% of the cities and counties during that period compared to 5% over the last five years. These changes are likely to occur in all geographic divisions of the country.

Among the other sectors of the economy, differing geographic trends are evident. Overall, the percentage of cities and counties that expect manufacturing to be their primary economic base for the next five years is slightly lower than the percentage that relied on manufacturing during the previous five years. Manufacturing is expected to lose its prominence in a number of New England and Mid–Atlantic jurisdictions but maintain its position elsewhere. It should be noted that although manufacturing is expected to slip overall, more than 46% of respondents pick this sector as the one they would most like to attract in the future.

Though the manufacturing industry may be the most economically desirable, it is apparently one of the most difficult to attract. Although over 70% (1,133) of reporting jurisdictions identify manufacturing as the focus of their economic development efforts (the highest of all sectors), few jurisdictions expect to register substantial gains in this area in the future. A significant amount of resources and effort are necessary simply to keep existing companies from relocating. Companies' willingness to shift the location of their operations has been previously demonstrated by the movement of many manufacturers from large urban industrial centers to the cheaper land of the suburbs. Given the mobility of this sector, the 23% of localities that listed manufacturing as their primary economic base for the next five years may find themselves struggling to meet their expectations for future economic growth.

One surprising result of the survey is the relative stability in the institutional category, which comprises government, military, and nonprofit organizations. Six percent of respondents describe their economic base as institutional during the last five years. This percentage dropped only slightly, to a little more than 5%, for the next five years. Given the difficult fiscal conditions local governments face across the country and the widespread acceptance of the need to adjust the size of the workforce at all levels of government, a more significant decline in this category may have been expected. Several factors may be at work. First, the number of respondents affected by military base closings was relatively small (4%). Second, future reductions in the governmental labor force may be offset by increases in employment in the not-for-profit community as the nongovernmental sector assumes a greater responsibility for "public sector" services. Finally, if the composite term *institutional* had not been used and separate categories for *military, nonprofit*, and *government* had been established instead, a sharp decline in government employment and an increase in nonprofit employment could probably have been traced.

OVERALL ECONOMIC GROWTH

It remains to be seen if the shift away from agriculture to more service-related sectors will put communities in a stronger economic position. Most of the respondents seem to think that their economies will improve in the future. In fact, local governments are extremely optimistic about their prospects: 82% believe they will experience some amount of growth over the next five years, even though only 68% registered any growth during the past five years. This optimism is exhibited in all geographic divisions of the country. Nevertheless it is somewhat surprising given the fiscal difficulties that localities have faced in the past few years and the generally conservative nature of their economic forecasting as influenced by bond-rating agencies. In this case, survey respondents may have perceived dire economic predictions to be self-defeating and therefore decided to err on the side of optimism.

The number of medium- to large-size cities projecting future economic growth is staggering. Ninety-two percent of large cities and counties (250,000 and over in population) predict some amount of growth during the next five years. Forty-six percent of jurisdictions in this population category expect growth of 10% or more. Slightly over 93% of medium-size jurisdictions (from 50,000 to 250,000 in population) are forecasting growth for the upcoming period.

There is substantial disparity among geographic divisions as to overall economic outlook. In five geographic divisions—East North Central, South Atlantic, East South Central, West South Central, and Mountain—at least half the localities predict economic growth of more than 10%. The survey indicates that localities in the East South Central division are in much better shape than their counterparts elsewhere in the country. This area had the largest number of rapid and moderate growth areas over the past five years and is expected to maintain a similar status during the next five years. The West South Central division respondents expect to have the greatest increase in economic growth, with 83% of the local governments forecasting growth in the upcoming period, whereas only 62% experienced such gains over the past five years.

The Mid–Atlantic and New England Divisions lag far behind, with only 25% and 26%, respectively, of localities in these divisions forecasting moderate to rapid expansion (rate of 10% and above). Jurisdictions in these areas have the least amount of land area zoned for commercial, industrial, and manufacturing uses. Conversely, jurisdictions in the Mid–Atlantic and New England divisions have the greatest percentage of land available for residential use. The percentage of localities focusing on manufacturing in their economic development efforts is also the smallest in these divisions. Such factors suggest that in their effort to overcome a relatively bleak economic outlook, the New England and Mid–Atlantic divisions should at least reexamine their land-use policies.

Impact of NAFTA

If survey respondents have the ability accurately to predict the twists and turns of their local economies, then a period of economic expansion is imminent. Local governments will have to be well prepared for many of the negative implications of growth, however, especially those that expect moderate or rapid growth. Depending upon the sectors driving economic resurgence, governments may experience greater strains on their already limited resources for infrastructure repair and expansion, pollution control, and public safety. The public sector faces the challenge of channeling growth into areas that maximize local tax bases but create minimal demands for costly enhancement of services.

Last year, a controversial treaty ratified by Congress was the North American Free Trade Agreement (NAFTA), which reduces trade barriers among the United States, Canada, and

Mexico. During consideration of the NAFTA legislation, one of the most heated issues was the eventual impact of NAFTA on American jobs. This debate was largely conducted at a national level, and its focus was on the effect of the agreement on the country as a whole. Given the disparity of opinions on this issue, it seemed that an examination of NAFTA from a local angle might provide new insight and reveal what changes, if any, city and county governments expect it to bring.

The survey shows that the majority of responding local governments (55%) believe that NAFTA will not affect their jurisdictions.

To the extent that NAFTA is expected to have an impact on localities, that impact is generally considered positive—either through job creation or increased revenues from U.S. exports. Furthermore, a greater percentage of large- and medium-size cities and counties believe they will be in a position to reap economic benefits from NAFTA than do their smaller counterparts.

Predictably, some of the most interesting variations in the survey data are geographic. Local governments in the West South Central and Mountain divisions believe they will be the prime beneficiaries of NAFTA as it pertains to employment. Of localities in the West South Central division, 48% report NAFTA will create jobs in their areas, compared with 4% indicating it will cause job losses. In the Mountain division, 37% of the respondents indicate NAFTA will increase the number of jobs, while 7% predict it will cost jobs. The East South Central division is the only area where the percentage of localities forecasting job loss as a result of NAFTA (25%) exceeds the percent expecting increases in employment (19%).

Although most localities do not believe that NAFTA will have an impact on them, the survey also indicates that many areas stand to gain from it. All this suggests that many local economies are not positioned to take advantage of the liberalization of trade restrictions NAFTA contains. The facts that respondents in West South Central division jurisdictions see themselves as the primary beneficiaries of job creation through NAFTA; that 37 out of the 137 jurisdictions responding from this division report moderate or rapid growth for the last five years, and that 70 of the 137 expect moderate or rapid growth for the next five years may be no coincidence. Certainly proximity (to Mexico) of the states in this division gives them a locational advantage, but no more so than those several geographic divisions that share borders with Canada.

Theoretically, the parts of the country that should benefit most are those that were doing business with these two countries prior to the enactment of NAFTA. During the next few years, it will be worth watching the localities in divisions that have either Canada or Mexico as neighbors to see if their economies change substantially in response to NAFTA. Finally, the ability of large- and medium-size cities to benefit from NAFTA further confirms the importance of foreign linkages and diversity in economic holdings in the pursuit of economic growth.

ECONOMIC FORECASTING

The survey data raise significant questions about the nature of economic forecasting in the public sector. State-of-the-art long-term economic development strategies are often predicated on developments in the economy that never materialize or trends that are short-lived. Yet plans that appear to be revenue winners in the short term are often criticized as being too shortsighted. Local governments that are surprised by changes in the economy are chastised as being unprepared.

Economic forecasting has never been a precise science. In the next five years localities will be confronted with changes in their economies that even the most sophisticated economists could not have predicted. Therefore, these entities must be flexible and make their best judgments about economic development policies based upon limited information. Such flexibility is dependent upon, among other things, discretion in land use, favorable political climates, and the willingness and resolve to enter into short-term agreements with businesses. Based upon the survey results, many areas would best be served by closely examining policies regarding land use and subsidies for manufacturing operations while exploring ways to modify their economies in light of certain national trends and developments—especially NAFTA.

Factors Influencing Economic Development

Each community confronts a unique set of economic circumstances that vary in impact and importance. The ways in which they choose to respond are as different as the circumstances themselves. Economic development programs, while still more reactive than proactive in nature, are a method by which communities can influence their

own destiny and, if necessary, alter the course of their economic evolution. When conducted in a comprehensive fashion, an economic development program addresses issues that go well beyond the economy itself. Physical, social, and environmental issues that are inherent in the economic development process are often included.

At the end of most decades, economic development pundits proclaim that a dramatic shift is occurring in focus and that the upcoming decade will emphasize different industry sectors, with new technologies and initiatives. In truth, although the thrust of economic development today is different from that of yesterday, programmatic transformations have been gradual and are a result of a myriad of factors both within and outside the control of the economic development practitioner.

SHIFTING ECONOMIC BASE

Perhaps the greatest external factor influencing economic development has been the steady shift away from manufacturing-dominated economies. In five of the nine geographic divisions, the combined retail and service sectors are anticipated by respondents to equal, if not surpass, manufacturing over the next several years. The gap is narrowing between the percentage of respondents who report economies based in the manufacturing and retail/service sectors during the last five years (23% and 18%, respectively) and those who predict such a base in the next five years (22% predict manufacturing and 21%, retail/service).

This shift away from manufacturing-dominated economies has forced localities to rethink the ways in which economic development services are packaged and provided. Many location-based attractions that may appeal to a manufacturing audience are often quite different from those of interest to service or retail sectors. While factors such as market access, local resource procurement, and cost sensitivity may be of central importance to each target audience, the degree to which they influence location decisions and help ensure facility operating success varies considerably, not only between these sectors, but within them as well.

A clear indication of shifting forces is in the name of the field itself. As recently as the 1970s, the term *industrial development* was most often applied to the attraction and retention of facility investment. Today, *economic development* is the most widely accepted term, and *industrial development* refers primarily to the provision of manufacturing-specific services.

COMPETITION

Another trend that has greatly influenced the economic development field is the shift away from central-city dependence and the "suburbanization" or "exurbanization" of the American economy. Ever-expanding transportation routes, reliance on telecommunications, and the migration of desirable labor to less costly surroundings have, in combination, had a dramatic impact on decisions to expand or relocate facilities. This phenomenon is particularly evident in the manufacturing sector. No longer do companies need to be within large cities to access the amenities necessary for operating viability. In many instances, the benefits of the operating climate in suburban or exurban locations far outweigh those of large cities.

Perhaps surprisingly, while the threat of suburban or exurban business competition is great, according to survey results, central locations do not fear this competition any more than they fear competition from locations in surrounding states.

By comparison, suburban locations appear most sensitive to competition in immediately surrounding areas, and independent locations focus most on in-state competition.

On average, only 9% of local governments report foreign countries as a source of competition for the attraction of investment. Foreign competition is feared the most in high-cost areas, such as New England, and in those geographic divisions where proximity and access to foreign markets is great, such as in the South Atlantic and Pacific Coast divisions. Central cities and counties are more sensitive to the influence of foreign competition than their suburban or independent counterparts, though far less so than they are to competition within the United States.

Several reasons can be cited to explain why concern over foreign competition is low among local economic developers. First, it is only fairly recently that the importance of globalization has entered into the consciousness of local economic development professionals, excluding those within the nation's largest cities. Second, inland communities and those that do not border other countries generally have had little international exposure. Even today, international linkages in local economic development programs often are limited to the relatively small presence of multinational companies within the jurisdictions.

BARRIERS TO
ECONOMIC DEVELOPMENT

While by no means a new phenomenon, efforts on the part of business to reduce ongoing operating costs continue to influence decisions about location and, correspondingly, influence the efforts of economic development professionals. Indigenous cost variations between locations are often the driving force in a company's decision to uproot or expand in one community rather than another. But where cost comparisons were once based primarily on easily quantifiable measures (such as labor, real estate, utilities, and taxes), today's sophisticated site seeker looks at many indirect or ancillary factors that often have a pronounced short-term and long-term impact on their bottom line. Government responsiveness, flexibility of regulatory and permit functions, labor quality and dependability, property and infrastructure readiness, quality of life, and community appeal for labor recruitment are but a few of the critical issues that are difficult to quantify but factor heavily into a company's ultimate operating cost structure. When asked to indicate what they believe to be the greatest barriers to economic development in their respective locations, the top four answers of survey respondents were lack of capital, availability of land, cost of land, and a lack of skilled labor.

In addition to cost cutting through facility location, facility investment decisions and organization reengineering are having a noticeable impact on local economic development. In efforts to improve the capacity, utilization, and efficiency of their existing facilities (particularly those that are manufacturing related), many companies are going through the exercise of facility consolidation, often at the expense of older facilities in more expensive locations. Such actions are reflected in the fact that survey respondents within urban locations expect manufacturing presence to drop appreciably over the next five years, whereas in suburban and independent locations they expect a range from relative stagnation to a modest increase.

Program Funding

Needless to say, a locality's capacity to fund economic development has a direct impact on its ability to attract investment and provide meaningful, lasting services to its existing business community. The most effective and most common economic development programs and initiatives are long term in nature. As the need for steady and controlled economic development continues to gain importance, so does the community's financial commitment to its economic development programs.

Although the funding of local economic development programs has come a long way in recent years, it is still hampered by common procedures that limit long-term program stability and continuity. First, local economic development programs tend to be funded, like most government programs, on an annual basis. Thus their funding cycles often do not coincide with the implementation periods of the programs that they are intended to fund. Further, although overall funding may continue from year to year, the funding levels often fluctuate greatly and are influenced by political considerations. Second, funding, especially as a result of fund-raising, is often specific to a particular economic development activity and not designated for discretionary use within the broader program. Targeted funding tends to discourage joint or leveraged activities and eliminate beneficial economies of scale that may otherwise occur. Third, financial contributions for local economic development are derived mostly from public sector sources, with private sector funding often considered supplemental. This imbalance tends to lessen private sector ownership in the economic development process. It also ties program funding to considerable public scrutiny and to the uncertainty of a local government's annual budget.

LOCAL GOVERNMENT ECONOMIC DEVELOPMENT BUDGETS

A rough correlation exists between community population size and the existence and amount of economic development budgets. All responding local governments 250,000 and over in population have funds dedicated exclusively to economic development (not shown). The percentage of communities with dedicated economic development budgets declines steadily as population size decreases. Additionally, according to survey results, annual economic development budgets for the largest communities, those 250,000 and over in population, averaged over $3 million in 1994. By comparison, communities with populations under 250,000 show average economic development budgets below $250,000. Economic development funding in central cities and counties averages six to twelve times that of suburban and independent locations, respectively. One explanation for this disparity is that programs within large cities tend to em-

phasize public sector contributions tied to relatively balanced tax revenue generation. Smaller, less urbanized communities may be hampered by a tax base that is both smaller and more reliant on residential taxpayers than on higher paying commercial or industrial taxpayers.

A comparison of funding levels among the geographic divisions indicates that economic development programs in the New England or West South Central divisions are woefully underrepresented and that programs that do exist tend to be underfunded relative to their counterparts. According to survey results, FY 1994 economic development funding averaged a scant $53,000 per local government in New England, and $158,000 in the West South Central division jurisdictions, compared with a national average of $316,000. Only 65% of New England locations report having any funds dedicated to economic development, compared to 73% for the West South Central division and the national survey average of 79%. In New England, one of the most significant impediments to public sector funding for economic development programs is citizen opposition. Almost 46% of survey respondents from New England jurisdictions listed this as an economic development barrier, compared with an average of only 34% of respondents nationally.

The Mid–Atlantic division has the lowest percentage of locations funding economic development (47%), but the average economic development budget is $277,000. The South Atlantic division possesses the highest percentage of communities with economic development budgets (86%) as well as the highest level of funding. The Mountain division actually has slightly higher percentages of communities with economic development programs; however, the funding level per program is on average more than $65,000 behind that of the South Atlantic division.

Private sector financial contributions to local government economic development marketing efforts are reported by 385 survey respondents (not shown). Of those 385 jurisdictions, 278 provided information on the amount of the contributions, with the average contribution approximately $55,000 per locality. The average private sector contribution is highest in jurisdictions with populations from 500,000 to 1,000,000 ($535,000), in central jurisdictions (approximately $178,000), and in the South Atlantic division ($98,000).

On average, almost half those surveyed expect their economic development budgets to increase over the next five years; only 6% expect budget cuts. South Atlantic division respondents, already laying claim to the second highest average budget, show the highest percentage of respondents (55%) expecting an increase in their economic development budget over the next five years. Local governments in the Mid–Atlantic division, where average 1994 budgets are among the lowest, are least optimistic about receiving additional economic development funding in the next five years.

FUNDING SOURCES

Public sector funding is most commonly derived from local tax revenues. However, funding from outside sources differs greatly by geographic division and population group. Economic development programs in the Mid-Atlantic and East South Central divisions rely heavily on outside funding from federal and state sources. North Central locations, as well as those in the Pacific division, are far more likely than their counterparts to utilize user-driven programs, such as tax-increment financing and special assessment districts. Further, revenue from bond issues (either general obligation or revenue bonds) is more widely used to fund economic development in the eastern than in the western United States. The use of bonds for economic development is also considerably more common among larger communities. At least 38% of those with populations 250,000 and over use some type of bond, whereas in communities under 25,000 in population, less than 10% do so. Conversely, with the exception of communities 500,000 and over in population, the smallest communities are most likely to use state-level funding for their economic development programs. On average, the larger the community, the more balanced its use of funding sources. Urban locations, for instance, are far more likely to combine many sources of funding for local economic development than is customary among their suburban or independent counterparts.

Program Staffing

The level of program funding is typically a good determinant of economic development staff size. Governments in the New England and West South Central divisions have both the smallest economic development budgets and the smallest number of individuals dedicated principally to local economic development. Conversely, the Pacific Coast and East South Central divisions possess, on average, both the highest budgets and the largest economic development staffs.

Population size, which frequently influences funding level, is a critical factor in economic development staffing. Although the average number of economic development staff in reporting jurisdictions is 2.8, the largest communities, those with populations 250,000 and over, on average had 15 or more employees who dedicate at least 70% of their time to economic development (not shown). In contrast, economic development programs in communities under 50,000 population average fewer than two staff members with 70% of their time dedicated to economic development. Similarly, central jurisdictions average over twice as many economic development professionals as suburban locations and almost four times as many as independent locations. Although size of professional staff often determines the amount of effort that an economic development organization is able to put forth, this is not always the case. Certain program activities are far more labor intensive than others. For instance, economic development organizations that use a sizable portion of their funds for the leveraging or for the capacity building of other programs may function quite effectively with only a skeleton crew. Programs with a large contingent of private sector involvement often rely heavily upon volunteer assistance, frequently on an ad hoc basis in lieu of the availability of full-time individuals.

Private Sector Involvement

The drive to ensure long-term economic vitality has prompted the private sector to play an active role in economic development planning and implementation. Though private sector participation in economic development is not a prerequisite for success, a program that lacks private sector input risks failure. As such, the multidisciplinary nature of economic development demands that those involved in the process possess a broad understanding of critical private sector issues and the acumen to respond to problems and opportunities quickly and effectively.

The economic development function has changed immeasurably from the early days of industrial attraction, or "smokestack chasing." Where once the primary responsibility of the organization was simply to provide timely and accurate information on the local business climate, economic developers today wear many hats, ranging from consultant to negotiator to ombudsman. The economic development professional often serves as the prospective business's advocate. This is especially important when dealing with regulatory, permit, training, or financial issues.

Changing demands of the end-user have brought a change in the economic development organization's structure. Today's typical program is an amalgamation of private and public sector resources and individuals working in tandem for the common good of the local economy. While the public sector still dominates the economic development landscape, few local programs can be found today that are not heavily influenced by, if not partnered with, the private sector.

Perhaps the greatest problem with the inclusion of the private sector is one of coordination. In many communities, private sector economic development programs have grown independently from those in the public sector, and periodically the two compete or conflict with one another. But programs that include the private sector in the economic development process have certain distinct advantages over those that are exclusively government operated. Private sector involvement often

1. increases and stabilizes long-term program funding,

2. provides expertise and direction from the end-user perspective, and

3. offers the potential for business-to-business marketing, which can greatly enhance program credibility.

Chambers of commerce provide input into the local economic development process of over 70% of reporting local governments. Perhaps the fastest evolving private sector participants are utilities. In several southeastern and midwestern states, the capabilities of the largest public utility rival those of the state's economic development organization. Utilities, and often chambers of commerce, are typically regional, and can thus address issues that transcend local political boundaries.

Perhaps surprisingly, respondents on average consider citizens and private businesses more active participants in local economic development planning than state agencies. While state economic development organizations typically possess the financial resources and skills to supplement local efforts, some communities fear that state involvement will dilute local initiative and bring in potential in-state competitors who would otherwise have been excluded. Local governments in the Mid-Atlantic and East South Central divisions report relatively active state economic development agencies, with those least active in the western United States.

A steadily evolving role of many state-level organizations is local capacity building. Rather than dedicate funds to an additional, often duplicative, marketing staff, state-level organizations financially support the educational and training infrastructure, and economic development efforts of local communities. State economic development agencies have considerable resources at their disposal, especially information, funds, personnel, and technology. The agencies that provide the greatest value to local economic developers are highly networked with other state agencies and regulatory bodies and are able to share and dedicate resources from many sources. While macro policy- and direction-setting is an important function of these entities, ability to support instead of compete with local development activities is typically the state agency's preferred role.

Private sector participation is far more common among large communities than among small ones. Several factors may contribute to this phenomenon, including the smaller communities' lack of a sizable base of corporate decision-makers and other parties likely to contribute to local programs. Private sector involvement, whether it be through individual businesses, chambers of commerce, or public/private partnerships, is far more common in urban areas than in suburban or independent locations.

Private sector participation takes a variety of forms. Many communities utilize the expertise of their business leadership to address issue-specific concerns that existing and prospective companies may have. One strategy that is becoming more popular is executive loan programs, where companies dedicate experts in specific fields on a part-time basis to support their local government's economic development programs. Under this program, banks may provide financial analysts or grant packagers, corporate or divisional headquarters may loan staff with marketing and promotional expertise, and real-estate companies may dedicate individuals to assist with industrial property development.

Educational systems and institutions are fast emerging as contributors to economic development programs. Vocational/technical establishments have long been key to the economic development process, but primary educational systems and local universities and colleges have not participated until fairly recently. Given the emphasis that businesses place on the availability of skilled and dependable labor, these entities can play a vital role in a community's economic development success. In addition to providing labor and coordinating future educational programs with local businesses, institutions of higher learning are beginning to provide valuable research and technology transfer services and leadership in a host of other critical areas.

Among the entities that remain woefully underutilized in most local economic development programs are labor unions, public libraries, and certain service sector businesses, such as accounting and legal services. In assembling active participants in the economic development process, the most savvy communities recognize the value of focusing on, and gaining the involvement of, their primary "stakeholder" organizations—those that have a stake in the community's economic future and can

contribute to its progress. A partial list of local public and private stakeholder groups would include:

> Chambers of commerce
> Civic organizations
> Economic development
>   organizations
> Educational organizations
>   (primary and secondary)
> Financial institutions
> Government officials,
>   regulators, and planners
> Industry and service sector leaders
> Public libraries
> Real-estate developers and builders
> Training institutions
> Unions
> Utilities

Economic Development Plans

The principal role of an economic development organization is to influence the direction of its local economy by fostering stability and growth. The intent of strategic planning within economic development is to ensure that the process is conducted in a logical and systematic fashion, emphasizing efficiency and effectiveness, in the context of predefined community goals and objectives. Whether the focus is singular in nature—stressing stability, diversity, or expansion—or multidirectional, the emphasis should be placed on applying the right level and mix of resources to enhance the location's economic climate and quality of life.

Strategic economic development planning is the only formal process that encourages participants to concentrate on critical issues, leverage support in a systematic fashion, implement a controlled set of targeted action steps, measure and monitor program effectiveness, and alter activities and emphasis in response to changing circumstances.

Given the undeniable value that planning adds to total economic development, one would expect an economic development plan to be at the core of every community's program; however, this is not the case. While most local leaders tout the virtues of strategic planning, only 41% of all cities and counties report the use of a formal, written economic development plan.

Economic development planning is far more common in local governments with populations 250,000 and above and in the Pacific Coast and Mountain divisions. Localities in the Mid-Atlantic and West South Central divisions are among the least likely to carry out economic development planning, a fact that could hamper their ability to enhance their respective economies.

Approximately two-thirds of all suburban locations surveyed do not utilize economic development plans, as compared to urban and independent locations, where economic development planning is considerably more common. Substantial economic growth in many suburban locations has occurred primarily as a result of proximity to more costly, perhaps less desirable, urban hubs and a position that enables them to capture investment from outmigrating businesses. But the lack of economic development planning for some suburban locations has resulted in severe labor shortages, congestion, and other problems associated with an inability to control or manage this rapid growth.

Loosely defined, strategic planning for economic development comprises three distinct yet mutually dependent phases: formulation, implementation, and evaluation. Although all phases are critical, economic development agencies routinely emphasize implementation, often to the virtual exclusion of the other two phases. Strategic plans should be updated regularly and treated as functional documents that facilitate establishment of priorities, confrontation of difficult choices, and regular self-examination.

Highly effective local economic development plans are those that are customized to address and capitalize on unique locational characteristics and operating circumstances. At the foundation of all economic development programs should be a keen understanding of a location's position relative to key competitors and, from the perspective of the target audience, whether the audience is existing or prospective businesses. All too often economic development plans prescribe a course of action with little basis in either community capabilities or the needs of the end-user. These are the plans that produce minimal, if any, positive results.

The participants in the planning process are as important as the plan itself. Those involved at the inception of the planning process are typically the ones who develop the strongest sense of ownership and remain the plan's staunchest supporters. Formal public-private partnerships are prime examples of this phenomenon. Economic development programs in communities where the public-private sector bond has been forged during plan formulation are typically characterized by broad business and government involvement, smoother coordination, less duplication of effort, and a longer-term vision for the future.

Increasingly, inclusion of the

general public in the formulation phase of the plan is a way in which communities garner widespread economic development awareness and support. In general, if the desires of the citizenry are reflected in the plan, the community in the aggregate is more likely to back its ongoing implementation. However, excessive community involvement can tend to slow or impede the planning process. It also can provide added opportunity for criticism and opposition. This is no more evident than in New England, where citizen advisory boards are the second greatest participants (beyond city government) in developing economic development strategy and are among the most frequently cited impediments to economic development success.

Once community issues and desires are clearly understood, organizational goals and objectives can be formed. It is not uncommon to see goals and objectives mentioned interchangeably in a strategic plan, though actually they are quite different. Goals reflect the aspirations of program participants and stakeholders. Objectives are targets that provide a framework and preferably a means for measuring specific actions.

Historically, the most common objectives among economic development organizations have been to create jobs and to generate tax revenue. Today, however, many communities are more concerned with labor shortages, out-migration of their best, brightest, and most educated residents, and fragility of economies too heavily dependent upon one industry sector or one institution. As such, objectives may have additional qualifiers, such as the quality or skill level of the job created, or the type of company attracted and its potential compatibility with existing companies, suppliers, and consumers.

While all objectives should be measurable, even if subjectively, economic development programs that state their targets in absolute terms often run the risk of undue scrutiny and failure. For instance, if the success of a program is measured solely by its ability to attract a certain number of firms or create a certain number of jobs, failure to achieve these numbers could result in unmet community expectations and, quite possibly, a reduction in funding. Furthermore, although effective economic development organizations have the ability to influence company decision-making, they neither control the ultimate decision nor the magnitude of the investment. In fact, careful scrutiny of apparent economic development "successes" in many high-growth communities may reveal that market trends and natural industry migration patterns are the driving location forces rather than the influence of local economic development programs. Still, the most astute organizations know how to leverage these forces and use them to their advantage.

IMPLEMENTING THE ECONOMIC DEVELOPMENT PLAN

The success of any economic development program is contingent upon its ability to identify realistic strategic actions that satisfy the demands of the targeted audience and at the same time comply with the prescribed objectives of the community. Among the difficulties in devising a game plan is matching available resources with local demands. Local economic development organizations often make the mistake of allowing community desires to dictate the strategies selected. The end result may be the selection of far more strategies than a city or county has resources to implement.

In an attempt to simplify the process, communities often distinguish between programs devised to assist their existing industry base versus those devised to entice new facility locations and accompanying location investment. In actuality, these efforts are inseparable because one of the most critical site selection factors is a community's ability to satisfy business needs once the move has taken place. In addition, many of the same principles, methods, and resources applied to one activity are directly transferable to the other.

Only 344 local governments report a written *business attraction* plan, and slightly fewer indicate *written retention* plans (297). Similarly, 1,337 local governments indicate the methods they use to attract business, and slightly fewer (1,204) provide information on their retention methods. On average, attraction programs are still more widely utilized than retention programs, though the gap is clearly narrowing.

BUSINESS RETENTION

Formal business retention programs are typically, and understandably, more common in older economies that are characterized by real or perceived compelling locational disadvantages that contribute to the pronounced outmigration of their businesses, particularly their manufacturers. For instance, while the Mid-Atlantic and New England divisions' resource dedication to business retention is, on average, less

than that of other divisions, it is greater than that which they dedicate to business attraction. The greatest disparity between retention and attraction is, however, found in the South Atlantic and Mountain divisions, jurisdictions, where, on average, the latter focus receives considerably more emphasis.

Existing industry programs, also known as retention programs, have seen a marked increase in popularity over the last two decades. The intent of these programs is to stimulate or support local economic development through efforts that help existing industry enhance its competitiveness and increase sales, employment, and profitability.

Effective existing industry programs are becoming increasingly important to local economic development efforts. Competition over the attraction of industry is more fierce than ever, and the frequency of company expansion through new facility development, especially within manufacturing, is considerably less than it once was. On average, over 75% of a community's job growth is generated from companies already residing within its boundaries. Against a backdrop of increased competition, decreased facility attraction opportunities, and ever-increasing foreign competition for U.S. company investment, many economic development agencies are turning their attention inward to tend to those businesses of most importance to their long-term viability.

As the name suggests, retention programs are heavily skewed toward preventing local firms from relocating. While most retention efforts tend to be reactive in nature, it is those that are preventive that stand the greatest chance of success. Once a firm decides to relocate, more often than not this decision is unchangeable. The local economic development challenge is to help foster a business climate that satisfies the needs of the business base and an array of existing industry programs and resources that lessen the temptation to move elsewhere.

The primary goals of most retention programs are to promote company stability, longevity and, where possible, growth. While typically not as critical for retention as for business attraction programs, increased jobs and tax revenue generation for the local community are often retention objectives. The success of retention programs may be measured by the number of jobs and amount of tax revenue prevented from leaving the local community. Calculating this can be tricky because it is difficult to establish links between economic development efforts and existing businesses that have not relocated.

When conducted in a comprehensive fashion, retention programs can serve as an accurate barometer of a location's business climate. Eliciting the input and opinion of a community's own businesses is the most effective mechanism for learning about important operating issues or problems that they may be experiencing. But determining the extent of local business satisfaction must be done with caution. A business leader's perspective, exposure to competing locations, facility working conditions, and a myriad of other issues can skew impressions of a local operating environment.

Strong retention programs are excellent complements to business attraction efforts. The importance of local government attention and customized service to a prospective investor cannot be overstated. In addition to the testi-monial value that can be realized by having satisfied businesses, a solid working relationship between retention and attraction speaks volumes about the way in which the prospect will be treated once the decision to locate has been made.

The benefits of a successful retention program far outweigh its costs, but costs do exist. On average, retention related activities are considerably more time and labor intensive than those dedicated to attraction. In the latter, the focus is often skewed toward promoting and generating the awareness of a location's business climate advantages. With the former, however, considerable personal attention becomes the norm. All-consuming projects for local businesses, such as regulatory assistance, trade development aid, skill enhancement, and infrastructure improvement measures can quickly convert a retention professional into an extension of the client company's staff.

A problem commonly voiced by retention professionals, particularly those whose task is fund-raising and program justification, is that retention efforts are perceived to lack "sex appeal." Whereas the attraction of a large labor-intensive company is a newsworthy event and often credited to local economic development efforts, the retention of a company already in existence may be viewed as merely a temporary measure with no net gain. Ironically, it is the latter success that is usually far more beneficial to the local economy.

BUSINESS ATTRACTION

Marketing cities and counties for the attraction of desirable industry has long been, and will continue to be, a vital element of local economic development. The basic premise behind business attraction programs is that communities are seen as products. As the consumer, corporate site seekers will shop for the most advantageous, highest quality, lowest cost product that is responsive to their long-term needs.

Given the magnitude and steady proliferation of competition for the attraction of businesses, communities are constantly striving for unique ways in which to "package" themselves and create a uniquely appealing identity. Evidence of this packaging is readily apparent in the ways communities describe themselves and the messages they attempt to convey.

Although no business attraction program can offer guaranteed results, if properly focused, supported, and implemented, the benefits of such a program can be substantial. While some question the value and effectiveness of expending substantial resources to attract businesses, much anecdotal evidence indicates that, if carried out properly, such programs can be quite beneficial. Communities that poll their newly located businesses to learn their reasons for choosing the new location occasionally learn that it was a particular promotional activity that sparked a prospect's interest and led to further investigation.

The marketing of a location has led to an all-out war between communities dueling for a limited number of facility locations. As the survey results indicate, cities and counties are no longer simply competing with jurisdictions of similar character and proximity. The competitive playing field for many of even the smallest locations has widened into other states and divisions, and for large

locations, competition stretches well beyond the country's borders.

When applied to local marketing campaigns, the term *competitive advantage* is overused and, more often than not, used improperly. Most locations will flaunt as their competitive advantages a high-quality workforce, central location, and pro-business attitude. These are hollow expressions when not supported by meaningful, quantifiable evidence and placed in the proper context. Often a location's true competitive advantage, whether it be a characteristic of the physical, economic, or political environment, is either only partially recognized, masked behind other, less important factors, or directed toward the wrong audience.

It is the act of identifying the right marketing audience and matching its operating needs with the location's operating climate capabilities that is the linchpin of a business attraction program. Given the range of location options and the specific nature of site selector needs, a generic approach to marketing may do little more than confuse its intended audience.

The challenge for the economic development marketer is to learn the specific needs of the site selector and then craft a direct response to satisfying them. This is the intent of a well-thought-out target marketing campaign. By dissecting and evaluating the typical needs of potential industry groups, the economic developer will be better able to focus only on those sectors most suited to what the location has to offer. By doing so, use of marketing resources can be limited to those industries and companies with the greatest likelihood of investing locally.

In the past, the primary rationale

for communities to engage in business attraction efforts was to boost local employment. A secondary rationale was typically to expand and diversify the local tax base. While these are still important goals, they are by no means the only ones. Some communities may turn to business attraction as a means to fill a local supplier or consumer gap to benefit an existing industry. Others may do so to introduce new technologies or to capitalize better on available workforce skills, underutilized economic development potential, or job training programs. Regardless of the rationale, the ultimate goal of business attraction is to match the needs and capabilities of the community with those of the prospective business investor and to foster a relationship in which both benefit from what the other has to offer.

INVESTMENT TARGETING

Economic development organizations have been very slow to alter their target focus in response to economic shifts. Although manufacturing is no longer the sole focus of the economic development profession, the emphasis of business attraction programs is still on the manufacturing sector. Survey responses to questions about business prospects show that 62% of all business prospects today are generated from sectors other than manufacturing. In three divisions, the Mid-Atlantic, Pacific, and Mountain, nonmanufacturing prospect activity exceeds 75% of the total activity. This suggests that although the *focus* of business attraction is on the manufacturing sector, the *successes* are derived from other sectors. The greatest amount of manufacturing prospect activity is found in the East North Central divi-

sion. However, even in this division, nonmanufacturing prospects exceed half the total. The percent of nonmanufacturing prospect activity tends to be highest in the northeast and western United States, as manufacturing continues its migration to the southeastern and central sections of the United States.

Even with the overwhelming evidence that manufacturing activity is declining in prominence, local economic development efforts remain heavily skewed in favor of the attraction of companies in this sector. Only 27% of all respondents put more than moderate emphasis on nonmanufacturing businesses in their business attraction programs. The Pacific Coast division respondents show the second highest percentage reporting current business prospects in nonmanufacturing activity and place the greatest emphasis on attracting business outside the manufacturing sector. Approximately 41% of jurisdictions responding from the Pacific Coast division emphasize nonmanufacturing in their attraction efforts, compared with 24% of localities responding from the neighboring Mountain division.

Although numerous opportunities remain for economic growth through manufacturing-sector development, the sector as a whole has expanded little in the last 20 years. In contrast, the service sector has virtually doubled during this period.

Economic development organizations have begun to take notice of the benefits of focusing on the service sector, but to many of them, identifying viable targets within this rapidly expanding audience remains a mystery. Whereas manufacturing targets break down neatly along industry lines, the service sector is much more difficult to segment. Standard Industrial Classification (SIC) codes that precisely categorize industries by product are of limited value in evaluating service industries. Segmentation of service industries along functional lines, such as information processing or telemarketing, will enable economic development organizations to understand better the factors that influence service sector location decisions. This, in turn, will allow them to position and market themselves accordingly.

Tourism and hospitality development may, in fact, be the next wave of economic development within the service sector. Successful strategies designed to enhance local tourism and hospitality industries often result in the attraction of such business amenities as hotels, restaurants, and conference centers that are of importance to the corporate decision-maker. Although the jobs created tend to be lower paying than those within traditional manufacturing or office settings, the multiplier benefits that ripple through the local economy can be sizable. Only 6% of the survey respondents report tourism/hospitality companies as active business prospects, but over 48% state that this sector is a focus of their economic development programs. Not surprisingly, in the Mountain, South Atlantic, and Pacific Coast divisions, where the tourism and hospitality industries are already an economic staple, the percentage of localities focusing on these industries is considerably higher than in other divisions.

Performance Measurement

Establishing and monitoring performance objectives is critical to a local government's effectiveness. Today there is a renewed interest in performance measurement at all levels of government. Spurred in part by tough economic conditions and taxpayer skepticism about service quality, public officials are becoming increasingly committed to demonstrating what is being accomplished with public dollars.

Performance measures play an integral role in the three administrative functions of nearly every government program—planning, budgeting, and management. Planning involves formulating program goals and objectives, defining action steps, projecting revenues and expenses, etc. To develop and utilize performance measures in the planning function, agencies must have plans. Only 41% of the survey respondents have written economic development plans, 17% have written business retention plans, and 20% have written business attraction plans. As previously discussed, the importance of such planning cannot be overstated, and survey respondents themselves support this point. As the survey data indicate, organizations that have had written economic development, business retention, and business attraction plans in place have experienced stronger growth in their economic bases over the past five years than those agencies without plans. Similarly, local governments that have plans in place today expect stronger growth in their economic bases over the next five years than those that do not. Although there is no concrete evidence that having an economic development plan guarantees success, survey respondents from localities with these plans have experienced and anticipate future programmatic achievements.

The budgeting function allocates financial resources among competing programs and services. As an example, the survey found that only 47% of the respondents conduct cost/benefit analyses before offering business incentives, and only 28% conduct cost/benefit analyses after offering business incentives. Again, although perhaps not surprising, this finding is disturbing. At a minimum, one would expect that the same number of agencies that conduct cost/benefit analyses before offering incentives would conduct analyses afterward to determine the effectiveness of the incentives and the accuracy of their original estimates. Such information would certainly be useful for making similar decisions in the future.

The management function typically focuses on the implementation of programs and the dedication of resources intended to achieve program objectives. According to survey results, only 17% of respondents use performance measures to assess and manage their economic development programs. Although unfortunate, given the amount of dollars involved and the importance of economic development programs, this finding is not surprising. It is generally consistent among most government programs because there are so many obstacles involved in establishing and maintaining meaningful performance measurement systems. Developing and implementing a system of performance measures is not easy. Data collection and integrity, staff resistance, and the types of measures to use are just a few of the challenges. Each of these problems is discussed below.

Performance measures require a consistent flow of reliable operational and financial data. Many economic development organizations lack the organizational and technical infrastructure required to provide such information. Even with such systems, data must be periodically audited to ensure integrity and accuracy. Since investments in operational and financial systems can be costly, governments must strike a compromise between the benefits of a high-quality performance measurement system and the costs of data collection and integrity.

The use of performance measures may be challenged and resisted by economic development managers and staff. Managers may feel threatened by measures for a variety of reasons. First and foremost is the increased accountability and capacity to be held to specific standards that often follow the implementation of performance measures. Such resistance can be valid, however, when the performance being measured is not within the direct control of the manager. But resistance can be entirely or partially overcome through the participation of staff in the selection and development of performance measures and the use of explanatory or qualitative data to explain external data or deviations from goals.

In general, there are four types of performance measures:

1. *Input measures* focus on resources needed to provide a program or service (e.g., expenditures, full-time equivalent personnel).

2. *Output measures* gauge the level of activity in providing a program or service (e.g., work-load measures).

3. *Efficiency measures* gauge the cost

(in dollars or personnel hours) per unit of output or outcome.

4. *Outcome measures* focus on whether a program or service is meeting its goals; used most often to evaluate program quality and effectiveness.

Of the respondents who use performance measures, 34% use input measures, 63% use output measures, and 62% use efficiency measures. In assessing the effectiveness of business incentives, for instance, many respondents measure the amount of job creation and local facility and labor investment provided by the targeted business.

Most organizations plan, budget, and manage their resources based on input, output, and efficiency data. Ideally, however, outcome information should be used, since such information relates directly to program objectives and priorities. But if resources are to be allocated based on program results, reliable outcome data must be collected. This is a difficult task for several reasons. First, there is often disagreement among stakeholders regarding the objectives of the programs or services. Unless consensus can be achieved, there likely will be different interpretations of performance outcome data. Second, outcomes tend to be difficult and expensive to measure compared to inputs and outputs. In situations where there are complementary or related programs, it is often unclear which program has produced the actual outcome. In addition, economic development outcomes often do not occur for several years, making it difficult to link them back to financial resources for budgeting purposes. Finally, whether or not an outcome has been achieved is often determined by public perceptions, changes in public behavior, or other qualitative indicators.

Nearly 87% of the respondents surveyed indicate that they use local government revenues to fund their economic development programs. As the public clamors for increasing accountability and improved services, performance measures will become more and more popular or, at a minimum, necessary evils. For measures to lead to program and service improvements, however, they must become integral parts of the planning, budgeting, and management functions and processes.

Conclusion

The changing nature of the economic development landscape is making it more difficult for professionals in this field to satisfy the needs of their respective communities. Businesses are demanding a higher and more customized level of government service. Funding sources and levels are inconsistent at best, with widespread budget cuts continuing to impede long-term program development and continuity. Competition for the attraction of desirable business investment is quite high and growing; increasing globalization of local and national economies is only exacerbating this condition. These constraints are coming at a time when the call for economic development program justification, demonstrable results, and accountability has never been louder.

The challenges facing economic development programs are further complicated by the relatively poor state of economic development planning at the local level. Fewer than half the survey respondents indicate they possess a formal written economic development plan to guide their efforts. Such plans are critical for well-focused, sustainable approaches. Without formal plans, local governments are far more likely to waste precious resources attempting to attract or retain industries that are not particularly well suited to their environments. In addition, few communities with economic development programs use meaningful performance measures. They therefore lack the ability to determine whether their efforts are satisfactorily achieving their prime objectives.

Survey respondents remain optimistic about the future economic growth of their communities. However, limitations and obstacles that they face suggest that these individuals may encounter difficulty in properly positioning their communities and directing this growth. Ultimately they may fall short of meeting their high expectations.

Local economic development practitioners are well advised to adapt their programs to the environment in which they operate. They should play to the unique strengths of their communities by focusing on those opportunities with the highest probability of success, rather than simply pursuing those that offer the greatest economic reward. Economic developers should expand their focus by incorporating information about international conditions and linkages into their existing activities. Given the high level of competition for investment as well as the multijurisdictional benefits associated with industry attraction and retention, more localities should develop cooperative agreements with neighboring communities to foster economic growth. Better ways to garner private funding and to encourage participation in the local economic development process should be sought. Finally, economic development professionals will see greater, more predictable returns on investments if they systematically plan their economic development strategies, cultivate useful ways to measure performance, and adjust accordingly.

CHAPTER 4

Issues Facing Small Businesses

Edward M. Marshall

Small business is a significant force in a city's economic vitality. But a city's small business development efforts need to be targeted to the specific needs of small businesses as they start up, grow and mature. An effective city small business strategy needs to address those factors that contribute to the failure or reduced profitability of small firms.

It is well known that 65 percent of all small, minority, and women-owned businesses fail within the first eighteen to twenty-four months of operation, a rate that increases to almost 90 percent within the first five years.[7] Why is the failure rate of small businesses so high? Six factors contribute to a high rate of small business failure.

• **Business Development Phases:** The lack of understanding about the phases of small business development and their specific needs from startup to maturity. Among the management skills needed are business planning, effective time management, cash flow management, market research, and board and staff development for small firms.

• **Management:** Poor management skills among top leadership. Entrepreneurs are often so involved with the survival of their business that they may not see or be able to plan for their businesses to go through various phases of development. If the company is growing rapidly, this lack of planning may seriously limit the company's ability to meet production schedules and quality standards,

Originally published as "Issues Facing Small Business," Chapter 2 of Small Business Partnerships, *1989. Published by the National League of Cities, Washington, D.C. Reprinted with permission of the publisher.*

putting it in a crisis management mode.

- **Capital:** Lack of access to sufficient venture and working capital at market or below market rates, particularly at the start-up and rapid growth stages.
- **Markets:** Lack of adequate access to markets, either in the private or public sectors.
- **Environment:** Environmental factors such as crime, location, and rents that drive up the costs of doing business.
- **Government:** Government regulations, red tape, and insufficient support, which reduce the flexibility and profitability of small business. Government red tape and paperwork can cause costly delays or increase the administrative costs of a business, thus cutting into the firm's profit margin.

The important point to remember is that if cities and towns want to strengthen and expand their small business sectors, their strategies and tools should be targeted to these specific issues as they affect small businesses at different stages in their development. Singular approaches or programs alone will not meet the diverse needs of small businesses as they grow. Tailored and targeted strategies are needed.

Phases of Small Business Development

The issues facing a small business vary depending upon the phase of its development. There are three basic phases:

Phase I—Pre-Startup: The entrepreneur has an idea that is assessed and developed for the marketplace. Market studies should be completed and capital generated. Business plans to guide the firm's development are in many cases not prepared, often hampering effective growth in the second phase.

Phase II—Startup/Early Growth: During the first three years of a company's existence, the product or service is intensively marketed and sales begin to take off. The firm seeks to establish its niche in the marketplace. Lack of access to capital or management expertise can severely hamper their ability to grow and mature.

Phase III—Maturity: After three to five years, the firm reaches maturity and one of three scenarios may be followed:

- **Scenario A—Stable Growth:** The firm develops its primary market, improves on its product or service and establishes a slow but steady growth objective.
- **Scenario B—Rapid Growth:** The firm's product or service catches on quickly in the market, with demand often outstripping supply. The firm may collapse because of lack of capital, be acquired by another firm, or obtain the capital necessary to fulfill demand.
- **Scenario C—Decline/Failure/ Bankruptcy:** The firm is unable to generate the necessary capital or market demand, provide the product, or manage the company to maturity or profitability. The firm "dies."

Not every small business goes through these phases of development in a lock-step manner. These phases represent a framework that local governments can use to tailor their strategies and tools to have the greatest impact on the development and profitability of their small firms. The types of problems a small business faces are also different in each phase of development. The key is to be able to tailor a small business policy and program to meet the needs of small firms at each point in their development.

Management Issues

The central issue for any small business is the management ability of the person running the business. In most cases, the entrepreneur gets into business because of a product, a technique, or a special expertise that he or she can sell. The entrepreneur is first and foremost a sales person for the product or service or an idea person—not a manager.

The management of a firm's development becomes even more difficult because entrepreneurs rarely seek small business management assistance. Instead, they typically hire an attorney and an accountant first. Then they develop a relationship with a bank, and proceed to sell their products. Before long, and very often during the second year in business, serious management issues arise, ranging from personnel problems to cash flow management or quality control. Crisis management becomes the *modus operandi*, and the firm begins to lose customers, employees, product quality, money, or a combination of these.

The survival of any small firm, particularly after the first eighteen months, depends on effective management that introduces systems and procedures to ensure that products or services are delivered on time. While effective management assistance is a logical solution to avoid crisis situations, few entrepreneurs see that need until it is too late. Table 1 outlines the types of management assistance needed at each phase of development.

Capital Issues

The central capital issue for small businesses is access to low cost financing in the amounts necessary to help them through each critical phase of development.

The National Commission on Jobs and Small Business found five capital problems for small businesses:[8]

- **Venture Capital:** The Joint Economic Committee of Congress has found that venture capital is largely unavailable for new firms.
- **Long-Term Financing:** Most small firms report a total lack of long-term funds (more than 60 months); even established firms have difficulty obtaining short-term financing at reasonable interest rates.
- **Bias Against Small Business Investment:** The financial community is often biased against small business because of the transaction costs of loans, the inability to take equity positions, and the lack of a secondary market for small business loans.
- **Raising Equity:** Securities regulations are cumbersome and expensive for small business.
- **Bias Against Minority Small**

Table 1
Management Assistance Needs at Each Phase of Development

Phase	*Management Assistance Needs*
I. Pre-Startup	Education Transition Assistance Design for Management System
II. Startup/Early Growth	Assessment Design/Install Management System Planning Board Training Staff Development Transition Assistance Consulting/Advising Problem Solving
III. Maturity **A. Stable Growth**	Assessment Staff Development Consulting/Advising
B. Rapid Growth	Assessment Planning Problem Solving Board Training Staff Development Transition Assistance
C. Decline/Failure/ Bankruptcy	Assessment Turn-Around Assistance Transition Assistance

Business: These problems are compounded, in some cases, for the minority community. There is a set of perceptions and attitudes in the financial community that minority small businesses are less credit worthy than their majority counterparts. Studies of loan default rates by the Comptroller of the Currency, however, find that minority small businesses default at the same rate as majority firms, or perform better.

In addition to access to capital problems, small businesses must also figure out how to get the kind of capital they need at each phase of business development when they need it. Timing is critical. The capital needs of small firms at each phase of development are summarized in Table 2.

In addition, small businesses need positive working relationships with their bankers as well as financial planning and management assistance. Even with adequate capital, new small firms may be susceptible to failure because of financial management problems.

Table 2
Capital Needs of Small Business at
Each Phase of Development

Phase	*Capital Need*
I. Pre-Startup	Owners' equity, seed capital, working capital and financial plan.
Start-Up/Early Growth	Seed capital, venture capital, working capital and short-term debt, receivables financing, inventory financing; financial management.
Maturity	
A. Stable Growth	Leveraging of fixed assets; working capital, short and long term debt; financial management system.
B. Rapid Growth	Venture capital, working capital, short and long term debt; fixed asset financing; financial growth management system.
C. Decline/Failure/Bankruptcy	Working capital, short and long term debt

The Tax Reform Act of 1986 also had a heavy impact on small business. Among the more important provisions are the following:[9]

• The elimination of tax-exempt industrial development bond (IDB) financing for certain kinds of private activities, and the reduced incentive for banks to participate in private IDB placements.
• Elimination of the provisions for long-term capital gains, with an increase in the rate from 28 percent to 34 percent.
• Elimination of the investment tax credit worth up to 10 percent of the cost of machinery and equipment.
• Longer depreciation schedules for writing off investment in plant, machinery, and equipment, meaning smaller deductions each year.
• A reduction in the research and development tax credit from 25 percent to 20 percent.

While there are some favorable aspects to the law, the new tax law appears to create a barrier for small business at precisely the time an expansion of capital for this important economic sector is needed.

Market Issues

The central market issue is market access. Small firms, starting up, particularly those that are not of the "Mom and Pop" variety, usually have been created because their owners have products or services that they believe are innovative or needed in the marketplace. On their own time, these entrepreneurs may have conducted some basic market research, but for most small businesses, survival and growth depends upon a serious investment in market research. This research tells them what the market is for their products or services, who the competition is, what the price structure is, what niches their products or services could fill, and what their competitive edges might be. With market data in hand, a firm can develop an effective strategy and public relations effort to generate new business. Most small businesses, however, cannot afford the time or the money required to do this kind of market research or strategy development.

In terms of export markets, small firms remain at a competitive disadvantage. Only 10 percent of American firms export, and a mere 250 companies ac-count for nearly 80 percent of all American exports, while there are 30,000 firms able to export goods and services. Further, between 1980 and 1982, small business experienced an absolute decline of 15 percent in real exports, twice the rate of decline in all U.S. exports. Finally, only one percent of SBA's loans were used for exporting from 1983 to 1985, and no export loans were made in 1986.[10]

Table 3 shows the marketing needs of small businesses at different stages of development and presents options for local government strategies to meet these marketing needs.

To enter the public market, small businesses will explore public procurement opportunities at the local, state or federal level. There are, however, a number of barriers:

Table 3
Marketing Needs of Small Businesses at Each Phase of Development

Phase	*Activity*
I. Pre-Startup	Develop realistic marketing plan Product/service analysis Segment/categorize markets Evaluate competition Assess firm's distinct competence/ success factors Assess industry trends/outlook
Start-Up/Early Growth	Implement effective marketing operation
Maturity	
A. Stable Growth	Evaluate new competition and revise plan Sustain/improve product
B. Rapid Growth	Resolve trade-off between market expansion and current profit

C. Decline/Failure/
   Bankruptcy
	Withdrawal from market to salvage
	   resources
	Retrench to core business
	Continuation of product strategy
	Liquidation

- Competition from larger firms with more established records.
- Preferential treatment for certain firms over others.
- High-cost bonding and insurance provisions as a requirement for bidding.
- Having to bid competitively against larger firms.
- "Hold out" provisions, under which the city retains 10 to 25 percent of the contract until the results are inspected.
- High-cost performance bonds
- Public agency failure to pay bills within 30 days.

Public procurement, however, remains an important market entry point for new small businesses and an important way for them to develop a track record and the confidence to compete in the private market.

Another market-related issue is the ability of small businesses to sell their products or services to either the public, private, or international markets. Effective public relations strategies are very expensive, and most small firms cannot afford to hire a sales force. Small businesses need to manage scarce sales resources effectively to build their images and reputations in the marketplace.

Environmental Factors

A wide range of factors outside the control of the small business and unre-

---

Table 4
Environmental Factors Affecting Small Business

Phase	Management Assistance Needs
I. Market Forces	High rents squeeze out small businesses Poor landlord-tenant relationships Commercial redlining by financial institutions Poor mix of retail businesses
II. Real Estate Factors	Poor design of buildings Large number of vacant buildings Large number of second-story buildings
III. Public Physical Infrastructure and Services	Inadequate or poorly managed parking High incidence of crime or public perception of crime Inadequate public physical infrastructure improvements Inadequate facilities or services to retain employees
IV. Private Business Development Factors	Negative image of commercial areas Poor marketing of business/city Inadequate organizational structures for small businesses

Source: Based on "The Small Business Retention, Expansion and Recruitment Project," National Trust for Historic Preservation, Washington, D.C. 1987

lated to government policy affect the survival and growth of small businesses. Table 4 lists some of these "environmental" factors; most are not tied to any given phase of development. Cities can make a major contribution to small business growth by addressing each of these environmental factors as part of an overall strategy.

Government Behavior

Knowledgeable city leadership is the best local ally small business can have.

By paying attention to the problems of small businesses, coordinating local programs, simplifying regulations and procedures, and providing targeted, on-going technical assistance that meets the issues that small businesses face in each phase of development, local government can create a healthy climate for small business growth.

At the local level, small businesses have a number of needs that fall within the scope of local government, among them:

- Simplified zoning procedures,
- Adequate physical infrastructure (roads, water, sewage, etc.),
- Access to public land for in-fill and development,
- Reduction of paperwork,
- Lower city taxes,
- Simplified regulations and one-stop permitting,
- Prompt payment of bills,
- Reduced costs for bonding and insurance,
- Preferential procurement for city-resident firms, and
- Small business experience in city business development agency.

PART II
Organization and Management

CHAPTER 5

Local Economic Development Practices

Cheryl Farr

Local governments in the United States play a substantial role in enhancing the economic vitality of their communities and job availability to residents through a complex set of proactive and reactive endeavors. Involvement in economic development is an integral aspect of local government. Regulatory and taxing powers as well as their expenditures on public infrastructure and facilities enable local governments to influence the economic and quality-of-life costs and benefits of various locations. Private sector decision makers consider local characteristics when choosing locations for their businesses. Many day-to-day local government actions can have a cumulative effect on the jurisdiction's long-run economic development opportunities, and it is frequently difficult to predict accurately these long-run results.[1] Recognizing that local land-use and development controls affect private sector actions that in turn influence the local economy, local officials weigh the economic, environmental, and other impacts of proposed regulatory changes.

Local officials respond to proposed new development plans by balancing the problems and the opportunities that growth brings. They look not only at the tax benefits but also at the consequences of new development like the effects on traffic, the ability of public services and infrastructure to meet new development needs, and the impact on environmental systems. Sometimes, officials must also weigh short-term against long-term benefits of a proposed development that requires changing existing local land-use plans.

Originally published as "Encouraging Local Economic Development: The State of the Practice," Chapter 3 of Municipal Year Book, *1990. Published by the International City/County Management Association, Washington, D.C. Reprinted with permission of the publisher.*

In addition to responding to private sector plans, local governments also serve as a catalyst for private action. Many seek to leverage public investment proactively by tying public commitments to private plans for the development, expansion, or rehabilitation of existing structures. For example, some local governments work with blue ribbon committees to plan downtown improvements and offer to provide municipal parking and upgrade sidewalk amenities if business owners commit to rehabilitating their stores, coordinating store hours, and cosponsoring special events. Other communities, aware of the importance of a skilled workforce, initiate efforts to help existing companies create on-the-job training programs or vocational training programs for students in an effort to strengthen work-force skills. Still others create programs to help provide loans or loan subsidies to businesses interested in expanding their operations or reinvigorating the community.

In addition to direct program development or support, local governments market their location to interested businesses. They visit prospective industries, develop brochures and videos, and serve as a clearinghouse for information on local services, workforce characteristics, transportation, available land, and other data that facilitate business decisions. Sometimes local governments conduct studies to identify community and regional market opportunities for private investment and then promote the results to encourage private sector investments. These efforts are often aimed at diversifying the local economy. Recognizing that heavy dependence on one industry causes the local economy to slump when that industry slumps, certain areas, especially those dependent on heavy cyclical industries like oil or automobiles, often adapt a strategy of encouraging other types of development in order to reduce the effect of business cycles in the community. These and many other tools enable local governments to help guide the course of community growth and economic activity in ways that they hope will strengthen the community's economic health.

Proactive and reactive efforts resulting from local government actions are intended to influence the primary force in local economic development: independent decisions of private sector actors within the free market economy. Since the economic strength of a community results largely from the level of funds coming into it from beyond the jurisdiction's boundaries and from how many times those funds circulate through the economy, local government officials want to understand the market activity and to facilitate its effectiveness. In recent years, planning successful economic development strategies has required local officials to focus far beyond their own jurisdiction's boundaries. It requires an understanding of the global economy; of federal and state mandates and policies; of regional trends, needs, and opportunities; and of local actors and the strengths they can bring to community efforts to influence economic growth. In 1989, ICMA surveyed local governments about their role in economic development. The survey asked local officials to identify their local governments' economic development goals, the activities they undertook to achieve those goals, the organizational structure they used to implement their programs, and the local governments' perceptions of their programs' effectiveness.

This chapter reports on the survey's findings regarding the respondents' top priority goals, their organizational structures, and the perceived effectiveness of local government economic development programs in meeting those goals. Information on population size, economic base, and other characteristics of responding communities is provided so that readers can evaluate the applicability of various local development activities to their own jurisdictions.

Methodology

The survey "Economic Development—1989" was mailed to 3,461 cities, towns, and counties in March of 1989. A second mailing was sent six weeks later to nonrespondents. The data represented here draw on the completed questionnaires received.

All cities 10,000 and above in population and 50% of the counties 25,000 and over received a survey. Not all survey respondents answered each questions.

Where possible, comparisons are made between the data collected from the 1989 survey and data collected by ICMA through a similar survey conducted in 1984.

Throughout this chapter, relationships among variables are discussed, and city and county places are combined into one pool of respondents. Population and regional information are two variables discussed frequently. Regional differences in economic development strategies and goals are highlighted because differences in characteristics like the skills of the existing workforce, natural resources, and access to markets may cause regional differences in pro-

grams and approaches. Population differences are discussed because this variable provides a useful proxy for the overall level of economic activity and of resources likely to exist in a given community. As a result, a link often exists between jurisdiction size and program activities.

Readers should not assume that causal relationships exist between variables without considering the impact that other variables may have on the relationship. For example, although information about where economic development functions are placed within local governments is presented in relationship to the top priority goals of the local economic development programs, the placement may be more a factor of jurisdiction size (and thereby budget and the local government's structure) than a function of the particular economic development activities. Because of the variation in the percentage of respondents from places with different population sizes, particular care should be taken when evaluating regional trends. In some cases, regional differences may result from the larger numbers of small places in regions (e.g., the Northeast as compared to the West).

This study examines the distribution of respondents by metro status and population size. These variables affect the economic multiplier—the number of times a dollar entering the local economy flows through it before leaving the jurisdiction's boundaries. Larger communities have concentrations of both population and businesses that provide greater opportunities for the repeated flow of funds within the community. Independent communities generally face little local competition for funds because buyers have fewer choices of jurisdictions in which to purchase goods and services: therefore, these communities tend to have a higher multiplier than suburban communities of similar size. These characteristics, as well as others that affect local economic development strategies, will be discussed in further detail.

Creating Partnerships

Many forces beyond the jurisdictional boundaries of a local government affect its economy, and local officials work in a variety of ways to influence and track trends. The need for local officials to function as mediators, facilitators, and coalition builders using a wide range of approaches is paramount to the design and implementation of effective economic development strategies.

International Factors. While some local governments pay scant attention to international influences on local markets, others see this arena as an opportunity for economic development and as a significant influence on their economy. Some local officials in California, for example, say that the impact of business decisions from Pacific Rim countries is one of the more significant influences on regional, and thereby local, economic health. Some local government officials actively encourage international trade and work to help local businesses develop international markets. A variety of jurisdictions operate these international trade programs, and many are joint ventures between local and state government, universities, and the business community. One example is the Louisville–Jefferson County Commerce and Trade Program, which seeks

out and develops markets for local business' goods and services. In its first year, the program recruited 2 foreign companies, created 50 jobs, and helped 140 local companies learn more about exporting. This joint venture is a partnership between the county's economic development office, local companies, the Chamber of Commerce, and two local universities.[2]

In the future, more of these partnerships will probably occur, as local and regional programs are created to respond to international forces or encourage more exportation of local goods and services. The differential impact of the global economy on specific regions is difficult to predict. Multinational firms manufacture products worldwide and draw on suppliers from many countries. Merchandise traded among industrial countries is nearly 30% of goods produced, but the percentage varies among regions.[3] The result is that the rise and fall of the dollar against other currencies has different effects on different industries and thereby on regional and local economies. And, as service businesses that rely on telecommunications rather than transportable networks become a larger part of the U.S. economy, the impact may be significant in unexpected locations.

Policies and Mandates. State and federal policies and mandates are variables that affect local economic development in ways that often appear more visible than do international markets and business cycles. Changes in federal policies have generally been perceived by local governments to have negatively affected their ability to achieve their local economic development goals in recent years. Significant among the changes that have affected local governments have been the reduction in Community Development Block Grant funding and the elimination of general revenue sharing and Urban Development Action Grants.[4]

State policies and the image of a state as a location for business are perceived as having a substantial influence on local capabilities to recruit and retain industry. Business climate factors are often discussed on a state-by-state basis. Factors that are discussed include "the attitude of working people to hard work, to quality work, to unionization; the attitude of government to business, as reflected in government aid in solving joint problems, and in regulations, tax rates, and financing; the attitude of government in managing itself, its services, its schools."[5] On balance, local governments have reported on the positive overall effect on local economic development activities of state policies and grants of home rule and municipal fiscal authority, of state infrastructure, and education improvement programs.[6]

Here, again, local officials must play the role of the broker-negotiator to effect (or prevent) changes that will facilitate local economic development programs. Through state leagues, the National League of Cities, and groups like the Council on Urban Economic Development (CUED), many local officials track legislative activity that could affect the tools available to local governments in creating economic development strategies. When appropriate, elected officials or their representatives lobby to influence state and federal policies and mandates that affect the local economy. Some local governments also lobby directly or engage in related activities.

Regional Solutions. Closer to home, local officials also promote economic growth by taking an active role in working with representatives of numerous public and private groups to develop and implement regional solutions to problems such as transportation, wastewater treatment, solid-waste disposal, and other issues that affect multiple jurisdictions. Sometimes, they form regional organizations or special districts to implement effective transportation systems, create good work-force education programs, and increase the availability of affordable housing—all significant characteristics in business location decisions. Structuring regional solutions to issues is becoming more common as resource limitations force local governments to seek the most cost-effective solutions to multijurisdictional concerns.

Community Solutions. Within the community, too, the current trend continues to be toward greater reliance on public-private partnerships to bring creative solutions to local issues. Strategic planning and consensus-building techniques are used extensively by communities to set agendas for the future and to strengthen the ability of the community to act rather than react to situations.[7] Many economic development practitioners feel strongly that the structured involvement of participants from all facets of the community is a critical ingredient in making local economic development policies representative and equitable.[8]

Depending on community size, community needs, and special interest groups, each community must create its own approach to public-private partnerships that will promote economic well-being in the community and leverage government resources. These projects may range from planning effective strategies to implementing specific new projects and providing management assistance programs for existing businesses. Cleveland is an example of a community using numerous public-private partnerships to revitalize its economy. The chief executive officers of 44 major Cleveland corporations worked together with the city in a public-private partnership called Cleveland Tomorrow. This partnership resulted in a range of programs, including counseling entrepreneurs and helping them find financing for their business ventures; promoting better labor-management cooperation; and increasing manufacturing firms' productivity through the efforts of leaders in education, government, and business. Other public-private partnerships in Cleveland have focused on helping small and medium-sized businesses obtain federal contracts and revitalize specific neighborhoods.[9]

The appropriateness of using public-private partnership efforts to promote economic development has been questioned by some researchers because those who stand to gain most from public action are often involved in planning the action. The concern is that economic development practitioners, who link public and private sector interests, measure their effectiveness by the number of businesses brought in, which could bias the practitioners' recommendations toward business interests rather than the public interest.[10] Despite this concern, the role of the local government official in a range of areas continues to evolve toward one of broker-negotiator with the public sector, and economic development programs are no exception. Local officials who use public-private partnerships to promote economic development are confident that this approach is in the public interest and that the most effective decisions and strategies are those resulting from cooperative efforts with the private sector. And, as the next section discusses, the use of this approach for local economic development is on the rise.

Community Leadership for Economic Development

Survey respondents in both 1984 and 1989 were asked which of three common approaches to community leadership for economic development efforts they relied on:

1. The local government is the most active group in local economic development.
2. There is a formal or informal public-private organization, or local development corporation, taking charge.
3. The private sector is the most active group in local economic development.

Local Government Activity. Forty-one percent of the jurisdictions identify the local government as the most active in promoting local economic development in 1989.

This is down from the number reporting government as most active in 1984 (55%). In 1989, the use of this approach was highest in the smallest communities. In places from 50,000 to 99,999, the use of this approach dropped 20 percentage points in the last five years. A smaller percentage of places in the South continued to report local government taking the lead than did other regions of the country. The largest regional decrease in the local government role was in the Northeast, where the level dropped 20 percentage points.

Formal Public-Private Partnerships. One of the significant differences between 1984 and 1989 local economic development activities, based on the data collected in the two surveys conducted by ICMA, is that the use of formal public-private partnerships has increased substantially. In 29% of communities, a formal, incorporated public-private organization took the lead in 1989, while in 1984 only 15% of communities reported using a formal, incorporated public-private organization. In places from 25,000 to 250,000 in population, the use of public-private partnerships roughly doubled. In the West, the percent using public-private organizations has more than doubled since 1984. The extent of such organizations is noticeably lower in the Northeast than in other regions. Central cities report a high increase in the use of public-private partnerships (up 21 percentage points from five years ago). There is a decrease in the percentage of respondents that use formal public-private organizations as population size decreases.

When a formal public-private partnership is created, a common approach is to create an Economic Development Corporation (EDC) or Local Development Corporation (LDC). LDCs are nonprofit organizations that can make loans to private businesses and carry out other related activities. A key benefit of an LDC is that its governing board (usually comprising public and private leaders) can be structured to provide for accountability in meeting public goals while enabling the local government to participate with fewer regulatory restrictions on day-to-day activities than it could without the LDC.

Private Sector Groups. In 1989, another quarter of the jurisdictions report reliance on a private business group such as the Chamber of Commerce or Board of Trade; the percentage reported in 1984 was 30%. The percentage using this approach is lowest in the communities from 100,000 to 249,999 and dropped by almost half in five years. Almost a quarter (23.9%) of all places over 250,000 in population say that the private sector is the most active in economic development at this time. The percentage of places using this approach is down by 11 percentage points in both central and independent cities.

Even when local governments are not taking the lead role in economic development, they provide financial support. Where there is a formal public-private partnership, the local government provides some funding in 92% of the communities. When private business takes the lead, the local government still provides some funding 64% of the time (not shown).

Economic Development Goals

Local economic development programs can be designed to achieve a wide range of goals. ICMA's survey listed nine of the most common goals and asked respondents to identify their jurisdictions' top priority goals from 1986 through 1989. The respondents ranked the following goals:

1. To attract new business
2. To retain or expand existing business
3. To encourage downtown development or redevelopment

4. To encourage neighborhood commercial development
5. To promote industrial development
6. To promote small business development
7. To encourage office development
8. To encourage service sector growth
9. To encourage minority business development

Business Attraction, Retention, and Expansion. Tied for top priority among all respondents were attracting new businesses (29%) and retaining and expanding existing businesses (30%). These two goals were listed among the top three priorities by more than three-quarters of the responding communities. Local governments attract new business to expand the local economic base. New businesses can strengthen the economy by bringing new capital into the jurisdiction, particularly when the businesses' primary markets are nonlocal. New business attraction is also a method to achieve economic base diversification, making the community less vulnerable to the business cycles of individual industry groups. New businesses can provide jobs for the unemployed or underemployed and expand opportunities for skilled labor, which in turn may help increase the local wage levels and thereby discretionary spending. New businesses can broaden the tax base, enabling the local government to provide a broader array of services without increasing property taxes.

Much has been written claiming that attracting business from elsewhere in the country is essentially a zero-sum game for the national economy since re-location does not generate new dollars but rather moves them from one community or region to another. Nonetheless, businesses continue to reevaluate their locations as they diversify their operations, as they change ownership, as their plants become outmoded, as businesses expand to new markets, and as they seek to maximize revenues and minimize costs in other ways. During the period from 1986 through 1989, nearly one-third of all communities made it their top economic development priority to woo these businesses.

While local governments continue to invest resources in attracting new businesses, they see supporting the growth and maintenance of existing businesses as equally important. They recognize that there are financial benefits associated with helping businesses currently in the community to broaden their markets, tap new markets, improve their management capabilities, or develop more effective ways to train new employees or upgrade employees' skills. Sometimes the costs of strengthening existing businesses are less than those of attracting new business. Local governments also are aware that people with businesses in the community have an existing commitment to the locale and an impact on residents that provides some unique benefits for business expansion.

Strengthening the Commercial Sector. Downtown development is the top priority of 18% and one of the top three choices for almost half of the communities that identified priority goals. Neighborhood commercial development, on the other hand, is listed as a priority, or goal, by many communities (53.5%) but has been the top priority of less than 1.0% of the respondents and one of the top three priorities for almost

8.0%. Creating viable commercial centers provides communities with more than just tax and license revenues. Service businesses create jobs as well as places for local residents and local business employees to spend discretionary income, which results in more dollars circulating more times through the local economy. Downtowns also play an important role in creating a sense of community, making them significant for more than financial reasons. The fact that local governments rarely make neighborhood-based commercial development their focus suggests that they, like researchers, see neighborhoods as primarily social, not economic, entities. Because of the lack of economic control of neighborhoods, programs designed to help a specific neighborhood strengthen its business sector are probably not effective strategies. Says one researcher,

> A melange of small business support programs (that) attempt to save failing firms and investment in cosmetic improvement of neighborhood shopping areas scarcely qualifies as a well-grounded strategy.... From an economic perspective, it is doubtful that anything (other than employment and training programs) can be more than a temporary palliative.[11]

In larger communities, the allocation of resources to support or upgrade neighborhood commercial areas versus downtown infrastructure can be a significant political issue. Neighborhood advocates often are at odds with one another, fighting for what they view as their fair share of community resources. And the central business district may be seen by neighborhood groups as getting an unfair share of local resources.

Broadening the Industrial Base. A diversified industrial base is an im-

portant factor in protecting communities from downturns in specific parts of the economy and provides a significant opportunity for jobs. Encouraging industrial development is the top priority of 16% of jurisdictions; 90% say it is a goal. Many local governments now use extensive analysis to determine the types of industries that can best thrive in their areas. Their efforts are targeted to specific industries that they think would benefit from their location, work-force skills, and other characteristics. Local governments then tailor their business attraction and retention programs to encourage specific types of industries.

Small Business Development. The top priority for only 1% of communities, small business development is listed as a goal for 89% of the local governments responding to ICMA's survey. One might expect that small business development would be a priority goal more frequently because this sector of the economy has a high rate of creating new jobs. In addition, entrepreneurs who create small businesses tend to stay in their communities rather than maximizing their financial return by seeking the ideal location for their businesses. Perhaps one reason for the low is that many local governments may consider small business development part of their business attraction and retention efforts but not a separate goal.

A specific approach to small business development that has received a lot of media attention in recent years is the creation of incubators—programs that provide new businesses with access to needed services at reduced costs, with advice on business management and, in many cases, with access to capital trust, which may help them move beyond the start-up phase to becoming a small business. One notable example is the Mobile, Alabama, Area Chamber of Commerce's "Jobs Creation System." A public-private partnership among the city of Mobile, the surrounding Mobile County, the chamber, and the University of South Alabama, this incubator resulted in 26 new business start-ups (4 from out-of-state) and 76 new jobs over three years. Six companies "graduated" during that period and left the incubator.[12]

Office Development. Another goal of local economic development efforts is office development. This is a goal for 72%, but the top priority for only 2% of respondents. Since almost three-quarters of local governments responding to the question reported office development as a goal, local officials probably continue to view new office buildings as an effective method for bringing new jobs into the community. But research suggests that much of the result of office development may be neither new business additions nor the expansion of existing businesses, but rather movement within the business community that is driven most often by a desire of businesses to upgrade their images. A study of one midwestern city found that of the rentable office space left behind by tenants moving into new buildings, half remained empty after two years. While new buildings can have a positive impact, excessive vacant space can create a negative perception of a business district in trouble. Local officials need to be leery of rosy projections about the job-generating effects of new office development.[13]

Service Sector Growth. Despite the indications that service sector growth is widely viewed as one of the primary areas for job growth potential for the 1990s, less than 1% of communities list it as their first priority; 6% rank it among their top three priorities, and 68% list it as a goal. Some of this may be the result of service sector employment being a sub-goal of business attraction and retention efforts rather than a goal in and of itself (either as a strategy to expand the economic base or to support the needs of manufacturing companies located in the region). But other factors may also come into play. In the past, service sector jobs were assumed to pay relatively low wages and to have little effect on the amount of capital from other jurisdictions coming into the community.

Recent research suggests that both of these assumptions may be wrong. More than 70% of the service jobs created in the mid–1980s were in the managerial and technical categories.[14] Other studies indicate that many service businesses have large nonlocal customer bases.[15] One study showed that a third of the Puget Sound, Washington, regional service sector employment is linked to export markets—and that small firms were just as successful in penetrating export markets as large firms.[16] Telemarketing, a growing employer in Omaha, Nebraska, and Des Moines, Iowa, has a substantial part of its local economy boosted by insurance industry revenues. These service industries find proximity to market location a less significant factor because they rely more on telecommunications to research their market. The quality of telecommunications infrastructure and community quality of life are increasingly significant factors in the business location decision.[17]

Promoting the Development of Minority Businesses. Encouraging the development of minority-owned businesses is a goal reported by 56% of respondents. However, this is not seen as a priority goal by most places, and 45% of the respondents reported that it was not a goal for their community during the last five years. Just one community responding to ICMA's 1989 survey said minority business development is its top priority—in fact, its combined percentage as first, second, or third priority is just 3%—far lower than the percentages for any other economic development goal. In ICMA's 1984 survey, approximately 18% of the responding local governments reported that they had some special programs aimed at encouraging economic development activity by minority groups. The low number of places listing this as a priority in 1989 suggests that the number of special programs has probably decreased during the last five years; reduced federal funding may have been a factor.

How Top Priorities Vary by Local Government Characteristics

Several characteristics can influence local government economic development programs. Population size and metro status can help create a sufficient market and encourage certain types of businesses. Regional transportation systems and market characteristics, plus the existing economic base, also influence the market and, as a result, the natural direction of the growth of the local economy. ICMA was interested in exploring the relationships among these variables and economic development program goals of the respondents.

Population Size. ICMA's survey data show the variation based on population size for local governments giving top priority to various goals.

Places ranging from 100,000 to 250,000 in population reported new business attraction as their top priority more frequently than any other goal. Correspondingly, a lower percentage of jurisdictions of this size identify downtown development or revitalization as their number one priority. Neighborhood commercial development is the top priority of only four places, all of them under 100,000 population. Industrial development is the top priority of a higher percentage of places under 10,000 population than other jurisdiction sizes. Not surprisingly, the only respondent to list minority business development as a top priority is above one million in population (not shown). Of those few places that have small business development, office development, or service sector growth as their top priority, they are predominantly places below 100,000 population.

Metro Status. Depending on the jurisdiction's metro status, its top priorities change.

For example, retaining and expanding existing business is top priority for 40% of independent cities but for only 24% of responding suburban places; downtown development or revitalization is a priority for 22% of suburban places and 7% of independent cities. And more than twice as many independent cities (25%) list industrial development as their top priority than do suburban jurisdictions (11%).

Geographic Region. Regional economic trends have significant influence on local economies. Regional growth and decline patterns have many causes. Among the significant ones are (1) competition within the global economy, (2) international inflationary and deflationary business cycles that affect goods-producing regions differently than more commodities-dependent regions, (3) the changing federal environment, and (4) how state practices within the region shift in response to federal changes.[18] Funds cross the jurisdictional boundaries of a local government as a result of many types of business activity. Tourism brings dollars from outside the community; retail businesses may bring in regional funds; and manufacturing firms may sell goods locally, regionally, nationally, or internationally and bring in substantial revenues. Residents who work outside the community but spend a large portion of their wages in local commercial and service establishments also contribute to the economic vitality of a community by providing a market for its goods and services.

Many business location decisions are based largely on characteristics beyond local government control—regional market demand, workforce, climate, and access to transportation are some of the more significant factors. So regional trends as well as state tax laws and business incentive programs affect choices. Federal programs to assist local economic development efforts have been cut during the past decade. But state and federal mandates that require local governments to adopt specific strategies addressing environmental, infrastructure, and other concerns create funding needs that differ for local governments depending on their regional location.

Across regions, there is some variation in top priorities. For example, 39% of places in the North Central region report retaining or expanding existing business as their top goal, while 24% of jurisdictions in the Northeast region report this as their primary economic development focus. Downtown development or redevelopment is a goal of 13% of places in the South and of 23% of places in the Northeast. Industrial development is a priority for nearly twice as many places in the South (22%) as in the West (12%). This may be at least partially due to the fact that the number of places reporting under 10,000 in population is substantially larger in the South.

Existing Economic Base

Effective economic development strategies build on the jurisdiction's strengths and minimize its weaknesses, increasing the desirability as a location for business enterprise. An objective look at the existing local economic base shows types of businesses that currently find the location advantageous, which enables identification of the types of businesses that could be attracted—either to support the existing businesses or because of the market for certain goods and services.

ICMA was interested in the relationship between the economic base, the growth rate of that base, and the local government involvement in local economic development. Because the current local economic situation affects the ability of a local government to achieve goals (particularly in the short term), survey respondents were asked to identify their primary economic base. This study examines the economic base of responding local governments according to population. The primary economic base—and the average growth rate of the economic base—among the responding places varies substantially. As would be expected, places reporting a primary agricultural or residential economic base are usually under 50,000 in population. Communities with an industrial or commercial economic base vary more in size.

Community Leadership and the Economic Base. Places with an agriculturally based economy report that formal public-private partnerships take the lead 38% of the time—more than any other group (not shown). In jurisdictions that are predominately residential in character, 50% of the time the local government takes the lead, and public-private partnerships are only used by 12% of places. When industrial activities dominate the local economy, the local government (37%) or a public-private partnership (36%) is favored over private business (20%) as the leader in economic development efforts. In commercially based economies, private business took the lead 28% of the time.

Priority Goal and the Economic Base. Comparing the top priority goal of the respondents to the economic base information they reported suggests that most jurisdictions seek to build on their existing strengths.

Those with industrial and agriculturally based economies give top priority to retaining and expanding existing businesses. Encouraging small business development is identified as a priority most frequently by places with agriculturally based economies. Respondents who report downtown redevelopment as their top priority typically rely on a commercial economic base or are from primarily residential jurisdictions. Those jurisdictions with a predominantly commercial base show relatively

little interest in industrial development as a top priority. Places with a primarily residential economic base are slightly more inclined to make attracting new businesses their number one priority than are those with other types of economic bases.

Growth Rate of Economic Base. Relatively few places (11%) report that their economic base has been declining during the last five years. Of those reporting significant decline, almost half are below 25,000 population, but smaller places tend to report more rapid growth rates as well (32.8%). The majority report their growth rate as slow (less than 10% change) to moderate (10% to 25%) over the last five years. Some of this is undoubtedly due to the fact that the relative impact of both business closings and new businesses is greater in small jurisdictions.

What is the relationship between the direction and rate of change in a jurisdiction's economic base and its top economic development priority. Places that have experienced rapid economic expansion over the past five years report that their number one goal is attracting new business (32%); retaining or expanding existing business is a distant second (21%). Some of these are undoubtedly places that are working hard to maximize the benefits of their location during a boom period; others may be in a mode of responding to private sector forces by providing various services but not necessarily trying to channel the growth in any specific ways. Jurisdictions that report moderate growth are somewhat more balanced between attracting new (33%) and retaining or expanding existing (26%) businesses, as are places that have experienced slow growth. This latter group also emphasizes retaining or expanding existing businesses (34%) over attracting new businesses (26%).

Places with a stable economic base over the past five years tend to give priority to keeping what they have: retaining or expanding existing business is the top priority of 37%, downtown development or redevelopment is the top priority of 25%, and new business attraction, the top priority of 24% of these jurisdictions. Places with a modestly declining economic base emphasize business retention somewhat more (39%) than those with other types of economic bases, but many continue to focus first on business attraction (27%). And those places that report significant decline over the last five years are split between retaining and expanding existing businesses (35%) and attracting new businesses (33%).

Leadership and Growth Rate of Economic Base. When growth is moderate to rapid, the local government is most often in charge of economic development efforts. Places experiencing decline in their economic base use public-private partnerships twice as often as do places with moderate to rapid growth. The private sector often takes the lead in stable environments.

Organizational Structure

The tasks that will be carried out by the local government are an important determinant in the placement of economic development activities within the local government structure. Some tasks will fit more logically in a manager's office, while others may be a logical extension of an existing department's functions. However, the history of relationships between the private sector and existing local agencies, departments, and their key staff is also an important consideration. These relationships will influence the private sector's (1) perception of the importance that the local government gives to the economic development functions and (2) confidence in staffs' ability to mobilize resources to complete tasks.

Where is economic development placed in the local government structure? Local governments were asked to choose among five options to describe how their government is organized to carry out economic development functions:

1. Economic development functions are within the office of the mayor/ city manager/chief administrative officer (CAO).
2. Economic development is centralized in a separate and distinct department.
3. Economic development is decentralized; functions are carried out by a variety of line departments.
4. Some economic development functions are part of a centralized department, and others are carried out by separate line departments.
5. Economic development is a function of a larger agency, such as a community development department, that has among its activities housing, zoning, inspections, etc.

In many small communities, the city manager, the finance director , and the economic development director are the same person, making location of the economic development function in the manager's office a necessity. Many moderate-sized communities traditionally place economic development in the chief administrator's office to give the function visibility and to demonstrate a "commitment from the top." This can be particularly important in places where relationships between the community development and housing offices and the private sector have been somewhat adversarial.

Decentralization of economic development functions into many different departments works best in places where established interdepartmental relationships enable effective matrix approaches. Decentralizing can be an effective way to provide a greater budgetary commitment that is less easily targeted for budget cuts, since the funding will be spread among several budgets.

This study reviewed the structure reported by the 1984 and 1989 survey respondents by population group. Overall, the most frequent response is that economic development functions are located in the office of the mayor/CAO/city manager (36%); the second most frequent response is in a separate department or division (27%). This is somewhat different from the structure reported by respondents in 1984. At that time, 40% reported placing economic development in the city manager's or chief administrator's office, and 11% reported that there was a separate department or division. The proportion reporting economic development as part of a larger community and economic development agency has declined from 25% in 1984 to 17% in 1989. The number reporting partial or complete decentralization of the economic development function has also declined slightly.

Among population groups, the largest places tend to show the largest amount of change in structure. In places with populations of 100,000 to 250,000, the percentage of places reporting a separate department increased 24.5 percentage points, and the percentage reporting a combined community and economic development department dropped by almost 20 percentage points. In places from 50,000 to 99,999 in population, the percentage reporting a separate department increased by 25 percentage points, and the percentage reporting a combined community and economic development department dropped by 20 percentage points.

The pattern of the largest change in organizational structure being an increase in the number of economic development departments also holds true for smaller places; there is an 8 percentage point increase in the use of separate departments in places from 10,000 to 24,999 in population. There is a drop of almost 5 percentage points in the percent of those smaller places that indicate a combined community and economic development department. The precipitous drop in community development block grant funding combined with the elimination of revenue sharing may have resulted in a scaling back of housing-related activities in many places and a focus on economic development functions.

Also reviewed is the relationship between the organizational structure and the top priority economic development goal identified by responding jurisdictions. When economic development is in the chief administrator's office, the top priority is most often new business attraction. When economic development is placed in a separate department, the top priority is most often business retention and expansion;

business attraction is a close second. When downtown development or redevelopment is the top priority, places tend to use a more decentralized structure. When economic development is part of a larger department's responsibilities, there is the most variation among the top priority goals the local governments are trying to achieve.

Having certain economic development priorities would influence who would be most involved in promoting local economic development. For example, if programs to attract new business are perceived to increase competition for a small pool of skilled workers and thereby raise labor costs, many existing business owners may see this as a threat and would not champion such efforts; the local government is more likely to be the leader. Conversely, if downtown business owners believe that their businesses will prosper by getting more foot traffic, which would be increased by a broader diversity of stores, then the business owners might be expected to play a significant role in encouraging the attraction of new commercial enterprises.

ICMA's survey suggests this may well be the case. When attracting new business is the primary goal, 43% of places have the local government taking the lead, 27% are formal public-private partnerships, and 23% are led by the private sector. The percentages are similar when retaining existing businesses is the primary goal. When downtown development and redevelopment or service sector growth are the focus, private groups like the Chamber of Commerce tend to take the lead more frequently.

Financing and Staffing Economic Development

Economic development program budgets vary dramatically; there are a wide variety of tasks that can be undertaken under the guise of economic development, and some require substantially more capital than others. Likewise, some programs are much more labor intensive than others.

Financing. Costs can be quite high if economic development activities include, for example, investment in infrastructure improvements for a commercial area plus direct loans or loan subsidies to individual businesses in that area to enable them to expand their operations or upgrade their properties.

Almost one quarter (23%) of the respondents report that their budget was under $25,000; most of those are places under 50,000 in population.

Not surprisingly, funding sources have changed substantially in the last five years.

Today three-quarters of all respondents report using general fund revenues for economic development (78%). Of those using general fund revenues, 64% report that they are one of the primary sources of funds for their economic development programs, and 39% report them as the primary source. In 1984, 61% of the respondents reported using general fund revenues for their economic development programs; 44% reported them as one of their three top sources, and 19% reported them as the primary source of funding for their programs. The use of local revenues has increased by about 12 percentage points in places under 50,000 population; it has risen by about 30 percentage points in places from 100,000 to 249,999 in population.

A substantial drop has occurred in local governments' reliance on federal grants-in-aid as a funding source. While more than half (53%) of places note that they rely on federal grants-in-aid for economic development activities today, a smaller number (about 42% of those using federal funds) report that those funds are one of their three primary sources of funding, and only 15% report that federal funds are their most important funding source. These figures are down substantially from five years ago, when 71% of the responding jurisdictions reported that they used federal grants-in-aid, and 56% reported that they were one of their three primary sources of funding. At that time, 27% reported federal grants-in-aid as the single most important source for their programs. The change has been to decrease use of this source in almost all population groups by 20 percentage points, except in the 50,000 to 100,000 population group, in which its use has decreased approximately 13 percentage points.

State grants-in-aid are a source of funding for 32% of jurisdictions, but only 4% report that this is the primary funding source. General obligation bonds, revenue bonds, tax increment financing revenues, and special assessment district revenues are all sources used, but account for a modest percentage of respondents' top revenue sources. While the 1989 data show some increase in the use of these tools over the 1984 survey, the level of increase is too modest to have statistical significance.

Staffing. In most places, modest staff resources are allocated for economic development. As one would expect, there is a link between staff size and the population of the responding jurisdic-tion. Fifty-eight percent of the respondents who report that they allocate one person's time primarily to economic development activities are places below 25,000 in population. Another third (34%) of places below 25,000 in population supplement that person with an additional one to two staff persons. Thirteen percent of places report allocating more than four professional staff (including the manager or director of economic development) to economic development activities, but more than half (58%) of places over 250,000 population report staffs of more than ten people in addition to the economic development director. More than half (56%) report that the economic development director works less than 80% of the time on economic development activities. The average salary for economic development directors was $43,752 as of January 1989.

Evaluating the Effectiveness of Economic Development Programs

How effective are efforts to encourage economic development, and how do local governments measure effectiveness? Overall, just one quarter of all places report conducting formal evaluations. There is a clear correlation between size of jurisdiction and the existence of a formal evaluation process. Obviously, the larger the program, the more resources the program managers may be able to devote to analysis—or the more desire there may be on the part of the manager, council, or commission to require a formal evaluation process. In places over 100,000 in population, about

35% use a formal evaluation process. In places under 100,000 in population, about 20% use a formal process.

The use of formal evaluations is apparently tied to available staff time, expertise, and other resources for evaluations that are available in larger places but cannot be allocated when staff size is limited. Among places where staff is limited to a single person handling economic development, only 15% said they conduct formal annual evaluations of their economic development programs. The percentages climbed steadily as the number of staff increased, but surprisingly, even in places where ten or more staff are working on economic development, only half of the places report formal annual evaluations of how effectively they are achieving their goals.

It's not simply the level of funding allocated to the program. This study revealed that 17% of those places that report spending less than $25,000 annually on economic development activities report using a formal process to evaluate their program effectiveness. But among those spending more than $100,000 on economic development, the percentage formally evaluating their programs never rises above 38%.

Whether or not the communities report using a formal evaluation process, most places can say whether their program met, exceeded, or fell short of expectations. Nearly half (49%) feel the programs meet their expectations. Almost a quarter say their programs exceed expectations, and another quarter feel their programs fall short. The major findings of this study are highlighted below.

1. Overall, the programs that most frequently exceed expectations are those focused on industrial development, business attraction, and business retention. Those that most frequently meet expectations are those focused on the goals (regardless of priority) of business retention, small business development, and neighborhood commercial development.

2. Business attraction program results most often exceed expectations when that area is the jurisdiction's top priority. But the results fall short of expectations just as often as they exceed expectations when business attraction is a goal but not a top priority.

3. Local governments report meeting or exceeding expectations more consistently for top priority business retention programs than they do for business attraction programs.

4. When downtown development or redevelopment is a goal but not the top goal, program results fall short of expectations close to 40% of the time.

5. For industrial development programs, the distribution is fairly even among local governments reporting the activity as first (30%), second (40%), or third priority (30%).

6. Among those most satisfied with their program results are the jurisdictions that rank small business development or service sector development as their top priority.

Conclusion

The economic growth potential of individual jurisdictions is increasingly difficult to predict. Certainly it will continue to be influenced by the existing industry and population base, the availability of suitable sites and infrastructure, and the quality of the labor pool and of transportation to markets. But these factors are becoming less significant for many service businesses. Telecommunications infrastructure and capabilities are of growing importance in the way many service businesses reach markets. Quality of life promises to be a much more significant factor in business decisions in the years ahead as the impact of telecommunications continues to change our concept of the workplace.

The impact of international economic activities on local economies will continue to increase. West Coast communities in particular have reported the substantial influence of Pacific Rim business investments and plans on their local economies. With the dramatic changes taking place in Eastern Europe, the 1990s promise to be a time of continued change in the influence of the global economies on U.S. local economies.

Changes in intergovernmental relationships, too, will continue to affect local economic development opportunities. Federal funding changes—perhaps most significantly the prospect of more mandated responsibilities for environmental impacts coupled with fewer funds for infrastructure development and maintenance—have changed the financial impacts of economic growth in substantial ways that will continue to show their effects in the 1990s. Because of both state requirements and local revenue limitations, the use of special districts and other approaches to addressing regional issues and the use of development fees are other trends that bear watching.

It is also increasingly difficult to identify all of the actors who will be involved in defining and implementing future local economic development programs. There is today a heightened expectation that decision-making processes will be inclusionary, and many communities have witnessed a substantial increase in the number of organized special interest groups coming to the table on almost every issue. Economic development planning is no exception.

The data discussed in this article provide a snapshot of the goals local governments sought to achieve during the 1980s and the organizational structures they have used to achieve them. Perhaps the most significant trend identified is that the use of public-private partnerships has increased. The role of local leaders in planning and implementing economic development strategies is that of a broker and negotiator for an increasingly diverse set of actors, and each local government is unique in the way that role is played. Local, regional, state, federal, and international information provide important background for defining effective approaches. The difficulty for practitioners lies in determining which information is important for decision making, in predicting how trends will influence their economy, and in translating that complex picture in ways that make the information useful to policymakers.

Notes

1. Ann M. Bowman, *The Visible Hand: Major Issues in City Economic Policy* (The National League of Cities: Washington, D.C. 1987): 1.

2. "A Salute to Imaginative Economic Development Programs," Council on Urban Economic Development, 23–74, NCUED.

3. R. Scott Fosler, "The Future Economic Role of Local Governments," *Public Management* (April 1988): 4.

4. *The Visible Hand.*

5. Roger W. Schraenner, *Making Business Location Decisions* (Englewood Cliffs, NJ: Prentice-Hall, 1982).

6. *The Visible Hand*, 22–23.

7. Several recent ICMA publications discuss these issues. For example, *Taking Charge: How Communities Are Planning Their Futures*, a detailed discussion of the use of consensus-building techniques in long-range planning. Numerous reports, such as "*Community-Oriented Policy*" (MIS, 1989) and "*Solving Community Problems by Consensus*" (MIS, 1989) discuss the use of public-private partnerships for other purposes.

8. Bernard L. Berkowitz, "The Politics of Local Economic Development: A Review of Selected Recent Literature from the Perspective of the Practitioner." *Economic Development Quarterly*, vol. 2, no. 4 (November 1988): 353.

9. Voinovich, "Commentary," Council of Urban Economic Development, 4.

10. Herbert J. Rubin, "Shoot Anything That Flies; Claim Anything That Falls: Conversations with Economic Development Practitioners," *Economic Development Quarterly*, vol. 2, no. 3 (August 1988): 242–50.

11. Michael B. Teitz, "Neighborhood Economics: Local Communities and Regional Markets," *Economic Development Quarterly*, vol. 3, no. 2 (May 1989): 113, 121.

12. "A Salute to Imaginative Economic Development Programs," 8–10.

13. Carl V. Patton, "Jobs and Commercial Office Development: Do New Offices Generate Jobs?" *Economic Development Quarterly*, vol. 2, no. 4 (November 1988): 316–25.

14. R. Scott Fosler, "The Future Economic Role of Local Governments," *Public Management* (April 1988): 4.

15. William R. Gillis, "Can Service-Producing Industries Provide a Catalyst for Regional Economic Growth?" *Economic Development Quarterly*, vol. 1, no. 3 (1987): 250–51.

16. William B. Beyers, Michael J. Alvine, and Erik G. Johnsen, "The Service Sector: A Growing Force in the Regional Export Base," Commentary (Fall 1985): (Washington, D.C.: Council on Urban Economic Development): 4–5.

17. *America's Boom Towns*, *U.S. News and World Report*, 13 November 1989, 54–66.

18. Bernard L. Weinstein and Harold T. Gross, "The Rise and Fall of Sun, Rust, and Frost Belts," *Economic Development Quarterly*, vol. 2, no. 1 (Newbury Park, CA: Sage Publications, 1988):13–16.

CHAPTER 6

How to Get Started

Nancy Stark and *Hamilton Brown*

Strategic thinking strategic planning, community visioning—most communities have participated in some sort of rational process to guide the path toward economic development. Yet, their experiences haven't always been rewarding.

Many community planning efforts go unfulfilled. Participants become discouraged as the process consumes countless hours; requires excessive energy, and takes too long to produce tangible results. People lose track of who was doing what, why and when. Citizens grow frustrated with unavailable or incomprehensible data. Planning team members are annoyed by a public that misunderstands or challenges their reports.

But the process doesn't have to go this way.

Thoughtful strategic planning or community visioning can bring great meaning and direction to a community, without wearing down its participants.

A bottom-up visioning process engages new talent, generates new ideas, and energizes the citizenry. Effective planning incorporates enough structure to keep people on track, but not so much structure that creativity is hindered. Understandable data, clear and measurable goals, and a balance of short-term and long-term projects produces insights and demonstrates progress along the way. Strategies for continuous learning create and sustain enthusiasm among planning participants. Also, techniques for stimulating a dialogue with the whole community keep citizens informed and engaged in the process.

Especially during times of economic dislocation or changing leadership, communities need a vehicle for reflection and redirection. Sometimes the requirement to update the comprehensive land use plan will propel a community into broader, more strategic thinking and planning.

Originally published as "Getting Started," Chapter 2 of Harvesting Hometown Jobs, *1997. Published by the National Center for Small Communities, Washington, D.C. Reprinted with permission of the publisher.*

According to the Oregon Visions Project, a thoughtful visioning process can help to accomplish four important tasks for a community:

- Understand the values of its citizens and use them as a basis for planning.
- Identify the trends and forces that are affecting the community.
- Articulate a big-picture view to guide short-term decisions and long-term initiatives.
- Develop tools to achieve its vision.

Economic development practitioners William Schweke and Graham Toft confirm that when strategic planning is done well, it achieves at least five outcomes: enthusiasm, unity of purpose, commitment to action, sustained leadership, and enhanced risk-taking.

How to "Harvest" Results

Within this chapter are references to numerous strategic planning and visioning publications, ranging from elaborate guidebooks with sample exercises and worksheets to short, inspirational pieces. Private and nonprofit organizations across the country teach strategic planning at conferences or through independent institutes. Many states operate certification and competitive grant programs for communities that undertake strategic economic development planning.

No matter what strategic planning process your community might follow, or which community visioning training session your leaders might attend, there is plenty of room for tailoring and improvement. This chapter identifies and describes 10 characteristics of successful strategic planning and visioning efforts— 10 features that differentiate dynamic, effective planning experiences from those that consume countless hours, but go nowhere. These 10 traits of effective planning/visioning are organized around three broad concerns:

1. Who is involved; how participants organize and manage themselves and make decisions.
2. How information is used to gain insights and demonstrate progress along the way.
3. How positive energy and commitment are preserved within the planning team and the larger community.

Get your community started by building these "best practice" traits into your strategic planning or visioning process. Despite failings in past efforts, regardless of how "planned out" the community might be, this next experience can be different. Consider this wise adage: "If you always do what you've always done, then you'll get what you've always got." Is that what you really want?

WHO IS INVOLVED, HOW PARTICIPANTS ORGANIZE AND MANAGE THEMSELVES, AND MAKE DECISIONS

Planning Team Is Truly Representative of the Community or Region. The traditional style of strategic planning tends to exclude, usually unintentionally, many of the community's most energetic and talented people. The process typically begins with the creation of a planning committee, composed of five or six people, representing key local interests: chamber of commerce, bankers, local industry, local government, agriculture, real estate, etc. These recognized leaders command power and resources, and have much experience working together.

Although this style of strategic planning can quickly organize activity, it is often ineffective and unsustainable in the long run. There is too much work for too few people. Feelings of burden and disenchantment set in; project proposals that have been defeated in the past resurface. With little diversity, the group has difficulty generating new ideas. Citizens distanced from the planning effort feel disenfranchised and unintentionally may sabotage the committee's hard work.

Communities with successful planning and visioning experiences go much deeper and wider in creating a planning team. They think and work "outside the box." Rather than relying only on traditional leadership, they uncover a dozen or so individuals representing a cross-section of the community: members of active grassroots organizations, church leaders, citizens who have played background roles in important projects, the young and the very old, people of different ethnic and racial groups, low-income citizens, concerned parents, and others who care deeply about the community's future.

People possessing specific skills and qualifications are invited into the process. Organizers seek to involve people who do not necessarily agree with them on every issue. Local business and government leaders are engaged as well.

The process of assembling a diversely skilled planning team may take some time, but it need not halt the visioning work. If an inspired startup group is ready and willing to get going, there is no need to wait until the team is fully in place. The group can go ahead and get the organizational work moving while simultaneously recruiting a diverse membership.

This eclectic group of a dozen or so citizens undoubtedly experiences bumps along the way, but it can more faithfully represent the needs and resources of the community. Members' talents are supplemented by others who attend a meeting or two, when their specific knowledge or skills are required, or who serve on special task forces or sub-committees.

Finding talented people who care deeply about the community, but have never before held leadership roles, requires imaginative thinking. Helen Lewis of the Highlander Research and Education Center, based in New Market, Tenn., has nearly 60 years of experience empowering citizen groups. She discovers new concerned citizens by knocking on doors, asking "Who's been doing stuff around here?" She identifies each and every small grassroots organization existing in the region: church groups, PTAs, recreation and sports leagues, informal groups organized around basic needs such as health or child care, arts organizations, women's networks, and more. One-on-one conversations and house meetings with neighbors locate and engage new, interested people. A smart strategy is to recognize the "hands" that have helped strengthen the community, not just the "mouths" who have spoken.

Individuals recruited for a planning team will have many questions, and may hesitate to get involved. Their initial reaction may be colored by past experiences with inadequately conceived projects that consumed precious hours. Sometimes people are unwilling to get involved unless there is money available to finance the project ideas they generated. Be prepared with clear answers to such inquiries as: What is the purpose of planning? What is the job of the planning team, and what will be expected of me as a member? How is this effort different from previous ones? Who else has agreed to participate? How much time will be required? Will it cost me anything except my time? How will it benefit me personally? How will the community benefit from my involvement?

Once the planning team is formed, concentrate on creating a comfortable and productive environment for everyone. Pick a meeting site that is "community space" and not strongly associated with any particular group or sector. The local community center, library or school are good possibilities. Choose a meeting time that is least likely to conflict with members' work schedules, keeping in mind that some people work evenings or at odd hours. See if child care can be arranged for parents with young children. Encourage people to dress casually, and arrange for snacks and drinks.

The tone established at the first few gatherings of the planning team is significant. Carol Kuhre of Rural Action Inc. in Ohio suggests that people set aside their papers and begin by sharing short personal stories of their lives in the community. Storytelling breaks the ice, begins building trust, and engenders feelings of comfort and confidence. Storytelling levels the playing field and reveals fascinating facts about participants' backgrounds and abilities. If people in power dominate the discussion from the start, others may hesitate to share their points of view.

A decision must be reached about when and how often the planning team will meet. Be sensitive to variations among people's work and family lives, and traveling distances. Volunteering is a sacrifice, especially for working parents with young children. Many planning teams meet on weekends, and cart along brown-bag lunches.

As planning progresses, money may follow. Watch out for power shifts, misinformation and personal agendas as the group acquires new dollars, contracts or land. Several Enterprise Zone/Enterprise Community sites experiences difficulties when grant funds arrived following an intensive, participatory planing process. As dollars flowed in, new players entered the scene and tried to take control. Weeks passed before the projects got back on track.

Of course, relationship and trust building cannot be rushed. Don't expect people to guarantee a commitment at the beginning of the process. They need time to ease into the process and gain faith that it will bring forth positive results.

When done well, planning will produce new, strong leaders for the community. "Participants aren't trained to be leaders; they become involved and committed through the ideas they contribute and the 'leadership acts' they take in the planning process," explain Schweke and Toft. "This indirect route to leadership and civic organization development cannot be achieved by a community that hires a consultant to prepare a completed strategic economic plan for it."

Ideas Are Generated by Reaching Wide and Deep into the Community; It's a Bottom-up Process. For many communities, strategic planning is often a top-down process. A committee of key decisionmakers examines the region's strengths, weaknesses, opportunities and threats—SWOT analysis—and crafts a vision for the future. The vision is translated into goals, packaged into specific projects, and presented to the citizenry. Consultation with the public takes the form of marketing the vision, goals and projects through newspaper articles, flyers and ceremonies after the plan is drafted. The public is informed, but not engaged.

Effective planning and visioning begins not with a committee of key decisionmakers, but with grassroots citizens; it's a bottom-up process. Even the most diverse planning team, truly representing a cross-section of the community, is a poor substitute for expansive grassroots involvement. The most diverse team is only a few citizens, with a limited number of points of view. Many more insights and inventive proposals may originate from the hundreds of citizens who are not team participants. To uncover these ideas, the planning team must reach wide and deep into the community.

"Significant community development takes place only when community people are committed to investing themselves and their resources in the effort," explain John Kretzmann and John McKnight, neighborhood development experts. "This is why communities are never built from the top down, or from the outside in."

Of course, not all projects require intensive community engagement. "Small, short-term, noncontroversial projects, such as planting flower pots on Main Street, can be derived, planned for and implemented without diverse in-

volvement," suggests Michael Kinsley, director of the Rocky Mountain Institute's Economic Renewal Project. "In fact, small, visible projects can help to inspire participation in larger, more significant bottom-up efforts."

People with Conflicting Views Search for Common Ground on Important Decisions. Most Americans have little experience in deliberating together to reach important decisions. We are schooled in debate and public hearings, where one person speaks loud and long to persuade the other, but the concept of creating "common ground" is largely unfamiliar. While opposing techniques may be effective in courtroom situations, they can exacerbate conflicts within communities—especially those immersed in planning their future.

"When individuals participate in public deliberation, they have an opportunity to learn a new perspective and gain new information to assist them in thinking through the issue of concern, some of which would never have occurred to them otherwise" explains Shanna Ratner, principal of Yellow Wood Associates based in St. Albans, Vt. As people think together, they come to define the problem in a wholly different way and find common ground where they thought it might never exist.

Strategic planning and visioning also may expose more puzzling and emotionally charged issues that demand great care and skill. When people of different perspectives congregate together to solve community problems, sparks may fly. Tension isn't necessarily a bad thing. "Most people spend most of their time meeting with people with whom they already agree. They seldom have an opportunity to try to talk through differences in a rational setting with their adversaries," laments former local elected official and author Bruce Adams. "People exchange attacks through the media and at public hearings, but they seldom talk with and almost never listen to people with whom they disagree."

An intriguing practice in active listening and creating common ground is worship sharing, used by Quakers. To resolve a problem, a group—small or large—assembles in a circle and begins with a short period of silence. As the silence resolves, each person has an opportunity to speak, but no one is compelled to speak. Each person speaks only once, drawing from his or her own experience. No time or attention is given to discussing, disputing, correcting, or answering the remarks of another.

Sharing proceeds around the circle, or in a scattered fashion. A minute or more of deliberate silence separates each speaker, when listeners concentrate on taking in what was just said. While listening actively to a speaker or during silence, people avoid thinking about what they might say when their turn comes. An hour or more into the process, a "sense of the meeting" emerges—a sense of how to best resolve the issue. To Quakers, this "sense of the meeting" reflects God's will.

Worship sharing is a spiritual pursuit for Quakers. For non–Quakers, worship sharing—or a variation of it—can be a powerful and meaningful practice for deliberating troubling issues. As each person has a say, separated by silence, a sense of what to do emerges, sometimes rather quickly. The common ground created is nearly always something different than what any single person could have imagined.

Planning Is Structured to Facilitate Action, Not Stifle New Ideas. What is the right amount of structure for planning and visioning? Too little structure can cause confusion and limit results. Too much structure may antagonize or overwhelm participants. Effective strategic planning incorporates enough structure so that people feel guided and supported, but not so much structure that new ideas never see the light of day. The emphasis is on structuring the process, but not the content. Effective planning also acknowledges and prepares for differences among individuals' attitudes towards structure.

People vary considerably in their need for, and comfort with, structure. Some people relish the order provided by thick, three-ringed strategic planning manuals, filled with sample exercises and data sheets. Others run screaming at the thought of following a how-to guide. Late arrivals and deviations from an ordered agenda disturb some meeting participants, while others are more troubled by caustic remarks or insufficient time for discussion. Culture often influences an individual's reaction to structured experiences. A linear, task-oriented approach may feel comfortable to a person of one cultural experience, but alienating to a person of a different heritage.

Helen Lewis cautions that the structure prescribed by many community development manuals can be excessively academic and restrictive. Especially when working in poor, marginalized communities, she picks and chooses among available materials, sometimes starting from scratch. Lewis is a strong advocate of popular education methods—training that empowers the learner. "People must be able to put things into their own words, and see them posted on newsprint," explains Lewis.

According to William Schweke, senior fellow at the Corporation for Enterprise Development (CFED), good planning achieves a healthy balance among four elements: linear planning/attention to tasks; brainstorming/creative thinking; care and feeding of the people/maintenance; and, gathering new information/intelligence. How much value is given to each element depends upon the planning group's history and culture.

Regardless of personality and cultural differences, effective strategic planning incorporates enough structure so that people understand who is doing what, and when. There is a "plan to plan" phase, including discussion and agreement on key goals, the division of labor, important dates, and so on. The "plan to plan" is especially critical if the community is approaching outside sources for financial support.

How Information Is Used to Gain Insights and Demonstrate Progress Along the Way

Action/Research Strategies Are Used to Collect Information About the Community, Analyze Available Data, and Draw Meanings That Are Understandable to Citizens. Too often, communities make economic development decisions based on incomplete or incomprehensible information, compiled from central data sources, and presented by outside consultants. Intelligent strategic planning is steered by the right amount and type of information, gathered from a variety of sources by both professionals and volunteers, and made understandable to ordinary citizens. By employing action/research strategies, local people learn how to collect data about their communities, in preparation for action.

The Internet is teeming with facts, figures and links to additional data sites. Detailed information about every county in the country is available from public sources such as the Bureau of Economic Analysis of the U.S. Department of Commerce; federal and state census data centers; state departments of economic and community development; some offices of local government; and local libraries. The challenge is to determine what data are particularly useful, and translate the data into language that has meaning for community people.

The most useful information will center on the community's population, demographic characteristics, employment and other economic measures, educational attainment, and social characteristics. A picture comes to life as the community's economic status and social trends are analyzed in relation to neighboring or similar communities—usually counties, the state, and the nation. Making such comparisons is essential; streams of figures presented without relationships to other places are confusing and meaningless.

Secondary, or published, data do not tell the complete story of any community. Some of the most intriguing and useful information for strategic planning comes from grassroots sources— surveys, interviews, observations and oral histories. Rural Action's Carol Kuhre calls this breed of data collection "action/research," and she has witnessed how citizen-directed, information gathering spreads education and ownership throughout the community.

Much Attention Is Focused on the Community's Assets, Not Just Its Needs. Northwestern University researchers John McKnight and John Kretzmann drew considerable attention in the early 1990s when they spoke out against popular community needs assessment tools, such as SWOT—strengths, weaknesses, opportunities, threats—a widely used framework for evaluating a locality's readiness for community and economic development.

The problem with needs assessment, say McKnight and Kretzmann, is that weaknesses and threats easily overwhelm strengths and opportunities, leaving citizens with a distorted view of their community. Deficiencies form a negative mental "map" that conveys a partial truth about the community, but is soon regarded as the whole truth. Especially in troubled neighborhoods and marginalized communities, this "needs map" determines how problems will be addressed, through deficiency-oriented policies and programs. "Citizens come to see themselves as people with special needs that can only be met by outsiders," McKnight and Kretzmann explain.

The assets-based development approach described in McKnight and Kretzmann's *Building Communities from the Outside* struck a nerve for many communities engaged in strategic planning. Concentrating first on what is present in the community, rather than what is absent, mobilizes local ingenuity and builds upon good works already underway. Recognizing and mapping community assets fortifies citizens to face the weaknesses and threats that will undoubtedly surface. Starting from a place of strength positions communities to use outside resources selectively and effectively.

McKnight and Kretzmann believe that every community boasts a unique combination of assets upon which to chart its future. They teach citizens to research and construct a three-part assets map—a drawing of assets possessed by local individuals, citizens' associations, and formal institutions. Inventorying the gifts, skills and capabilities of community residents unearths a broad array of talents useful to community development. Developing a profile of all citizens' associations—religious and ethnic groups; service clubs, youth groups, parent-teacher associations—identifies many under-involved groups with leadership capacity.

Accounting for all local institutions—businesses, schools, parks, libraries, police, fire stations, hospitals, social service agencies—enlists formal establishments in the process of community development. In this assets-based development process, citizens use the map to identify specific community-strengthening opportunities and to "capture" resources within the community.

Even communities wedded to more traditional SWOT-style assessment are re-balancing their strategic planning approaches to accent assets. Refocusing on building communities from the inside out adds flexibility and energy to strategic planning.

A Participatory Evaluation Process Is Set in Motion. Perhaps the most common and legitimate criticism of strategic planning/visioning is that it consumes more in the way of time and energy than it produces in tangible results. Participatory monitoring and evaluation is a strategy to circumvent this obstacle. By engaging citizens in identifying goals, indicators, monitors and measures, planning becomes grounded in tangible accomplishments. People see what they are striving for, and what they have achieved.

The current push for evaluation and measurement arises from several sources: funding sources, who wonder if their financial investments have achieved meaningful results; elected officials and policymakers, who question the impact of particular local, state and federal programs; and citizens, who want to see concrete results on the local level, such as an increase in the number of jobs created for local citizens.

A new evaluation vocabulary has emerged in guidebooks, training programs, journals and newspapers. There is much talk of accountability, performance measurement, benchmarking, and measurable outcomes. Communities seek to model Tupelo, Miss., which grew from poverty in 1940, to a thriving city in the 1990s, driven by 10-year plans and annual goals. And, innovative state initiatives, such as Oregon Benchmarks, use quantifiable performance outcomes to gauge how well the state is progressing.

Participatory monitoring and evaluation differs considerably from the appraisal process familiar to many people. Most evaluations are undertaken by outside experts, who examine the success or failure of a program after it has occurred. For example, a researcher evaluates the impact of the Head Start program on children's academic performance five years thereafter. Participatory monitoring and evaluation is community-directed and continuous. It engages citizens in ongoing assessment, and regularly feeds information back into the program, to incorporate changes and improvements along the way.

An exciting experiment in participatory monitoring and evaluation is the Rural Empowerment Zone/Enterprise Communities (EZ/EC) Learning Initiative. The Learning Initiative is a national project designed to monitor and measure the impact of the EZ/EC program, and to document lessons to be learned for community development. Signed into law by President Clinton in 1993, the EZ/EC initiative charges local communities with developing their own unique vision for change, based on their own strategic plans. Participating EZ/EC communities represent a cross-section of some of the toughest problems facing rural and urban America, as well as some of the best attempts by citizens to revitalize their cities and towns through intense community involvement.

The Learning Initiative's evaluation team considered a number of different approaches to monitor and evaluate a national program like the EZ/EC initiative. Since the EZ/EC program emphasizes "bottom up" participation and planning, the team chose a citizen-directed, participatory evaluation design over a more traditional assessment approach directed by outside experts. The team concluded: "Since the goal of the EZ/EC program is to enable communities to develop their own strategic vision and capacity for change, it is also important that communities learn how to monitor and measure their own progress towards these goals."

Citizen Learning Teams in 10 pilot EZ/EC sites are collaborating with regionally based researchers and lead staff at the University of Tennessee to carry out participatory monitoring and evaluation at the local level, by:

- Selecting two or three of the most important *goals* of the EZ/EC initiative in their particular local community. A *goal* is a purpose toward which effort is directed; an objective. An example of a goal is good health.
- Identifying *indicators* of success. An *indicator* is an actual activity or condition you can monitor or measure in some way, to assess whether progress is being made toward a goal. For example, possible indicators of good health are blood pressure, minutes per week of exercise and weight loss/maintenance. There can be, and usually is, more than one indicator that must be met in order to achieve any goal.
- Determining ways to *monitor* and *measure* progress towards the goals.

  Monitoring means "to check, watch, or keep track of." It is an informal approach to gathering information by watching, reading and listening. For example, a way to monitor good health might be to observe how a person looks, or inquire about how he or she feels.

  Measuring means "to mark off the dimensions, quantity of, or capacity of." It is a more formal process, requiring forethought and precision. A *measure* is the actual bean-counting or analysis necessary to measure an indicator. It requires a standard unit of measurement, e.g., inches on a yardstick, and a consistent baseline. A measure starts with words such as "number of," "presence of," "quality of." For

example, if the indicator of good health is weight, a measure could be the number of pounds, percent gain in pounds during the past 12 months, or the number of pounds over or under the average weight for a particular height.

- Exploring how to use *action/research strategies* to collect and analyze information for monitoring and evaluation. Refining methods through field testing and continuous improvement.
- Identifying key *lessons* from the project, and sharing them with the community.

Communities that are frustrated by strategic planning/visioning that produces few tangible results might achieve far more with a citizen-directed, participatory evaluation design. As grassroots citizens learn how to monitor and measure progress towards community-generated goals, responsibility and authority for evaluation shifts to where it belongs: in the hands of the community.

Planning and Action Occur Simultaneously. "Vision without action is merely a dream. Action without vision just passes the time. Vision with action can change the world." Joel Barker's wisdom underscores a struggle inherent in community development: citizens either act too long before they plan, or—in the case of ineffective strategic planning—they plan too long before they act. In an effort to "dot all the i's and cross all the t's," they set short-term projects aside. When planning sacrifices action, people lose faith and interest, and the process dies on the vine.

The solution to balancing planning and implementation is to act while you plan. Communities that identify and carry out immediately doable projects early in the planning process are better able to generate and sustain citizen support. Early successes follow the P-A-S-T-A principle—they are Popular, Affordable, Short-Term, and Achievable.

Even the community's most far-reaching goals must, in the end, be achievable. Citizen workshops conducted by South Carolina's Penn School for Preservation dramatize the creative tension between a community's current reality and its vision for the future. Using rubber bands to demonstrate the gap between present and future, participants learn to conceive community goals that create the right amount of creative tension—not so little tension that the community stands still; but, not so much tension that motivation breaks, the goals become elusive, and the community's dream flies away. As management expert Peter Senge explains: "Individuals, groups, and organizations who learn how to work with creation tension, learn how to use the energy it generates to move reality more reliably towards their visions. Without vision there is no creative tension."

HOW POSITIVE ENERGY AND COMMITMENT ARE PRESERVED WITHIN THE PLANNING TEAM AND THE LARGER COMMUNITY

Strategies for Continuous Learning Sustain Enthusiasm Among Planning Participants. Only rarely are the energy and creativity stirred up by strategic planning/visioning sustained over time. Communities start out with great hope and overflowing ideas. Often,

an outside intermediary is brought in to facilitate grassroots visioning. Once the vision is crafted, plans are made, and projects commence. People feel engaged and confident. At some point, however, usually after several projects have been completed and the outside intermediary turns its attention elsewhere, the burst of energy fizzles out. The pace of insights and new ideas slows down. Something meaningful is missing.

This loss of momentum has long troubled the Community Capacity Building Learning Cluster, a group of 15 experienced community development practitioners. But in reviewing published materials and their own experiences in communities, the Cluster discovered something intriguing about energized places: communities that sustain enthusiasm and effort over time are communities where people are engaged in learning—they are *learning communities.*

The disclosure that people are most creative and productive when they are learning has tremendous significance for strategic planning/visioning. It means that learning should happen in everyday places: at strategic planning meetings, training workshops, and citizen forums. But, how does a community consciously build "learning" into the front end of its agenda? What strategies can a community employ to sustain learning over time? The Cluster's exploration of learning communities generated the following recommendations for more vibrant meetings, workshops, and citizen forums.

The most powerful learning happens when individuals make their own discoveries, not when they are fed conclusions, no matter how accurate the conclusions might be. If citizens become immersed in data and become skilled in making educated observations about their community, they cannot help but learn. Then, the "Ah-ha?" of self-discovery breeds enthusiasm. But, if a consultant runs the numbers without citizen involvement and presents the findings to the public, learning may not happen.

People learn best in an atmosphere of relaxed alertness, when feelings of tension are balanced with feelings of personal safety. Rearranging chairs in a meeting room before people re-convene, or asking direct questions of participants creates a state of relaxed alertness, and promotes learning. When the level of tension rises too high, emotions take over, people grope for safety, and learning stops.

Learning and doing go hand-in-hand, and reinforce one another. A powerful learning principle, supported by extensive research, is that people learn best when they are actively involved in the learning process. Traditional, instructor led teaching rarely results in powerful learning because, according to Edgar Dale's Learning Cone of Experience, most people generally remember only 10 percent of what they read, and 20 percent of what they hear. But, if print and spoken information is interspersed with hands-on exercises requiring use of the information, the recall rate climbs to nearly 90 percent.

Opportunities for reflection bring wisdom and strength to learning. As New Mexico community organizer Luis Torres explains, people learn best at the *resolana*—a Spanish word meaning the sunny side of a building, out of the wind, in a sheltered place. Short spells of reflection offer meeting or workshop participants time to absorb new infor-

mation, gather their thoughts, and refresh their souls.

Effective learning touches our emotions. Celebrations and other rituals enhance learning by connecting the mind and the heart, in a break from tasks and time tables. Research shows that classical music, especially Baroque, inspires reflection and reinforces learning. To sustain effort over time, people must feel emotionally invested and supported by their community work.

Innovative Communication Techniques Capture the Public's Attention, Promote an Ongoing Dialogue. In its study of 10 state-sponsored strategic planning/visioning programs, the North Central Regional Center for Rural Development discovered that effective communication with the public about ongoing community visioning initiatives is sorely lacking. Half of all study respondents declared that more and better promotion and public awareness is needed to secure the public's understanding and support of community planning efforts. "In certain situations, the (planning) program is seen as exclusive or almost secretive. Yet, broad community understanding and support is key to long-term success," the researchers noted.

Promotion and public awareness of strategic planning/visioning projects typically takes the form of press releases, periodic news reports, bulletins, and other public information vehicles. The problem, however, is that "keeping the public informed" is insufficient. For strategic planning/visioning to succeed, communication devices not only inform the public, they also absorb the public. Rather than supplying facts and stories in a passive way, communications should captivate the public's attention, draw them into a dialogue about the community's work, and inspire people to ask questions and bestow ideas, even if they have had little involvement in the planning process.

When a communication vehicle is effective, it presents information in an innovative, lively and compelling way, and promotes an ongoing dialogue within the community. Consider the following techniques for captivating the public's attention and promoting an ongoing dialogue about the community's strategic planning/visioning initiative:

- Engage elementary school children to design and paint a large public mural depicting the town's rich history of its exciting future, now unfolding.
- Enlist high school students to write and publish a town newsletter featuring interviews, stories, updates, and editorials pertaining to the community's visioning work.
- Sponsor an art, essay, poster, videotape, or photography contest in which children and/or adults show and tell what they love best, or find most unique, about their community. Display top entries at several prominent locations, such as the public school, library, town hall, and county courthouse. Award prizes of savings bonds, gift certificates from local retail and service businesses, or scholarships to area colleges. Use the awards ceremony as a media event.
- Create a slogan and/or logo for the town's visioning initiative, and use it in all communications.
- Because a picture is worth a thousand words, make certain that all print materials are visually appealing, engaging, and informative. Graphics are a powerful communications tool. Use maps, tables, graphs, charts, and architectural renderings to draw comparisons and explain trends, display data in understandable ways, reinforce key points, and bring images to life.
- Construct an inventory of the many informal ways in which information is channeled through the community: over morning coffee at the local cafe, on community bulletin boards, at mothers' gatherings with young children, etc. Identify someone within each channel to spread planning news through it.
- Assemble a list of all area service clubs and neighborhood organizations. Appeal to clubs and organizations to publish short information items about the community's planning/visioning initiative in their monthly bulletins. Possible titles include "Ten Interesting Facts About Our Town," or "Test Your Knowledge About Our Community: A True or False Quiz."
- Recruit five volunteers to form a speakers bureau for short presentations to local service clubs and school classes. Create a 15-minute outline of planning project highlights, with a few overhead transparencies, for volunteers to use.
- Take advantage of the growing movement of civic journalism in which newspapers and television and radio stations are nourishing citizen involvement and public

deliberation. Approach area journalists about sponsoring a series of stories telling citizens how they might add value to the community's visioning process.

- Produce a video documenting the community's planning work, with help from the nearby community college or cable television station. Screen it at a large town meeting or celebration, and on public access television.
- Ask the local radio station to host a call-in show to publicize citizen participation opportunities and invite questions and comments.
- Engage computer-savvy volunteers to develop a free-net—a no-cost service computer that users can access to gather electronic data and communication through electronic mail. Free-nets typically provide electronic access to a range of information about community issues, local government regulations and procedures, school announcements, job listings, planning and zoning applications,

crime reports, etc. Many networks offer "chat" features and "meeting places" for people with similar interests. Citizens can access the free-net through their own computers, or at computer terminals situated in public libraries, chambers of commerce, and public schools.

Explore using new and emerging technologies to produce exciting, "real time" graphics for presentations at community gatherings or in print materials. The latest generation of computer, graphic, and audiovisual technologies may be available at nearby colleges or universities, architectural consulting firms, or state planning offices. These new technologies include: Geographic Information Systems (data presented in computer-generated maps), digital imaging (photographs enhanced, changed or manipulated), multimedia technology (sophisticated presentations using video, audio and animation), and virtual reality (computer software which allows the user to "enter" and "experience" imaginary environments).

CHAPTER 7

Municipal Government's Role

Pat Noyes

Of all the organizational issues that face Main Street programs in America's small towns, perhaps the most fundamentally important is a program's relationship with city hall. Regardless of a program's age, the interaction between local government and the downtown's private interests requires careful definition, especially in assigning and understanding roles, if efforts to improve downtown are to succeed over the long term.

While most people agree on the significance of and need for a "public-private partnership," it is in defining that relationship—particularly at the outset of a program—where misunderstanding, program problems and, sometimes, real controversy arise. The problem seems to lie with the community not fully understanding what city government does best versus what the private sector does best. In fact, automatic assumptions are often made about city roles and responsibilities that, if acted upon, can thwart progress in a downtown program.

Although situations differ from town to town, the socio-political conditions necessary for a solid downtown program are more similar than they are different in small towns nationally. Therefore, the most common misconceptions regarding the proper role of local government can be identified and clarified as a community undertakes and sustains a downtown program.

Originally published as "Local Government's Role in Downtown Revitalization: Clearing Up Misconceptions,"Main Street News, Issue No. 45, April, 1989. Copyright 1989 by the National Trust for Historic Preservation. Reprinted with permission from Main Street News, *National Main Street Center, National Trust for Historic Preservation, Washington, D.C.*

City Hall Has No Obligation to Revitalize Downtown. Wrong!

This belief, often held by city hall itself, could not be further from the truth. A community's downtown represents millions of dollars of government investment in public property and infrastructure. A public entity has the same responsibility to maintain and improve its property as does a private owner to care for his or her property; actually, more so, if one remembers that the public investment derives originally from the private taxpayer.

A revitalization program protects public as well as private capital investment downtown and so requires public-sector cooperation, involvement and support. A downtown program, in fact, maximizes public investment by providing an opportunity to increase land values which, in turn, increases the city's revenue in the form of property and retail sales taxes. In short, a city stands to gain greater earnings.

Cities usually identify job creation as a priority in economic development planning. Because most downtown programs undertake projects and services that stimulate business development, which in turn creates and retains jobs, a city can count this activity toward meeting its employment creation goals.

Generally, a healthy and attractive downtown experiences fewer safety and security problems. In terms of health and welfare issues, therefore, it is in the city's best interests to support endeavors that protect the downtown environment for shoppers and workers.

Finally, in most communities the downtown represents the commercial and cultural center of town. As such, the downtown projects an image of the community as a whole, good or bad, to residents and visitors as well as investors. A positive community image is as vital to city government as it is to the private sector in terms of quality of life issues and long-term financial gain. So, while the downtown may in fact never again be the largest—much less the only—commercial district in the community, its role in terms of image alone requires that local government support efforts to keep that image healthy and appealing.

City Government Can't Give Preference to One Commercial District Over Another. Wrong!

As a matter of fact, in order to realize progress in a community, city governments shift project priorities all the time. Usually, a local government gives priority to those areas of a community that have the greatest need or to projects that provide the greatest communitywide benefit. Therefore, a city government policy that advocates equal treatment of all business districts at all times fails to address real needs and reasonable resolutions to them. It also calls into question the elected body's ability to exert leadership on behalf of constituent needs.

It is a political reality that a city cannot *always* give a downtown program top priority. But, because of the reasons discussed above, downtown can and should be recognized by the local government as having sufficient communitywide impact to warrant status as a major priority much of the time.

Giving downtown a priority status, however, does not mean giving downtown a handout. The city's preferential treatment of downtown is matched several times over by investment from the private sector. Property owners upgrade their buildings and store owners improve their inventory and business practices and increase their advertising. With the city's cooperative support, an atmosphere of positive change instills confidence in the private investor.

City Hall Holds All the Decision-Making Cards: Main Street's Its Responsibility. Wrong!

Both the public and private sectors hold this view when downtown revitalization is narrowly defined as consisting of only physical improvements. The private sector must understand that it has the most to gain in investment returns and, thus, should serve as a real and active partner with the city, both financially and in terms of program management. In many ways the private sector balances the city in the decision-making process.

City hall, on the other hand, needs to cultivate the financial and organizational involvement of private citizens in order to leverage public funds (ideally viewed as seed money) to be invested in the downtown. This will also help city hall avoid the difficulty and sometimes inappropriate role of real estate agent on behalf of downtown. Given that the private sector can respond faster to changes in market conditions, it is the private sector that provides the greatest opportunity for positive change. The private

sector should be viewed as the city's *required* partner if long-term, positive change is to occur. The responsibilities of the public and private sectors may be different, but they are nonetheless shared.

The Only Thing Cities Have to Offer Downtown Programs Is Money. Wrong!

It is true, however, that money is likely the first item discussed when the city is approached to help downtown, whether the request comes from city staff or a resident. In reality, city hall can be a valuable partner to a downtown program because of the range of assistance it can provide *other than* money.

- **Technical expertise.** The city offers a wealth of information and staff abilities in terms of planning; land use and development standards; public works and engineering; redevelopment law; economic development strategies; market research and other demographic data; design review; and the permit process. City staff can be directed to focus on projects involving the downtown, thereby establishing program priority and providing necessary labor.
- **Political/legislative policy.** City hall can support a downtown program by the way it interprets and formulates policies affecting downtown, such as: waiving user fees; prioritizing development projects; forming assessment districts; establishing zoning and land use policies for infill and new commercial construction; offering tax

rebates; monitoring parking management; enforcing safety and security procedures; qualifying projects to receive public funds; placing downtown in a redevelopment district; supporting the retention of public offices in the downtown; and giving the downtown priority in the city's capital improvement budget each year. For example, any plans to expand existing or new commercial districts outside the downtown automatically need to be weighed against their impact on the overall health of the downtown area.

- **In-kind contributions.** In lieu of funds, city hall can lend some of the materials and staff time a downtown program needs such as furniture and supplies, computer time, Xeroxing services and clerical assistance. Some cities are able to offer insurance coverage or personnel benefits to revitalization program staff.

If City Money Is Involved, the Downtown Program Must Be Housed in City Hall. Wrong!

In fact, with few exceptions, there is very good reason *not* to place a downtown program in city hall. This holds true even if a new program is receiving the bulk of its operating money from a single public revenue source. It also holds true even when the city is investing in downtown public improvements that require city staff attention. While the above example demonstrates real city commitment, it does not automat-

ically define the best case for effective ownership of a comprehensive program.

To attract and retain support from downtown businesses, property owners and the community at large—support that translates into private reinvestment, volunteer participation and private leadership endorsement—a downtown program needs its own identity. For the reasons stated above, it is difficult for a city to serve as a credible advocate for downtown private interests, which it is forced to do when a Main Street program is part of city government. Ideally, a Main Street program should be housed in its own nonprofit corporation.

At the same time, because of its public investment downtown, city hall has every right to be concerned about the management and results of a separate revitalization program. City hall's concern will be even greater when it is planning projects for downtown while also giving money to the program. In such instances, it is appropriate for the city to require a contract that specifies the scope of work the Main Street program will undertake. It is also appropriate in such cases for a representative from the city, ideally an elected official, to sit on the nonprofit group's board of directors. A city official serving in an ex officio, nonvoting capacity on the board performs an important liaison function for both the nonprofit and the city, providing information both ways.

In any case, a nonprofit Main Street program must realize that it is accountable to *all* funding sources for program results and especially to the city, regardless of the level of funding.

The City Already Has an Industrial Economic Development Corporation—It Can Run the Main Street Program. Wrong!

Downtown requires full-time management and focus. A revitalization program is best sustained and achieves maximum results when it has its own identity and the ability to make responsible decisions. City government, a chamber of commerce and an economic development agency all have geographic areas of program concern and ranges of political issues that far exceed the boundaries of downtown. While these entities are all stakeholders in downtown and a credible downtown program needs to establish a strong relationship with each of them, a downtown program needs to be self-managing.

There are exceptions to this principle, as in communities with populations under 5,000 or in downtown districts with fewer than 50 businesses. In such instances, there might be a chamber of commerce already primarily serving the downtown. Human and financial resources being more limited in such circumstances, it can make sense to house a downtown program within the chamber or city hall.

City Hall's Involvement Ends After Three Years. Wrong!

Three years is the usual time frame associated with programs given demonstration status by a state Main Street program. Local revitalization program participants from both the public and private sectors often mistakenly assume,

however, that the end of three years of intensive on-site assistance from either the state or National Main Street Center means that the local program is either finished or that the local program is now on its own.

In the first place, downtown is never "finished." On the contrary, as its market is in constant flux, downtown demands permanent management if it is to stay attractive and economically sound. Commitment to this level of long-term management must, therefore, be permanent. The public-private partnership that is necessary to initiate a downtown program is the same partnership that is needed to permanently manage the program. Roles may shift slightly and activities change, but the relationship must exist. City involvement is particularly important because public policy involvement continues.

In addition, a city's financial commitment to the downtown program should continue. While local government can rightfully expect a Main Street program to attract private funds for program operation, thereby reducing the need for city funds, the city is not off the hook altogether. Experience nationwide shows that Main Street program budgets increase annually due to added project costs, and in only a very limited way due to added overhead costs. It is often these projects that attract private financial support to a program. In fact, it is easier to raise private money for specific projects than for overhead. (Although, in approaching funding sources, it is important for a Main Street program to market its organization as an integral part of the program services, projects and products it offers.)

If, then, it is easier to attract public monies to cover nonprofit overhead, it is not inappropriate for a Main Street program to request and receive some financial support from the city, even if eventually that level is very small. As it is, a successful downtown program usually reflects the reality that city hall is making necessary public improvements to the downtown, which is a significant commitment in and of itself.

In the final analysis, whether the city's financial involvement focuses on Main Street's operating budget or on needed public improvements, city hall's involvement never ends. It is all the more essential, therefore, that Main Street and the city continue to carefully define the nature and extent of their partnership.

CHAPTER 8

Creating Small Business Partnerships

Edward M. Marshall

The issues facing small businesses are substantial, complex, and interrelated. An effective small business strategy requires leadership from the city and the careful building of a long term partnership with the private sector and other institutions in the community. The city is both a catalyst for the development of a strategy and a major partner in its implementation, which is the focus of this chapter. Specifically, the following three issues will be examined:

- Why a small business strategy is important and the critical things that must be in place for it to work.
- What a small business strategy is and the steps involved in developing it.
- What a small business partnership

is, the key actors in it, and the roles they play.

Why Have a Small Business Strategy?

A small business strategy, if carefully developed, is one of the best ways a city can create jobs, expand the tax base, and increase long-term economic stability. Public officials understand the importance of a vibrant small business sector to the survival and growth of their local economy. Hard economic times in all parts of the country and new market realities, however, require new policies and approaches to ensure a city's long-term economic stability and growth by harnessing its entrepreneurial energies. A local economy that is booming could

Originally published as "City Strategy and a Small Business Partnership," Chapter 3 of Small Business Partnerships, *1989. Published by the National League of Cities, Washington, D.C. Reprinted with permission of the publisher.*

go bust five years from now. An economy that is declining now could be reversed. Or a local economy could remain relatively constant over time, neither booming, growing, nor declining.

While some public officials do not believe local government should intervene in the private market at all, others see the necessity of direct participation to ensure the survival or stability of their local economies. Furthermore, many local governments have some kind of small business strategy, whether it is formal or informal. If a city wants to significantly expand its commitment to small business development to meet the new economic challenges, however, there are a number of questions public officials may want to consider before they put a strategy together. Several of them are listed in Table 1.

These questions can be answered not only by research, but by participants in a citywide small business partnership including: the mayor, city council, the local chamber of commerce, organized labor, educational institutions, nonprofit community agencies, financial institutions, and manufacturers.

These questions can be used to start the decision-making process necessary to determine if and to what degree the city gets involved in an expanded small business development initiative. As these key players answer these questions and formulate a strategy, they need to consider the following characteristics of an effective small business strategy:

- There is a firm commitment from the city's top public and private sector leaders to substantially expand investment in small business development.
- There is a recognition that public participation is an investment in the economic infrastructure of the community, not an expenditure.
- Risk-taking that is based on a carefully developed plan is essential.

Table 1
Questions for Local Government Officials
Regarding Small Business Development

- What is the health of my community's economy now? What is it projected to be in five to ten years? (Measures include: unemployment, underemployment, aggregate income, wage levels, level of private investment, tax revenues.)

- What is the economic health of the small business sector? What is it projected to be in five to ten years? (Measures include: new start-ups/year, failures or bankruptcies/year, gross annual sales, profitability, employment.)

- What are the priority economic and social needs and goals of my community now, and in the future? What will they cost? How will we pay for them?

- What level of public and private investment do we have available to be able to replace every job in this community in the next five to ten years? Is the private sector willing to participate actively in a partnership?

- Are my government departments prepared and able to design and implement a full scale small business policy and program? How can it be incorporated in programs and departments already in place?

- There is an entrepreneurial orientation that rewards innovation and individual risk-taking.
- There is a comprehensive process that addresses the specific needs of small businesses at each stage of their development.
- The strategy is market- and reality-based.
- It builds on existing resources and is tailored to individual needs on a planned, long-term basis.
- There is a community consensus that is perceived as legitimate and is backed by public and private sector leadership.
- The strategy generates a return on investment to the community in the form of jobs, increased tax revenues, and new private sector investment.
- Federal, state and private resources are coordinated.
- Small business concerns are integrated into other city programs and supported by existing economic development initiatives.
- The community as a whole and small business in particular benefit.

Defining and Building a Small Business Strategy

A small business strategy is a comprehensive approach that a city's small business partnership adopts to address the specific problems of small business by generating financial and technical resources, designing, tailoring and implementing programs, and ensuring that the small business sector grows. Specifically, a strategy consists of the following ten items:

1. **A policy statement,** which clearly and concisely sets out the local government's commitment to assist small business and the goals it intends to achieve.

2. **A package of legislation,** which addresses all aspects of small business development as a top priority of the jurisdiction. Cities may opt not to pass legislation since there are many initiatives that can be employed without legislative action.

3. **Advocacy** for the interests of small business at several points in local government: the mayor's office, as a committee of the city council, and as an agency in the city government.

4. **A community consensus** that exists among all key city players to support the partnership.

5. **A small business development plan,** which builds on a market study of the local and regional economy, and spells out the priority objectives and strategies to be employed to achieve the goals set forth by the policy statement.

6. **A comprehensive set of programs,** which addresses the money, market, management, and public policy issues facing small businesses.

7. **Financial resources** that are identified and available to underwrite the development of the small business initiative and also to invest in business ventures and those programs necessary to support them.

8. **Public and private investment,** both direct and indirect. Direct investments include loans, grants, land or equity participation in a given business, or cash outlays to provide management and technical assistance. Indirect investments are those that support small business development but do not go directly to firms, such as street and water

services needed for a small business incubator.

9. **Management and technical assistance** needs to be made available to any small business.

10. **Maintenance of effort,** monitoring and evaluation systems need to be put in place to ensure an on-going, high level of program performance and effectiveness.

Within this framework, many cities may adopt sub-strategies that focus on a particular type of small business development. Many cities, such as Indianapolis or Philadelphia, have commercial retail strategies that target resources to certain neighborhoods or commercial areas. Minority- and women-owned business development is another important focus for many cities, such as Oakland, Boston and Miami. Still other cities, like New Haven and San Antonio, are focusing on a high-tech/low-tech small business strategy. Regardless of the focus of the strategy, these strategies have the basic characteristics outlined above, and these cities have had to develop their approach with the full support of their key public and private sector leaders.

While there is no cookie-cutter approach to strategy development—it must be tailored to local circumstances and needs—the process follows twelve easily identified steps.

1. IDENTIFICATION OF THE OPPORTUNITIES AND ASSESSMENT OF NEED

The first step is the most important since the definition of need will set the framework for action by the partnership. Substantial research and data gathering is done to identify data already available in the city and its small business community and gaps that exist. Subjective or perception-based surveys of small businesses and business organizations provide an important complement to analytical data. The key point is to develop a consensus on the needs of local small businesses.

2. FORMATION OF A SMALL BUSINESS PARTNERSHIP

During data collection, key leaders will emerge as spokespersons for the various constituencies in the city. A leader, usually the mayor, council president, or city manager, needs to convene the members of the partnership.

3. DEVELOPMENT OF A COMMUNITY CONSENSUS

The partnership, once organized, can then approach the community to discuss the needs of the small business sector and use community forums to build a consensus and political support for action. In large cities this might be done by neighborhood.

4. INITIAL RESOURCE MOBILIZATION

Every partnership effort will cost money. Partners should be asked in the beginning to pledge a sufficient amount of funds or in-kind services to cover operating/staff and consultant costs for up to one and one-half years.

5. CONDUCT A MARKET SURVEY

Data needs identified in Step 1 should be filled and analyzed in terms of the market needs for small business development in the city and/or its neighborhoods.

6. DEVELOPMENT OF A SMALL BUSINESS DEVELOPMENT PLAN

All the data is now organized into a small business development plan which specifies quantifiable results to be accomplished within a given time frame (three, five, or ten years), and priorities are given to these desired results. The plan is formally adopted by the small business partnership.

7. DESIGN OF THE STRATEGY

Once approved, the partnership spells out in detail the steps that will be taken to achieve each result, and determines who will be responsible for each activity.

8. IDENTIFICATION OF SPECIFIC TOOLS TO USE AND INITIAL PROJECTS TO BEGIN

For each desired result, specific projects are then identified and tools from the tool kit are matched with the project to ensure that the projects are effectively accomplished. (See Chapter 19 for a discussion of small business development tools.)

9. RESOURCE MOBILIZATION FOR IMPLEMENTATION

The small business partnership then uses the plan and strategy to mobilize private and public sector resources.

10. CREATION OF A SMALL BUSINESS SUPPORT SYSTEM

Beyond the planning and politics, the partnership needs to develop an ongoing management, financial, and technical support system geared to meet the needs of small businesses in each phase of their development.

11. IMPLEMENTATION OF THE PLAN

The partnership turns over implementation to an existing, highly skilled and competent business development organization, or creates an independent corporation to carry out the plan on an on-going basis.

12. MONITORING AND EVALUATION

The partnership members can serve as a de facto "board of directors" that meets quarterly to ensure that the plan's targets are met.

Many cities have the staff capabilities to complete many steps in this strategic planning process. Many do not. In any case, objective outside expertise may be needed to facilitate Steps 1, 2, 3, 6, 7, 8, and 12. This expertise should be brought to bear on those parts of the process where local interests compete for control, where there is the need for consensus and conflict resolution, and where the experience of other communities can be brought to bear on this community.

The essential ingredient for an effective small business strategy, however, is the commitment of the community's top public and private sector leadership to having small business

development as a priority. Once that commitment is made, a small business partnership becomes the vehicle for a comprehensive policy and program approach.

Small Business Partnerships

A small business partnership is the vehicle by which the key public and private sector leaders come together to develop a small business strategy. The purpose of the partnership is to mobilize the private, community and public consensus and resources to make small business development a local priority.

One technique for initiating a partnership is for the mayor, the president of the city council, a bank president, and the director of the chamber of commerce to call a meeting of the top fifteen to twenty leaders in the community to discuss the city's small business needs and to chart the course through the twelve-step process. The partnership can be formalized or be an ad hoc task force, but it is the chief elected official who calls and runs the initial meeting.

The partnership should define its goals clearly, appoint a chair and vice chair, select committees, identify support staff, and set up a calendar of regular meetings (monthly) for the duration of the strategy development process.

The city is the focal point for the initial effort because it is the city's legitimate responsibility to identify a community's primary concerns, determine who can do something about them, and be the catalyst that brings those people and resources together. Many cities, large and small, have taken this leadership role—for example,

Cleveland, Pittsburgh, Baltimore, Indianapolis, Lima, Ohio, and many more. In each instance, the city's leadership role and the private sector's cooperation have produced dramatic turn-arounds in the city's image and business fortunes.

There are at least nine key players in the partnership, each with a different resource base and role, as indicated by the diagram on page 113.

Each member of the partnership plays more than one role in moving small business development from the idea stage to reality. Earlier, twelve steps were identified in the process of developing a small business strategy. When these steps are cross-referenced with the nine players, a matrix of roles and responsibilities can be derived that ensures the adoption of an effective strategy. Chart 1 shows the typical participants in a small business partnership.

Chart 2 shows the degree of cooperation required among all players at each step of the way. The mayor and city council take the leadership role, while the department of economic development or planning provides staff support. The chamber of commerce has a key role in all eleven steps, while financial institutions are involved in all but two steps. Clearly the city, the financial institutions, and the chamber of commerce are at the core of the process.

The key to any successful small business partnership is recognizing that there is a problem and an opportunity and making a commitment to address it. The city plays a critical role as a catalyst and partner, and once the strategy has been developed, helps to mobilize resources to implement it. The specific tools a partnership may use will vary from city to city, but there is a substantial array of options available. It is

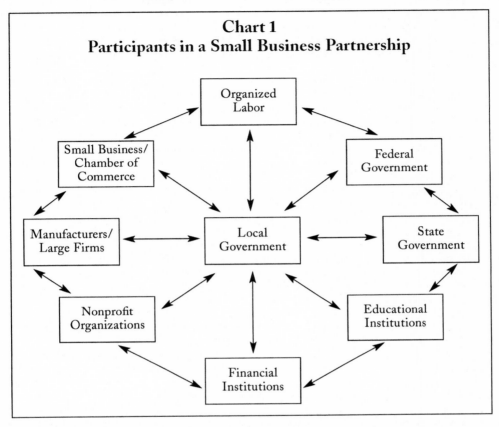

Chart 1
Participants in a Small Business Partnership

important, however, to note that every small business partnership should carefully select its tools based on the goals it has set for itself and tailor the tools accordingly.

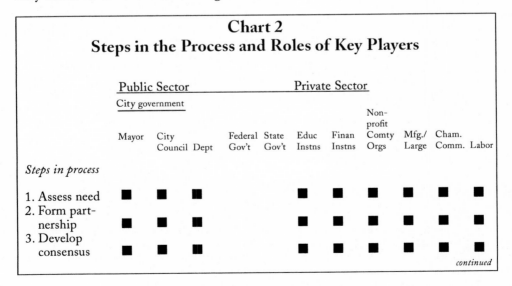

Chart 2
Steps in the Process and Roles of Key Players

	Public Sector			Private Sector							
	City government							Non-profit			
	Mayor	City Council	Dept	Federal Gov't	State Gov't	Educ Instns	Finan Instns	Comty Orgs	Mfg./ Large	Cham. Comm.	Labor
Steps in process											
1. Assess need	■	■	■			■	■	■	■	■	■
2. Form partnership	■	■	■			■	■	■	■	■	■
3. Develop consensus	■	■	■			■	■	■	■	■	■

continued

Chart 2, continued
Steps in the Process and Roles of Key Players

	Public Sector					Private Sector					
	City government										
Steps in process	Mayor	City Council	Dept	Federal Gov't	State Gov't	Educ Instns	Finan Instns	Non-profit Comty Orgs	Mfg./ Large	Cham. Comm.	Labor
4. Mobilize resources	■	■		■	■	■	■	■	■	■	■
5. Market study			■							■	
6. Develop plan	■	■	■			■	■	■	■	■	■
7. Design strategy	■	■	■							■	
8. Identify tools/ projects	■	■	■				■			■	
9. Create support system			■		■	■	■			■	
10. Implement plan			■				■			■	
11. Monitor results	■	■					■			■	

CHAPTER 9

Conducting a Community Self-Evaluation

Al Gobar

The key to a successful economic development program is to generate early winners, while keeping an eye on clear, quantifiable long-term goals. But, many economic development efforts have reflected effort more than achievement and style more than substance. Such programs suffer from a lack of clearly defined goals, strategies to achieve these goals, and implementation processes which build on existing resources to achieve the most effective outcome.

Crucial to an action plan for community development is the simple Biblical admonition, "Know thyself." Here's a story to illustrate how important this is: A highly placed policymaker in one California county with an enviable record of economic growth was concerned about the county's job base being composed primarily of "hamburger flippers," when, in fact, the county has more manufacturing jobs per thousand jobs than any other area in Southern California. An economic development strategy based on the erroneous assumption that the area's population was composed of fast food service personnel would have been fruitless.

Therefore, a precondition to an efficient and successful economic development effort is an audit and evaluation of current conditions and the establishment of very specific goals.

The initial self-study process should

Originally published as "How to Evaluate and Build on Your City's Assets," Western City, Vol. LXIX, No. 8, August 1993. Published by the League of California Cities, Sacramento, California. Reprinted with permission of the publisher.

define a specific reason for an economic development effort that is carefully and objectively articulated. In an oversimplified form, the problem can be reduced to the following simple queries:

1. Why do we want economic growth?
2. What resources do we have that other communities do not have that would be especially appealing to specific engines of economic growth?
3. Would these elements of potential economic growth contribute to the basic reasons we want to expand the local economy in the first place?
4. Who are these elements, how do we reach them, and what is our most appealing message?

Economic development goals should be quantified in specific terms such as a target increase in property tax base per capita population, a defined increase in sales tax revenue, increases in local employment opportunities, and removal or mitigation of community limitations.

The first step in this process is a community appraisal of a wide range of objective measures of the community's advantages and limitations. For instance, many communities have consumer support bases well in excess of the level of retail sales activity within their boundaries. That means residents are shopping elsewhere, and their communities are losing retail sales tax revenues, *ad valorem* property tax revenues, and business license revenues to surrounding communities. More successful exploitation of existing and future consumer support increases city revenues from local taxes and provides a source of local jobs.

The City of Apple Valley's retail sector, for example, captures only about 40 percent of the retail expenditure potential of the community, but the scale of the town's population would permit a maximum effective capture rate of approximately 80 percent. Achieving this level of efficiency in the retail sector would double sales tax collections, create more local jobs, and enhance *ad valorem* taxes and business license revenues.

Similarly Tustin and Fountain Valley identified underexploited retail opportunities not only in their own cities' populations but the surrounding population, resulting in a substantial increase in sales tax revenues from the development of such new retail facilities as the Tustin Marketplace, the Price Club, etc.

Another important element is understanding where local employed residents actually work. Antelope Valley's economy, for example, is largely supported by commuters to jobs located in the more urban portions of Los Angeles County. The city loses the *ad valorem* tax base associated with work places and long commutes impose a burden on local residents.

Availability of land is also an important factor. Evanston, Illinois, for example, is bounded by other cities and Lake Michigan. So there is no land available for expansion. As a result, the city's economic development strategy involved reuse of previously developed land to achieve the city's specific economic goals of enhanced property tax base, expansion of local government opportunities based on the skills of local residents, and higher convenience for the people of Evanston.

Public service facilities and infrastructure capacity also represent a community advantage in some instances but a limitation in others. Adelanto has capitalized on abundant land by installing infrastructure to accommodate industrial development, giving the city a significant competitive advantage over communities without adequate and similarly priced inventories of immediately developable industrial land. Irwindale is another example of a community in which economic development has been facilitated by the installation of infrastructure.

Communities that provide an attractive residential environment attract high-energy decision-makers who like to live close to their jobs, which generates more local business, increases tax revenues and raises the level of local job opportunities.

Specific elements to be considered in this category include general neighborhood characteristics including household income profiles, educational levels of local residents, and other factors. Executives work hard and play hard, so recreational opportunities are important to such movers and shakers. They also are concerned about the availability of superior schools and a broad-based cultural program, including churches, Lions, Kiwanis, etc.

Such executive amenities have been important to Orange County as a whole, which has a higher ratio of manufacturing employment per 1,000 jobs than any other part of Southern California as well as a higher ratio of employment to population than any other part of California—despite the area's high housing prices and traffic congestion. Its success in attracting manufacturing jobs can be traced to one factor: Corporate executives like to live there. They don't like to commute, and manufacturing jobs grew in this area because decision-makers

were attracted to the community as a place to live. This resource is not typically identified in the establishment of a data base for long-range economic development plans.

The Temecula-Murrietta area experienced a mini-boom in industrial development in large measure because of the area's ability to market itself to upper-income, entrepreneurial households as a place to live and eventually to establish businesses. Irvine is another example, as is Newport Beach.

A user-friendly, cooperative local political climate—while difficult to quantify—is another advantage associated with economic growth. A commercial developer we know, whose entitlement process in one California city has now endured for more than four years, has stated that he would "never, ever attempt to develop another project in that city." Executive "flight" is especially problematic when a nearby city is not only passive with regard to new and desirable development, but also active in providing subsidies through sales tax rebates or other techniques which have become increasingly common.

Effective economic development also takes advantage of the city's natural resources. Big Bear Lake—home to two major ski resorts and one of the few major recreational lakes in Southern California—enjoys a substantial advantage in generating economic growth. Modesto experienced a boom in the mid–1980s by promoting its central location to attract distribution and warehouse facilities to serve much of urban California. Ontario has capitalized on the confluence of four major freeways and the existence of a major airport by spurring massive development of distribution facilities.

Barstow, Lake Elsinore, and the unincorporated Imperial Valley community of Cabazon have capitalized on their locations adjacent to major freeways but removed from urban areas to support the development of factory outlet centers. The Oxnard–Port Hueneme area has benefited from its proximity to port facilities by encouraging distribution activities.

Many of the limitations to economic development are simply the flipside of the advantages described above. Limited infrastructure or lack of available land implies a redevelopment strategy as distinct from an economic development strategy. Inadequate availability of low-cost housing either within the community or nearby has an indirect, adverse effect on the availability of a suitable labor force. Remote locations with no nearby, easily accessible market imply a strategy aimed at generating businesses which produce products and services with a high value-to-weight ratio to overcome this limitation. Lack of executive housing has also been a contributing factor to the slow economic development of some areas which otherwise have substantial advantages and resources.

Many of the elements described here can be defined objectively and with sufficient accuracy to facilitate decision making on the basis of relatively inexpensive research methodologies. Some of these are as follows:

• Standard retail site analysis techniques are useful in defining underpopulated consumer markets which represent an immediate potential for economic development. The process models retail sales expected within the community in light of its structure, population base, surrounding area population base, etc., in relationship to sales tax patterns and the existing inventory of retail facilities. Retail development in Fountain Valley, for example, was inhibited by the city's proximity to two regional shopping centers and a major auto plaza. Almost by default, the most effective retail development except for some minor fine-tuning was the attraction of a major "big box" retailer. Through a focused effort, Fountain Valley was able to attract a Price Club which, in turn, stimulated an influx of other hyperefficient retailers. National City had the potential to support regional shopping center facilities. Community support surrounding Murrietta was more than adequate to justify consideration of a conventional regional shopping center there. The High Desert region of San Bernardino County has an inadequate number of new car dealerships in relationship to its market, so targeting such high ticket retailers could be a productive strategy there.

• The 1990 Census data provides a rich source of information from which to define the study area's affluence, its labor force characteristics, commute patterns, employment by industry, and a variety of other elements related to skills, education, and age. This information provides the data base that is a prerequisite to effective economic development. The socio-demographic analysis potential inherent in the data is also useful in evaluating the compatibility of the community with high-income, executive-type residents.

- Analysis of published data regarding land sales, prices, etc., is a reasonable method for identifying the limitations and advantages of a community's land and infrastructure resources.

Evaluation

An audit of local community resources and limitations can be compared with other communities or with averages for the larger area in which it is located. These comparisons define the special advantages and limitations of the local community against potentially competitive local economies. A simple financial analysis of city revenues and costs in the context of a peer group of cities is another useful indicator in defining limitations, resources, and the political climate. Cities with a high per capita cost of development services in relationship to historical development levels typically are communities in which development is difficult. A simple history of building permit activity at the city level as compared with peer group cities in similar locations is also often a useful diagnostic tool.

The results of the audit process can be integrated with input from local community leaders to define and prioritize specific goals of an economic development effort. Examples of goals that can be defined by this process are:

Expanding the community's retail section. This captures sales tax dollars escaping the community by attracting specific types of retailers for which there

is a viable market opportunity. The experiences of Tustin, Fountain Valley, National City, and Evanston illustrate this example.

Attracting industrial employers. This achieves a better job-to-population balance and minimizes long commutes for local residents. Adelanto has made substantial progress through a program of infrastructure development specifically oriented to industrial users, a process preceded by the establishment of a strong and financially efficient redevelopment agency. Identification of local residents working in the finance sector in Antelope Valley contributed to the attraction of a major national financial printing organization.

Increasing the areas' value-to-weight ratios in products and services. The thinking of many planners involved in community development continues to focus on the outmoded, over-estimation of the economic value of local manufacturing jobs. Although they are a source of job-to-population balance, they are not the solution for all communities. Manufacturing jobs provide little in the way of fiscal benefit to the communities in which they are located, and frequently, the cost of securing a manufacturing job (dictated by the large number of communities competing for these jobs) exceeds their value to the community not only in a quantitative sense but probably also on a subjective basis.

The process of defining resources and limitations would, for example, highlight the limitations of some communities that are located at some distance from major markets. Ideal export industries for such communities would include the types of products that are "shipped" electronically and services and specialized goods which exhibit a high value-to-weight relationship, etc. Credit card processing organizations, for example, have selected such remote locations as the Dakotas, Phoenix and Las Vegas, based on those areas' tax structures and labor force availability because their product is essentially information.

Conceiving a practical implementation program is a relatively simple matter once the community's advantages, limitations, and goals are defined. The most effective implementation programs are highly focused. The process also should result in specific goal prioritization and implementation processes that build on one another. The achievement of an early goal provides a platform for the achievement of more difficult goals ahead through focused marketing efforts targeted at industries that have a special affinity for the specific attributes of the community.

The entire process should be reviewed on at least a five-year cycle, if not more frequently, to measure progress toward achieving specific goals, to provide a basis for reevaluating the practicality of achieving certain goals, and to redefine the goals in light of the achievement of intermediate goals. This regular review and updating is not often a part of a long-range economic development strategy.

Pre-conditions for an efficient and successful economic development effort include the following:

Goals should be specific and carefully articulated. Such goals could include a target increase in property tax base per capita population, specified increases in sales tax capture, defined ratios of local jobs to local labor force, and defined new development by type—70 percent residential, 22 percent commercial, 8 percent industrial, etc.

An effective development plan also includes an objective definition of the community's resources and limitations.

The next step is a realistic appraisal of how available resources can be mobilized to exploit special opportunities defined by the pattern of resources and limitations. One community with which we are familiar, for example, has a strongly established medical industry economic base which can be built upon to attract retirees and to fill in gaps in the representation of specific types of medical service capability.

Another has ample excess capacity in resort facilities during the third quarter of each year, which would accommodate an increase in visitor population. A small investment in new facilities would contribute to the overall economic efficiency of the facilities themselves as well as the entire community.

Another community, located on the western edge of a population base, is not now served by adequate retail facilities, causing this hinterland population to pass through the community to other, more established retail sectors located to the west of the city in question. Targeting retail business would improve the city's economy.

A commuter city's population base includes a substantial number of residents employed in the finance sector who travel long distances to work. That implies the city has a skilled available labor force which could help attract backroom financial service activities.

Too often communities engage in promotional activities without having a clear-cut definition of their message or their specific target audience, let alone of the appropriate media to reach this target. This means that a valuable community resource for economic development is an objective, comprehensive, and continuously updated data base available to all agencies and private sector elements interested in promoting the local community. Once that information has been gathered and evaluated, then a community can begin to effectively market itself to the business sector.

CHAPTER 10

Managing Development and Growth

Nancy Stark and Hamilton Brown

A national task force, after examining the environmental needs of rural America, concluded that, "Small towns are not just smaller than large ones, they are different." The small town and rural economic development strategies presented in *Harvesting Hometown Jobs* are different too, in scale and in the level of commitment expected from the communities which will benefit. In contrast to many urban dwellers, rural people do not commute to work from a place they live, to a place in which they have no personal investment. Because work and personal life are located in the same general setting, small town economic development involves preserving the people and the place, as well as the livelihood of current and future residents.

When rural communities were largely agricultural, or dependent on single industries such as timber, mining or manufacturing, there was little discussion of public disagreement that what was good for the core industry was good for the entire community. With fewer people, more expanses of underdeveloped land, less pollution of the land, air and water and less knowledge of the future impact of current practices, many towns accepted without question the course of the community's future.

Times have changed. For most small town and rural governments, the decline of key industries and/or the pressure for unplanned growth from metropolitan areas have brought large and controversial issues, such as the size and

Originally published as "Managing Development," Chapter 7 of Harvesting Hometown Jobs, 1997. Published by the National Center for Small Communities, Washington, D.C. Reprinted with permission of the publisher.

type of development and land use planning, to center stage.

In examining how to manage development, these issues need to be addressed:

- The distinction between sustaining and depleting essential community resources;
- The tools to achieve shared community goals; and
- The procedures to reconcile differences among competing interests and distribute benefits across the spectrum of those who contribute to community life.

To Preserve and Sustain

Even when rural communities were dependent on a single industry, business interests and conservation interests often seemed to work at cross purposes. In recent years, the debate has sharpened in many communities where the traditional economy has simply collapsed; or where there are immediate financial returns for residential and commercial development driven by the expanding collar surrounding major population centers. The U.S. Department of Agriculture now classifies only 556 of America's 2,276 rural counties as primarily dependent on agriculture, and even within these counties, only one of 10 residents, on the average, lives on a farm.

Nationwide, nearly one million acres of agricultural land are lost each year to some form of development. If a small community is to remain one that still feels like home, then the key is to manage growth or development in a way that is consistent with the will of the community and assures that resources remain for the future.

There is now a national, even international, movement to reconcile necessary economic development with the preservation of environmental resources in a way that serves the needs of the whole community. Perhaps the best known phrase to describe the dynamic relationship among these concerns is "sustainable development." [We use a number of other terms in this chapter, should "sustainable development" acquire a limited or negative connotation.]

One of the first explanations of sustainable development is among the most balanced and useful. In 1987, the World Commission on Environment and Development offered this definition: "to meet the needs of the present without compromising the ability of future generations to meet their own needs." It does not say "no growth," and it does not say all new industry must be "green," or have zero environmental impact. At the same time, it challenges present-day businesses and individuals to look at the definition of need, in light of what we now recognize as limited resources. As many a planner has observed, "they're not making any more land, air or water." And, as experience shows, the cost of reclamation or cleanup far exceeds the cost of initial protection.

Strategies for managing growth, compatible development and sustainable industries are essential approaches for any community anticipating change. They may be especially important tools for making decisions in those towns faced with extraordinary pressure for development or job creation. For example, when a major entertainment conglomerate proposed construction of a multi-million dollar theme park near tiny

Plains, Va., there was plenty of sentiment that "any job was a good job."

Local authorities approved many of the procedures which would have cleared the way to bring up to 30,000 visitors a week to an area where the central town's population was 300. While elected leaders generally sided with the developers, citizens circulated and publicized traffic studies which suggested that the existing interstate virtually would have to be renamed as "the corporate parking lot" when the predicted gridlock occurred. Other projections seemed to confirm that the minimum wage jobs created at the theme park would never generate the revenues to pay for the required expansion of local services.

The corporation backed off when faced with such fierce opposition from people whom it considered a primary target audience for its theme park. Would this proposed project have been all bad? No one will know, but it would have radically changed the face of an area, even a region, that satisfies its citizens and attracts a manageable flow of tourists through its unspoiled rural atmosphere.

Likewise, a number of economically depressed communities and chronically poor states have welcomed large scale chicken, pork and beef producers and processors. Many of those small communities now wrestle with what are known collectively as Confined Animal Feedlot Issues (CAFI), which include odors; animal waste products contaminating surface and ground water; and the overuse of gravel roads by heavy vehicles carrying livestock.

Also, food processing plants often place a huge strain on existing water treatment facilities. The waters of the Potomac River near Washington, D.C., show signs of contamination from chicken rendering operations hundreds of miles upstream in West Virginia.

Should all meat producing activities be avoided when considering how to strengthen the local economy? Like any other option, there should be some community criteria or benchmarks that establish the nature and size of what is acceptable and a decision, upfront, of certain activities that simply will not meet these future goals.

According to a study by Anthony Downs, cited in the Lincoln Institute for Land Policy's *Managing Growth and Change*, 90 percent of the population want to own a detached, single family house. Virtually every adult and teenager want to own a vehicle in which they can reach major sources of goods, services and entertainment in 20 minutes or less of congestion-free driving. [Between 1975 and 1990, vehicle ownership increased 30 percent, vehicle miles driven rose 62 percent while the population rose only 15 percent.] Many newcomers to rural areas, who still commute to an urban workplace, will push for access roads and four-lane highways to the city, providing yet another push for out-of-control development.

When faced with the need for or inevitability of economic change, the first challenge is to incorporate the often competing interests of business and the environment into a vision that shares common goals. The second challenge is to find the tools that will enable these goals to be achieved locally.

What Is Sustainable Community Development

In its guide, *Communities by Choice*, the Mountain Association for Community Economic Development of Berea, Ky., says there are three Es that help build prosperous communities over the long term: Economy, Ecology and Equity. The *economy* involves the management and use of resources to meet individual and community needs. *Ecology* concerns the interaction between living things and the environment—primarily the relationship of human beings to their surroundings. *Equity* involves fairness in the way in which communities make decisions and distribute benefits from common efforts and shared resources. Keeping these forces in balance is what characterizes a community that can weather difficult times and keep its citizens committed to common goals.

Local governments can play a critical leadership role in these fields individually, as well as in managing the competing or conflicting goals that can cause tensions within the community. Particularly in rural areas, local land use management practices have a profound impact on: the local economy; the prudent use and protection of natural resources; and the equitable assignment of the costs and benefits related to development.

Certainly, development is a responsibility of many parties, private and public, individual and organizational, if it is to truly be community-owned. But where large tracts of private land are yet to be developed, local governments usually must take the lead because of the unique powers they may exercise over future land use. The reluctance to act because some in the community may actively resist, must be measured against the consequences of not acting at all. In looking at how government may carry out this role, it is critical to come to agreement on the terms "manage" and "development."

There are few times when local economic conditions are so consistently favorable that the best policy is to leave well enough alone. Small and rural communities generally find that they are experiencing either economic decline, economic stagnation or economic growth, all of which are likely to have some unintended or undesirable consequences. While each of these circumstances calls for active local management, the strategies chosen are going to be very different. The authors of the Lincoln Institute's *Managing Growth and Change* offer some observations on the local government management of land that are applicable to the thinking for rural economic development, in general.

> In this nation, ... the overwhelming majority of development decisions are private ones. Given this inherent right to develop, the intent of government intervention is to alter how private and public investments are made in order to produce a more socially acceptable result. Often, this is by specifying the end result an owner must achieve if he or she chooses to develop a property (i.e., single-family homes, construct a place for neighborhood retail activities, etc.). More recently, the focus has been shifting from the specified end result of development to the transaction itself, as in impact fees or performance systems. In either approach, when markets are strong, regulation or market restraint is the normal mode of intervention and when markets are weak, public incentives or inducements are employed.

This quotation points up three key considerations when a community moves from merely reacting to economic change, to structuring long-term economic activities in a dynamic relationship with shared environmental and social goals. First, the recent publicity given to the property rights movement is a reminder that many long-time property owners—particularly of large, family held lands—believe that government should have a very limited say in how land is used by current or future owners. Second, however, government has the right, and often the responsibility, to restrict certain activities on private land that would harm others who are affected by how local land, air and water are used; or, to promote activities which serve a general public good. Land use restrictions on hazardous waste disposal, for example, would fall in the first category; a requirement that developers set aside a certain percentage of property for park and recreation land would fall into the second. Finally, whether intervention is in the form of restrictions or incentives, economic goals should be directed towards the creation of lasting jobs that do not deplete community resources; and land use decisions should, ideally, benefit the many, rather than the few.

There is a town, famous throughout New England, that has two motor speedways within its corporate limits. The predictable traffic, public safety and litter problems materialized as soon as the first track opened for business. As a result, the town now has relatively strict zoning laws governing its commercial and residential development, which never enjoyed public support in the past.

Other small cities have passed ordinances requiring a minimum of 40 acres for a residential lot, that, in effect, hold farm families hostage from selling smaller parcels of land, even if agriculture can no longer support full time farming operations. Other towns have passed such strict limits on commercial development that they preclude the

business community from contributing to a reasonable expansion of the local economy.

Neither extreme of too loose nor too strict an approach to zoning seems a good model to follow. Like land use planning, development strategies may polarize communities, if they are only presented as a choice between extremes. There are the champions of "no growth," who see each new resident or business enterprise as threatening community character or draining the public budget. On the other end of the spectrum are advocates of "all growth is good growth." Often, pro-growth leaders maintain that they are advocates only for small, clean, well-paying industries or for residential development that will pay its way. But a number of people who have studied economic development trends suggest there are new ways to view economic development and to assess its true costs and benefits to your community.

Michael Kinsley of the Rocky Mountain Institute in Snowmass, Colo., says in the Institute's *Economic Renewal Guide*: "The assumption that economic prosperity requires growth seems so reasonable that most of us don't think much about it. The trouble is, the word 'growth' has two fundamentally different meanings: 'expansion' and 'development.' Expansion means getting bigger; development means getting better, which may or may not involve expansion."

Even within smaller communities, it is easy to think of examples where growing bigger resulted in the loss of something special: The move of the main street diner to a modern new building with three times the seating; or the purchase of the family-owned hardware store by a national chain that doubled sales volume with deep discounts and that replaced knowledgeable sales people with a computerized inventory system.

The *Guidelines for Sustainable Development*, reprinted here, are drawn from Kinsley's book and offer some general rules for implementing sustainable development in your town or region. They may help local community and business leaders recognize actions that are already underway or which could easily be added to current efforts.

Links to Other Efforts

The principles of managing growth in a sustainable manner introduce another dimension, both to the planning process and to the consideration of actual economic development strategies. This way of thinking may be incorporated into visioning or other long-term approaches to planning. It may be used to refine the way that a community carries out specific job creation or infrastructure projects. Many of the development strategies discussed in other chapters reflect a sustainable development approach.

For example, recreational and ecotourism at manageable levels do not require or exhaust resources to the same degree that permanent manufacturing facilities or residential development are likely to. Stopping retail leakages and adding value to homegrown products before they are shipped to market keep dollars circulating for local benefit and enable local jobs to grow in dollars earned—but not necessarily in number. Business visitation programs and the encouragement of entrepreneurs may lead

to more and better jobs in the future, while drawing upon community resources at approximately current levels.

Even business attraction can be gauged according to a standard that renewable resources cannot be used at a rate faster than they can be renewed. [The lumber and fishing industries are two examples where the widespread exhaustion of resources in the past have finally prompted efforts to assure that demand does not exceed the exhaustible supply.] As a flexible and adaptable process, the sustainable management of growth allows for its incorporation into virtually all small town job creation strategies.

But managing resources in a sustainable manner is not exclusively associated with economic development decisions. Of equal importance, local governments have major responsibilities for the protection of public health and the preservation of land and water resources where concerns about sustainability also must be aggressively pursued.

Water is perhaps rural America's most precious natural resource, critical to agriculture, current and future business and residential development, recreation and general public well-being. In many parts of the country, however, water has become contaminated, more costly to provide and increasingly scarce. Contaminants from industry—past and present—agriculture, underground storage tanks and numerous other sources have been found in a number of the nation's surface and underground water supplies.

Often, these contaminants are colorless, odorless and tasteless, giving no evidence of their harmful presence without sophisticated testing. The monitoring requirements in the Safe

Drinking Water Act of the federal government, and its recent 1996 amendments, assign major responsibilities to public water systems for the identification and removal of both chemical and bacteriological contaminants to levels posing no threat to human health.

There are ways that local governments can manage natural resources, just as they would economic development, which are better, but not necessarily bigger. If drinking water contamination is expected to increase in the future, the problem could be handled by building a bigger treatment facility. Yet many water systems are developing source water protection programs that focus on the prevention of pollution in the first place and the wise use of water in homes, business and agriculture.

Source water protection programs typically identify actual and potential sources of contamination and then develop mandatory and voluntary strategies to remove or control the causes. A gallon of petroleum can make a million gallons or more of water undrinkable. Therefore, many communities now identify all abandoned underground storage tanks and have them removed by the owners; or with public dollars when an owner cannot be located.

Runoff from agricultural chemicals and animal waste products is the single largest contributor to rural non-point source pollution [that type of pollution which does not originate from an identifiable point, such as a sewage treatment plant]. Local government leaders and farmers now meet in many areas of the country to work out voluntary best-management practices to minimize the impact of runoff from agricultural sources on streams, rivers, lakes and underground water supplies.

Preservation Strategies

Another key area of growth management in which rural governments can work with community partners is the preservation of farm land and open spaces. Statistics on the annual loss of farm land to development and the overwhelming home owner preference for single family houses with a yard, would seem to place agricultural interests and new residential development on a collision course. But there are several promising approaches that do not stop development altogether, and locate growth on nonagricultural lands where public services can be provided at the least cost and with the least impact on the environment.

Many smaller governments, such as Washington Township in Berks County, Penn., have recently discovered a zoning tool that allows landowners in preservation areas to permanently sell or transfer their development rights to landowners in development areas—a concept known as the transfer of development rights (TDR). A common thread can be found in successful programs across the nation: a concerted effort to induce developers in the private real estate market to purchase development rights from landowners in a preservation area, or sending area, and transfer them, and the potential development they represent, to a development area, or receiving area.

By using the TDR concept, small and rural governments have a powerful incentive to preserve and protect virtually any natural resource the community has identified as invaluable and irreplaceable, including agricultural land, forest land, park land, and recreation and conservation areas, and simultaneously increase development densities. A locality interested in incorporating TDR into its zoning ordinance must begin by first identifying the priority preservation and development areas of its jurisdiction.

With the sending and receiving areas identified, a township must then allocate to landowners in the preservation areas a pre-determined number of development rights, which they can sell to landowners who want to develop their own land. But to provide an incentive to sell these rights, landowners in the preservation area must normally be allocated rights for more dwelling units than they would be permitted to build under the township's current zoning.

Washington Township proved to be one such "natural fit" for a transferable development rights program. A largely rural community of 2,800 residents near the eastern tip of Berks County, Washington Township surrounds the small Pennsylvania boroughs of Bally and Bechtelsville. The township managed to escape the development boom of the 1980s, but the board of supervisors realized early on that their rural community lay directly in the middle of an area ripe for development. The board also agreed that just sitting back and waiting for development to hit would quickly lead to disaster.

According to Sandy Moser, who has served Washington Township for 21 years as secretary, the supervisors felt they could better facilitate cooperation among the farming interests, members of the planning commission, other township residents, and the township's planning consultant by taking the lead role in the revision of the comprehensive plan and update of the township's zoning ordinance.

In response to concerns regarding the cost of infrastructure to support the higher-density development created by the TDR program, the board argued that villages in the township were already in need of sewerage and that sewers would be more affordable for everyone if the villages were the core of the TDR receiving area. More development to share the costs would eventually lead to lower sewer bills for many township residents. And, lastly, in response to reservations voiced about the impact of higher-density development on the township's rural roads, the supervisors reasoned that a successful TDR program would deflect development pressure away from the most rural areas of the township, thus providing the only hope of preventing unmanageable traffic levels.

These and many other concerns were expressed time and time again throughout the process by both supporters and opponents, explained Moser. The board questioned everything as it proceeded cautiously through the project. Under the direction of the board of supervisors, the township's planning consultant delineated endless possibilities of sending and receiving areas and considered several different development densities before the TDR concept was written into the township's zoning ordinance. John Weller, planner for Systems Design Engineering, the township's planning consultant, noted that the endless hours of research and planning eventually paid off for the township.

The resulting zoning ordinance outlines a number of procedures and tools to implement the TDR concept, including provisions for a high-density residential and village district as the receiving area for development rights. Single-family, detached dwellings and two-family dwellings with traditional lot sizes and densities are allowed in the district, but smaller lot sizes and higher building densities are allowed with the purchase of TDRs. The number of development rights required for other uses varies.

The zoning ordinance specifies that transfers of development rights must be approved by the township board of supervisors and the rights must be officially transferred by a deed recorded in the Berks County Office of the Recorder. Purchasers of development rights must also pay any municipal real estate tax due to the township. Ninety-five development rights have been created and recorded, and four subdivision plans have been proposed recently using TDRs. "The township is reviewing those subdivision plans now," said Moser, "and public sewer and water service is going into the receiving areas outlined in the zoning ordinance. These improvements and the availability of the development rights from the agricultural district should begin to attract more developers who are interested in building higher-density housing in Washington Township's TDR receiving area."

Weller, the township's consultant, warns that townships should thoroughly investigate the TDR concept before proceeding with any significant zoning ordinance changes that incorporate the concept: "Any growth management concept must be specifically appropriate for the community." And TDR is very community-specific—above everything else, you must have the support of the community. Even elected and appointed officials can only go so far in their support of a project before being perceived as being in pursuit of their own agenda.

"In Washington Township's experience and the experience of other communities that have implemented TDR," noted Weller, "I am convinced that TDR would never have been adopted without the constant support of all of the groups who faithfully attended the many work sessions and participated in the process of planning and zoning."

The Washington Township case study was documented in a series of articles on "Preserving Open Space" which appeared in the *Pennsylvania Township News*, in the July, August and September 1995 issues. The series also described several other local and state initiatives to protect farm land. They include: agricultural protective zoning; the outright purchase of farm land by local, state or nonprofit entities; agricultural easement purchase programs [a public sector version of the transfer of development rights program]; and open space, which clusters development in a way that minimizes the land required for homes and infrastructure, but which provides home owners with visual and physical access to the land which remains undisturbed.

Inclusion and Resolution

In this guide, economic decisions are presented as deliberate choices that are consistent with the wise use of community resources and with future community goals. Virtually all resources can renew themselves—given time and use which do not exhaust or irreversibly contaminate them. Of the three Es involved in building a sustainable community, there remains the issue of equity. It is a word that should cast a wide net. If used in a restrictive or self-serving way, equity can be a divisive, rather than inclusive, process.

Equity at its core is about fairness. It involves the distribution of economic and social benefits across the community. It recognizes the range of economic needs within the community and allows affected parties to be heard, as choices on development initiatives are presented, debated and made. If consensus cannot be reached on issues such as the line between the use and misuse of local resources, then an equitable solution may require establishment of an independent dispute resolution process or an outside mediator.

An equitable view for sustaining the community, for example, will recognize that jobs must be available for young people graduating from high school or risk that many of the community's future taxpayers and leaders will settle elsewhere. As another example, the transferable development rights ordinance adapted by Washington Township enables farmers to receive some of the financial benefits that their land would bring, if developed for business or residential purposes. But in exchange for selling these rights to a developer who can use them on non-agricultural property, the farmer is legally bound to keep the land in agriculture, as a sustainable community resource.

Equity involves looking out for more than just a worker's paycheck. In Vermont's Mad River Valley, town leaders from Warren, Waitsfield and Fayston have worked successfully in partnership with the Sugarbush ski resort since the 1970s to make development compatible with town life and the environment. Yet the popularity of the area steadily drove up the cost of housing to the point that many young families who staffed the resort could not afford to live in the area. When approached about the problem, the owners of Sugarbush donated a parcel of land located off the mountain slopes, which is being developed by a volunteer, non-profit community group, as a site for affordable housing.

Efforts are underway to attract tourists to the resort on a year-round basis, so that many of the seasonal jobs will become year round jobs. [Chapter 8, *Creating Small Business Partnerships*, documents this and other partnerships among local governments, community groups and business interests.]

Equity provides everyone a place during the discussion of decisions that affect them. If a controversial facility such as a prison or landfill is to be located in your town, make certain that its placement is not imposed on a group or area that is unable to mount effective resistance. If the project is a good one for the community, then open discussion should make people stakeholders, not opponents.

In some small towns, there may be strong traditions or incentives not to open up the decision-making process. Often a small, recognized group has, over the years, taken the lead for determining the community's future. The leadership group is familiar, if not always content, with the way its members conduct business. In some communities, citizens are content to let those willing to serve take all responsibility.

Yet when decisions will affect current and future residents, their livelihood and the quality of community life for years to come, these decisions must be made by as broad a base of citizens as possible. Inclusiveness is one of the benchmarks of sustainable communities and one of the keys to success.

To Avoid or Accept

When issues are as all-encompassing as how land will be used for generations to come and what kinds of jobs and businesses may or may not meet community criteria, conflict is almost inevitable and this fact is better faced early on in the process.

History demonstrates that the cost of avoiding conflict is high. In the late 1930s, Neville Chamberlain, Prime Minister of England, was known as the Great Compromiser, who averted conflict with Hitler's Germany through a series of appeasements that sacrificed many a nation's freedom. Chamberlain is now recalled with disgrace, however, for not forcing an early diplomatic showdown that might have led Germany to seek a political rather than a military solution to territorial disputes.

At a more local level, while unnecessary arguments expend time, energy and people's inability to work with one another, on many issues, conflict is inevitable and must be recognized and worked through. Rather than dreading conflict, local leaders should utilize the opportunity to fully examine and resolve issues that may fester and resurface if ignored. Volumes have been written on conflict or dispute resolution. There are some general rules, however, that apply to most public conflict, including those involving sustainable growth decisions.

- *Define the issue.* Often, conflict is over a choice of words or emphasis within a generally acceptable solution. Norman Mailer once observed that two people meeting face to face are still looking in opposite directions. When opposing views of a contentious issue are first verbalized, they frequently are full of inflammatory language. Generally, it is good to let people speak as forthrightly as they want in order to clear the air. The moderator may want to record each position on a flip chart, but also restate the key points in less loaded language. "I hear you saying this...," or "You seem most concerned about this..." are two ways of introducing such restatements without putting words in the mouth of the original speaker; or passing judgment on what was said initially. Sometimes the issue itself cannot be agreed upon and discussion may move on to other dimensions of the resolution process.

- *Determine if information, emotion or personality is at the root of the conflict.* A lack of convincing information is often the basis for conflict, and its presence is also the key to resolution. The impact of economic development, positive or negative, on property values and quality of life concern most citizens. Additional study, or reassurances from towns which have had parallel experiences, may resolve the issue. Some issues are argued on purely an emotional basis. Landfills and low-level nuclear waste sites, for example, generate almost immediate opposition. Sometimes, emotional resistance to a local issue cannot be resolved to everyone's satisfaction, although it may help to identify the consequences of not landfilling solid waste. A possible resolution would be for the community to undertake a large-scale effort to recycle and to collect household hazardous waste for separate disposal outside the community.

Personality conflicts may be the hardest public disputes to resolve, because both parties are often willing participants. The root cause may have little to do with the issue under discussion and much to do with family or business transactions in the far past. If a member of the decision-making body, such as the town council, becomes embroiled in the dispute, he or she should not serve as the moderator, for example, and should perhaps be asked to be excused from a role in making the decision itself. If a real issue lies behind the public conflict of personalities, local leaders may move discussion ahead by asking both parties what they would choose as a general outcome. This question forces people to refocus on the issues. This same approach may work when a group or public forum is having problems defining the issue. Occasionally, it helps to work backward from where you hope to end up.

- *Allow all sides a chance to be heard and to be heard seriously.* Many individuals or organizations will press their position in a disruptive way if they believe they have been ignored or disrespected. Public meetings should be well-publicized and different interests encouraged to schedule an appearance. Groups representing minorities, smaller constituencies or disadvantaged residents should not purposely be scheduled when few are in attendance or attention spans have grown short. Most people and organizations are willing to accept that dispute resolution involves giving up some goals to achieve others that are shared with the rest of the community. But first, all parties who will be committed to what emerges as the common good must sense that their views have been heard and weighed in the final decision.

- *See if a consensus is emerging.* In full and open discussions, a combination of information, logic, cross fertilization of ideas and respect for others' view points often opens the way for consensus. It is best for one of the parties in dispute to suggest initially the outline for a resolution since some people will not move from their original position until they see movement from the other side. Group leaders may try to structure the suggestions that come from different interests in ways that appear to be equitable, but that remain consistent with overall community economic development goals. Most people are willing to work towards and accept consensus, if they have been included from the beginning and do not feel they are being conspired against when choices are made.

- *Engage an outside mediator for complex, highly-divisive and legally high-risk situations.* Some conflicts either start or become so charged with implications that they are best handled by an experienced, outside, neutral party. There is no check list to determine when this type of situation has arrived. But if most of the decision-makers feel overwhelmed with the prospect of peacefully resolving an issue, or the financial and legal consequences of the decision are substantial, then a professional mediator may be the best option. It is important before the mediator is chosen to have the different parties agree that they will accept the outcome of the mediator and that they will have some input into determining the skills which the mediator should bring to the negotiating table.

Ideally, managing growth in a way that is consistent with community concerns for the environment and with the equitable involvement of all citizens should bring the community together, not apart. It may prove to be an important part of your community's unfolding history when job creation is linked directly to quality of life issues; and when land use planning preserves the century-old view of croplands free from development into the foreseeable future. With sustainable development as a goal for growth, we can be more certain that what we value from the past will live on; and in our ability, "to meet the needs of the present without compromising the ability of future generations to meet their own needs."

PART III
The Tools

CHAPTER 11

Assessing Development Potential

Kevin T. McNamara and *Warren Kriesel*

During the 1960s and 1970s, many manufacturers looked to rural communities as a source of low-skill, low-wage labor. Today manufacturers for whom this is a high priority often locate in third-world countries. Manufacturing employment has lost its predominance in the U.S. economy while employment in service industries has expanded (Rosenfeld et al., 1985; Johnson, 1984; Deaton & Weber, 1986).

Despite this trend, local economic development groups in rural communities continue to focus on recruiting manufacturers (Smith & Fox, 1990). They often fail, but such failure could be avoided by more thorough preliminary analysis. How can local leadership incorporate estimates of their community's probability of attracting manufacturing investment into their assess-

ment of appropriate development policy? This chapter addresses this key question by presenting a model which community leaders can use to assess their community's attractiveness to industry.

Plant Location Decisions and Local Recruitment Strategies

A footloose[1] manufacturing firm's decision process is a multi-stage process that begins when the firm decides to invest in a new manufacturing facility (Smith, 1981: Schmenner et al., 1987). The first stage of the process involves selection of a geographic region that optimizes the firm's location with respect

Originally published as "Assessing Local Industrial Development Potential," Journal of the Community Development Society, Vol. 24, No. 1, 1993. Published by the Community Development Society, Milwaukee, Wisconsin. Reprinted with permission of the publisher.

to factor supply and product markets. This region could be a state, a multistate area, or other area depending on a specific firm's requirements. From a community perspective, until this regional location choice is made, local policy can do little to influence the firm's site selection decision.

Once a firm has selected a specific region, it searches within the region to identify a specific site that will minimize the firm's cost of production. This search may include evaluation of a variety of sites within the identified region that meet some criterion deemed critical by the firm influencing its cost of production. Selection of a specific site within the region is based on cost factors that include labor availability and costs, agglomeration economies, community's eagerness for industrial development, access to input factors and product markets, and miscellaneous firm cost factors (Kriesel & McNamara, 1991). Quality of life factors also influence a firm's location decision (Hekman, 1982). It is during the site-selection stage of the search process that state and local actions can influence location decisions.

Understanding the factors that influence manufacturing firm location at the county level provides leaders with insight into what local development policy options influence new manufacturing investment. Community location factors presented in Table 1 can be divided into two types, those that cannot be locally controlled and those that can be influenced by local government policy. As leaders examine their community's potential for attracting new industry, they should consider how their community compares to other communities in regard to both types of location factors. Investments in factors that

the community can influence, like industrial site quality, may be fruitless if the community lacks other attributes that are important to firms.

A general conclusion from location studies is that a community's attributes influence location choices for new manufacturing investment. Communities can make policy decisions to improve their attractiveness to industry. Industrial site quality, local taxes and local public services are three categories of local determinants that local policy can influence. Efforts to develop industrial sites with more services, to lower property and inventory taxes, and to expand local school, public safety, and fire protection services have positive impacts on a community's probability of attracting new manufacturing investment. Communities considering manufacturing recruitment as a strategy, however, should be aware that these investments may not help communities overcome disadvantages, such as poor highway access and a small labor force. Local leaders' expectations of the potential returns to various investments must be well thought out before any such investments are made. Location decisions are based on firms' assessment of how well specific industrial development sites meet some minimum cost and other location criteria.

The next section of the paper uses a model developed by Kriesel and McNamara (1991) to illustrate how community leaders can 1) assess their probability of attracting manufacturing investment, and 2) examine how their probability of attraction will change in response to local investment which improves community characteristics.

Table 1
Community Location Factors

A. Agglomeration factors
       population (1), (3), (5), (6)
    population density (5)
    commercial employment (1)
    number of manufacturing plants (5)
    distance to SMSA (2), (3)
B. Labor quality/cost/availability
    labor force size (2)
    unemployment rate (4), (8)
    wage rate (1), (5)
    percent of adult population with high school diploma (6)
    labor productivity (1)
    distance to vocational school (5)
    distance to four year college (2), (7)
C. Transportation facilities
    interstate highway access (2), (4), (5), (7)
    distance to airport (5)
D. Access to capital
    bank assets (5)
    bond financing (2), (7)
E. Site facilities and services
    site quality (2), (7)
    public site ownership (2), (7)
    site price (4)
    sewer capacity (5)
    zoning (5)
    location incentives (8)
    funded development group (6)
F. Taxes
    property tax rate (3), (8)
    inventory tax relief (4)
G. Public services
    per pupil school expenditures (2), (7)
    high school math achievement test score (6)
    fire protection rating (2), (4), (7)

A County Level Industrial Location Model

A county level industrial location model was estimated by the authors to determine a community's probabilities of attracting new manufacturing investment, and to identify community factors that impact firms' location decisions.[2] The manufacturing location model included community location factors classified as either a) factors that are beyond a community's ability to influence or, b) factors which communities can directly control and change through local investment. A county-level ordered, categorical logit model was used to estimate the probability of a Georgia county attracting a manufacturing plant. The model and complete empirical results are described in Kriesel and McNamara (1991). The analysis was conducted over the 1987–1989 period, during which 92 of Georgia's 159 counties attracted one or more new manufacturing facilities.

Table 2 illustrates use of the statistical analysis to examine the relative influence of each location factor on firms' decisions. The first column lists the location factor and the second column describes a change in the location factor. The third column gives the percentage increase in probability (for *average* Georgia county) from a specified change.[3] For example, the average county with no interstate highway had a 75.9 percent chance of attracting a plant. With an interstate, its chance is 82.7 percent, an increase of 6.8 percent.

A location factor's importance is judged by two things: a) its effect on location probability and b) the certainty of that effect, signified in the third column with the [sig] symbol. Table 2 indicates that factors most closely related to location decisions are the percentage of black population, passage of the inventory tax referendum, the fire protecting rating and the price (quality) of the industrial site. The effects of these six factors on probability are large and they are

Table 2
Effects of Location Factors on Probability of Attracting Manufacturing Plants and Certainty of the Effect

Factor	*Description of Change*	*Effect on Probability of Getting One Plant*
Non-Controlled Factors		
Interstate Highway	County gets a new interstate highway	+6.8%
Weekly Manufacturing Wage	Wage increases by $50, from $289 to $339	+0.7%
Miles to College	Distance increases from 26.6 to 46.6 miles	−3.2%
Miles to Metropolitan Area	Distance increases from 18.9 to 38.9 miles	−2.2%
Unemployment Rate	Rate increases by 2%, from 6.4 to 8.4	+7.4%
Percentage of Black Residents	Percent increases from 29.9% to 37.9%	−8.0%
Community-Controlled Factors		
High School Completion Rate	Rate increases from 61% to 71%	−2.5%
Effective Tax Rate per $1,000 Property	Rate increases by $5.00, from $8.68 to $13.68	+4.1%
Inventory Tax Relief Referendum	County passes the referendum	+7.8%
Fire Protection Rating	Rating improves from 6 to 4	+9.4%
Per Acre Price of Industrial Site	Price (quality) of site increases from $1,000 to $5,000 per acre	+2.2%

statistically significant at the 95 percent level. The remaining five factors are also important, due to either conceptual grounds or the previous research that showed them to be important. However, in the context of this Georgia research the influences of these other factors are less certain than are the six most significant factors.

The local unemployment rate was included in the model as a measure of labor availability. Its significance suggests that firms consider local labor availability in location decisions. The inclusion of racial composition is suggested by Till's research (1986), where counties with a high proportion of blacks were found to attract fewer manufacturers.[4] The interstate mileage variable was included as a measure of access to transportation routes. While these variables do not measure location factors that community leadership can directly impact, they provide valuable information to communities considering manufacturing recruitment as a local development strategy. Communities that have a small labor force or lack interstate highway access, for instance, should be aware that they are at a competitive disadvantage.

Other factors which influence manufacturing location can be controlled by a community. Three of these variables in the model were statistically significant: passage of inventory tax relief referendum, local fire protection rating, and the quality of local industrial development sites. Communities which enact inventory relief (which reduces a firm's local tax liability) will increase their probability of attracting new manufacturing investment. Improved fire protection serves to reduce a firm's insurance premiums. Furthermore, the upgrading of a community's fire protection is usually accompanied by the improvement of its water, sewer and related public services which directly benefit businesses.

The third locally-controlled variable associated with the firm's location decisions was a measure of local industrial site quality.[5] Communities can invest in one of several industrial site attributes to increase a community's attractiveness to firms seeking industrial sites. Site quality is related to three site specific attributes: lot size, the site's distance to an interstate highway, and the distance to an airport with air service. Community characteristics also influence the site's quality. These include educational attainment of adult population, the size of the local manufacturing base, the civilian labor force size, and whether or not the community is in a metropolitan area. While communities can improve the quality of local industrial sites by purchasing larger tracts of land that have good highway and railroad access, community characteristics limit the impact that communities can have on improving the quality of their industrial sites.

All but two of the location factors from Table 2 have the expected influence on location decisions. The two factors which influenced in an unexpected direction are both insignificant variables. The manufacturing wage has a positive effect, contrary to expectations. If this model had accounted fully for the quality (or education level) or labor, then higher wages should have negatively influenced plant location. The high school completion rate was also a negative influence. This was not expected because employers should expect higher production and profits from better educated workers, and counties with better educated workers should be more attractive to new manufacturing investment. Even with these unexpected effects, the overall statistical model can correctly predict 76 percent of plant locations in all 159 Georgia counties between 1987 and 1989.

It should not be a surprise that the effective tax rate has a positive effect on location. Counties that tax themselves are able to raise revenues which finance better public services that companies need. An example is the fire protection rating used here, plus police service, sewer and water.

APPLICATION OF THE LOCATION MODEL TO LOCAL DEVELOPMENT PLANNING

A county's leadership can use the results of a manufacturing location model to evaluate a) their chances of attracting a manufacturing plant to their county and b) alternative strategies of attracting a plant. For example, with an estimate of a Georgia county's probability of attracting new manufacturing investment, leaders from that county can consider the expected returns from various recruitment investments. They can make an estimate of the local tax revenue cost that would result from passage of a local inventory tax relief ordinance and compare it with costs of other development options such as further development of an industrial site or improvement of the local fire protection rating. Comparing the probability increases with the associated costs will indicate which investment is the most cost effective.

An analysis of 34 Georgia counties with an estimated probability of plant location of less than 50 percent indicates that passage of the inventory tax relief referendum, improving the county's fire protection rating, and increasing the quality of a local industrial site would increase the county's probability of attracting a new plant (Kriesel & McNamara, 1991). Substantial improvements in existing industrial sites (approaching $1 million) would be needed to increase their probability an additional five percent. Improving the fire protection by one rating point in the same community increases probability of attracting new manufacturing investment by nearly eight percent. Therefore, if a county can achieve the one point improvement in its fire protection for less than $1 million, than investment in fire protection (and similar public services) would be more cost effective than investing in industrial site improvements for increasing the community's probability of attracting a new firm. Adopting local inventory tax relief increases the county's probability of attracting a firm by about eight percent. The cost associated with this policy option can be estimated with local tax records and compared to the costs of other strategies aimed at improving the community's attractiveness to industry.

It is important for county leadership to realize a vital distinction between investing in industry-specific items versus public services that impact firms' costs. A speculative shell building, paved access roads or industrial tax breaks yield benefits *only if* the county actually attracts a new plant which uses those investments. On the other hand, local investment in public services, such as police and fire protection, schools and public utilities, provides benefits to county residents even if they do not attract a plant.

The Georgia counties' probabilities of attracting new plants are not easily transferable to localities in other states or regions because of variation in the general attractiveness of regions to industry, and in the types of and numbers of industries locating in different states of regions. The importance of specific community attributes in attracting firms, however, does provide insight into which local policies have the greatest impact on a community's attractiveness to industry. It also suggests which types of communities have higher probabilities of attracting new manufacturing plants.

In order to gain more general information about local recruitment prospects, probabilities were computed using the mean values of county factors for Georgia counties grouped by Beale's urban-rural continuum (Butler, 1990). Beale's ten categories were collapsed into seven categories because of limited observation in three categories. Location probabilities were estimated for the resulting categories (Table 3). The number of counties in each category is reported along with the estimated probabilities of attracting one new manufacturing facility (Probability 1) and two new facilities (Probability 2).

In Georgia, a state that has been among the leaders in attracting new manufacturing investment throughout the past thirty years, even the most remote county has a probability of attracting new industry that is greater than 50 percent. Even in Georgia, however, industries have a strong urban bias in selecting sites. County codes 6 and 7, representing the 44 most rural counties, had probabilities 37–40 percent lower than the code with the highest probability of attracting a new plant (Code 1—urban counties), and 15–18 percent lower than the Code 5, the next less remote group of rural counties. The differences for Probability 2 were 49–68 percent for Code 1 and 17–36 percent for Code 5. These estimates suggest that rural communities are at a disadvantage

Table 3
Probability of Attracting New Manufacturing Investment for Georgia Counties by County Type

County Type*	Number of Counties	Probability**	Probability†
Code 1	18	.93	.86
Code 2	20	.81	.70
Code 3	8	.90	.82
Code 4	27	.73	.57
Code 5	42	.71	.54
Code 6	21	.56	.37
Code 7	23	.53	.18

*County types are based on an urban-rural continuum code presented by Butler (1990). Nine classification codes were collapsed into seven because two codes had less than 5 observations.
**Probability of attracting one new manufacturing plant.
†Probability of attracting two or more manufacturing plants.

in competing with urban communities for new manufacturing investment. The more remote and smaller the rural county, the greater the disadvantage.

Summary and Conclusions

Location trends and recent location research provide general insight into a specific community's potential for attracting new manufacturing investment. An agglomeration of population and economic activity, labor availability and quality, air and highway transportation facilities, industrial site quality, and local public services were important location factors in most of the research cited. In general, communities with larger economies and populations are more attractive for manufacturing firms because many firms can operate at a lower cost of production at these sites. These communities should consider industrial recruitment options as part of their local development strategy. Local policy can influence a community's probability of attracting new manufacturing investment and its ability to compete with other communities for manufacturing investment. Analysis of a community's location attributes can help local leaders target industrial recruitment spending to get the greatest increase in the community's location probability per local dollar spent.

Small and rural communities are often less attractive to industry than urban counties. Rural communities in some regions of the United States, however, have successfully attracted manufacturing plants in the late 1980s. Three factors that are beyond local control, interstate highway access, available labor, and regional location, tend to be key factors in these plant locations.

Notes

1. A footloose firm is one that is not restricted to a specific location because of supply or demand related constraints.

2. The focus of these studies has been community or state factors that influence firms' location decisions. The analysis has not considered specific needs of firms by industry or type, such as by standard industrial classification (SIC) code. The limited number of location observations of any particular SIC code is not sufficient in any one state to permit cross sectional analysis.

3. The probabilities are calculated by evaluating a first degree polynomial: $z = a + b1X1 + \ldots + bkXk$, where a and b1 are estimated by the logistic regression, and the X1 are the location factors. The probability is found by inserting x into the logic transformation formula: Probability $= 1/|1 - \exp(-z)|$.

4. This negative association between the proportion of minority population and industry location could be due to several factors. Among these are racial discrimination, a perceived higher propensity for Blacks than Whites to unionize, or a perception that areas with high minority populations lack skilled and educated workers.

5. The measure was derived from a hedonic price analysis of industrial sites throughout the state.

References

Butler, M. A. 1990. *Continuum Codes for Metro and Nonmetro Counties.* Staff Report No. 9028. Washington DC: Agriculture and Rural Economy Division, Economic Research Service, U.S.D.A.

Deaton, B. J. & B. A. Weber. 1986. *The Changing Rural Economy of the States.* Blacksburg, VA: Department of Agricultural Economics, Virginia Tech.

Heckman, J. S. 1982. What are businesses looking for? *Economic Review* (June).

Johnson, T. G. 1984. *Off-Farm Employment of Small-Farm Operators: A Strategy for Survival.* Proceedings of the Forty-Second Professional Agricultural Workers Conference, December 2–4. Tuskegee, AL.

Kriesel, W. & K. T. McNamara. 1991. A county-level model of manufacturing plant recruitment with improved industrial site quality measurement. *Southern Journal of Agricultural Economics* 23:121–127.

Rosenfeld, S. A., E. M. Bergman, & S. Rubin. 1985. *After the Factories: Changing Employment Patterns in the Rural South.* Research Triangle Park, NC: Southern Growth Policies Board.

Schmenner, R. W., J. Huber & R. Cool. 1987. Geographic differences and the location of new manufacturing facilities. *Journal of Urban Economics* 21:83–104.

Smith, D. M. 1981. *Industrial Location.* New York: John Wiley and Sons.

Smith, T. R. & W. F. Fox. 1990. Economic development programs for states in the 1990s. *Economic Review* July/August: 25–35.

Till, T. 1986. The share of southeastern black counties in the southern rural renaissance. *Growth and Change* 17:44–55.

CHAPTER 12

Community Reinvestment Act

Virginia M. Mayer, Marina Sampanes, and James Carras

The Community Reinvestment Act, commonly known as the CRA, was enacted as Title VIII of the Housing and Community Development Act of 1977. Its passage was the culmination of years of grassroots community activism, research, and regulatory protest dealing with bank lending practices in cities around the country. Financial institutions in Chicago, Cleveland, New York, Boston, Baltimore, and other cities were accused of "redlining," or refusing to make mortgage loans in lower-income, often minority, inner-city neighborhoods.

The vigorous community and activist scrutiny of the banking industry led the Senate to hold hearings to investigate the redlining allegations and determine if the industry was discrimi-

nating against certain communities. During the course of the hearings, Congress was told that bank disinvestment, coupled with a decline of basic services such as transportation, health care, public safety, and retail stores, intensified the decline of older urban neighborhoods. This trend of large-scale disinvestment and shifts in racial and ethnic mix heightened the urgency for financial institutions to ensure that they meet the banking needs of their communities.

The Community Reinvestment Act reinforced the message, spelled out in bank charters, that federally insured and regulated financial institutions have the inherent obligation to meet the convenience and needs of their communities. The CRA reinforced this basic tenet and required that financial insti-

Originally published as Local Officials Guide to the CRA, *1991. Published by the National League of Cities, Washington, D.C. Reprinted with permission of the publisher.*

The Community Reinvestment Act

The CRA, enacted in 1977, requires each federal financial supervisory agency to use its authority when conducting examinations to encourage the financial institutions it supervises to help meet the credit needs of the community. Specifically, a regulatory agency conducting an examination of a financial institution must:

(1) assess the institution's record of meeting the credit needs of its entire community, including low- and moderate-income neighborhoods, consistent with the safe and sound operation of the institution; and
(2) take that record into account in evaluating an application for a charter, deposit insurance, branch or other deposit facility, office relocation, merger, or holding company acquisition of a depository institution. 12 U.S.C. § 2903.

Simply stated, the CRA and the implementing regulations place upon all financial institutions an affirmative responsibility to treat the credit needs of low- and moderate-income members of their communities as they would treat any other market for services that the bank has decided to serve. As with any other targeted market, financial institutions are expected to ascertain credit needs and demonstrate their response to those needs.

Source: Joint Policy Statement.

tutions not only meet depository needs but also credit needs of local communities, including low- and moderate-income communities (see box above). The CRA applies to all federally chartered and insured depository institutions: bank holding companies, national banks, savings and loan associations, and federal savings banks (all referred to as "banks" in this chapter.

The CRA gave communities the opportunity to help modify bank lending practices. The law encouraged every bank to identify the credit needs of its community, including low- and moderate-income neighborhoods; develop or adapt products to respond to those needs; and market the services to those communities.

While the CRA was a helpful first step toward increasing bank investment in low- and moderate-income communities, several problems limited its effectiveness: the language was vague, giving few specific guidelines; the law had no teeth—there were no concrete incentives

for complying and no immediate penalties for not complying; and scrutiny and enforcement were often lax. In an effort to spur full enforcement of the act, community-based organizations and coalitions challenged or protested bank applications for mergers, acquisitions, and branch openings. Since 1985, with the advent of interstate banking, community organizations used the regulatory system to leverage more than two hundred lending agreements, most of them with large regional banking institutions. These agreements spelled out specific commitments for mortgages, affordable housing, and small business lending.

Two factors brought renewed attention to the CRA in the late 1980s. The lack of federal funds for affordable housing and community development forced local development agencies and community-based organizations to intensify their search for private financing resources. In their efforts to gain financing, they often used CRA as a leveraging tool to encourage bank participation in community investment programs and partnerships. During the same years, new studies of bank lending patterns in several major cities, alleging that redlining and discriminatory practices continued to exist, received extraordinary press coverage (for example, in Atlanta, Boston, Detroit, and New York). The renewed public focus on investment practices resulted in an important regulatory policy statement in March 1989, and then in August 1989, in new legislation that increased the enforcement and power of CRA.

Federal Regulators' Statement on CRA

In March 1989, the four federal bank regulatory agencies—the Federal Reserve Board, the Federal Home Loan Bank Board (since replaced by the Office of Thrift Supervision), the Office of the Comptroller of the Currency, and the Federal Deposit Insurance Corporation—issued a Joint Statement on the Community Reinvestment Act to clarify the responsibilities of banks and community-based organizations. The significance of this policy statement extends beyond the printed words. It was the first comment by regulators on the CRA since a brief informational statement in 1980.

The document was carefully crafted to detail regulatory expectations and guidelines to both financial institutions and their communities. The twenty-three page Joint CRA Statement details:

- The basic components of an effective bank CRA policy;
- The need for periodic review and

documentation by lenders of their CRA performance (use of expanded CRA statements); and
- The need for ongoing communication with community organizations.

The Statement noted that all federally regulated financial institutions (referred to as "banks" throughout this chapter) must be far more proactive in communicating with their low- and moderate-income communities and "assessing their credit needs." In other words, financial institutions must have a better understanding of their communities' credit needs, resources, and concerns—and banks must respond to these needs with responsive loan products and programs. Effectively, banks need to look at the CRA from a strategic point of view and develop a plan of action.

Components of an effective bank CRA policy. A bank's CRA Statement, available to the public by law, generally outlines the description of its lending community and the types of credit offered (see box following). In their 1989 policy, the regulators encouraged financial institutions to expand their CRA Statements to elaborate on CRA efforts and describe their CRA performance, including:

- The methods and results of ascertaining the community credit needs;
- Steps taken to meet the needs, such as special credit-related programs, educational or technical assistance programs; and
- Descriptions of their outreach, product development, and marketing efforts, plus a summary documenting their results.

CRA Statements of Financial Institutions

CRA Statements describe the financial institution, its community, and the products and services offered. Federal regulators strongly encourage financial institutions to expand the contents of these Statements, which are reviewed by bank management on an annual basis. CRA Statements must be available to the public at all branch locations.

Cities should review the CRA Statements of local banks and thrifts to keep informed of how the institutions view themselves and what they are doing in the community. Basic elements of a CRA Statement include:

> Description of the financial institution and its branches;
> Delineation of its community (with a map) and how it was determined;
> List of specific types of credit and services the institution is prepared to extend within each community;
> Copy of its CRA Notice;
> Minutes of the Board meeting in which the Statement was approved.

In addition, an expanded CRA Statement may include the following:

> Methods used in ascertaining community credit needs;
> Results of the credit needs assessment process;
> Steps taken to meet identified credit needs;
> Special programs (i.e., educational or technical assistance)
> Community outreach efforts;
> Product development efforts;
> Marketing techniques to reach low- and moderate-income communities;
> Results of the institution's Internal CRA Review;
> Community development projects in which it is involved;
> Community leadership activities with community-based development organizations;
> Charitable contributions to support community-based activities for low- and moderate-income communities.

The regulators also recommended including a summary of the results of the bank's Internal CRA Review. Such documentation in the CRA Statement serves as the framework for public comment on an institution's CRA performance. American Security Bank of Washington, D.C., and Bank of America, California, have expanded CRA Statements that can serve as models for other institutions. The CRA Statement may be a good first step to learning of the activities and community philosophy of each bank. A note of caution: not all banks have expanded their CRA statements, which may indicate a lack of awareness on their part.

Bank/community relationships. The most effective community investment initiatives have come from discussions among lenders, local government, and community groups. In many cases, these discussions or negotiations have resulted from either challenges to bank expansion applications or publicized mortgage lending studies done by grassroots community advocates and coalitions.

The Joint CRA Statement encourages banks and community groups to engage in dialogue and establish ongoing relationships without the acrimony of past CRA protests of bank applications for mergers or acquisitions. Interested parties, such as city governments and community groups, are "strongly encouraged" to comment on bank performance and to bring their concerns and issues "to the attention of the institution and its supervisory agency at the earliest possible time."

One method of communicating concerns to a bank is to use the bank's Public Comment File. Banks must maintain a Public Comment File containing any CRA statements in effect during the past two years, a copy of the most recent CRA Performance Evaluation (conducted on and after July 1, 1990), and all comments on bank performance copies must be sent to the appropriate federal agencies. This file is open for public review.

Financial Institutions Reform, Recovery, and Enforcement Act of 1989 (FIRREA)

In August 1989, five months after the regulatory statement was issued, Congress passed the Federal Institutions Reform, Recovery, and Enforcement Act (FIRREA), focusing attention on its role in restructuring the nation's thrift industry and the cost to taxpayers. The hefty document also included new CRA disclosure provisions that could have a profound impact on communities around the country and their quests for increased bank involvement in their minority and low- and moderate-income neighborhoods. FIRREA amended the CRA and the Home Mortgage Dis-

closure Act (HMDA) to increase the amount of information available to the public by

- Revising the CRA rating system,
- Requiring disclosure of CRA ratings and evaluations, and
- Expanding HMDA reporting requirements.

New CRA rating system. The regulators use twelve assessment factors to review bank CRA performance. These assessment factors are grouped into five performance categories:

- *Ascertainment of community credit needs:* activities conducted by the institution to determine the credit needs of the community, including efforts to communicate with the community about credit services, and the extent to which the institution's board of directors participates in formulating policies and reviewing performance with respect to the purposes of the CRA.
- *Marketing and types of credit offered and extended:* the extent of marketing and special credit-related programs to make members of the community aware of the bank's credit services; origination of residential mortgage loans, housing rehabilitation loans, small business or small farm loans, and rural development loans, or the purchase of such loans originated in the community; participation in governmentally insured, guaranteed or subsidized loans programs for housing, small businesses, or small farms.

- *Geographic distribution and record of opening and closing offices:* geographic distribution of credit extensions, credit applications, and credit denials; the record of opening and closing offices and providing services.
- *Discrimination and other illegal credit practices:* any practices to discourage applications for types of credit set forth in the bank's CRA statement; evidence of prohibited discriminatory or other illegal credit practices.
- *Community development:* participation, including investments, in local community development and redevelopment projects or programs; ability to help meet community credit needs based on its financial condition and size, legal impediments, local economic conditions, and other factors; any other facts that bear upon the extent to which the bank is helping meet community credit needs.

In the past, banks received a numerical rating for each of the five categories, from which a composite rating (from one, the best, to five, the worst) was derived. The grading criteria for each category were not specific, and the weighted value of each category in relation to the composite rating was not clear. The lax enforcement of CRA was demonstrated as the composite ratings tended not to reflect much analysis; virtually every institution received a passing grade. Less than 3 percent of all banks received less than passing grades. The regulatory agency's evaluation process and ratings for each institution were not publicly disclosed.

The FIRREA amendments changed the grading system to replace the earlier numerical scale with a four-tier descriptive rating system. The new ratings are:

- Outstanding record of meeting community credit needs
- Satisfactory record of meeting community credit needs
- Needs to improve record of meeting community credit needs
- Substantial noncompliance in meeting community credit needs

All four regulatory agencies now use this uniform set of CRA disclosure guidelines and the same rating system. These new guidelines provide consistent and better defined parameters for the new ratings. For example, CRA evaluations now include findings and supporting facts for each category, as well as overall conclusions. In addition to being more qualitative, the ratings are now disclosed to the public.

Disclosure of the CRA ratings and evaluations. The new disclosure policy created by FIRREA is important to city officials because it provides a new tool for increasing bank community investment. Under the new regulations, lenders are required to make the CRA evaluations public within thirty business days of their receipt from the regulator. The evaluation must be placed in a financial institution's CRA public file at its main office, and also at one designated office in each community it serves. It must be made available to anyone who requests the information. The institution may also include its response to the evaluation in the public comment file, if it so chooses. (See box on next page.)

CRA Ratings Go Public Under FIRREA

As of July 1, 1990, CRA ratings are no longer on a numerical basis; rather they are written evaluations using a four-tier descriptive system:

> Outstanding record of meeting community credit needs
> Satisfactory record of meeting community credit needs
> Needs to improve record of meeting community credit needs
> Substantial noncompliance in meeting community credit needs

Each financial institution will have its performance reviewed in five major categories:

1. Ascertainment of community credit needs;
2. Marketing and types of credit extended;
3. Geographical distribution and record of opening and closing offices;
4. Discrimination and other illegal credit practices; and,
5. Community development.

An "outstanding" rating will be achieved only by financial institutions that demonstrate certain qualities, including leadership in ascertaining community needs, participation in community revitalization, and affirmative involvement in planning, implementing, and monitoring their CRA-related performance. Most CRA observers agree that "outstanding" ratings will be difficult to achieve.

CRA Evaluations can be found at an institution's main office and designated branch in each of its local communities. They are not, however, required to provide free copies.

Expansion of the Home Mortgage Disclosure Act

The Home Mortgage Disclosure Act was passed in 1975, early in the debate over redlining, to create a national system under which regulated financial institutions were to report mortgage loans.

The lack of home mortgage availability, especially in urban areas, resulted in charges of discrimination or "redlining," the systematic exclusion of certain geographic areas as viable communities for bank investment. The allegations of redlining centered around minority communities. Community leaders used creative but elementary means to demonstrate bank disinvestment through maps of neighborhoods marked where mortgages had been made. Lenders had no systematic method to indicate where specific mortgages had been made. Early in the debate, the Home Mortgage Disclosure Act (HMDA) emerged. HMDA instituted a national reporting system of mortgage loans by regulated financial institutions.

HMDA required financial institutions to disclose information on their mortgage originations and purchases. Banks were required to submit summary reports of their mortgage loan activity by geographic area. The reports, however, lacked detail in reporting information to reflect loan activity with respect to expressed demand (loan applications). Also, rapid investment in lower-income communities often resulted in gentrification, displacing residents for newer, more affluent buyers and investors. Financing for gentrification alone does not fulfill institutions' obligations under the Community Reinvestment Act.

HMDA's limited effectiveness as

an analytical tool resulted in efforts to amend the Act. Eventually, changes to the HMDA were implemented through the Financial Institutions Reform, Recovery, and Enforcement Act (FIRREA) of 1989. The changes to HMDA will make it a valuable tool for cities and towns as they define their community needs.

Reporting requirements. HMDA now requires financial institutions to disclose the race, gender, and income level of all applicants as well as borrowers by census tract. Institutions must also report on the disposition of each loan request and may, if they choose, indicate the reason if the application is denied. Loans sold to the secondary market must be noted according to the category of purchaser.

The first set of expanded reports is due to the supervisory agencies by March 1, 1991. Each agency, in turn, gives the data to the Federal Reserve, which will produce a series of data tables for each reporting institution. Each bank's report will be sent to the bank; the bank will subsequently make the report available to the public upon request. As in the past, the regulators will also continue to provide these reports to local HMDA depositories in each metropolitan statistical area, where copies of the HMDA data for each local institution are available for inspection or copying by the public.

These reporting requirements extend to virtually all mortgage lenders, including mortgage and home finance companies, banks, savings and loans, and credit unions. The only financial institutions exempt from these new requirements are those with assets of less than $30 million (including assets of the parent organization). In addition, the

U.S. Department of Housing and Urban Development (HUD) requires all FHA lenders, regardless of size or affiliation, to comply with the new HMDA requirements. FHA lenders must report HMDA data on all FHA activity to HUD, regardless of reporting to any other regulatory agency.

Bank Activities/Responses Encouraged by Regulators

In their 1989 statement and their subsequent actions, the regulatory agencies have encouraged financial institutions to undertake many activities in their banking and CRA efforts.

In general, the following actions are encouraged:

- Participate in various government-insured lending programs and other types of lending programs, such as conventional mortgage loans with private mortgage insurance to help meet identified credit needs.
- Develop and advertise services to benefit low- and moderate-income persons, such as government check cashing and low-cost checking accounts.
- Target an advertising and marketing strategy to inform low- and moderate-income groups of the loan and deposit services available to them. Identify means to reach these groups (for example, small newspapers, radio, television, community/church organizations, non–English literature).
- Establish a process involving all levels of management in efforts to contact governmental leaders,

economic development practitioners, businesses and business associations, and community organizations to discuss the financial services that are needed by the community.

• Participate and provide assistance to community development programs and projects.

• Invest in state and municipal bonds.

Some bankers need to be reminded that CRA-related loans and activities are safe and sound investments in the community. The agencies discourage "give-away programs" that would place an institution at undue risk—and they offer many approaches lenders can take to address community credit needs. City government should evaluate local lenders' CRA programs using their own criteria.

CRA evaluations for all CRA examinations commenced by bank regulatory agencies after July 1, 1990, will be made public. This is a large number of evaluations, and it will take some time before evaluations for all banks are available. As examinations are completed, the public evaluations will be sent to the banks by the regulatory agency. The bank will then have thirty business days in which to release the evaluation to the public.

To determine whether a particular bank's CRA Evaluation is available to the public, contact the bank directly or consult the bank's primary supervisory agency. Each supervisory agency now periodically publishes lists of those banks for which CRA evaluations are available.

The New CRA Environment

The efforts by community organizations to change policy to mandate public disclosure of CRA ratings were opposed by the banking industry. Proponents for public disclosure (community organizations, state and local governments, and the National League of Cities) say such information will be helpful in several ways.

• Disclosure places pressure on regulators to make their examinations more thorough.

• Public disclosure provides communities with more information and encourages banks to be more active.

• Disclosure will make CRA efforts a more competitive element among local lenders.

• Lenders with solid CRA programs will be duly noted and can promote their record.

• The descriptive information in the evaluation identifies the strengths and weaknesses of an institution's CRA program and policies.

• The public can assess its impact on the financial institution's CRA policies.

• Access to such information indicates the emphasis on and interpretation of certain elements of CRA by the supervisory agencies.

In opposing public disclosure, the banking industry claimed that ratings could be misinterpreted by consumers (possibly confusing CRA with safety and soundness evaluations, which are not disclosed publicly) or misrepresented by others to cast aspersions on an institution's community record.

As more examinations are released, it seems certain that some financial institutions will incorporate them into public relations and marketing strategies. For instance, Bank of America in California, which was rated "outstanding," issued a press release and aggressively distributed copies of its examination findings. The public may request a meeting with the regulators and place letters to financial institutions in their public comment files (with copies sent to the regulatory agencies) prior to the anticipated examinations. All of the effects of public disclosure have yet to be seen, however.

What the New CRA Environment Means Locally

The new CRA environment spells opportunity. It also means more information, more communication, and more collaboration among the public, private, and nonprofit sectors.

Implications for lenders. Many lenders must now respond to the new CRA environment. Lenders are seeking to minimize the politicizing of the CRA issue by institutionalizing community reinvestment practices as a normal course of business. This is accomplished through aggressive community outreach that facilitates dialogue and that can in turn help identify and take advantage of sound market opportunities. A receptive bank attitude fosters goodwill and cooperation between the lending institution and its community. All this can result in good business for the lender and economic growth and vitality for its community. As the First National Bank of Chicago discovered, a neighborhood lending operation can be a strong profit center.

Local officials who give increased attention to the CRA, however, should view it in the context of today's uncertain economic climate and the banking industry's losses, especially in real estate lending. The declining financial condition of many institutions has increased federal regulators' scrutiny of loans. In turn, lenders have reduced all types of lending. As a result, many lenders feel they are receiving mixed signals from regulators who are, on one hand, scrutinizing all lending and, on the other hand, encouraging banks to undertake community development lending. Though the two are not mutually exclusive, this environment appears to be somewhat confusing for lenders.

Implications for local governments. Together, the CRA Policy Statement, increased regulatory enforcement, and disclosure of CRA ratings and HMDA information provide new tools to help local governments and community organizations make sure that financial institutions invest in low- and moderate-income areas.

The need for ongoing dialogue across the interested sectors is an obvious part of identifying needs and developing responses to those needs. Local government officials can establish a constructive process to work on community reinvestment issues with local lenders and community representatives. Local government and the lenders share the mutual interests of complying with federal regulations while building the local economy and community development base. Armed with more complete information on local lenders' performance and a local credit needs assessment, city officials can work confidently with the banking community on specific issues affecting targeted low- and moderate-income neighborhoods.

The Role of Local Officials

Often, public offices, functions, and programs are generalized under the catch-all category of "government." Different government interests identify priorities, needs, and solutions based on their respective interest or expertise. For instance, the priority "development" issues of the Mayor may differ from the immediate concerns of the City Council, while the Planning and Community Development departments may be focusing on different phases and elements of the community economic development process. Government is always blending political agendas with planning, policy, and programmatic policies. It is important, however, not to send mixed messages to residents, banks, and other interests. Making sure that all parties are working under the same message is a key element in success.

Notwithstanding the different perspectives, functions, and concerns, city leaders need to take advantage of the current CRA climate by assuming a variety of roles. Leadership takes many forms, depending on the local personalities and political climate of the community.

City as advocate. City officials can be the advocates for community reinvestment, raising the credit issues that need to be addressed by financial institutions. The city can increase awareness of the need for investment initiatives through studies, such as a community credit needs assessment and or analysis of HMDA data; planning documents; public hearings on issues; and community meetings. The city can provide uniform demographic data to all financial institutions so that all are working from the same base when they develop their plans. As an advocate, the city should be prepared to ask the questions and exert pressure on local financial institutions to respond to the community credit needs.

City as architect. The city may also choose to be the architect of a comprehensive community investment strategy or specific program. With the needs of the community identified, the city can develop an investment strategy that maximizes the city resources by investing with private sector actors. Get a head start by formalizing the goals, objectives, and potential responses discussed within local government. Through these efforts, the city sets the agenda and framework for discussion. The resulting strategy or plan can be the basis for discussion with local lenders and community-based organizations.

City as facilitator. City leaders can serve as the facilitators and brokers, building bridges between the local financial institutions and community-based organizations and building consensus based on common interests. The city assumes this role by sponsoring hearings, forums, and smaller meetings among interested parties. Community-based organizations know what their needs are, and the financial institutions need to understand them. The education that comes from discussion among the public, private, and nonprofit sectors helps construct a community investment program that is doable and beneficial. As facilitator, the city can build consensus among groups with very different perspectives.

City as provider. Local governments can be the provider, as well, of public resources to be used with new bank commitments to increase their impact and reduce the risk for private lenders. Such participation can include loan guarantees, loan programs, loan participations, technical assistance services, and community outreach.

City as partner. Most important, in all situations, and along with any other roles it may take on, the city can be a partner in the development and implementation of a comprehensive community investment program. Working with all interested groups, the city can establish a process, participate in the process, and help get a community investment program off the drawing board and into the community. Local officials can help create new vehicles and intermediaries that facilitate bank participation in community economic development.

Prepare for your roles. Whatever role or roles the city chooses to assume, the greatest success will occur when city officials are prepared. Being prepared in the following areas can demonstrate the local government's leadership in the community reinvestment process.

- *Get the facts.* Know your community and its credit needs.

- *Set the agenda.* Armed with the knowledge of the needs in the community, local officials should identify their goals and plans for the city. Specific projects in which participation by the private sector can leverage precious public dollars can be used as the initial areas of focus for discussion with local lenders.

- *Dedicate staff time.* As with any city plan or program development, consider committing staff time to working on this process in two areas: meetings with local lenders and community organizations; and program/product development to consider for your city.

- *Research product and vehicle options.* Financing products require creativity and resourcefulness. Learn what is working and what has not worked elsewhere; explore initiatives in other communities. The National League of Cities can serve as a peer-to-peer referral resource for local officials interested in learning from colleagues in other areas.

CHAPTER 13

Downtown Revitalization

Dolores P. Palma

Downtown revitalization is on the upswing all across the country. In communities of all sizes, there is a growing understanding that the health of Downtown is directly related to the health of the community as a whole. Hundreds of communities all across the country have on-going Downtown revitalization programs in place. And, the tale these communities have to tell is that there are certain initiatives which seem to bring about the greatest success in revitalizing our nation's Downtowns.

The top ten initiatives which appear to result in Downtown success—regardless of a community's population or geographic location—are shown below. In short, these initiatives show that the Downtown enhancement programs which are experiencing a great deal of enthusiasm and success, seem to

have strong management and business-oriented initiatives in place.

Initiative #1: Private-public Partnerships—Over the last twenty years, many communities have formed public-private partnerships whose mission was to enhance Downtown. In these partnerships, the public sector, the business sector, and the civic sector joined together, made decisions together, and each carried their weight to reinvest and reinvent their Downtown. Going beyond that, the most successful Downtown revitalization programs today are forming private-public partnerships. What is new about these partnerships is that they are driven by the private, rather than by the public, sector. The Spirit of Anniston is one such partnership. Created with the Downtown's private sector taking the lead and the City

From Municipal Maryland, *Vol. 23, No. 4, November, 1994. Published by the Maryland Municipal League, Annapolis, Maryland. Reprinted with permission of the publisher.*

of Anniston as a strong partner, "The Spirit" defined a Downtown Business Plan and raised $1.2 million to implement the Business Plan. And, showing private sector leadership and commitment, only $30,000 of these funds will come from the public sector each year.

Initiative #2: Downtown Vision—Waiting until the handwriting is on the wall and then reacting to it is the old way of doing business. The newer, more proactive and successful way of revitalizing Downtown is to define a clear vision of where you want your Downtown to go—a vision that is realistic and that is shared by the business community, the local government, and the citizens of the community—and then aggressively pursuing that vision. In Grand Haven, Michigan, the Central Business District Downtown Development Authority spearheaded an inclusive out-reach effort to define a shared community vision for its CBD. That effort resulted in a vision that has been embraced by the residents, the civic sector, the business community, and City Hall and a partnership has been formed to make that vision a reality.

Initiative #3: Market-driven Business Plan—Market analysis is THE critical first step for successful Downtown revitalization. The Field of Dreams Approach to Downtown revitalization—"If you build it they will come"—has proven not to work. Instead, the successful approach is much more business-oriented—know who your customers are, who your POTENTIAL customers are, what they want today, what they will want tomorrow—and provide those things.

But knowing Downtown's economic potential is not enough. For greatest success, an aggressive course of action—or a Downtown Business Plan—must be defined. The purpose of the business plan is to enable Downtown to capture economic potentials revealed in the market analysis. In other words, the market analysis findings must drive all Downtown improvement actions—all of the private sector's business decisions and the public sector's governance decisions—including how to market the Downtown, which business hours to keep, which types of streetscape improvements to make, etc.

The City of Americus, Georgia, realizing the importance of market knowledge, is undertaking a comprehensive market analysis that will identify the retail, office, and housing potential for its Downtown. And, knowing that taking this step is not enough, Americus is using the market knowledge to define a comprehensive and aggressive business plan for its Downtown.

Initiative #4: Unique Niches—In the most successful Downtowns, the business community knows that "doing business as usual" has led to Downtown's decline. And, the business community knows that they can't out mall the mall AND they can't out discount the discounters. Instead, for Downtown to succeed it must create, carve out, and become known for its particular niches in the marketplace. Embracing an "adapt or die mentality," Downtown can reinvent itself and successfully co-exist with other commercial giants.

Old Town in Alexandria, Virginia, is an excellent example of the adapt or die mentality. With multiple shopping malls, shopping strips, and neighborhood business centers—as well as the largest discount mall in the world—within close range, Old Town has carved out its own niche. Now known for its specialty restaurants, home furnishing stores, and gift stores, Old Town attracts area residents as well as millions of tourists each year.

Initiative #5: Business Attraction—In all Downtowns that have experienced economic decline, attracting additional businesses is a primary goal. However, the Downtowns where this goal is met are implementing aggressive, targeted, and personalized business attraction campaigns. Such an approach to business attraction requires the market analysis and identification of niches, mentioned above, as well as identifying, calling, and hosting targeted business prospects who match the Downtown niches being created. An example of this initiative can be seen in Downtown Tupelo, where Tupelo Main Street recruited 27 businesses in one year by implementing an aggressive business attraction campaign that was based on market analysis findings.

Initiative #6: Business Counseling—The most progressive Downtown enhancement programs are those that understand that keeping your existing businesses is as much economic development as attracting additional businesses. And, the most successful way to ensure that existing businesses are retained is to nurture them through one-on-one personalized counseling. Business counseling can be used to address specific issues facing a particular business owner such as how to use the findings of the market analysis to boost sales; how to adjust hours so that they are market-driven, how to become distinctive through exceptional customer service, how to develop an in-house customer mailing list, and how to cross-advertise with other Downtown businesses. The counseling is best provided by the Downtown director or by local service providers, such as a Small Business Development Center.

Initiative #7: Focus Groups—A tool long used in the advertising industry, focus groups are now widely used in the most aggressive Downtown efforts. Focus groups allow the Downtown partnership to assemble a small group of Downtown customers or potential customers and ask what they like and don't like about Downtown. The lesson here is, for success, don't try to guess what your customers want. Ask them!

Focus groups can be arranged to engage a wide variety of Downtown customers and potential customers. For example, teen focus groups were held in Downtown Grand Haven, Michigan, to discuss whether or not to build a teen activity center; university student, faculty, and administration focus groups were held in Murfreesboro, Tennessee, to discuss how Downtown could better meet their shopping needs; a focus group of medical center employees was held in Robbinsdale, Minnesota, to discuss how Downtown could be made more appealing to them as a nearby customer group; and a Downtown employee focus group was held in Oscoda, Michigan, to determine how Downtown could embrace this built-in market.

Initiative #8: Downtown Housing—The most successful Downtown enhancement programs are those where housing development is being encouraged once again. In its early stages, this usually involves renovating buildings into housing units. And later, as Downtown and its housing market are strengthened, this often entails constructing new, infill residential buildings in Downtown or on its perimeters.

It must be pointed out that this

initiative has been successful in small communities as well as in large communities. For example, Peabody, Kansas, with a population of 1,410, and Westminster, Maryland, with a population of 17,000 have both created market rate apartments in the upper floors of older commercial buildings on their main streets.

Initiative #9: Formal Marketing Campaigns—Downtown's customers and potential customers are sophisticated and smart consumers who have many shopping options. And, they are constantly being bombarded by sophisticated marketing messages. The most progressive Downtown efforts in the country today are those that have realized the need to implement a marketing campaign that is every bit as professional and comprehensive as the competition's. For greatest success, the campaign must be of high quality, professional, and must stress Downtown's economic themes and overall image. CITY-CENTER Danbury decided to take the plunge into a professional crafted marketing campaign. The organization hired a professional to help them define a strategic marketing campaign and, after successfully raising the necessary funds, the organization retained a public relations firm to implement that campaign in conjunction with the group's marketing committee.

Initiative #10: Management Techniques from the Malls—While our Downtowns should not try to—and are not able to—compete head-on with malls and win, most successful Downtowns are those that have learned and borrowed the best management techniques from the malls. These include:

- Having the Downtown partnership function much as a mall management company does;
- Hiring a full-time, professional, experienced Downtown director who would be the equivalent of the mall manager;
- Defining and implementing a leasing plan for Downtown so that businesses that can share customers are clustered together;
- Making sure Downtown is appealing by keeping high standards of maintenance for both private and public spaces;
- Putting into place a financing mechanism that ensures adequate, predictable and reliable funds to implement the Downtown revitalization effort.

Figure 1, developed in conjunction with the National League of Cities, sets forth a simple test to evaluate the health of your downtown. Details concerning the scoring of this test are explained at the bottom of this figure.

Figure 1
The Test of a Healthy Downtown

Please indicate if you strongly agree, somewhat agree, somewhat disagree or strongly disagree with each statement.

	Strongly Agree	Somewhat Agree	Somewhat Disagree	Strongly Disagree
1. I am very pleased with the variety of businesses that are Downtown.	_____	_____	_____	_____

continued on p. 162

Figure 1 (continued)
The Test of a Healthy Downtown

	Strongly Agree	Somewhat Agree	Somewhat Disagree	Strongly Disagree
2. I am very happy with the selection of goods and services available Downtown.	_____	_____	_____	_____
3. I am very happy with the price of goods and services available Downtown.	_____	_____	_____	_____
4. I am very happy with the quality of goods and services available Downtown.	_____	_____	_____	_____
5. I am very happy with the service I receive from Downtown businesses.	_____	_____	_____	_____
6. I am very happy with the hours that Downtown businesses are open.	_____	_____	_____	_____
7. I am very happy with the parking situation Downtown.	_____	_____	_____	_____
8. I am very happy with the overall physical appearance of Downtown.	_____	_____	_____	_____
9. I am very happy with the appearance of buildings Downtown.	_____	_____	_____	_____
10. I am very proud of the image Downtown portrays of our community.	_____	_____	_____	_____

How to Score the Test Results:

Developed in conjunction with the National League of Cities, this simple survey and scoring system can be used to determine the health of your Downtown. The "test" should be given to community residents (by phone) and to Downtown business owners. The resident and business tests should be scored separately so the results can be compared.

The test results can be scored using the following point system:

- 4 points for each response of "Strongly Agree"
- 3 points for each response of "Somewhat Agree"
- 2 points for each response of "Somewhat Disagree"
- 1 point for each response of "Strongly Disagree"

The number of points received by each question should be added together. In other words, if 100 people were surveyed, the number of points each person gave to question #1 would be added together and divided by 100 to yield an average score. The maximum average score for each question would be 4 and the minimum would be 1. The average scores allow you to diagnose the patient's illness—in other words, what is the particular disease Downtown is suffering from, according to those participating in the survey. For example, an average score of 3 to question #1 would indicate that, on the

continued on page 163

Figure 1 (continued)
The Test of a Healthy Downtown

whole, survey participants were not completely pleased (or were somewhat displeased) with the variety of businesses found in Downtown at the time of the survey. The diagnosis for each question can be looked at in the following way:

- An Average Score of 4: No Disease
- An Average Score of 3–3.9: Time to Look at Preventive Health Care
- An Average Score of 2–2.9: The Disease Has Broken Out; Quick Action Is Needed
- An Average Score of 1–1.9: Put the Patient Into Intensive Care!

CHAPTER 14

Downtown Safety Strategies

Dolores P. Palma

Safety is becoming a prominent issue in downtowns all across the country today. When dealing with this issue, downtown leaders frequently find that downtown safety concerns are more often rooted in perception than reality—meaning that the issue must be addressed and resolved if our downtowns are to thrive economically.

A downtown that is unsafe—or that is perceived to be unsafe—will not be able to attract the customers, users, and investors needed for that downtown's economy to flourish. Therefore, the issue of safety must be addressed as part of an economically-driven downtown enhancement effort.

Contributing Factors. Research has shown that a variety of factors contribute to the perception that a downtown is unsafe. These tend to fall into the following three categories:

- *Physical and Environmental*—These items involve the condition of property, the presence of litter and graffiti, the physical layout of public spaces, and downtown lighting levels. A downtown that is in poor physical condition gives the impression of being abandoned, and therefore, unsafe.

- *Social*—These items involve the presence of homeless individuals, people "hanging out" on the street, the public use or sale of drugs and alcohol, and the presence of panhandlers. These situations tend to be intimidating to customers who, therefore, try to avoid the areas of downtown where social issues exist.

- *Image Related*—These items involve the frequency of media reports and the message conveyed

Originally published as "Effective Strategies for a Safe Downtown," Municipal Maryland, *Vol. 24, No. 7, February, 1995. Published by the Maryland Municipal League, Annapolis, Maryland. Reprinted with permission of the publisher.*

in these reports concerning safety issues in and related to downtown. Media reports about downtown tend to heighten the potential downtown customer's awareness of what is—and what is not—occurring in downtown.

It is ironic that the physical, environmental, social, and image-related items discussed above often carry greater weight—in terms of a downtown being viewed as unsafe—than incidents of real downtown crime. This is because the items above are extremely visible in a declining downtown. Downtown's customers, clients, employees, and visitors see these items on a daily basis and, therefore, constantly have their perceptions reinforced of downtown as abandoned, scary, or intimidating. On the other hand, real downtown crime (muggings, robberies, bad checks, etc.) is comparatively invisible—it occurs in a very finite time period and all visible evidence of the occurrence is often gone immediately.

Effective Safety Strategies. According to recent national research, strategies to effectively deal with downtown safety issues primarily fall into the seven categories discussed below. It must be noted that, first, these safety strategies are most effective when they are implemented as part of a comprehensive downtown enhancement effort. And, second, safety strategies must be tailored to the specific needs of each downtown.

- *Community Policing.* A discussion of safety cannot take place today without mention of community policing—the "hot" law enforcement "buzz word" of the 1990s.

    Community policing, in its simplest form, is getting back to the basics—to local police personnel and citizens working together to address and resolve the problems facing their community. Community policing is a "user-friendly" form of policing that is based on the philosophy that the community, as well as the local police force, have a responsibility and a role in preventing crime. This partnership between community and police force creates a strong community which is the best weapon against crime.

    Community policing typically involves establishing and maintaining a highly visible and personal police presence. Common ways of accomplishing this often include making a shift from car patrols to foot and bicycle patrols; police substations; and crime "watch" programs.

    Developing a personal relationship between police officers and area residents and business owners is an integral part of community policing. This approach has been embraced based on the belief that an individual's feeling of safety is enhanced by knowing police officers personally. Community policing is being used in business districts to afford business owners and employees an active role in both controlling criminal activity and addressing the public's fear of crime.

- *Communication and Networking.* Most efforts being implemented to address downtown safety issues include communication and networking. The goal of such efforts is to open lines of communication—between the downtown organization, downtown business owners, community residents, and the local police force—in order to identify, address, and resolve safety issues. One example of this safety strategy is the Downtown Security Fax Network in Phoenix, AZ. Operated as a collaboration between the downtown Phoenix Partnership and downtown business people, the fax network allows immediate dissemination of information about crimes reported in downtown Phoenix.

• *Education and Training Programs.* Several downtown organizations have developed programs that go a step beyond networking and improved communications. These organizations provide educational programs for downtown business owners and employees regarding how to deal with safety issues. An example of safety education and training can be seen in Baltimore. The Downtown Partnership of Baltimore employs a retired police officer to conduct crime prevention seminars and training programs for merchants. The training sessions are aimed at providing a variety of business-related security tips—such as how to improve security through store layout.

• *Physical Improvements.* Physical eyesores—such as dilapidated vacant buildings, uncontrolled litter, and graffiti—are often viewed by the public as indications that downtown is unsafe. Therefore, many downtown organizations have instituted aggressive maintenance, clean-up, and beautifi-

cation programs in the belief that a clean, well-maintained, and inviting physical environment is one of the best deterrents to crime and fear of crime.

Examples of communities making physical improvements to address safety follow:

• The Trenton Downtown Association implements a highly visible maintenance program. Four full-time personnel work six days a week cleaning, sweeping, picking up litter, etc., in downtown. The Association has found that these efforts persuade people not to litter by setting a good example and make downtown's users feel more comfortable and secure.

• The Downtown Berkeley Business Association has a program specifically aimed at graffiti removal. The "Graffiti Kit" was developed in cooperation with a local paint company. The cardboard kit—which is shaped like a building and is part of the Association's "Grime Stoppers" campaign—includes a can of color-matched paint, a paint brush, a mixing stick, rags, wet paint signs, and a throw-away plastic tarp—everything needed to "get it clean and keep it clean."

Addressing Social Issues. Today, the social issues that exist in downtowns are being addressed not only as social concerns but as economic concerns. Social issues often associated with downtowns include homelessness, panhandling, public drinking, public urination and defecation, public solicitation and use of illegal drugs, disorderly conduct, and lewd behavior. Those downtown

organizations seasoned in addressing social issues seem to unanimously advocate taking a "tough love" approach and
working directly with social service agencies. Examples include the following:

- Launched by the Center City District as part of the Mayor's comprehensive policy on homelessness, downtown Philadelphia's
  Campaign for Real Change has
  proven to be a highly visible and
  successful initiative with over 800
  downtown retailers participating.
  The campaign seeks to educate
  the public so that any donations
  which might be made to panhandlers are redirected to non-profit
  and charitable organizations in
  the business of helping people
  move from the streets to more
  productive lives.
- The Security Task Force of the
  Downtown Phoenix Partnership
  implements a program in which
  downtown guides distribute cards
  to panhandlers and homeless
  people. The cards contain information about social service agencies and programs that provide
  relevant assistance.

Enhancing Police Presence. While
downtown organizations are becoming
more involved in downtown safety issues, it is important to note that their
efforts are not meant to supplant the
local police force. Instead, the safety
efforts of downtown organizations are
usually implemented through close and
continued cooperation with the local
police force. In addition, the safety
efforts of downtown organizations are
often aimed at increasing "user-friendly"
police presence in downtown.

An outstanding example of this is
the Escondido, CA, bike patrol which is
administered by the local police department and supported by the Downtown
Escondido Business Association—
through financial contributions toward
equipment, helmets, and winterization.
Escondido's police officers regard the
bike patrol as the "foot beat of the 20th
century" and cite mobility as the biggest
asset of bike patrols. Being able to travel
where cars cannot, the downtown Escondido bike patrols have an average response time of under 40 seconds.

Augmenting Police Presence.
The safety strategy most commonly
used today to augment police presence
in downtowns is the downtown "guide"
or "ambassador" program. Downtown
guide programs are generally implemented to supplement the efforts of
local police officers by serving as additional "eyes and ears on the street" or by
serving as downtown ambassadors—
thereby relieving police of this "hospitality" function.

Examples of downtown guide and
ambassador programs follow:

- The downtown Trenton guide program is operated through an
  agreement between the local
  community college and the Trenton Downtown Association, so
  that college students have the opportunity to be downtown
  guides. Each guide is assigned a
  specific section of downtown to
  patrol and is expected to observe
  any safety-related behavior or incidents, report suspicious behavior, and serve a hospitality role by
  providing information to visitors
  and other downtown users. In addition to being paid an hourly
  wage, downtown Trenton's guides

are reimbursed for 100% of their tuition, up to $600 per semester, if they carry at least 12 credit hours per semester and maintain a 2.0 grade point average.

- Three years ago, CITYCENTER Danbury—the private sector organization that represents downtown Danbury, CT—began a downtown guide program. While the program was successful in addressing safety issues and perceptions, it ran into financial difficulties. To remedy this, the Danbury Police Department gave CITY-CENTER Danbury a grant to finance 40% of the guide program cost.

- The downtown guide program in Long Beach, CA, is operated by the downtown organization. The distinguishing feature of this guide program is that the Downtown Long Beach Association obtains guides through a contract with an arm of Wells Fargo Security. Downtown guides work closely with local police in fulfilling their primary mission, which is to address disorderly street behavior and provide hospitality services.

CHAPTER 15

Historic Rehabilitation Tax Credit

Kennedy Smith

Since 1981, the historic rehabilitation tax credit has generated more than $12 million in tax savings for the owners of approximately 12,000 commercial buildings in America. More than 70 percent of all these tax act projects were carried out by people with annual incomes of less than $100,000—not the "big guys," but individuals with ordinary incomes investing in their own communities.

With figures like these, there is no doubt that the rehabilitation credit has had a major impact on downtown revitalization. And, in spite of the restrictions placed on real estate development financing by the Tax Reform Act of 1986 (see "The Impact of Tax Reform on Downtowns," *Main Street News*, No. 20, January 1987), the tax credit will continue to be one of the most effective tools for redeveloping traditional commercial buildings. The following examples show how the rehab tax credit could produce substantial savings for property owners in downtown or neighborhood business districts.

- Jane Doe has owned 201 Main Street—a three-story 1885 Victorian commercial building—for 42 years. She has operated Jane's Dress Shop on the first floor since the day she bought the building, and makes an adjusted income of about $40,000. Because Jane has owned the building for so long, it is fully depreciated. She's invested very little in repairs for the past 20 years, so the building needs some major improvements.

Originally published as "Reinvesting in Downtown: The Historic Rehabilitation Tax Credit," Main Street News, *Issue No. 39, September, 1988. Copyright 1988 by the National Trust for Historic Preservation. Reprinted with permission from* Main Street News, *National Main Street Center, National Trust for Historic Preservation, Washington, D.C.*

Now, Jane wants to retire. If she sells the building, she'll have to pay a substantial capital gains tax on the proceeds. Plus, she may need to make repairs in order to attract a buyer—repairs that could eat up any profit remaining after the capital gains tax. Rather than incur these expenses, Jane unfortunately has decided to demolish the building and sell the vacant lot to her next-door neighbor for parking.

- John Jones owns an insurance agency downtown. He's been in business eight years, and the agency is doing well. He rents the ground floor of a two-story 1926 Art Deco building at 416 Market Street for $500 per month, the maximum amount he feels comfortable paying.

The property owner is willing to sell the building for $30,000. John would like to buy it, rehabilitate the vacant second floor for his office and rent the ground floor to a retailer. He estimates that rehabilitation will cost about $50,000. Of the $80,000 needed for the whole project, he can put down 10 percent ($8,000) and wants to finance the balance, $72,000. But the monthly mortgage—at 10 percent interest and a 20-year term—would be $694, almost $200 more than he now pays in rent.

In both instances, the rehab tax credit could make the difference between a project that works and one that fails. In the first example, Jane could rehabilitate her building and rent it to new tenants, offsetting the taxes on her rental income with savings through the tax credit, increasing the building's value and delaying the capital gains tax for several years, when she will probably be in a lower tax bracket. In the second case, the tax savings from the rehabilitation credit would reduce John's income tax liability and, despite the higher monthly debt service payment, make the project's cash flow work.

How to Use the Credit

To be eligible for the rehabilitation tax credit, a building must be a "certified" historic structure, meaning that it must be:

- individually listed in the National Register of Historic Places
- located in, and contributing to the character of, a local or state designated historic district that meets National Register criteria

To certify that a building listed in a historic district, the owner must file Part I of the Historic Certification Application (OMB Form No. 1024-0009). This form can be obtained from the state historic preservation office (SHPO) or the National Park Service (NPS), the federal agency that administers the National Register. After it is reviewed by the SHPO, the form is sent to the National Park Service for final approval.

Just certifying a building, however, does not mean that the property owner can get a tax credit for any building improvements. The plans must be reviewed by the SHPO, then sent to the Park Service for certification before the improvements are begun. In communities with design review boards, the proposed changes may also have to be reviewed locally. In reviewing a proposed project, NPS and the SHPO use *The Secretary of the Interior's Standards for Rehabilitation*, 10 standards that describe the desired effects of rehabilitation activity.

Part II of the certification application is used to certify the proposed rehabilitation. On the form, briefly—but thoroughly—describe each step of the project and the specific processes that will be used. For instance, it's not enough to simply state that masonry will be repointed; describe the exact mortar mix that will be used, the way in which old mortar will be removed and the profile of the finished mortar joint.

Be sure to take *plenty* of photographs of the building before rehabilitation begins. At a minimum, there should be pictures of every exterior and interior wall, plus photographs of significant interior and exterior details. In particular, take several pictures of walls or features that will be directly affected by the rehabilitation. The photos attached to the certification application should be black and white and clearly labeled; however, it's a good idea to shoot some color slides or photographs as well, particularly where color of material is important. Also include architectural plans and specifications showing proposed changes. Paint chips to show color may also be included with Part II of the application. Finally, attach a check for the required filing fee. (Fees are based on the project's total cost.)

In all cases, the property owner should consult with the SHPO before and during the process of developing rehabilitation plans. The SHPO can provide advice on proper rehab techniques

and point out cost-effective methods. Also, the SHPO can steer the property owner away from alterations that might prevent the project from being certified—and, in turn, from qualifying for the rehabilitation tax credit. SHPO staff members will sometimes visit the site during the project to make sure the rehabilitation techniques are, in fact, the appropriate ones.

When the rehabilitation is completed, the property owner should file Part III, the final section of the rehabilitation certification forms. Part III asks for photographs and descriptions of the completed project. Like the photos and written descriptions submitted with Part II, those prepared for Part III should be as thorough as possible, highlighting the rehabilitated areas of the building. At this point the SHPO and/or NPS staff members may visit the building to make sure Part III adequately illustrates the rehabilitation and that the project was completed correctly.

Once the National Park Service has approved the completed rehabilitation, it will send the property owner a certificate verifying that the project has been completed and that it is eligible for the tax credit. The property owner needs this certificate to actually get the credit. Although the certificate does not have to be attached to the owner's federal income tax return, he or she must be able to produce it if the tax return is audited. And, a high percentage of people who use the credit are, in fact, called in for an audit.

Ways to Lose the Credit

Proper rehabilitation of traditional commercial buildings has many benefits.

In the first place, it ensures that buildings will be preserved for future generations in a way that will not distort their original character. Secondly, thanks to the rehabilitation tax credits, it provides real financial benefits for investors, which in turn boosts reinvestment in the commercial district and contributes to the area's economic resurgence. Finally, it focuses public attention on the qualities that make the district unique.

Occasionally, however, rehabilitation projects involving downtown or neighborhood buildings are "decertified"—i.e., the NPS and SHPO revoke or deny the building's status as a certified historic structure, which then prohibits use of the rehabilitation tax credits because of inappropriate rehabilitation work. In traditional commercial areas, some of the most common errors that can lead to decertification include:

Window treatment. Changing the design character of windows is a common error in building rehabilitations. Because storefront display windows are such a prominent feature of traditional commercial buildings, even minor modifications can dramatically change the overall appearance of the storefront. In general, avoid enclosing storefront windows, dividing them up into smaller panes of glass or converting them to a new window type; for instance, changing fixed windows to double-hung windows.

Masonry cleaning. For years, many people have sandblasted buildings to clean off dirt, paint or debris. Unfortunately, sandblasting cuts away the hard-baked protective outer surface of brick, exposing the softer masonry core to moisture, wind and extreme temperatures, which gradually erode the building. Once a building has been sandblasted, there is little that can be done to protect it from deterioration. On the other hand, there are a number of cleaning methods that will not damage masonry—for instance, a low-pressure water wash with a mild detergent and soft-bristled brush, steam cleaning or some types of chemical solvents. Property owners and contractors should be urged to use one of these methods; sandblasting a building virtually guarantees its decertification.

Changing entrance or window locations. Moving doors and windows drastically changes the appearance of most traditional commercial buildings. Some common mistakes include the following: opening new doors and windows along the sides of corner buildings; creating outside entrances to upper-floor spaces that interfere with the original storefront configuration; and recessing or protruding door or window openings in ways that conflict with the original design.

Applying false historic themes or styles. The original design of a building reflects an exact moment in time. For that reason, buildings tell the history of their community's development. Unfortunately, to many people, "historic" often means "Williamsburg" or "Galena" or some other city well known for its restored or recreated historic buildings. As a result, well-intentioned builders have frequently applied the architectural style of these buildings to commercial structures in their own communities, regardless of the original ages or styles of their buildings. Imitating historic building styles or elements misleads the public, giving them a false perception of their community's history. Thus, when an original building element is missing, many SHPOs prefer that its replacement blend in with the building but be clearly identifiable as modern design.

How a Main Street Program Can Help

There are many ways a Main Street or other commercial revitalization program can help property owners rehabilitate their buildings properly *and* earn an income tax credit for their efforts.

Providing information. Revitalization programs can encourage appropriate design change by: gathering and sharing information on proper rehab methods; holding workshops to teach building contractors how to treat historic commercial buildings; conducting site visits to successful rehab projects in other communities; and teaching property owners, contractors and tax accountants how the rehab tax credits work.

Helping property owners certify their rehab projects. To property owners unfamiliar with the certification process—or with historic preservation in general—having a building certified can be a nightmare. Frequently, the revitalization program's staff can act as intermediary between the property owner, contractor and SHPO to ease the process for all concerned.

Monitoring rehab activity. Because local builders and designers are often unfamiliar with preservation methods, it's important to monitor construction while it is taking place. If some techniques or design modifications seem inconsistent with *The Secretary of the Interior's Standards for Rehabilitation*, the downtown or neighborhood manager or a design committee volunteer can usually intervene and correct the procedure before it endangers the project's eligibility.

Promoting proper rehabilitation and the use of the rehab tax credits. By advocating historic preservation as an economic development tool, the revitalization program can help break the cycle of disinvestment and can find ways to make traditional commercial buildings economically viable again.

CHAPTER 16

Keeping Retailers on Main Street

Kathleen Les

During the 1960s, large scale urban renewal projects symbolized our national attitude that downtowns were disposable. In the 1970s the thrust of redevelopment, as we began to call it, was toward systematically disposing of large sections of downtown in the name of removing blight. Now, during the 1980s, we willingly embrace the wholesale preservation of our downtowns, but we struggle with finding the best solutions.

Back at the turn of the century when many of our downtowns were coming into existence, they served as a focal point in the community in a way that is hardly understood in the new age of suburbanization and decentralization. In the 1920s, when you went downtown, you not only could shop, but you could go to the theater, eat at a restaurant, go to church, visit your service club, go to the bank, visit your doctor, catch a train out of town or watch a parade all in the space of a few blocks. With all this going on, downtown streets were the crossroads of pedestrian activity that nourished a vibrant retail shopping district.

During the post–WW II years and through the 1970s when these auxiliary services and activities moved to the suburbs and, more important, with competing shopping malls springing up alongside the new suburban housing tracts, many downtown retailers saw their market share drop off and their business volume dwindle. Today with a renewed appreciation of their strong sense of place and their historical importance, city planners, decision-makers

From Western City, *Vol. LXIV, No. 10, October, 1988. Published by the League of California Cities, Sacramento, California. Reprinted with permission of the publisher. For information about subscribing, please call 916-658-8223 or visit the magazine's website at www.westerncity.com. Subscription information is also available by calling 1-800-572-5720 and asking for document #45.*

and business owners are making downtowns the object of many of their economic development efforts.

What is the inherent economic value of a downtown business community to a city? In 1986, the National Trust for Historic Preservation commissioned the first comprehensive study on downtown retail retention, recruitment and expansion successes. Conducted by Armentrout & Associates, Inc., in association with Doyle Hyett, AICP, the study found some very revealing information.

Their survey of recent data on the subject of job growth found that as many as two-thirds of all new jobs nationwide occur in small businesses and principally in firms made up of four or fewer employees. Most downtowns are full of these small businesses. A town with as few as 10,000 people typically has 400 to 500 people working downtown. Says Hyett of Hyett-Palma, Inc., "We should think of downtown as a company of 500 and do what's necessary to keep that company healthy and in town."

At a time when cities in California are increasingly dependent on sales tax as a form of revenue, downtowns should not be overlooked as an important slice of the sales tax pie.

What are the main reasons businesses leave a downtown? The study found two primary reasons. First, businesses leave because of inadequate physical conditions. They either outgrow the space in which they are located or the surrounding neighborhood deteriorates, presenting a poor marketing image. The second predominant reason businesses leave is due to diminished market support for the merchandise they sell. Either they have too much outlying competition or a poor retail mix downtown reduces the incentives for customers to come shop there.

The highest attrition rate is among businesses that sell items with a small ticket size. Those that sell ice cream cones at a dollar apiece are more likely to fail than a jewelry store selling thousand dollar rings. Many more businesses fold, though not necessarily due to bankruptcy, than relocate. For any number of reasons, many small businesses close their doors within the first three to five years of opening.

The National Trust study evaluated 12 cities to determine why these cities met with success in their retail retention and downtown revitalization efforts. The study found the common denominator was not that the same strategy and same ingredients were used in all cases, but that each city took the time to develop a fundamental understanding of its own unique problems and took action first toward remedying these with a specific program to address each problem. These cities did not pick programmatic solutions out of the air just because lots of other cities were using them. They implemented programmatic solutions, such as a loan program for rehabilitating historic buildings, because they addressed fundamental needs in their revitalization strategies.

In improving a downtown retail climate it must be understood that downtown revitalization is a contextual process. The problems are many and no one solution or project can be expected to remedy all ills. Attention to the physical appearance of the public streets and private property is important, but so are the quality and spread of business types as well as the planning and economic development incentives that make a downtown attractive for businesses locating there. If your downtown itself were a business, to meet with success, its physical appearance must project an exciting image, you must have a winning product for sale and your marketing must be convincing.

In developing revitalization strategies, cities all too often have emphasized making physical improvements to public and private property and left little time or money for business improvement and marketing activities. More and more we are realizing the importance of improving businesses internally so that they, along with the appearance of a downtown environment, will attract customers.

So how do you elicit cooperation and get your downtown retailers to get serious about doing business? How do you keep them a vital ingredient in your downtown chemistry? Here are my best tips and strategies.

Make Your Gospel These Three — Leadership, Consensus Building and Persistence

Cities with successful downtowns follow this gospel. Leadership is the springboard of all successful projects. Leadership must be present in both the public and private sectors, but if one is foundering, the other should move ahead and independently accomplish what it can. Success almost always breeds enthusiasm, new commitment and additional leadership.

The need for consensus building is true of all facets of city planning, but it is especially true in downtown revitalization where change depends on a shared vision and a commitment to making that vision happen. Downtown merchants are a particularly fickle bunch and attempts to ramrod change will only result in great dissension. Where leadership comes into play is in pulling diverse points of view together and finding a common ground on which to move forward so everyone feels like a stake holder.

Everything takes time, and only persistence will get you to the finish line. It took nearly 30 years for downtowns to decay, and they certainly won't be reborn in six months. Downtown Hanford, which today sports handsomely restored buildings, lovely street furnishings and a flourishing retail economy, has been over ten years in the making and hard work is still going on. This small central California town probably has undergone more dramatic transformation than any other town in the state, and it can be fairly said that Hanford has done it all right. How has it happened? Through a continual public-private partnership with effective leadership and repeated give and take in both sectors.

In 1975 when the Hanford Improvement Association agreed to a doubling of the business license fees to create a Business Improvement District, the city agreed to give back all the business license monies collected by the city to the HIA. When the city committed sizable dollars to remodeling the streetscape, property owners matched the dollar commitment by undertaking major rehabilitation work on their historic buildings. When the buildings were rehabilitated, business owners rose to the occasion, and to the rising rents, by upgrading their businesses to be on par with the attractiveness of the buildings. In 1985, Hanford won the League's coveted Helen Putnam Award for Excellence and today boasts a strong downtown with an unusually high sales tax per capita. Retail activity from tourists is on the increase as well. Hanford's secret, according to Planning Department Director Jim Beath has been, "the public and private sectors each forging ahead in their respective realms and operating with a determination and persistence; each side gave a lot and reaped a lot in return."

You Must Deal with Crime

Unfortunately, many of our downtowns are beleaguered by high crime or the perception of it. This has come about for many reasons, one of which is all too often a turn-the-cheek attitude on the part of police administrators. The thinking goes: "If we allow crime enhancing uses, such as bars, to be concentrated in the downtown that will also concentrate criminal activity there and make it less prevalent in other parts of town."

This strategy does in fact often work, but to the detriment of downtown. In Porterville, where four existing bars contributed to three murders in six months, Main Street Project Manager Carl Kaden, worked with city officials to pass an ordinance requiring a conditional use permit for all bars and lounges and creating a provision for closing down bars if enough complaints are received from neighbors.

"You can't revitalize an area if there's crime," says Kaden. "You have to deal with crime first before you can expect customers to feel comfortable patronizing downtown stores." Today, as a result of the ordinance, all four bars have been closed down and the historic hotel in which one was located is now the object of a $2 million restoration project.

Think of Your Downtown as a Shopping Center

According to James Ratner, President of Forest City Development, marketing and merchandising innovations are the key ingredient of successful malls, not enclosed buildings and parking. Major malls have marketing and merchandising plans based on professional analysis done at regular intervals.

The key here is that malls offer what the public wants in the way of goods, and malls merchandise those goods in a way the customer finds irresistible. And this effort is based on analytical formulas. Can the same be said of your downtown? Probably not. How can you, as city officials, help determine realistic market niches for downtown businesses. Again, thinking of your downtown as a business, it is necessary to understand its market draw and the kind of goods and services that market needs. This valuable information can help downtown businesses better their market, but this data is very expensive for them to obtain on an individual basis. One word of caution here: There are many market analysis consultants. Be sure to get one who really understands the economics of downtowns.

Don't Overestimate Your Market

A market profile is useful primarily because it will help present a possible vision based on realistic expectations rather than wild, unattainable dreams. We all would like our downtowns to be havens of upscale shops and restaurants, but only a few very wealthy communities in California can sustain such businesses.

A large population and high disposable income are the two primary ingredients needed to support upscale retailers. If you don't have this, don't be discouraged. Many seemingly "low income" businesses are quite successful. They do a high volume by catering to low-end spenders. You can generate just as many sales tax dollars this way and still have a flourishing downtown.

The City of Ventura, as an example, has had the courage to recognize the limitations of its downtown and has performed a comprehensive market study in-house from which a sound retail plan and recruitment effort has been launched. Recognizing that the disposable income immediately adjacent to the downtown is low, city planners now see the downtown as having a minimum of neighborhood-serving retail uses and more emphasis on businesses lacking in the region, particularly those for which shoppers are willing to drive a greater distance. The market study showed it was possible for downtown Ventura to be a center for home furnishings and décor with the nucleus being existing antique shops which were originally perceived to be a low-end use. "Downtown has large spaces and cheap rent ideal for businesses selling home furnishings," explains Mariam Mack, Economic Development Coordinator. "We now see this as a usable asset, and we plan to capitalize on it." Last year the well-known Scandinavian store Danica House decided to locate in a 10,000 square-foot building downtown.

Many Downtown Businesses Need a Good Housecleaning

"The biggest problem with many downtown retailers," states Carl Kaden, "is the way they let obsolete inventory accrue for which there is no buyer interest. The less of the old inventory they sell off, the less capital they have to buy new goods, and a vicious cycle of dependency on outmoded stock develops."

Kaden, himself a retail expert who for years was on the management team of J.C. Penney, recently has been responsible for some of the most innovative downtown retail planning in the nation in his capacity with the Porterville Main Street program. Working with a third-generation family-owned furniture store there, he helped the owners make the transition from near bankruptcy to a 60 percent increase in sales in one year. He found that 73 percent of their inventory was outdated and worked with them to liquidate their old stock and acquire new merchandise to be sold at competitive prices.

Sounds like an obvious and straightforward approach, but actually Kaden spent many, many hours researching the best market and merchandising angle for the store. Most business owners are so caught up in the day-to-day management of their operations, they have no time, not to mention money, to hire a retail planning expert the equivalent of Kaden. This is not an excusable situation, but it is one that requires special assistance. Cities should begin to think about funding business planning experts to work with existing retailers to aid them in becoming more profitable. The cost of services might be reimbursed down the line when the store is operating at a higher profit level.

In short, downtown retailers need to learn to work smarter, not harder. They need to find new market niches and new ways to reach customers other than just depending on pedestrian traffic. The days are over when downtown retailers can just float off the foot traffic outside their doors.

Poorly run businesses do a downtown—and a city dependent on their sales tax revenues—no good. But business owners, for a variety of reasons, will be resistant to changing their operations. Sometimes the best approach is to offset these lagging businesses with new retail recruits who are not likely to be as sour on the downtown as those who have struggled for years.

Work to Help Foster Merchant Unity

It's true, most downtowns suffer from strong disagreement among merchants on what's best for the downtown. Interestingly, merchant surveys repeatedly show that retailers themselves identify greater merchant unity as a high priority. They know they need organizing, but, they aren't always capable of doing it themselves.

The City of Davis strongly desired to see their downtown business community better organized and recognized they needed a boost to do so. In the two-and-a-half-year period beginning in February 1987, they will have allocated over $75,000 in Community Development Block Grant (CDBG) funds to hire a Downtown Coordinator. The

principal responsibility of this position is to work with downtown merchants in organizing promotions and to ready the business community for adoption of a Business Improvement District. When the BID is formed, the downtown association will have their own funds to carry out management and promotions.

How does this help with retail retention? Business owners have a great desire to pitch in and work for the betterment of the downtown when they feel the downtown association is working in unity and with attainable goals. And they are more likely to push their own businesses farther when they see fellow retailers working in concert and see a tangible commitment on the part of the city. Self-improvement is the best form of retail retention.

There Are No Formulas and No Magic Answers

It would be nice if you could call in a consultant who would wave a magic wand and make your downtown retailers blossom again. The closest thing we have to a workable formula is the National Trust Main Street Program, a four-point program involving urban design, economic restructuring, community organization and marketing and promotions. Now in its tenth year, the Main Street approach is a proven model for improving downtown retail trade, but it works only when all four aspects of the program are emphasized equally.

The success of the Main Street program is that it provides a model so that each city can move in a direction best suited to them. The problems from downtown to downtown tend to be similar, but the solutions are always unique to that city.

Reviving Main Street retail is more of an art right now than a hard science. After several decades of severe decline of our older business districts, we are faced with restoring the retail climate and physical appearance of our downtowns. Commitment, hard work and a willingness to take risks are the only guarantees of success.

Chapter 17

Parking Facility Management

John W. Dorsett

Parking is not just a convenience, it is a necessity—one that many customers and tenants take for granted. There are real costs associated with providing parking, and they can significantly affect real estate projects and even block their development. When shopping centers, office buildings, and hotels do not charge for parking, there is the popular misconception that it is free; however, someone must pay for the parking facility—as well as for the land under it and the lighting, insurance, security, and maintenance needed to keep it functioning—and that money must be recouped. There also are design, testing, and contracting fees, as well as financing costs, developer's costs, and surveying costs. On top of all that, owners of parking facilities often pay property, sales, and parking taxes.

If these costs are not covered by parking fees, they are passed on to the facility owner and ultimately to the facility users. For example, to cover parking costs at a shopping center, the owner charges tenants higher rents and common area maintenance fees. In turn, the tenants charge consumers higher prices for their services and merchandise. Hotels indirectly bill the cost of parking to their guests as part of the cost of overhead. In short, just as there is no such thing as a free lunch, there is no free parking.

Identifying Need and Clients

Many owners do not worry about parking facility finances until they think they need a new facility. Before

Originally published as "The Price Tag of Parking," Urban Land, Vol. 57, No. 5, May, 1998. Published by the Urban Land Institute, 1025 Thomas Jefferson Street, N.W., Suite 500 West, Washington, D.C., 20007-5201. Reprinted with permission of the publisher.

exploring financing options for new development, however, owners should make sure that existing parking spaces are not going unused because of poor management. Is a new lot or garage really needed? If it is, then the owners should be able to pass on all or part of the project's capital costs and operating expenses to parking patrons, or financing may be difficult to secure.

Owners also must determine what type of parking facility will be most efficient. The cost of construction of a parking garage runs five to ten times higher than the cost of surface parking; however, if a proposed structure is in an urban location where land is at a premium, a multilevel parking facility, which requires less land, should be considered. Other options that could be considered before constructing a parking garage include the following:

- If it is cost effective, provide shuttle-bus service to transport parking patrons from a remote surface parking lot to their destination.
- Restripe existing parking facilities to increase the number of parking spaces, and implement additional parking management strategies (such as shared parking, which minimizes the number of reserved spaces) that allow existing parking resources to be used more efficiently.
- If a loss of green space is acceptable, build a surface lot on existing vacant property.

After choosing either a structure or a surface lot, the question remains: Can the project generate sufficient revenues to offset operating expenses and poten-tial debt service? If not, how can the operation be subsidized? Structured parking facilities that are not profitable often are subsidized by companion office buildings, hotels, or retail shops.

When projecting revenues for a prospective parking facility, it is important to identify user characteristics. Who will use the garage? Considerations that will help identify likely patrons include:

Cost. What are the customary parking rates within the immediate area? What rates could be supported at the proposed parking facility?

Traffic and pedestrian circulation. Is the parking facility easy to get to? If it is located on a one-way street that makes access awkward, fewer motorists will use the facility than would if it were located in a more convenient spot.

Ease of use. Can patrons enter and exit quickly? Can they find their way around the facility easily? Can they easily locate their vehicles?

Cleanliness. Is the parking facility clean? If it is dirty and the one across the street is clean, patrons could be lost to the tidier facility.

Ancillary services. Does the parking facility operator provide services within the garage such as car washing and/or detailing, vehicle repairs, oil changes, or a dry cleaning pick-up/drop-off facility? Such benefits often can sway patrons toward a facility.

Safety and security. Is the parking facility perceived by patrons to be safe and secure? Is it well lighted? Is the facility equipped with security features appropriate for its environment?

Figure 1
Examples of Parking Space Solutions

Shopping Centers: Instead of employees occupying spaces closest to the stores, create remote parking facilities for employees and establish protocol that discourages employees from parking in "shopper designated" parking areas.

Mixed-Use Parking: Hotels and office buildings can experience a shortage of parking spaces. Hotels have shortages during evening hours, while office buildings have shortages during business hours. Instead of each having exclusive parking privileges, they can negotiate an agreement to share their parking with each other, thereby circumventing the need to develop additional parking.

Remote Parking: To increase the use of remote parking, develop a tiered-pricing scheme that requires higher parking rates for convenient spaces and lower parking rates for spaces in remote locations.

Site and Market Area Characteristics

The parking facility's site and market area determine, to some extent, its ultimate success or failure. Factors that need to be considered when projecting revenues include:

Parking space supply and demand. How many parking spaces exist in the market area of the proposed parking facility? Are they now being used? Are there a lot of inexpensive, unused spaces? (See Figure 1).

Nearby land uses. What land exists within a block or two of the proposed site? Will those uses generate significant numbers of patrons?

Building occupancy. What is the building occupancy rate in the market area? Is it expected to increase significantly in the future, thereby creating additional demand for parking?

Future developments. Are any proposed developments slated for construction in the near future? How will they affect future parking demand?

Competition. Who provides parking in the market area? What rates are charged? Are those rates subsidized? If so, how does that affect the feasibility of a new parking facility?

Measuring demand for a garage involves identifying the number of patrons who will use the garage by hour of day, day of week, and month of year. This includes an estimate of how long patrons will park, how many times each space will be used during a 24-hour period, and when demand will occur. Does the surrounding environment consist primarily of offices in which most employees work 8:00 A.M. to 5:00 P.M. on weekdays? Are there other uses such as retail stores, restaurants, hotels, or entertainment venues that create evening and weekend demand?

Figure 2
Distribution of Parking Garage Operating Expenses

Maintenance	13.5%
Utilities	14.5%
Miscellaneous	19.4%
Cashiering and Management	53.0%

Development and Operating Costs

Development and operating costs of parking projects differ widely. Construction costs vary depending on geographic area because of differences in labor rates, materials, and construction methods. Typically, developers can count on construction costs ranging from $6,000 to more than $15,000 per parking space for a garage built below grade. Land costs affect development costs; for that reason, structured parking facilities instead of surface parking lots often are built. Soft costs such as design and testing fees and financing costs also must be considered during the project planning stage.

Since few parking projects are paid for in cash, the cost of financing becomes an important factor. Most parking projects are financed at fixed interest rates with no equity. The interest rate is determined by the debtor's credit history, the amount of collateral, and possibly the amount of insurance purchased to secure the loan. Currently, parking projects are being financed as both tax-exempt and taxable facilities at rates ranging from 6 percent to more than 10 percent. The customary term for most loans is 20 years.

Operating expenses of parking facilities also vary dramatically. Variations are due to geographical location, size of facility, staffing patterns, method of operation, and local legal requirements. These expenses include the cost of utilities, supplies, daily maintenance, cashiering, management and accounting services, on-site security, structural maintenance, and insurance. Types of insurance coverage include comprehensive liability, garagekeeper's legal liability, fire and extended coverage, workers' compensation, equipment coverage, money and security coverage (theft occurring on the premises), blanket honesty coverage (employee theft), and rent and business interruption coverage (structural damage resulting from natural phenomena). Annual operating expenses for structured parking facilities typically range from $200 to more than $700 per space. (See Figure 2).

Development and operating costs together determine the revenue necessary for the project to generate a positive or break-even cash flow. The monthly revenue needed to reach the break-even point usually ranges from $42 to $196 per parking space, excluding land costs.

Parking facilities frequently are not profitable ventures and therefore must be subsidized. For that reason, parking authorities or city parking departments often become active in their ownership and operation. Public sector involvement typically is motivated by a desire to encourage economic development by keeping parking rates artificially low rather than charging market rates. Parking authorities and city parking departments sometimes have the advantage of not having to pay debt service on older parking facilities. In addition, public entities often supplement off-street parking operations with revenues generated by on-street spaces and through parking violation fines.

While many people believe that parking should be provided free of charge, parking is expensive and the costs must be recouped by the owner, whether by direct or indirect means. Owners should explore less costly options before deciding to build a new parking structure. If a new structure is

Figure 3
Monthly Revenue Needed to Achieve Breakeven*

Construction Cost/Space	Annual Operating Expense per Space					
	$200	$300	$400	$500	$600	$700
$1,500	$ 42	$ 50	$ 58	$ 67	$ 75	$ 83
5,000	74	82	91	99	107	116
6,000	85	94	102	110	130	139
7,000	97	105	114	122	130	139
8,000	108	117	125	133	142	150
9,000	120	128	136	145	153	161
10,000	131	140	148	156	165	173
11,000	143	151	159	168	176	184
12,000	154	163	171	179	188	196

*Construction cost inflated by 35 percent to include contingency, design, testing, and financing cost; bond financing terms assumed on 8 percent annual interest for 20 years (ten years for surface lot).

necessary, the next question is whether or not it is affordable. Determining project affordability can be difficult due to problems in projecting operating revenues and costs. Care should be taken to budget for realistic operating costs and debt service. Because of variations in these factors, some parking facilities provide lucrative investment opportunities while many others must be subsidized. (See Figure 3.)

CHAPTER 18

Rural Banks and Economic Growth

Deborah M. Markley and *Ron Shaffer*

As rural community banks chart their futures, they are challenged by economic and financial change. Today's rural communities are no longer isolated from global and national economic trends. Competition from abroad has hurt profit margins for rural businesses. Technical innovation, while boosting productivity, has softened the demand for rural labor. Many of the most educated rural businesses are being drawn to urban centers where they can be closer to suppliers and customers.

Just as the economic landscape is changing, so is the financial environment in which rural community bankers must operate. Deregulation and new technology have brought larger financial institutions into the rural marketplace. And, as the regulatory burden on banks continues to change, rural bankers are finding it harder to compete on their home turf.

This chapter explores the challenges that face rural communities and their community banks. The chapter also discusses strategies bankers might use to help themselves in the changing environment. The chapter concludes that to survive and prosper, rural community bankers need to play a more active role in fostering economic growth in their communities.

Fundamentally, the success of rural community bankers is closely tied to the economic health of their rural communities.

Originally published as "Rural Banks and Their Communities: A Matter of Survival," Government Finance Review, *Vol. 10, No. 4, August, 1994. Published by the Government Finance Officers Association, 180 N. Michigan Avenue, Suite 800, Chicago, Illinois 60601 (312-977-9700, fax 312-977-4806, e-mail GFR@gfoa.org). Annual subscription $30. Reprinted with permission of the author.*

Changing Financial Environments

Just as the national economy is being shaped by changes in the global marketplace, the economies of rural communities are being shaped by national and global economic trends. As a result, a rural location no longer provides a buffer against the ebb and flow of distant markets. Indeed, many rural communities find themselves disadvantaged by recent economic and financial change. Bankers in rural communities also are finding themselves buffeted by change. Deregulation and the changing regulatory burden continue to redefine the competitive environment for banks, while advances in technology, products and services are creating new opportunities and new challenges.

Globalization of the U.S. Economy. Advances in technology, travel, communications and financial markets have created a global marketplace for most goods and services—a marketplace that offers both incentives and challenges to rural economies. Low-wage, low-skill rural manufacturers face stiffer competition from developing or emerging economies in the rest of the world. As rural communities adapt to the competitive pressure, those with a diversified economic base are likely to prosper. In contrast, the loss of a plant to an offshore location, for example, could cripple a rural community that lacks other employment opportunities.

Trade agreements may have a disproportionate impact on rural communities. While the effects of the North American Free Trade Agreement (NAFTA) cannot yet be adequately measured, some researchers suggest that the plants most likely to move as a result of NAFTA are concentrated in rural communities. At the same time, NAFTA may give a boost to communities in the heartland that depend on agricultural production.

Industrial Restructuring within the United States. Several key changes in the world's industrial sector are reshaping the way that rural businesses must operate to remain competitive. As the industrial structure of rural communities evolves, rural community bankers must develop new tools to meet increased credit needs. And bankers must make difficult decisions about whether to lend to nontraditional businesses.

One key change occurring in the national economy is the shift away from goods-producing industries toward service producing industries. In rural areas, goods producers and low-skill, service-sector activities still tend to predominate. Attracting higher-wage, higher-skill producer services to rural communities will depend on a community's location, its quality of educational and job training resources, and its infrastructure investments, particularly in telecommunications.

To remain competitive, U.S. firms are being forced to rethink almost every aspect of the manufacturing process. Flexible manufacturing has become the objective for many firms. This change entails reorganizing the production process so that the firm can respond quickly to changes in final demand. The emphasis is on smaller, more adaptable production facilities, lower levels of inventory, higher skill levels for workers and the latest technological innovations.

With the trend toward smaller and more flexible operations, outsourcing has become a more dominant practice. The emphasis now is on external economies of scale, that is, on developing relationships with other enterprises to permit flexibility in manufacturing and to take advantage of specialized production facilities in other firms. This change suggests that proximity to other potential suppliers is becoming increasingly important for many manufacturing firms.

Changes also have occurred in the traditional basic industries of rural America—agriculture, forestry and mining. Consolidation in agriculture has resulted in fewer farms, fewer supplies and fewer processors of farm products. The search for increased productivity in forestry and mining has led to technological innovation and less demand for labor. Moreover, in all three of these traditional industries, expanded environmental regulations have made it difficult to match concerns for productivity and profitability with the need to protect the environment.

Another key feature of industrial restructuring is the rising importance of the small-business sector. Small businesses are producing more jobs and greater economic diversity, particularly in rural economies. Recognizing the key role of smaller enterprises has helped refocus on economic development activities. Emphasis has shifted away from attracting large manufacturing firms toward assisting the creation and expansion of home-grown businesses.

Increased Importance of Agglomeration Economies. In an era of globalization and industrial restructuring, agglomeration economies take on heightened importance. Agglomeration economies refer to a concentration of related business activities in one place. Concentration allows companies to benefit from networking and pools of resources, such as labor. Agglomeration economies may be particularly important for high-skilled, producer-service industries. The lack of agglomeration economies may limit the ability of rural communities to attract these service firms, continuing their dependence on low-wage, low-skilled manufacturing and service-sector jobs.

In the 1970s, industry tended to decentralize from cities to more rural areas. More recently, the value of agglomeration economies has increased, shifting the competitive advantage back to urban areas for some types of enterprises. Whether a rural community can cope with such a trend may depend on its particular characteristics. For example, a rural community may be better able to attract new firms if its industrial base is diversified. One research study found that rural areas with highly skilled labor, amenities and proximity to urban areas will be able to compete for modernizing firms, while rural communities without such a base are at a competitive disadvantage.

The challenge for community bankers will be to help create mechanisms that enable rural businesses, nonbank and bank alike, to capture the benefits of agglomeration. In addition, recognizing the importance of agglomeration economies to particular local industries may help community bankers assess the potential viability of a business and the economic development consequences of such lending.

Changes in the Financial Services Industry. As rural economies undergo fundamental change, so does the financial services landscape. Several factors have dramatically altered the face of banking over the past 10 years.

Banking deregulation has prompted

much of the evolution in financial services. Mergers have decreased the number of lending institutions while increasing their size. Statewide branching and interstate banking have redefined the competitive environment, particularly for isolated rural community bankers.

Community bankers must now compete for increasingly sophisticated customers with other local and nonlocal lenders. To stay competitive, community bankers must consider offering the same mix of services as their larger competitors—for example, credit cards and leasing. And they must focus on meeting credit needs in a particular market niche.

Advances in technology, products and services have created new opportunities and sources of competition for rural community bankers. Increasingly, rural residents have access to the same type of financial innovations available to urban residents. Credit card customers are solicited by mail, and money market funds can be established and accessed by phone. Close proximity to customers no longer guarantees rural community banks their traditional deposit base. As a result, local deposits may prove insufficient, and gaining access to external funds may soon become critical to rural community banks.

As local bankers attempt to plot strategy for the next decade, questions arise about expanded regulation, particularly as it applies to banks reinvesting in the community. Because most rural community banks lend almost exclusively in the local community, they are less likely than urban banks to face official challenges through the federal Community Reinvestment Act. But the reporting requirements in the act still increase costs for community banks. Moreover, some states have begun to review and enact new legislation on community reinvestment and interstate banking—laws that will apply to rural community banks operating within their borders.

The increased reporting requirements resulting from the changing regulatory burden could require local bank staff to spend more time on paperwork and less time on assisting potential borrowers. For small community banks with limited specialized staff, the added cost of meeting regulatory requirements may make it even more difficult to compete with large regional and money center institutions that open branches in rural communities.

Responding to Change

Rural community banks are in a unique position to respond to the economic and financial changes sweeping rural America and the financial services industry. No one knows the local rural economy better than the community banker. And, while deregul.ation has raised the specter of large banks entering rural markets, the reality is that most communities remain dependent on the community bank to finance their futures. Thus, rural community bankers and businesses must work together to respond to a rapidly changing economic and financial environment. In many cases, the future of both the bank and the community is on the line.

Community bankers can use several strategies to improve growth prospects for themselves and their communities. Rural community banks should, of course, continue their traditional role of lending to local businesses. But equally important, community bankers have special knowledge and skills that can be deployed more broadly to foster economic development. Banks can help find the capital—both debt and equity capital—that businesses need to modernize and remain competitive. Banks also can offer financial expertise to rural entrepreneurs who need help in starting small businesses. They can serve as an information link about credit and other programs available to encourage business development and economic growth. And, rural community bankers can provide leadership to help the community develop a vision for adapting to economic change.

Accessing New Sources of Capital. To meet the challenges ahead, rural communities and businesses must have access to capital. Rural communities need capital to support new business startup and expansion, and rural businesses need capital to modernize and remain competitive. While community bankers are the primary source of debt capital for local businesses, the ability of banks to meet new demands for capital may be limited for two reasons. One, traditional financial institutions continue to be constrained from providing equity capital. For startup enterprises and expanding industries, future capital needs may be for equity-like capital rather than debt. Two, regulated community bankers must always be sensitive to the risk involved in lending activities. As such, lending to support community economic growth may involve loans with limited or nontraditional collateral, loans to new enterprises with limited business experience or loans to existing firms that want to expand into new markets. This type of lending requires increased innovation by community bankers.

To meet the capital needs of local entrepreneurs, community bankers can form partnerships with other private and public entities. These partnerships can be forged with public-sector institutions, such as state development finance programs, with private-sector community development institutions or with alternative financial institutions. These partnerships are necessary to pool limited resources and leverage funds to support economic growth. These relationships also are helpful in allowing banks to become more involved in financing local economic activities without incurring unacceptable levels of risk. Not only are funds pooled through these partnerships, but risk is shared as well.

Two prime examples show how partnerships can help banks provide access to new sources of debt capital to support community economic activities. Community bankers in Michigan are able to make moderately risky business loans through their participation in the Capital Access Program, an insurance pool funded by state programs, private lenders and borrowers. Most of these bankers are making business loans that would not be made without the program. And in Illinois, community bankers can make loans to small businesses, including women-owned and minority-owned businesses, in partnership with a state lending program. Banks also can make loans to individuals, with state funds serving as a second mortgage for the borrower.

Access to equity-like capital is considerably more limited in rural communities. Community bankers, however, can develop partnerships with alternative financial institutions. For example, banks in North Carolina purchased stock to capitalize an alternative financial institution that provides debt and equity-like financing to businesses.

Assisting New Business Formation. Community bankers have more than capital to offer a potential business borrower. The banker's financial expertise is an additional important resource to rural entrepreneurs since access to business assistance services in rural communities can be difficult. Yet, several surveys suggest that many smaller firms feel they are not being served by their local bank or are unaware of services offered. Community bankers must be more focused on reaching out to the small business community and playing an active role in local economic development.

Small businesses represent a continuing experiment by individuals who think they have an idea the market will support. Often these ideas require serious revisions. While experienced business managers can anticipate potential financial pitfalls, new business managers or owners may not. The community bank can play a crucial role during the business formation process, therefore, by increasing access to management counseling and support.

Banks could pursue several options for providing this support. The bank could support business management education programs for new and current small business customers. Community banks can create separate affiliations, such as community development corporations and small business advisory committees, that enable the bank to actively support small business development while maintaining an "arm's length" relationship with potential borrowers.

Many private, nonprofit community development corporations also provide business assistance. Local bankers can work with these technical assistance providers, outlining the bank's lending criteria, discussing necessary financial documentation and referring potential borrowers to other professional advisers, such as marketing consultants. Having a local economic development organization share in these costs reduces the costs of making small business loans.

Providing Community Leadership. New economic realities are signaling that the days of passive community banking are over. Bankers must aggressively identify entrepreneurs, encourage and prod community leadership in the pursuit of economic growth, and support economic development activities. In other words, community bankers need to provide leadership to the community and help develop a vision for how the community can adapt to economic change.

Successful communities develop comprehensive strategies for guiding economic changes. Community bankers have an important role to play in formulating and implementing these strategies. Bankers can engage community groups in determining how the bank can respond to emerging community needs. Bankers can lend needed financial expertise in support of economic development endeavors and make prudent lending decisions in support of community economic change. Communities need to identify the internal investment opportunities that are necessary for successfully adapting to economic change. Communities need to identify the internal investment opportunities that are necessary for successfully adapting to economic change. In turn, community bankers must weigh the potential returns from making short-term investments outside the community against the need for supporting the long-term investments identified as being necessary for growth within the community.

Community bankers in Wisconsin are active participants in the University of Wisconsin–Extension's Community Economic Analysis program, which seeks to help communities build economic development strategies. Their participation involves contributing to the discussion of major issues facing the community, building strategies to address priority issues, and supporting implementation efforts that often require bank personnel and expertise rather than bank financing.

One particularly important way rural banks can demonstrate leadership in their communities is by relaying information. In most cases, the local bank is the first stop for a business needing capital for startup, expansion or modernization. Bankers can serve as an information link for these enterprises by maintaining information about state development finance programs, equity investors in the state or region, technical assistance providers, university or state industry modernization programs, and other relevant business assistance providers.

In the early stages of business development the banker may be able to as-sist a business most by providing information rather than capital. For example, bankers in Texas actively refer small businesses to business-assistance resources available through the Business School at Pan American University. The small businesses can receive assistance in preparing business plans, evaluating financing needs and preparing the financial documents necessary to apply for a bank loan.

Conclusion

The pace of change in the national and global economies demands that rural communities and rural community bankers find new ways of doing business in order to survive. Unfortunately, there is no single model for banks and communities to follow.

This chapter explored several strategies rural community bankers might embrace to become more active participants in their communities' economic development. Each community banker can customize these strategies to the unique set of circumstances under which the bank operates. The strategies provide a way to meet both fiduciary and community economic development objectives by accessing new sources of capital for rural businesses, assisting new business formation and providing leadership to the community.

CHAPTER 19

Small Business Development Tools

Edward M. Marshall

An effective small business partnership focuses on the critical needs of small firms and uses tools appropriate to meeting their needs at each stage of their development. The partnership's goals need to be clear, and the strategy must be tailored to achieve those goals. The partnership now turns to address the practical questions of strategy implementation. How do you know what type of small business development to encourage or which tools and resources to use? In this chapter, the following elements will be considered:

- The factors that need to be considered in deciding what type of small business to encourage,
- Specific tools a city can use to encourage small business development,

- Six types of programs cities can adopt to promote new small business growth, and
- The types of federal and state resources available to a city to pay for the development and implementation of the strategy and eight ways to access them.

What Type of Small Business Development Should We Have?

Not all small businesses are created equal. Small high technology companies will not generate the same effect on a local economy as "mom and pop" stores, and a small manufacturing company does not use the same type or amount of labor as a wholesale distribution

Originally published as "Tools for Small Business Development," Chapter 4 of Small Business Partnerships, *1989. Published by National League of Cities, Washington, D.C. Reprinted with permission of the publisher.*

warehouse. It is critical, therefore, that cities clearly determine what types of small business development are best suited to their local economic needs and resources. To do so requires market research, which allows the city to determine its small business competitive advantage.

The first step in determining this advantage is a survey of the small business community. Until the city understands the needs of its own small businesses, it cannot effectively develop a growth strategy. This survey should ask questions in at least twelve areas (see Figure 1):

Figure 1
Key Elements of a Small Business Survey

- Perceptions of City Hall
- City small business policies or plans
- Organization and management of small business programs
- Access to capital—working and venture
- Access to public markets
- Employee training needs
- Access to land and new sites
- Regulations
- City's quality of life
- Quality of public services
- Public physical infrastructure
- Business assistance programs

In addition, the survey should determine what each business plans to do in the next one to two years—for example, hire new employees, expand its facility, branch out into international markets, scale back/close down, or relocate.

A second type of research should include a survey of the largest employers in the city's economic market, which may extend up to a 100-mile radius around the city. This survey should focus on the supplies or services those businesses need and where they now get them. In Lima, Ohio, for example, market research found that the city's largest employers purchased more than 70 percent of their goods and services from outside the Lima economic market. Information on the supply and service needs of local businesses, the prices being paid and quality control needs, made it possible to open up a major new market for entrepreneurs.

A third type of research should focus on industry growth and decline trends. Several years ago, surveys showed that health-related industries were a high growth part of Philadelphia's economy, and that San Francisco's economy was becoming a service-based economy. Knowing which major industries will grow in your economy allows you to encourage those small businesses that will serve as producers and suppliers.

Armed with this data, the city and the small business partnership should be able to quickly identify existing small businesses that need assistance, new private market opportunities, and new directions for small business investment.

In making the decision to promote certain types of small business development, the partnership may wish to consider giving priority for assistance by using the following guidelines:

1. Small businesses that can be profitable within the existing market area.

2. Small businesses that increase exports outside the local market.

3. Small businesses that supply goods and services to local, large employers.

4. Small businesses that diversify the local economic base.

5. Small businesses that use local labor.

6. Small businesses that meet the community's needs for a safe and clean environment.

Using these guidelines, the partnership can begin to formulate a strategy which is truly based on the sensitivities of the local market and local needs and resources.

Small Business Development Tools

Once the city has completed its initial research and adopted its plan, the next step is to determine what tools are needed to address the city's liabilities and enhance its assets. There are twelve types of non-financial tools that cities can use to generate new small business investment. Not every city will need to use all of these tools, but may wish to consider them when adopting a comprehensive plan.

1. To Improve Perceptions of City Hall:
- Provide high-level leadership and support for efforts.
- Involve small business in a task force or commission.
- Mount a public relations campaign to build city image.
- Sponsor small business fairs.
- Demonstrate a positive attitude toward business.
- Form a small business partnership.
- Appoint an ombudsman for small business in city hall.

2. To Improve Planning and Policy Making:

- Establish a comprehensive policy with goals and objectives.
- Conduct a survey of small business needs.
- Involve small business in planning.
- Undertake economic research, analysis, and forecasting.
- Target selected types of small business for development.
- Target certain areas of the city.

3. To Improve Organization and Management of Small Business Programs
- Establish a small business development authority.
- Ensure that all city resources are coordinated to emphasize small business development.
- Link state and federal programs with local efforts.
- Develop networks with financial institutions, business leaders, labor, and others.
- Employ skilled staff who have small business experience.
- Monitor and evaluate program efforts.
- Provide continual training for staff.
- Contract with an outside small business adviser to provide perspective and expertise to your strategy.

4. To Improve Access to Affordable Capital
- Establish bank consortium and loan pooling agreements.
- Establish partnerships with financial institutions.
- Deposit city funds at banks that invest in small businesses.
- Target community reinvestment programs for small business interests.

- Access state and federal resources.
- Encourage organization of bank community development corporations.

5. To Improve Access to Public Markets:

- Establish a public procurement information/bidding system. Use regional and national systems.
- Eliminate or reduce bid-bonds.
- Establish a bond guarantee and liability insurance program.
- Create local purchasing preferences from firms whose owners live in the community.
- Establish and enforce prompt payment legislation.
- Provide technical assistance to small business on the city bid and procurement process.

6. To Improve Human Capital:

- Harness the Job Training Partnership Act program to meet small business employment needs.
- Develop entrepreneurial training programs at local universities and secondary schools.

7. To Improve Availability of Land/Sites:

- Land banking; use city land to leverage private investment and generate a public sector equity stake in small business development.
- Survey available sites and maintain a data bank.
- Assemble parcels.
- Provide incubator space—old public/private buildings that are rehabilitated and opened up to new businesses at substantially reduced lease or sales prices.

- Establish small business parks.

8. To Improve Regulatory Climate:

- Create a one-stop permitting center.
- Reduce paperwork.
- Expedite processing.
- Eliminate nuisance regulations.
- Modify zoning to promote small business development.
- Identify an ombudsman.

9. To Improve the Quality of Life:

- Upgrade educational institutions.
- Expand recreational opportunities.
- Encourage sports franchises.
- Upgrade cultural opportunities.
- Improve health care.
- Provide day care.

10. To Improve Public Service:

- Upgrade visible services like police and fire protection and combat crime.
- Contract with small businesses to provide city services.
- Target services to small business areas or commercial strips.
- Reroute public transit to serve small business areas.

11. To Improve the Infrastructure:

- Adopt a long-range capital improvements program.
- Rehabilitate and/or construct roads, bridges, and water lines.
- Upgrade public transportation.

12. To Improve Business Assistance:

- Create a management assistance center for small business.
- Provide training for entrepreneurs using local educational institutions.

- Provide ongoing management technical assistance.
- Underwrite management services to small businesses.

New Small Business Growth

The entrepreneurial city is always looking for new ways to increase opportunities for its entrepreneurs and to put people who are not working back to work. The following six tools are new areas of small business development or are potential areas where cities can make a difference: small business incubators, bank consortium/small business partnerships, export trade, youth enterprises, public housing small business development, and welfare self-sufficiency projects. In all six areas, the city can play a critical role as catalyst and partner.

SMALL BUSINESS INCUBATORS

According to the Small Business Administration, incubators are buildings where a number of new or growing firms can locate and conduct business at a much lower cost than in conventional, market rate space. Incubator firms share centralized clerical and administrative services, business assistance, conference rooms, or loading docks. Incubators are most effective for startups where overhead costs are high and markets are not yet fully developed. In some instances, incubators can also serve an economic revitalization purpose by being located in abandoned but rehabilitated factories, or in historic preservation districts where abandoned office or commercial buildings need new life. Cities can identify potential incubator facilities, pack-

age the project, underwrite its rehabilitation for small business use, promote its use, and provide management assistance to the firms once they have located in the facility.

BANK CONSORTIUM/SMALL BUSINESS PARTNERSHIPS

Partly in response to the Community Reinvestment Act (CRA) requirements for more community lending, and partly because of the need to reinvest in urban neighborhoods and businesses, banks and savings and loans across the country are forming consortia to promote small and minority business development and low income housing. Since 1982, the Development Credit Fund in Baltimore has been making working capital loans ranging from $5,000 to $750,000 to high risk businesses that normally would not be eligible in the private market. The six largest banks in Maryland, led by Maryland National Bank, pooled over $22.5 million, which is now supported by a Small Business Administration loan guarantee program, to share the risk, reduce transaction costs, and build a bridge to the small and minority business market. Other bank consortia in Oakland, Atlanta, and Pittsburgh are looking to expand access to capital for this underserved population of businesses.

EXPORT TRADE DEVELOPMENT

Greater small business access into the export market is needed. The National League of Cities has suggested a number of ways cities can do this:

- Providing leadership to encourage and assist local businesses to mitigate or expand international business activities.
- Conducting trade missions.
- Encouraging direct foreign investment.
- Forming a foreign trade zone.
- Forming an export trading company.
- Developing an export trading company.
- Establishing ties with universities overseas to further develop information on export markets.
- Providing information on trade fairs, exhibits, government-sponsored trade missions.
- Encouraging international tourism.

Any or all of these actions depend upon the city's competitive advantage in exports.

YOUTH ENTERPRISE DEVELOPMENT

To develop the entrepreneurial talents of the next generation, cities can establish young adult community development corporations (CDCs), which can be subsidiaries of an existing CDC or the city's SBA 503/504 corporation. Youth CDCs bring the business world to young adults in a way that generates a sense of ownership and builds business skills. They provide a positive alternative to subminimum wage jobs.

PUBLIC HOUSING SMALL BUSINESS DEVELOPMENT

Public housing projects, particularly larger ones, have an untapped market potential. Hundreds of millions of

dollars each year flow from these projects to commercial and retail firms without benefiting the micro-economy of the project. At the same time, the projects often have empty buildings suitable for incubators, people who need work, and services that need to be performed for the project itself or that could be sold outside the project. Cities and their housing and welfare departments could consider converting economically distressed projects into havens for new enterprise development.

WELFARE SELF-SUFFICIENCY PROJECTS

Several cities are experimenting with putting welfare recipients with entrepreneurial talents into business for themselves. Once a venture idea is identified by a welfare recipient, the city and its small business advisers work with the recipient to start up the new business.

Potential Resources

Mounting a significant, long-term strategy will require upfront investment by the members of the small business partnership. Every member is a potential contributor to underwriting the costs of the strategy. The contributions can be either in cash or in kind. Here we will focus primarily on the kinds of assistance federal and state governments can provide, and what cities can do to access and coordinate those resources.

There are eight basic types of federal and state government small business development assistance for cities: legislation, advocacy and research, fiscal aid, expenditures, regulations, financial aid, programmatic assistance, and non-financial aid.

1. Legislative: The power to draft and lobby for specific legislation to support small firms to enhance the capabilities of local governments to aid small firms—for example, home rule.

2. Advocacy and research: It is essential for small business to have a political voice at the top echelons of government at least comparable to the influence of big business or labor. The U.S. Small Business Administration has an Office of Advocacy that identifies, researches, and supports the concerns of the small business community. State economic development agencies and governors either already have the advocacy/research capability to assist cities and small businesses, or they can create it.

3. Fiscal: The tax and revenue sharing powers of the federal and state governments are among the most powerful tools available for developing a vibrant small business sector. Tax policies should: (a) reduce barriers to the efficient operation of capital markets; (b) be stable and certain; (c) be evaluated regularly to ensure positive impact. Federal and state revenues can be distributed to communities in greater economic need, local governments can be reimbursed for federally and state-mandated programs, while statutes can be passed to enable metropolitan revenue and tax base sharing programs.

4. Expenditure: Federal and state governments are the largest consumers of goods and services in the economy, responsible for over one-third of the GNP. They spend hundreds of billions of dollars annually, only a small percentage of which goes to small business. Procurement policy and programs need to be directed to small and minority firms and targeted to firms in economically distressed communities. Public facility siting can boost local government and small business revenues. Public pension funds can be used as a source of investment or even as a guarantee for a secondary market for small business financing.

5. Regulatory: In the areas of banking, insurance, environment protection, land use, licensing, permitting, and paperwork reduction, federal and state governments can reduce regulatory barriers that impede access to money and markets. For example, these governments can facilitate interstate bank competition, permitting bank equity investments in business ventures, and enforce the Community Reinvestment Act bank investments in small businesses located in distressed areas.

6. Financial assistance: Federal and state governments have available to them a wide range of traditional and non-traditional financial assistance other than tax policies. Table 1 lists several of these options.

7. Programmatic assistance: Specific programs or initiatives, with or without financial assistance, can be developed on the premise of supporting the development and growth of small firms. These include: foreign export development, interregional market development and trade, enterprise zones, small business incubators, public physical infrastructure improvements, fostering neighborhood and community development corporations, or other forms of targeted assistance to specific types of small business or to particular places.

8. Nonfinancial assistance: Here

Table 1
Public Sector Financial Aid to Small Business

Grants
Loans and loan guarantees; pooling consortia
Revolving loan funds
Interest subsidies
Bonds, taxable and tax-exempt
Equity and near-equity financing
Business site development assistance
Customized job training
Tax incentives, credits, and abatements
Venture capital institutions
Development finance institutions

coordination with their existing resources.

Access is particularly important. All too often the resources are scattered among agencies, each with different purposes, requirements, and paperwork. Once a small business partnership has decided to develop a plan, the city should be asked to identify and access the key federal and state resources.

Table 1 suggests steps a city can take. The partnership should also spend time regularly (every three months) to brainstorm new ways to bring these resources to bear. The point is to keep federal and state attention focused on your city's small business needs.

Coordination is also critical to a successful small business program, particularly between the state and city governments. The initiative for coordination needs to come from the city and is best located in the mayor's office or the city's office of intergovernmental relations. If the city does not already have an intergovernmental staff member who has expertise in small business, the city

again, federal and state governments can provide the management and technical assistance so essential to small firms. They can act as information and referral clearinghouses, and provide public relations or marketing assistance. They can also act to enhance the coordination and partnership capabilities of local governments. Public sector assistance is available, depending upon the state. The two issues cities face are access and

Table 2
Accessing Federal and State Resources

- Determine the specific types of assistance needed and when they are needed (for example, planning funds needed immediately, project funds in a year).
- Conduct an agency inventory to find out which agencies have the kind of funds or assistance needed, their requirements and deadlines.
- Identify key gaps between city needs and federal and state resources, and let the executive and legislative branches know.
- Focus on state department of economic development/commerce financial assistance to small business. Establish relationships with top officials.
- Become aware of state agency allocation formulas and how they can benefit your city; determine if you are getting your "fair share."
- Submit solicited and unsolicited proposals to key state agencies regularly for assistance.
- Increase the number of industrial development bond applications for small business projects that qualify (check per capita limitations).
- Invite federal and state officials and your congressional delegation to tour the city, meet with the partnership, and conduct forums or hearings on small business needs.

may want to consider hiring one. This person should serve as a liaison and communications point, coordinate all grant or program applications, and make sure that all small business gaps identified are filled. Table 3 provides a state-by-state analysis of the typical small business assistance programs provided by each state.

The tools available for small business development are significant, and new approaches to finance, management, and self-help are emerging every year. Public and private sector resources are also substantial and can be carefully crafted into a comprehensive tool kit for small businesses to use at each stage of their development. Paying for these tools, yet another challenge for the partnership, is the focus of a subsequent chapter.

Table 3
State Small Business Assistance Programs

	State 503 Development Cos.	Business Incubators	Small Business Office	Loan Program	Procurement Program	Government Liaison	Advisory Board	Small Business Economic Revitalization Program
Alabama	■	■	■	■	■		■	
Alaska	■		1		■			
Arizona	■	■	■	■		■	■	■
Arkansas	■	■	■	■		■	■	■
California		■	■	■	■	■	■	■
Colorado	■	■	■	■			■	
Connecticut	■		■	■	■	■	■	■
Delaware			■			■	■	
Florida	■	■	■			■	■	■
Georgia	■	■	■	■	■	■	■	■
Hawaii			■		■	■	■	
Idaho			■	■	■		■	
Illinois	■	■	■	■	■	■	■	■
Indiana	■	■	■	■	■	■	■	■
Iowa	■		■	■		■	■	
Kansas	■		■	■	■		■	
Kentucky	■	■	■	■	■	■	■	
Louisiana	■	■	■	■	■	■	■	
Maine	■	■		■	■	■	■	■
Maryland	■	■	■	■	■	■		■
Massachusetts		■	■	■	■	■	■	■
Michigan	■	■	■	■	■	■	■	■
Minnesota	■		■	■	■		■	
Mississippi	■	2	■	■	■		■	■

continued on page 202

Table 3, continued

	State 503 Development Cos.	Business Incubators	Small Business Office	Loan Program	Procurement Program	Government Liaison	Advisory Board	Small Business Economic Revitalization Program
Missouri			■	■	■			
Montana			■	■	■			
Nebraska	■	■	■	■	■	■	■	■
Nevada	■		■	■	■		■	
New Hampshire		■	■					■
New Jersey			■	■				■
New Mexico	■	■			■	■	■	
New York	■	■	■	■	■	■	■	■
North Carolina		■	■		■	■	■	
North Dakota	■	■	■	■	■	■	■	■
Ohio	■	■	■	■	■		■	■
Oklahoma		■	■	■	■			
Oregon	■		■				■	■
Pennsylvania		■	■	■	■	■	■	■
Rhode Island	■		■	■	■		■	
South Carolina		■	■	■	■	■	■	
South Dakota		■	■	■	■			■
Tennessee		■	■	■	■	■	■	
Texas		■	■		■	■		
Utah		■	■				■	
Vermont	■	■	■	■		■		
Virginia		■	■	■	■	■		
Washington	■		■			■	■	
West Virginia	■	■	■	■	■	■	■	■
Wisconsin		■	■	■	■	■		
Wyoming	■		■	■	■	■		■
Puerto Rico				■	■	■		
District of Columbia				■	■			

1. Incorporated into the Office of Enterprise, Dept. of Commerce and Economic Development
2. 1985 legislation authorizing establishment; funded through state, city, and private sources; it is only in the initial consideration stages at the present time

Source: The Guide to State and Federal Resources for Economic Development, Northeast Midwest Institute, 1988, p. 394.

CHAPTER 20

Strengthening Downtown Businesses

Dolores P. Palma

Each community must tailor its business retention and expansion strategy to the identified needs—and the identified potentials—of its local business community. With this in mind, it is helpful to consider the initiatives which are most often included in downtown business retention and expansion strategies today. Those initiatives are shown below.

One-on-One Business Counseling

Business district professionals and leaders all across the country have found that technical assistance and professional assistance can often make the difference between small business success and failure. In addition, it has also been found that small business owners are not very likely or able to attend seminars in order to obtain this information. Therefore, personal contact is essential to get the attention of small business owners and to make sure they get the information they need to survive and thrive.

One-on-one business counseling usually involves assistance on business matters considered to be private, such as business planning, business financing, record keeping, computerization, etc. For this initiative to be a success, follow-up with business owners—to make sure they got the information they needed and were able to use that information—is essential.

Originally published as "Retaining and Strengthening Existing Downtown Businesses," Municipal Maryland, *Vol. 25, No. 3, October, 1995. Published by the Maryland Municipal League, Annapolis, Maryland. Reprinted with permission of the publisher.*

Business Visitation Teams

Long used in programs aimed at industrial retention and expansion, visitation teams are a technique that has been borrowed by downtowns. The visitation team usually involves two to three people who call on the owner of a local business. The purpose of the visit is to first, determine the needs of the business owner and, second, to meet these needs by linking the business owner with information sources. As with one-on-one business counseling, follow-up is essential for this initiative to be effective.

Referrals to Service Providers

Many downtown organizations provide assistance to existing businesses by referring them to appropriate local service providers such as a Small Business Development Center, a SCORE chapter, municipal government agencies, etc. The rationale here is that the downtown organization cannot be all things to all people and should not try to reinvent the wheel. Instead, business owners and local service providers both benefit if the downtown organization acts as a liaison between the two. Again, follow-up is essential for this initiative to be effective.

Seminars, Workshops, Forums and Conferences

Often offered to business owners on a quarterly basis, these sessions have long been used to convey information that is of interest to business owners as a group. Topics usually covered in such sessions include coordinated marketing, building rehab, effective window displays, interior design and merchandising, etc. Many downtown organizations are holding fewer sessions of this type, since it is often difficult for the independent, small business owner—for whom the sessions are usually held—to attend. The trend that is emerging is to hold one or two sessions a year, with well-known speakers or "experts" who act as a "draw," instead of regular, quarterly sessions with low-profile speakers.

Employee Training

A popular business retention tool in many communities is seminars and workshops for employees of existing businesses. Such programs can focus on the orientation of new employees, training of new employees, and the re-training of existing employees. Often, these programs will focus on topics such as providing excellent customer service, referring customers among businesses located in downtown, and providing information about downtown goods, services, and activities to downtown users. The key to the success of such programs is threefold. First, to determine the seminar topics in conjunction with business owners. Second, to present them to employees as a tremendous opportunity rather than as a chore. And, third, pay employees for the time they spend attending the sessions.

Secret Shopper Programs

Long used by shopping centers and department stores, secret shopper programs have come into use in downtowns. Such programs involve individuals who are asked to, first, anonymously shop at a particular downtown store and then to evaluate the quality of that shopping experience. For these programs to be effective it is essential to hold a training session with each secret shopper, to direct the shopper to shop at a particular store and/or department within that store, to have a standardized method for the shoppers to rate and evaluate the shopping experience, and to maintain strict confidentiality of the results.

Retail and Office Market Analysis

A retail and office market analysis is a critical element of business retention and expansion programs because it reveals the potential of the business district. In addition, the analysis is critical because it provides information which small business owners must have to succeed—but which they commonly do without because they lack the time or money to acquire this information. When the downtown retail and office market analysis is completed, its findings should be widely distributed to downtown's business owners. Ideally, business owners would use the market information to:

- Learn the characteristics and buying habits of customers and office users in their trade area;
- Determine the most appropriate customer groups or office users for their business to target;
- Learn who their competition is and what their competition is offering in the trade area;

- Make decisions regarding changes in the type of merchandise they sell, services they offer or space they rent;
- Test additional merchandise lines or services; and
- Expand their business and its offerings.

Guidelines and Assistance

Many business retention and expansion programs provide guidelines to assist business owners who want to make physical improvements to their facilities. Such guidelines often cover topics such as appropriate exterior rehab, effective window displays, effective interior layout and design, appropriate business signs, etc. Where time and money allow, many business retention and expansion programs provide technical and professional assistance that is related to the guidelines.

Financial Incentives

Local efforts aimed at the retention and expansion of small businesses often focus on providing technical assistance, professional assistance, and financial counseling prior to—or along with—providing financial assistance. The reason for this is that while financial incentives can provide businesses with a competitive edge, they do not normally help businesses develop the human and technological skills needed for long-term gains in competitiveness.

Financial incentives that have long been used as part of business retention efforts include revolving loan funds, grants for facade rehab and signs, tax abatements, interest subsidies, and supply give-aways (such as paint programs). Today, financial incentives are also likely to be provided through programs such as the Community Reinvestment Act initiatives of the local lending community, through energy audits and subsidies provided through the local government and utility systems, and through design services that help businesses make smart renovation investment decisions.

One-Stop Shops

Realizing that the saying "time is money" is a truism for business owners, many local governments have created one-stop shops—an office where business owners can obtain all required permits, licenses, and approvals. The aim of these shops is to cut both the cost and time business owners spend going through government review and approval processes.

Marketing Campaign

As was said earlier, the findings of the market analysis should be used by a downtown's individual business owners to guide their marketing decisions. In addition, the findings of the market analysis should be used to define a marketing campaign for the downtown. This will allow the business district to be marketed as a single economic entity— much as a shopping center is—and to be positioned in the mind of the consumer as a "special" commercial district. The marketing campaign should be used to strengthen the business district as a whole and, therefore, to strengthen each of the district's businesses.

A comprehensive marketing campaign should include:
- Print pieces which can be used to promote downtown and its businesses;
- A public relations strategy which creates and reinforces downtown's desired image; and
- Collective and coordinated advertising which portrays downtown as a varied and convenient shopping district.

Awards Programs

Often, business retention and expansion strategies will include awards programs for two reasons—first, awards reinforce the positive actions taken by the award recipients and, second, awards market the fact that improvements are being made in downtown.

Award programs are most typically used to recognize outstanding physical improvements, business improvements, volunteer efforts, and employees.

Owner-Match Programs

An emerging downtown business retention initiative is one that involves linking soon-to-retire business owners with entrepreneurial individuals who are interested in becoming business owners. This is a particularly important business retention issue since many downtowns lose their most successful businesses when their independent owners retire without heirs who are interested in taking over the business.

The key to this match effort is to identify future retirees *early* so that prospective successors can be found and nurtured *before* the business is closed. Ideally, prospective buyers are found early enough so that they can join the current owners in running the business for a year or two, and, thereby, be groomed by the successful owners before they retire.

The ten steps necessary to start a downtown business retention and expansion program are highlighted below. These simple steps will help public officials, merchants, and citizens alike begin the journey leading to a successful business retention and expansion program for the downtown in their community.

Step 1: Form a Partnership Between Downtown and City Hall. If they are to succeed, business retention and recruitment efforts cannot—and should not—be the purview of either the private sector or the public sector alone. Instead, both sectors have an investment in downtown and both have a responsibility to protect and enhance that investment. Therefore, successful business retention and expansion efforts require a partnership between the private and public sectors. The role of the partnership should be to assess the area's needs and potential, define an appropriate strategy, and see that the strategy is aggressively implemented.

Step 2: Identify Sponsoring Organization and Staff. For best results, the business retention and expansion effort should be sponsored by a local organization that is actively involved in downtown and well-respected by both the private and public sector leadership of the community. The role of the sponsoring group is to lend credibility and champion the effort.

It should be noted early on that the effort will require the attention of at least one professional staff person who is experienced in downtown business development.

Step 3: Define and Implement a Public Relations Strategy. The business retention effort—and its successes—must be regularly publicized. Doing so will result in businesses, resource providers, investors, etc., seeking out the sponsoring organization and staff so that they do not always have to be the initiator of actions. When this occurs, it is a true sign of success. Therefore, a thorough, on-going public relations strategy should be defined early in the effort and relentlessly implemented throughout.

Step 4: Complete Business Needs Assessment and Market Analysis. A business needs assessment should be completed to determine the needs of the downtown's business owners and their perception of the business district. In addition, a market analysis should be completed which details downtown's potential for retail and office businesses.

Step 5: Analyze and Interpret Results of Assessment and Market Analysis. The needs assessment and market analysis are data collection methods that will involve compiling a great deal of information about downtown and its businesses. However, this information will be useless unless it is analyzed and interpreted to *make decisions about specific business retention activities to carry out.* Remember, data collection alone is a futile exercise. Data collection must be taken to the next step of analysis and interpretation of data so that these findings can be used to drive the business retention effort.

Step 6: Respond to "Red Flags" Uncovered. The needs assessment and the market analysis might reveal issues or situations that require *immediate* attention. These so called "red flags" often mean that action must be taken at once to avoid losing a business. For example, during the process it might be determined that a significant downtown business must find space to expand into or it will have to relocate outside of downtown in order to continue operation. This would be a project which requires immediate attention—thus a "red flag" project. Staff and volunteers should be detailed to quickly respond to red flags before moving on to the next step of the program.

Step 7: Select Appropriate Initiatives. Based on the needs assessment and analysis conducted, a business retention strategy must be defined. The strategy should be composed of specific initiatives selected because they allow the effort to address business needs and capture the market potentials identified.

Step 8: Define an Implementation Schedule. Once the appropriate initiatives have been selected, an implementation schedule must be defined. This is a management tool that details when each initiative will be started and completed; who will take the lead in implementing each initiative; how much each initiative is expected to cost; and the source of funds for each initiative.

Step 9: Monitor Progress of Effort. The sponsoring organization and staff should establish a method for continually monitoring the progress and success of the business retention and expansion effort. This will ensure that implementation runs smoothly and stays on course.

Step 10: Update Business Needs Assessment and Market Analysis. Approximately every two years the needs assessment and market analysis should be updated. This is necessary since the characteristics of downtowns and their businesses—as well as their users—are constantly changing. Therefore, the needs and the potentials of the downtown and its businesses will similarly change over time. To stay abreast of these changes—and to ensure that the retention effort is appropriately designed to address needs and potentials—the data on which the effort is based must be updated.

CHAPTER 21

Tax Increment Financing

John E. Greuling

With the cessation of important federal and state urban redevelopment programs, increasing pressure is being put on local units of government with declining Central Business Districts, "Downtowns," to devise innovation financing mechanisms for redevelopment projects. These projects range from rebuilding the falling public infrastructure to rehabilitating (and in some cases, replacing) the commercial buildings that gave viability to downtowns.

One innovation being employed by municipalities in many states is tax increment financing, or "TIF." The basic tenet of tax increment financing is that any redevelopment activity in an urban area usually creates higher property values in the redeveloped area, and, thus, increases the property tax revenues from that area. Tax Increment Financing Programs are designed to use the increased property tax revenues generated by a redevelopment project—the "tax increment"—to finance a portion of the costs associated with the project. The purposes of this article are to describe this development tool, note some of its uses, to present its advantages and disadvantages and to conclude with some recommendations.

The information for this chapter was obtained from both primary and secondary sources. The author contacted many individuals with direct experience in the use of tax increment financing. These included legislative attorneys, financial consultants, bond counsels, city officials, planners, and downtown business and property owners. Lengthy

Originally published as "Tax Increment Financing: A Downtown Development Tool,"Economic Development Review, Vol. 5, No. 1, Winter, 1987. Published by the American Economic Development Council (AEDC), 9801 W. Higgins Road, Suite 540, Rosemont, Illinois 60018 (847-692-9944, website www.aedc.org, e-mail aedc@interaccess.com). Reprinted with permission of the publisher.

interviews were conducted with individuals with special knowledge of key tax increment projects in Illinois. Additional information was collected from secondary sources on tax increment financing, including published and unpublished reports, articles and papers, state statutes and other enabling legislation, newspaper reports and information brochures.

Tax Increment Financing

DEFINITION

Tax Increment Financing (TIF) can be defined as a relatively new mechanism (in most states) for providing funds in urban areas by capturing the incremental increase in tax revenues from new development to pay for public investment to assist that development.[1] TIF programs, in short, are designed to use the *increased* property tax revenues generated by an urban development (the tax increment) to pay for the public costs of that development.[2]

The growth in the use of TIF has come because of a declining source of federal and state funds for redevelopment and an increasing local need to obtain funds to: (1) strengthen the local tax base and spread the cost of tax services, (2) salvage a declining area and create a new economic climate, and (3) improve housing, rehabilitate commercial and industrial areas and create new job opportunities.[3] TIF provides both a new source of funds *and* the local control and flexibility that has long been needed in funding community development programs.[4]

In a TIF project, the tax increments generated by the project are used solely to pay for "public costs" associated with the project. These public costs of development can be defined as those costs associated with either the public portions of the redevelopment project (e.g., infrastructure reconstruction) or the public "incentives" offered to make redevelopment of a particular area attractive to developers (e.g., land assembly). In the case of the former, rebuilding and/or replacing the aging infrastructure (streets, water and sewer lines) are "added" costs that often make redevelopment less financially attractive than new development. In the case of the latter, TIF funds can be used as a "carrot" for redevelopment by paying for land assembly and preparation costs, including demolition of existing buildings, with the land then being sold to the developer at a financial loss.[5]

It is these public costs that are financed by a TIF program, either by using the annual increment of revenues to pay for the improvements or by pledging the increment to repay bonds which are used to finance improvements.[6]

HOW IT WORKS

Although the TIF program is essentially local, state enabling legislation is required before the program can be initiated. Twenty-eight states as of 1984 allow their communities by statute to use TIF. Although there are distinct differences in use and application between states, generally the TIF process is the same.

To use tax increment financing in a state legislated for it, the city must first designate a "blighted" or deteriorating residential neighborhood, business district or industrial area for redevelopment.[7] The total assessed valuation is determined for all property in the designated TIF "district."

Once the district is established and the assessed value determined, the city (or redevelopment agency) makes the necessary public improvements. As noted above, this might include the assembly of land, preparation of it and construction or reconstruction of the "public" infrastructure, including streets, parking garages and pedestrian malls. These improvements might be paid for from general revenue funds or through the issuance of bonds or tax anticipation warrants.

The city or agency then sells some or all of the property to a private developer who builds the industrial, residential or commercial project. The selling price to the developer may be substantially less than the acquisition and/or improvement costs were to the city with the resulting loss being recouped with tax increment funds.[8]

The public and private investment in the project area results in an increase in the assessed valuation of the area. Taxes generated by this increase in assessed valuation—the tax increment—go into a special tax increment fund (also called a "tax allocation" fund). This fund is used to pay the public costs associated with the project.

While these *increased* tax revenues go only to the city (or development agency) to cover the costs of the public improvements, the amount of taxes collected *before* the project started continue to go to the other taxing bodies in the district, such as the county, township, school district. This is because the original assessed value that these bodies based their taxes on is frozen at the level it was prior to the start of the project.

Although the assessed value is frozen, the amount of taxes these taxing bodies may collect can increase if they increase their tax levy.[9]

When the redevelopment of the area is completed and all debts incurred by the city to pay for the public improvements have been repaid with tax increment funds, the TIF district is dissolved and property taxes based on the full increased assessed valuation of the area go to all taxing bodies.

There is no guarantee that the public investment paid by TIF will always generate new private investment. This risk is an important consideration in the utilization of tax increment financing. If new private investment does not occur or is less than anticipated, it is possible that enough tax increment will not be realized, and the financing can become a serious community liability.

TIF and the States: A Comparison

As of January 1984 some 28 states permit TIF in their local communities. While "Tax Increment Financing" is conceptually the same in all states, there are several key differences in regard to TIF procedures, financing and planning limitations. The following is an overview of those differences.

ENABLING LEGISLATION

Most states had existing urban renewal legislation prior to allowing tax increment financing. In many instances, it was amendments to these laws that were the primary vehicle by which TIF was institutional.[10] In some cases, such as California and Oregon, constitutional amendments were required before TIF could be allowed. In states without existing urban renewal laws, TIF legislation has been adopted separately.[11]

TIF AGENTS

In all states the primary local government responsible for implementing TIF programs is the municipality. However, in eight states, housing or urban renewal agencies are given authority to use TIF, and in four states county government is permitted to use TIF.[12]

The local government agents directly responsible for TIF administration is usually one or more of the following: city council, special TIF development commission, city planning office, housing and redevelopment (community development commission), industrial/economic development commission.[13]

TIF DISTRICTS

All states require some degree or possibility of blight and deterioration in an area before a TIF or redevelopment district can be created. This is the case because in all states TIF is justified from a constitutional perspective by the "public purpose" it serves.[14] Since the decline of housing, commerce and industry in urban centers has a deleterious effect on the economic base and overall quality of life in a community, it follows that a program designed to eliminate "blight" serves a justifiable public purpose.

What constitutes a "blighted" area is usually spelled out in the particular state's enabling legislation, but generally include the following elements: building deterioration and obsolescence, high vacancy rates, declining tax base, lack of new investment, infrastructure inadequacy and deterioration, and lack of an overall area "plan" for land use.

In California, blight alone is insufficient reason to justify designation of a TIF district: "According to state legislation, the 'blight' in a proposed district must create a burden on the community that could not and would not be remedied by the private sector."[15] In Illinois TIF district designation is not limited to blighted areas: "Conservation areas," or areas most likely to become blighted areas but are not now, also qualify.

The size of the TIF districts varies among states and ranges from a single site to a TIF district that includes the entire municipality. In some cases there are no district size limitations whatsoever; in others, the states limit the size of the TIF District as: a percentage of total land area of the city, a percentage of total tax base of the city, or a set acreage figure allowed per city.[16]

TIF DISTRICT PLAN

Once the area proposed for TIF has met the "blight" criterion, all states require that a TIF or Redevelopment Plan be prepared describing the projects to be undertaken within the district.[17] A number of states have mandated that the TIF plan include safeguards against abuses that might occur as a result of redevelopment:

> Both Minnesota and South Dakota require a fiscal impact analysis for all contributing taxing jurisdictions, while California law necessitates the filing of a neighborhood impact statement for a TIF district and adjacent areas. Illinois and Kansas require all TIF plans to state the specific dates of

project initiation, completion and the retirement of all related debt.[18]

In the case of Minnesota, extensive guidelines are given in the TIF legislation for the plan and its contents, including: a needs statement, relevant real estate data, procedures for clearing, improving and marketing a site, and a full disclosure of project costs.[19] Many states require planning commission review prior to city council adoption.

In addition, all states require that a public hearing be held to discuss the plan, its impacts and future amendments to the plan.[20] These hearings for the most part are the only formal provision for participation by local residents and affected taxing jurisdictions in the TIF process.

While public hearings on TIF projects are mandated in all states, recourse for affected parties varies:

- In Maine, TIF law requires an "advisory board" for each development district, and more than half of the members of this board must own property or residence in the development district (or adjacent to it). Community residents approve the district by referendum;[21]
- In Utah, if three-fourths of the project area's property owners object to a TIF plan, it must be approved by voters before the project is begun;
- In Kansas, TIF projects cannot proceed if objections are filed at the public hearing (or within 30 days of it), by affected counties or school districts.[22]

RECEIPT OF
TAX INCREMENTS

As a general rule, most TIF laws provide for full tax increment payments to the TIF agent over the life of the project. As described above, the tax increment is generated by applying the property tax rate for each unit of government to the increased property value within the TIF district. In one state, Illinois, any retail, service and utility taxes generated within the district can be captured a part of the tax increment over the life of the district, if the district is established prior to January, 1987.

In at least four states, provisions are made to return a part of the tax increments from the project area to affected local taxing jurisdictions.[23] This is done only after all the TIF indebtedness outstanding is paid for the particular year, and the remaining tax increment is shared proportionately (as determined by tax rates) by the overlying taxing jurisdictions.

In all states tax increments are only generated when district property values exceed their value at the time the district was created. If property values do not increase after project initiation, no tax increment revenues are collected.

Tax increments are generated by all taxing bodies having taxing authority within the redevelopment district, including the local municipality, county, schools, special districts.[24] In a few states, school districts are exempt from the tax increment process:

> This can be done by not including the school tax rate in determining each year's tax increment calculation (as in Florida), by returning calculated tax increments directly to school districts (as in South Dakota),

or by compensating school districts indirectly through state school aid formulas (as in Wisconsin).[25]

In the first two, tax increments are affected dramatically since school taxes often make up a large portion of the total property tax rate for an area. In Wisconsin, the state becomes a contributor to the local TIF process.

The length of time for tax increment capture also varies among states. In some cases it is open ended, or until blight is "eliminated," but most states set time limit requirements. These requirements are either for a set period of time (15–25 years) or until a particular project is actually completed and the bonds are repaid. In Wisconsin and Kansas, projects must be started and public funds expended within five years after plan adoption.

ELIGIBLE DEVELOPMENT ACTIVITIES

All states restrict the type of development or redevelopment activities allowed in the TIF district. Most states allow TIF to be used in residential, commercial or industrial projects: Kansas and Maine restrict the use of TIF for commercial areas only; South Dakota prohibits the use of TIF for residential development.[26]

The particular activities that are eligible for funding under TIF legislation comes under the guise of "public improvements" and normally include any (or combination) of the following: land assembly, relocation of tenants, demolition, site preparation, land cost writedown, street, sidewalk, curb and gutter construction, utility repair and replacement, water and sewer lines, planning,

engineering fees, debt service on bonds/ warranties.[27]

FINANCING METHODS

Allowable financing methods for TIF improvements projects vary only slightly among states. Generally, these financing sources can be broken into four categories:

1. General Obligation Bonds— G.O. Bonds are issued by the municipality, with bond proceeds used for the public improvements. This is a very common method of financing TIF programs; it is also very attractive because the bonds are secured by the full faith and credit of the municipality.

2. Tax Increment or Allocation Bonds—Most states provide for TIF Bonds, which are excluded from local debt limitations (unlike G.O. Bonds) and are secured by the full faith and credit of the city or by the project area itself. The proceeds are used solely within Tax Increment Districts.

3. Other Long Term Financing Methods—Most states also allow the use of lease-revenue bonds, industrial revenue bonds, special assessments and other municipal improvement bonds for TIF projects. Revenue bonds are secured solely by the project area, the developer and/or the tenants within the project area.

4. Annual Expenditure Increments—This method uses no bonds; instead the TIF project improvements are made and funded as tax increments are received. It is almost impossible to finance large projects using this method.[28]

In some cases, municipalities can (and do) enter into agreements with developers that guarantee that there is no revenue shortfall in meeting debt service on TIF bonds (i.e,. the developers finance the increment "gap"). This limits the public "exposure" on such issues, and gives additional security to the bonds improving their marketability.

TIF: The Pros and Cons

Historical utilization of TIF has shown that it is flexible enough to meet each state's particular goals relative to redevelopment. It has also shown itself to have several advantages and disadvantages:

ADVANTAGES

- TIF can provide significant capital to some types of development projects which are economically feasible.
- The community (and taxing bodies) do not lose tax revenues which were being collected prior to the development program.
- Property owners do not pay more than the normal tax burden.
- Tax Increment Bonds, when used, are not counted against the city's bonded indebtedness.
- Development is financed from increased tax revenues that the project generates rather than being subsidized by taxes from other areas.
- Once the project is complete, and bonds retired, the full tax base and revenues become available to all taxing bodies.
- Since the sale of bonds is required for most TIF projects, economic feasibility of the project is closely scrutinized by potential bond purchasers.
- In most cases, no public referendum is required of bonds issued for a TIF project.

DISADVANTAGES

- Under TIF there is no increase in tax base (and tax revenues) for taxing bodies until the bonds have been retired.
- If TIF or Revenue Bonds are used, they will be more expensive to use (higher interest rates) than G.O. Bonds because of greater risk.
- TIF has been abused—Cities have designated large areas as TIF Districts in order to capture increments not directly related to the public improvement financed.
- If TIF is not limited in some way (either by area or length of time to capture the increment), TIF can extend indefinitely and never return any benefits to the community.
- If the increment does not materialize, other sources of revenue must be used to retire bonds (including a general revenue tax increase).
- Citizens have little say on the use of TIF.
- It is difficult to use TIF with certain development incentives a community might offer to a developer, such as tax freezes or tax abatements.
- Once TIF Bonds have been issued, it is difficult to change development plans because of obligations to the bond holders.[29]

Recommendations

The following are some recommendations the author would present to communities contemplating the use of tax increment financing as a *part* of an overall downtown redevelopment program:

- Use care to avoid abuses. Design TIF programs to attract new investment, not to take advantage of projects that would have occurred anyway without TIF.
- Set realistic goals for the redevelopment program with the careful planning of projects to meet those goals. The planning stage should explore how the redevelopment can act as a catalyst to private investment. Don't over plan—it's too costly.
- Be sensitive to the realities of the private development process and markets. This will insure the infusion of public dollars at the right time.
- Do not expect TIF redevelopment to be cure-all for all municipal problems. Other improvement programs must be carried out simultaneously.
- Make sure the redevelopment (TIF) district is adequately sized to capture all tax increments due to the project improvements.
- Offer the proper (and needed) incentives to the private developer to insure investment. These include offers of pre-assembled land at reduced costs, necessary site improvements, adequate offstreet parking, regulatory relief, low-interest financing, etc. The private developer is in search of a fair return on investment, and the project needs to offer this.
- Be ready to make a long term commitment to the program. The TIF district will likely be in place for more than twenty years, with very little return on investment in the early period.

The use of tax increment financing by communities will continue to grow. With this additional use will come a greater sophistication in the use of TIF, with added flexibility in its application. In addition, there will continue to be a greater awareness that financing downtown development should not depend exclusively on one method of financing or source of funds.[30] This will result in a more balanced, and ultimately, a more effective way of financing the redevelopment of downtowns.

Notes

1. Douglas A. Harbit, Tax Increment Financing, National Council for Urban Economic Development Information Service, no. 1 (Washington, D.C.: National Council for Urban Economic Development, 1975), p. 1.

2. Benjamin Jones, Tax Increment Financing of Community Redevelopment, Council of State Governments Research Report, no date, p. 1.

3. Richard G. Mitchell, "Tax Increment Financing for Redevelopment: Is It Bad as Critics Say? Is It as Good as Its Proponents Claim?" *Journal of Housing* (May 1977): 226.

4. *Ibid.*, p. 227.

5. Jones, Tax Increment Financing of Community Redevelopment, p. 1.

6. Harbit, Tax Increment Financing, p. 1.

7. Illinois Department of Commerce and Community Affairs, Tax Increment Financing (unpublished report), p. 1. (Mimeographed.)

8. *Ibid.*, p. 1.

9. *Ibid.*, p. 1.

10. Jack R. Huddleston, "A Comparison of State Tax Increment Financing Laws," *Capital Financing Strategies for Local Governments*, ed. John Matzer, Jr. (Washington, D.C., International City Management Assoc., 1983), p. 130.

11. *Ibid.*, p. 130.

12. *Ibid.*, pp. 130–131.

13. Harbit, Tax Increment Financing, p. 1.

14. Huddleston, "A Comparison of State Tax Increment Financing Laws," pp. 131–132.

15. Casella, Tax Increment Financing, p. 3.

16. Huddleston, "A Comparison of Tax Increment Financing Laws," p. 134.

17. *Ibid.*, p. 134.

18. Harbit, Tax Increment Financing, p. 1.

19. Huddleston, "A Comparison of Tax Increment Financing Laws," p. 134.

20. Casella, Tax Increment Financing, p. 3.

21. Huddleston, "A Comparison of Tax Increment Financing Laws," p. 134.

22. *Ibid.*, p. 134.

23. *Ibid.*, p. 131.

24. Harbit, Tax Increment Financing, p. 1.

25. Huddleston, "A Comparison of Tax Increment Financing Laws," p. 131.

26. *Ibid.*, p. 136.

27. Harbit, Tax Increment Financing, p. 1.

28. *Ibid.*, p. 1.

29. *Ibid.*, p. 6.

30. Mitchell, "Tax Increment Financing for Redevelopment," p. 229.

Bibliography

Conley, Gary N. *Attracting Private Investment Into the Inner City Through Development Subsidies*. Washington, D.C.: National Council for Urban Economic Development, 1976, reprinted 1978.

Department of Community Development Services. *Urbana Downtown Tax Increment Area: Conservation—Redevelopment Plan and Projects*. Urbana, no date.

Downtown: Urbana's Future. City of Urbana: Urbana, Illinois, 1979.

Greuling, John. "Tax Increment Financing in Illinois: A Downtown Redevelopment Tool." *APA Newsletter* (November, 1982): p. 3.

Hulkonen, John. "Tax Increment Financing: A Total Community Approach to Economic Development," *AIDC Journal*, Vol. IX, No. 2 (April, 1974), pp. 49–67.

Illinois Department of Commerce and Community Affairs. *Everything You Wanted to Know About Tax Increment Financing (Well, Most Everything)*. Springfield, IL, 1983 (unpublished).

Illinois Department of Commerce and Community Affairs. *Tax Increment Financing*: DCCA (undated and typewritten).

Illinois Revised Statutes, Chapter 85, "Industrial Building Revenue Bond Act." Illinois: 1975.

Illinois Revised Statutes, Chapter 74, Public Corporations—Interest Rates. Illinois: 1975.

Illinois Revised Statutes, Chapter 24, Municipal Code, Section 11, Division 74.4, "Real Property Tax Increment Allocation Redevelopment Act." Illinois: 1977.

Jefferson, Gary H., and Tee Taggart. "Tax Increments Criticized," *Journal of Housing*, January, 1975, pp. 5–6.

Jones, Benjamin. *Tax Increment Financing of Community Redevelopment*. Department of Research, the Council of State Governments.

League of Kansas Municipalities, *Downtown Redevelopment Through Tax Increment Financing, Proceedings of a Seminar, July 10, 1980*, Topeka, Kansas: League of Kansas Municipalities, 1980.

Mitchell, Richard G. "Tax Increment Financing for Redevelopment: Is It as Good as Its Proponents Claim?" *Journal of Housing* (May, 1977): pp. 226–229.

National Council for Urban Economic Development, Information Service. *Tax Increment Financing*. September, 1975.

Perloff, Harvey S., et al. *Modernizing the Central City*, Cambridge, Mass.: Ballinger Publishing Company, 1975, pp. 327–343.

Quincy, Illinois Central Business District: Tax Increment Redevelopment Plan and Projects. City of Quincy and Urban Programming Corporation of America. Quincy, IL, 1982.

Stifel, Nicolaus & Company, Inc. *Tax Increment Financing in Illinois*. St. Louis, MO: Stifel, Nicolaus & Co., Inc., 1981 (typewritten).

Swide, James N., "Tax Increments Supported," *Journal of Housing*, February, 1975, p. 52.

Trimble, Gerald M., "Tax Increment Finance for Redevelopment: California Experience Is Good," *Journal of Housing*, November, 1974, pp. 459–463.

PART IV
The Case Studies

CHAPTER 22

Creating "New" Main Streets in California, Florida, and Illinois

Charles Lockwood

Throughout the 1980s and 1990s, hundreds of towns—both large and small—embarked on main street revitalization programs to strengthen their communities. Now, post–World War II suburbs throughout the United States are building main streets from scratch in a bold attempt to give identity to an anonymous suburban sprawl. By doing so, they hope to gain an edge in competing with other towns for future development and increased tax revenues.

Several dozen new main streets are under construction or in the planning stages in suburbs across the country. They are *not* intended to be outdoor shopping malls masquerading as main streets. Like pre–World War II, small town main streets, they contain a full range of everyday uses and activities—including office, retail, entertainment, hotels, housing, and civic institutions such as public libraries—all integrated within a pedestrian-friendly environment.

New suburban main streets are sprouting up in virtually every kind of postwar community—from unplanned, sprawling suburbs like Schaumburg near Chicago, to new towns like Valencia outside Los Angeles, and to picture book new urbanist communities like Haile Plantation in Gainesville, Florida,

Originally published as "Retrofitting Suburbia," Urban Land, *Vol. 57, No. 7, July, 1998. Published by the Urban Land Institute, 1025 Thomas Jefferson Street, N.W., Suite 500 West, Washington, D.C. 20007-5201. Reprinted with permission of the publisher.*

and Disney's new town of Celebration, Florida. These new main streets take many forms—from streets several blocks long to tree-shaded town squares and village greens.

These developments mark the wane of an old trend and the emergence of a new movement. Since World War II, most suburban development has ignored the broader, historic role of the street as a key component in a shared public realm. Rather, development patterns have reduced the street to a pedestrian-intimidating, single-purpose traffic arterial. The last few generations of Americans rarely have had the experience of coming together on a tree-lined street to shop, to walk after dinner, or to talk with friends.

Today, the pendulum is swinging another way. More and more people want to return to the traditional main street, particularly as their lives become more mobile, more global, and more computerized. Despite all the talk about "going virtual," people still need to feel they belong to a community.

Why Retrofit Suburbia?

Why are a growing number of suburbs, which previously celebrated their shopping mall/automobile-dominated lifestyles, building new main streets?

The "Tin Man" Syndrome. Like the Tin Man in *The Wizard of Oz*, more and more American residents are complaining that their postwar suburban towns have no heart. They feel cast adrift, with nothing to hold onto except a steering wheel. A main street, whatever its scale or architectural style, is the heart of a community. Reston Town Center in the new town of Reston, Vir-

ginia, for example, serves not only as a downtown that brings the Reston community together but also as a regional center for residents and workers from neighboring suburban communities that lack multiuse public gathering places.

Identity. As look-alike suburbs increasingly compete for residents, jobs, conventions, and tourists, many of them are regarding the addition of new main streets as one way to create an easily recognizable—and marketable—identity and character that will attract new businesses, development, and shops, as well as generate increased sales tax revenues.

Suburban Renewal. Many 1950s and 1960s inner suburbs are declining, just as urban neighborhoods did a generation or two ago. The suburb of Park Forest outside Chicago watched its population decline by 14 percent in the 1980s and its median household income shrink by 3 percent when the nation was enjoying a 7 percent increase in median income. The 695,000-square-foot Park Forest Center regional mall has been plagued in recent years by a 70 percent vacancy rate. Now, most of the mall buildings have been bulldozed as Park Forest builds a new main street in its place to help revitalize its community.

Program Overload. Many people are turning away from overstructured, formulaic places that look alike to the diversity of traditional main streets. Big buildings, small buildings, a few ugly buildings, and some standout ones work together to make main street a real place where people can feel connected.

Changing suburban retail trends are another key factor fueling the new suburban main street trend. Medium-sized, higher-end stores like Williams Sonoma, Barnes & Noble, and Crate & Barrel no longer want to locate inside typical suburban malls. They prefer a separate identity, which means having their own building on a pedestrian-oriented main street. According to *Stores* magazine, "The revitalization of main street has caught the imagination of retailers, who see neighborhood locations as a viable means of growth.... Main street stores are answering shoppers' demands for convenience, efficiency, and something new while avoiding the sense of sameness that frequently seems to fill many suburban centers."

The Gap, Saks Fifth Avenue, Sears, Limited Stores, Express, Victoria's Secret, Bath & Body Works, and Abercrombie & Fitch are a few of the increasing number of retailers that have rediscovered the profit potential of main street. But not all retailers are appropriate for a new suburban main street, or for any main street for that matter.

"You cannot have major stores or big-box retailers on a pedestrian-oriented street," notes Kalvin Platt, chairman of the SWA Group, an international land planning and landscape architecture firm. "Their buildings and their parking lots are simply too big for the pedestrian-oriented main street scale."

Blazing the Trail: Three Pioneers

Construction of one of the first suburban main streets began in 1987. Fields Point Development Company hired architects Andres Duany and Elizabeth Plater-Zyberk to redevelop the circa–1960 New Seabury Shopping Center in Mashpee, Massachusetts, into a three-block-long, pedestrian-oriented town center called Mashpee Commons,

complete with stores, housing, a library, and a church.

In 1991, Crocker & Company completed the first phase of pedestrian-oriented, mixed-use Mizner Park in Boca Raton, Florida, on the site of the failing 420,000-square-foot Boca Raton Mall. Architects Cooper Carry & Associates created an instant community hub by designing a two-block-long village green ringed by low-rise buildings with shops and restaurants and entrances to them on the ground floors. The upper floors have offices or apartments.

In 1991, Mobil Land Development Corporation completed the first phase of Reston Town Center—the "big city" version of a traditional main street. The town center includes 530,000 square feet of office space, 200,000 square feet of stores and restaurants, an 11-screen movie theater, a 514-room Hyatt Regency Hotel, and a one-acre central plaza with a fountain. Parking structures and surface lots are located behind the buildings.

Schaumburg, Illinois: Municipality as Main Street Developer

Sometimes, a municipality—rather than a developer—is the catalyst behind a new main street. In recent decades, Schaumburg, Illinois, near Chicago's O'Hare International Airport, became one of the nation's largest, most successful edge cities. However, it had no town center, no unifying core. Then, several years ago, Schaumburg's village government purchased a run-down, half-empty retail center at Roselle and Schaumburg roads, the community's traditional crossroads, along with several nearby parcels.

Land assemblage for this 29-acre site took several years. "Although we initiated condemnation proceedings on some properties," says Mayor Al Larson, "we did not go to court. Instead, we ended up negotiating the prices, using money from the larger tax-increment financing (TIF) district to purchase and redevelop the land." After completing site assemblage in 1995, the village of Schaumburg began selling parcels to developers. "We didn't want to own the center," Mayor Larson explains. "We just wanted to create a development plan to reflect our vision for the site and the community, and then sell the parcels to developers who would build our vision."

The key was attracting strong anchors to Town Square. Larson wanted one of these to be the Schaumburg Township Library, the second busiest library in the state. He knew the library wanted to relocate, and he sold it on Town Square. A 70,000-square-foot grocery store serves as the second anchor. Together with the library, it will generate strong retail traffic for the restaurants, stores, and other businesses that will surround the central square. A nearby residential project, with more than 100 upscale townhouses and some single-family houses, will bring additional foot traffic.

Schaumburg's new Town Square, designed by Hitchcock Design Group, is rapidly taking shape. An amphitheater, a park, ponds, and waterfalls have been built in the central square. A 55-foot-tall clock tower, the traditional icon of town squares for centuries, is already standing. The grocery store is open, and the shops and professional space on the south side of the square are completed and 80 percent occupied. Parking has been placed behind the buildings, so that visitors are not confronted by an ocean of parking when they arrive. The library, which will open this September, is expected to attract an estimated 1 million patrons a year.

Village Commons: Vernon Hills, Illinois

Several postwar Chicago suburbs are following Schaumburg's lead by planning and building a wide variety of new main streets. One of these is Vernon Hills, 35 miles northwest of Chicago. Incorporated in 1958, Vernon Hills has more than 3.5 million square feet of retail space. With a population of 20,000 and rising, it has been one of the fastest-growing municipalities in the state for the last two decades. Still, the village wanted to improve its ability to compete with surrounding historic towns.

Vernon Hills is reviewing plans for the Village Commons, which will have a village green, a library, a hotel, retail space, residential uses, and a senior center. "We are trying to create some history and a sense of place," says Craig Malin, the village's assistant manager.

Part of the funding for Village Commons is coming from a $200,000 CMAQ (congestion mitigation air quality improvement) grant, which uses federal Intermodal Surface Transportation Efficiency Act (IS-TEA) funds. Using CMAQ formulas, the village was able to show that reconfiguring land usage and constructing a town square would reduce automobile emissions in Vernon Hills. The Chicago Area Transportation Study, CMAQ's Chicago metropolitan planning organization, is funding this new approach to pollution reduction.

Town Center Drive: Valencia, California

In the new town of Valencia, 30 miles north of downtown Los Angeles, the Newhall Land and Farming Company is now building a half-mile-long, pedestrian-oriented main street called Town Center Drive, directly adjacent to the enclosed Valencia town Center regional mall, which opened in 1991.

"The Valencia master plan, which was completed by planner Victor Gruen in 1965, designated this location as the community hub," explains James S. Backer, senior vice president of Newhall Land's commercial and industrial real estate division. Many industry leaders were thinking of an outdoor retail mall for this location, but Thomas L. Lee, Newhall Land's chairman and CEO, Tom Dierckman, president of Valencia Company, and Backer were main street boosters from the start.

A key component of the site plan was linking Town Center Drive with the Valencia Town Center regional mall. John Kriken, a partner with Skidmore, Owings & Merrill, LLP, had advised Newhall Land to break the traditional ring of mall parking and set aside an area for the mall's main entrance, with movie theaters, a working carousel, and fountains—all waiting to connect to Town Center Drive.

Wide sidewalks, shade trees, and benches line the new main street. The first two Town Center Drive buildings are already open and seven other buildings are under construction, including the 250-room Valencia Hyatt Hotel, an entertainment/retail complex, and office buildings, as well as several hundred apartments on the western end of the street.

Haile Village Center: Haile Plantation, Florida

In 1992, architect and developer Robert B. Kramer and his partner Matthew Kaskel began building a five-block-long main street at Haile Plantation, a master-planned community outside Gainesville, Florida. Kramer laid out Haile Village Center and designed about three-quarters of the relatively small white clapboard, tin-roofed professional buildings, most of which have apartments on the second floors.

The 50-acre project uses a network of bike paths to link Haile Village Center to the surrounding subdivisions. Popular events like a weekly farmers market to help lure residents to the new village center. More than 40 buildings already line the street. About half of the commercial property is owner occupied.

"We have the traditional mix of main street uses—plenty of shops, including a corner grocery store, a dry cleaners, a post office, a dentist, a stockbroker," says Kramer. "We didn't create a list and say 'We've got to have those people.' They came to us, so there must be a demand for our kind of main street." Future development projects include a town hall, a 100-unit apartment complex, an assisted-care facility, and a 75-unit lodge and conference center.

Roadblocks to Success

For all its benefits, the new suburban main street trend faces several roadblocks, including:

Expense. Many developers and municipalities cannot afford to fund such large, long-term development projects, particularly when they must pay today's high prices for land even as municipalities struggle with dwindling tax bases.

Site Assemblage. Like Schaumburg, most suburban cities will have to assemble their own main street sites. Will other municipalities have sufficient political support—and funds—to assemble these sites through negotiation or eminent domain?

Traffic Codes. Many jurisdictions require overly wide streets that spoil the intimate scale of pedestrian-oriented main streets and introduce high-speed traffic into their roadways.

Too Many Clones? The real estate industry's mania for formulas also threatens the success of the new suburban main street trend. Developers and municipalities are notorious for replicating successful projects, rather than creating a distinctive streetscape that reflects their area's market, history, and demographics. Others take the main street "formula" and strip it down to cut costs, leaving residents with a cheap outdoor mall. "Big developers are already jumping on the main street bandwagon," warns Plater-Zyberk, "without understanding or appreciating the many intricate components that can make or break a public realm."

Too Little Too Late? Finally, trying to create a traditional, pedestrian-oriented main street in the midst of sprawling, automobile-dominated postwar suburbia may be impossible for most communities. Without careful planning, the results can be little more than nostalgic window dressing, like the faux turn-of-the-century storefronts in a typical suburban mall.

But there is more upside than downside for this development trend. Touring developers and architects, for example, are flocking to Haile Plantation. "They come here," says Kramer, "and tell me, 'We don't have Disney's money to do something large and all at once, like Celebration. But if you can do it in small, market-driven increments, I guess we can do this kind of main street development, too.'"

Equally promising, developers of some vast mixed-use complexes are making new suburban main streets a key feature in their projects. The focal point of the Winmar Company's just-completed Redmond Town Center outside Seattle is a five-block-long new main street. Built on the site of a former golf course in Redmond, Washington, this 1.375-million-square-foot, mixed-use project, designed by LMN Architects, contains retail space, office buildings, multifamily housing, restaurants, an eight-screen cinema complex, a hotel, and 40 acres of parks and open space.

Main streets are also being included in large downtown redevelopment plans. Rockville, Maryland, is in the beginning stages of replacing a failed downtown mall that physically divided its central business district with a $300 million, 1.5 million-square-foot, mixed-use development. Designed by Hellmuth, Obata & Kassabaum, the project includes a new four-block-long main street whose purpose is to unite and revitalize the downtown and create a community hub for the entire city. (See "Rockville Center: Creating a New Town Center," *Urban Land*, July 1997.)

"Building a main street from scratch," says Philip J. Enquist, a partner at Skidmore, Owings & Merrill

LLP, "takes a total commitment from the city, the developers, and the community. Fortunately, dozens of communities are making that commitment. We are the only American generation to live without main streets. We may not have to live without them for much longer."

CHAPTER 23

The Santa Monica, California, StreetscapeProject

Charles Lockwood

Downtown Santa Monica is a hodgepodge. The area includes some of Southern California's most popular destinations, including the recently rejuvenated Santa Monica Pier; the two-mile-long Palisades Park; and the Third Street Promenade, a revamped and highly successful pedestrian mall. At the same time, some sections of the downtown are run-down and deserted at night and on weekends.

That picture could soon change. In late July, the Santa Monica city council approved a five-phase, $18.7 million downtown streetscape plan prepared by the ROMA Design Group of San Francisco. The plan is aimed at improving traffic and transit patterns, creating stronger pedestrian and transit linkages, and luring new shops and restaurants to the 28-block downtown core. It envisions wider sidewalks on several key streets, improved landscaping, and new street furniture and lighting.

City officials say work is scheduled to start this month on the plan's $500,000 first phase.

Inspiration

If Santa Monicans want proof that change is possible, they need only look at the Third Street Promenade.

Once a thriving main street, the old Third Street had seriously declined by

Originally published as "Onward and Upward in Downtown Santa Monica," Planning, Vol. 63, No. 9, September, 1997. Published by the American Planning Association, 122 South Michigan Avenue, Suite 1600, Chicago, Illinois 60603-6107. Reprinted with permission of the publisher.

the mid–1960s as shopping malls in other communities drew customers away. In 1965, in an effort to compete, the city followed the prevailing planning wisdom and converted three blocks of Third Street into a pedestrian mall.

For a while, the strategy worked. The problem was that adjacent blocks kept declining, pulling the Third Street mall down with them. The mall also had some serious design flaws, including its 600-foot-long blocks and 80-foot-wide pavement.

The final blow came with the opening in 1980 of a new enclosed shopping center, Santa Monica Place, at the south end of Third Street. The center became one of the nation's most successful shopping centers, while the Third Street mall became a concrete wasteland.

The Promenade

In 1986, the city commissioned the ROMA Design Group to come up with a revitalization plan for the pedestrian mall. "Our design for Third Street Promenade was based on the premise that a city's public spaces—its streets, parks, plazas, and other gathering places— are the principal stages on which the life of the city is acted out," says Boris Dramov, the design principal for the project. Following the plan, the city installed new 30-foot-wide sidewalks to encourage strolling while lessening the impact of the mall's excessive width. New sidewalk cafes soon followed. The city also planted dozens of trees and hung banners from poles. And it created a new "mixed-use zone" down the center of Third Street, a place for kiosks, newsstands, art displays, seating areas, and even topiary dinosaurs. The mixed-

use zone broke up the long blocks into smaller, more welcoming activity areas.

To complement—not compete with—the popular Santa Monica Place, the 1986 plan gave priority to entertainment and food rather than retail, says former mayor Dennis Zane. At the same time, the city put zoning controls on commercial development in other areas. Among other things, the new zoning forbade the construction of new movie theaters anywhere but on Third Street.

Success came quickly. The first new occupants—several multiplex theaters and a group of moderately priced restaurants—became magnets for other new businesses, including a number of specialty shops. Thanks to a zoning incentive—an increase in floor area ratio— apartments were built atop a new restaurant and entertainment complex. Retail sales have risen every year since 1989, even during the recession years of the early 1990s. In 1992, ROMA's plan for the mall won a national urban design award from the American Institute of Architects.

This summer, the promenade had a 100 percent occupancy rate, reports Kathleen Rawson, executive director of the Bayside District Corporation, the management entity created by the city. Shops, restaurants, and movie theaters generated more than $1.3 million in local sales taxes in 1996. Some 20,000 shoppers and visitors flock to the mall on a good weekend, Rawson says.

The makeover is not without its critics. One target of their complaints is national retail chains such as Disney and Banana Republic, which moved in several years ago, displacing some of the locally owned businesses that gave the Third Street Promenade a distinctive character.

Another often-heard complaint is that Third Street caters to tourists at the expense of Santa Monicans. A particularly irksome feature, critics say, is the increasing number of noisy street performers. "What started out as a very innovative and cute feature that attracted people has gotten overloaded, almost chaotic," says Paul Rosenstein, city council member and chair of the downtown urban design plan steering committee.

Moving On

Now the city hopes to capitalize on Third Street's success and solve some of its problems at the same time. "One of the key goals of the new streetscape plan," says ROMA's Boris Dramov, "is to transfer some of Third Street Promenade's energy and crowds onto nearby streets." The hope is that lower-rent Second and Fourth streets will attract local merchants and the unusual stores and cafes that many residents and visitors look for.

The plan also seeks to create strong pedestrian activity on streets like Santa Monica Boulevard to balance the crowds that gather on the Third Street Promenade.

A second goal, says Dramov, is to restore downtown streets to their original role as public meeting places. Parades, farmers' markets, street fairs, and sidewalk sales are all part of the picture.

To improve traffic circulation and reduce congestion, the plan calls for making two one-way streets, Fifth and Broadway, two way; redirecting traffic onto other underused streets; and ensuring slow-speed vehicular access throughout the downtown. The idea, says Dramov, is to make sure that pedestrians, not drivers, get top priority on downtown streets.

In an effort to define the downtown core, the plan recommends that a richly landscaped formal gateway be created at the Fifth Street exit ramp from the Santa Monica Freeway. The plan also recommends that palms and flowering trees be planted along Ocean, Colorado, Lincoln, and Wilshire boulevards, streets that define the core.

Finally, street furniture—including specially designed transit shelters—should be installed to bolster the impression of a community-oriented space, Dramov says. For instance, benches would be placed in clusters facing away from street traffic. The plan also includes design guidelines for elements that open to and interact with the street—entries, courtyards, gardens, windows, and signs, for instance.

Getting Into Gear

Phase one, which includes restriping Fifth Street and Broadway to make them two-way, and adding curbside parking on Fourth Street as a traffic calming measure, is expected to be complete by Thanksgiving. The city will use already budgeted general funds for this work, according to planning department sources.

The $5 million for phase two, which is likely to begin in mid–1998, is also budgeted. This phase involves more extensive streetscape improvements, with big changes for Santa Monica Boulevard between Ocean Avenue and Fifth Street.

"We will take a lane of traffic out of Santa Monica Boulevard, and all curbside parking will be eliminated in these four blocks," Rosenstein explains. "We will widen the sidewalks on each side by 12 feet to create a pedestrian promenade with plenty of space for sidewalk cafes. The center of the roadway will have one lane of traffic in each direction. One curbside land will be designated for transit. The other curbside lane will be set aside for cabs, valet parking for restaurants, and loading activities."

The redesigned boulevard will lead people past the Third Street Promenade intersection, two blocks down to Ocean Avenue and Palisades Park, and then over to the Santa Monica Pier, which boasts a new Ferris wheel and roller coaster.

Uncertainties

Funding for subsequent projects could prove more difficult, particularly since last year's passage of Proposition 218, which requires California municipalities to win the approval of affected property owners before they can impose special assessments.

Nonetheless, the outlook for implementation of the downtown streetscape plan is good, given Santa Monica's excellent fiscal condition and good planning and development track record. According to the city finance department, Santa Monica is the only California municipality with an AAA bond rating.

"Most cities are so economically strapped that they will do anything to get new development," says Rosenstein. "They can't be choosy about developers or design issues. Sometimes, they're not even aware of the best thinking on urban design. So they take whatever happens."

In contrast, he says, Santa Monica has a clear vision of what it wants to be. "We have a dream of what our downtown could be like—a vibrant place where all kinds of people can live, shop, work, and recreate—and do it safely, without having to dodge traffic at every step."

CHAPTER 24

Bringing Back Neighborhood Streets in Boulder, Colorado

John M. Fernandez

Boulder, Colorado, has a problem shared by cities across the country. Too many of its streets divide rather than integrate. They are single-purpose arteries, emphasizing cars over people. They despoil the environment with their expansive impervious surfaces. They encourage speeding. And they support faceless suburban development patterns guaranteed to worsen traffic congestion.

Residential streets are key determinants of neighborhood quality. They offer a place to walk, to play—and of course to park. yet ever since the start of the post–World War II housing boom, residential streets have become increasingly devoted to traffic movement. The wide lanes required by today's codes lead to higher speeds, more accidents, and greater urban fragmentation.

In recent years, many planners—and even some traffic engineers—have begun to question whether wider streets are as functional as their advocates claim. Increasingly, designers, public officials, and developers—often spurred by neighborhood activists—are considering the virtues of a hierarchical street classification that would provide for a variety of residential street types, each reflecting different traffic conditions.

Local History

Like many western cities, Boulder was laid out, in 1859, on a grid based on

Originally published as "Boulder Brings Back the Neighborhood Street," Planning, Vol. 60, No. 6, June, 1994. Published by the American Planning Association, 122 South Michigan Avenue, Suite 1600, Chicago, Illinois 60603-6107. Reprinted with permission of the publisher.

a 400-foot block and 25-foot lots, a pattern admirably suited to speculation. It should be noted, however, that the Boulder City Town Company set high rates for town lots, up to $1,000 for a 50-by-140-foot building site. Even then, it appears, Boulder favored slower growth.

The post–World War II subdivisions disrupted the grid pattern, with larger lots and blocks set along curvilinear streets, and no alleys. In the 1960s and 1970s, more cul-de-sacs appeared, with fewer connections to adjacent development. Today, the city is characterized by a high rate of car ownership (two vehicles for every three people) and a significant jobs-to-housing imbalance. Boulder's employment-to-population ratio is 0.83, more than 40 percent higher than the figure for the eight-county Denver metropolitan region. If current trends continue, total employment will exceed population by 2010.

Boulder also has several recent examples of more sensitive residential planning. In 1983, a local developer built The Cottages, a 37-unit affordable housing project. The 5.3-acre site abuts city-owned open space on the north side. And in 1990, another local developer, William Coburn, built Walnut Hollow, a high-end infill project consisting of nine Victorian-style houses— with detached garages—arrayed along an 18-foot-wide street just each of downtown.

But these projects, both planned unit developments, resulted largely from individual initiatives and not from a communitywide vision of what constitutes better urban development. Moreover, neither would be allowed under the current regulations. In the past, the city's planning department used the PUD or-

dinance to vary street standards. But as concerns grew over liability, policy makers were unwilling to grant individual waivers in the absence of new citywide street standards.

For the most part, recent new subdivisions have complied absolutely with the letter of the Boulder rules, laid down in the zoning code and subdivision regulations adopted in 1971. The result: three-car garagescape uniformity, the "loops and lollipops" pattern exhibited so well in the city's expanding northeast quadrant.

In 1992, the planning department, aware of the community's growing unhappiness with the look and operation of the new subdivisions, decided to take a more aggressive role in the neighborhood design. The staff noted that the city's 1989 transportation master plan called for new residential street guidelines to enhance neighborhood safety and livability.

As it happened, a large new project had just been proposed for the northeast edge of the city—the 140-acre Four Mile Creek. The planning department hired Peter Brown, AICP, an urban designer in Houston, to conduct a design charette before the project entered the development review phase. Brown toured the site and interviewed the developers, a consortium of local builders. Then, working with other team members, he compared construction costs for both a conventional subdivision and a neotraditional design, complete with narrow streets and pedestrian paths, and drew sketch plan alternatives.

The plan that resulted was then presented to the developers, and they used many of the neotraditional design elements in their annexation application. (The annexation ordinance was the legal device used to vary the city's street standards.) The 309-unit project is now under construction. Its gridded street plan includes both boulevards and narrow streets. It also features short blocks; motor courts (oblong cul-de-sacs with central landscaping and parking); a raised intersection (road surface matches elevation of crosswalk); traffic circles; and an alley. There is also an extensive bicycle and pedestrian path network.

The Four Mile Creek exercise was considered a success in that it convinced the city to move beyond simply responding to proposals to assuming a leadership role in defining a vision for development. Under the leadership of its new planning director, Will Fleissig, Boulder is now attempting to relate its street design standards to an overall community planning and urban design program.

Complete Overhaul

The vehicle for this new approach is the Resident Access Project (RAP), which was initiated jointly in the spring of 1992 by the city's planning and public works departments. The impetus was the increasing restiveness of neighborhood residents concerned about traffic congestion. At that point, the planning staff proposed to broaden the residential street guidelines to include the entire movement network in residential areas and to create urban design guidelines.

The entire project is being carried out in house, with no special funding except for a small graphics budget. Both the public works staff member—a transportation planner—and I devote about a fifth of our time to RAP. We report to an interdepartmental steering committee.

The first part of the two-phase project was aimed at devising a statement of purpose and a richer menu of street standards. The project staff has spent the last two years researching standards in other cities and involving residents in a collaborative planning process. A spinoff effort, the neighborhood traffic mitigation program, will encourage the use of traffic calming measures.

In March of this year, the planning board endorsed the staff's recommendation that the city's one-size-fits-all street standard be replaced. The current standard requires 12-foot travel lanes, six-foot parking lanes, curb, gutter, and sidewalk in a 48-foot right-of-way. The new standards would offer four classifications, all of them narrower than the current requirement.

The two lowest classifications would be low-speed (15–20 m.p.h.) "queuing" streets. They could be as narrow as 20 feet, and they would allow on-street parking. To mollify fire officials, the standards provide for fire set-up areas (pads long and wide enough to accommodate fire trucks and close enough together so fire hoses can reach the back of all dwellings).

The standards would also allow alleys, which are officially discouraged in the current subdivision regulations. The planners noted that Boulder residents consistently rate traditional neighborhoods with alleys as most livable.

The planning board also endorsed the staff's recommended street purposes statement. A clear definition of intent is expected to guide all those involved in administering the new regulations.

The final proposal for phase one is to be presented to the planning board this month. The next step is to translate the proposal into an ordinance for consideration by the city council. That's expected to be done this summer.

Phase two of RAP will address the broader topic of residential-area design, including the building-street relationship, network standards, and "shared" streets (such as the Dutch woonerf). A set of performance-based standards will parallel the new prescriptive standards.

The planning department is putting the draft standards to the test in a subcommunity plan now being prepared for north Boulder. With 9,200 residents spread over 2,300 acres, "NoBo" is the least developed of the city's nine subcommunities. It was annexed four years ago, and its many vacant and underutilized parcels are considered ripe for redevelopment.

At a five-day public charette held the first week of May in the National Guard Armory, more than 300 citizens suggested ways of intensifying the movement grid and reconnecting streets. Their recommendations included both boulevards and skinny streets. A Miami-based urban design consulting firm, Dover, Kohl & Partners, is incorporating their recommendations and many of the RAP concepts into the plan being prepared for city council consideration in July.

Searching Out Models

There seemed to be few models when Boulder started this project two summers ago. Most jurisdictions still use some variation of the highway-oriented street standards that arose in the late 1930s with the creation of the Federal Highway Administration and the "Green Book" published by AASHTO,

the American Association of State Highway and Transportation Officials.

Recently, designers associated with the movement coming to be known as "the new urbanism"—Andres Duany, Anton Nelessen, AICP, Peter Calthorpe, and others—have received considerable media attention. But most of their work has been on large tracts of raw land, not the infill projects that are typical of places like Boulder.

There are other models with broader applicability to the situations in which most planners find themselves: infill, redevelopment, and fringe-area development.

One such example is an early one, the "performance streets" standard adopted by Bucks County, Pennsylvania, in 1980. It provides a model ordinance that includes a rich hierarchy of street types, although its use as a model is limited by the emphasis on cul-de-sacs and loop streets, and its lack of attention to alternative modes of travel.

The performance streets concept is also the basis of a new set of supplemental standards for residential neighborhoods now being considered by the city of Houston and surrounding Harris County. The city currently has only two types of residential streets: a 28-foot pavement section with a 50-foot or 60-foot right-of-way. The new standards would create eight street types and allow narrower streets in new subdivisions, with such design elements as "chicanes" (jogs to slow traffic) and flareouts. The standards were prepared by Peter Brown in collaboration with Patricia D. Knudson & Associates and Terra Associates, both of Houston.

Portland, Oregon's 1991 "skinny streets" ordinance applies to residential blocks where lots are over 5,000 square feet. It allows 20-foot-wide streets with parking on one side, or 26-foot-wide streets with parking on both sides—thus overturning the long-entrenched idea that all streets must provide at least two through lanes of traffic. City engineer Terry Bray reports that 30 blocks of skinny streets were built in the first two construction seasons.

Olympia, Washington's state capital, has approved transportation policies that prohibit new cul-de-sacs. The policies, adopted in 1992, are an outgrowth of a visual preference survey and urban design plan undertaken with the help of New Jersey consultant Anton Nelessen.

Nelessen also prepared the urban design guidelines now being reviewed in Santa Fe, New Mexico. The guidelines offer 16 distinct land-use and circulation prototypes. Widths range downward to 18 feet, sometimes with no building setback requirement, and curb radiuses as tight as four feet. Frank Diluzio, the city's newly appointed fire chief, says he supports the standards provided that new streets "pretty much keep a 20-foot clear zone," meaning that no parking rules must be strictly enforced.

In Squim, Washington, a retirement community on the Olympic Peninsula, a "block standard" includes a 12-foot alley in a 20-foot easement. Public works director Richard Parker says the alleys work well for utility placement and the city's automated garbage collection system.,

Another model is the west end of Vancouver, British Columbia, where traffic calming measures have proven to be an important adjunct to street standards. Street closures and diverters have created a pleasant walking environment in a high-rise district flanked by busy shopping streets.

But the most promising model is an Australian one: the code for residential development prepared in 1992 by the planning and housing department in the state of Victoria. This exemplary document covers the entire residential environment, from lot orientation to regional street networks, and it defines a broad hierarchy of local streets.

The Victoria code includes both performance-based and prescriptive standards, and is specific about details like deflection angles (for speed control). It also requires that all dwellings be located no more than 700 meters (about 2,300 feet) and three "junctions," or intersections, from a major street to balance the amount of time motorists are forced to spend in low-speed environments.

Most important, the code requires development planners to plot out pedestrian and bicycle lanes as well as the usual environmental constraints and opportunities—before the street system is laid out. In this, the Australian planners echo the advice of California architect Christopher Alexander, who says that in urban design, pedestrian spaces should be designed first, then the buildings, then the roads.

Wendy Morris, the senior urban designer in the department's Melbourne offices, described the code in Alexandria, Virginia, last October at the first Congress on the New Urbanism. She said a key to making it effective has been interdisciplinary workshops: "We found that to make real change in building patterns, those who make design, permitting, and development decisions must be involved and retrained."

Ready for Change

Back in the U.S., the Florida Department of Community Affairs has undertaken an ambitious project to develop "community design guidelines" for everything from energy conservation to affordable housing to streets. The project's principal researcher, Reid Ewing, of the Joint Center for Environmental and Urban Problems at Florida Atlantic University/Florida International University in Fort Lauderdale, says the "overriding rationale is to make the street more livable, less energy-consumptive, and environmentally sound." His team has proposed a 20-foot wide standard for all local streets.

Ben Starrett, the director of strategic planning and policy coordination for the community affairs department, says he expects the guidelines to be published soon.

Even the Institute for Transportation Engineers, long a holdout against alternative street standards, is becoming part of the solution. In February, the institute's technical committee on neotraditional town design issued an "informational report" entitled *Traffic Engineering for Neotraditional Neighborhoods*. Frank Spielberg, a traffic engineering consultant in Annandale, Virginia, who chairs the committee, says members hope that ITE will endorse the "recommended practices," which include narrower streets in some cases, within the next year.

As to liability, the bugaboo of city officials, one member of the ITE committee, Walter Kulash—a traffic engineer in Orlando—contends that "legal obstacles to narrow streets are a red herring." He notes that a 1993 study he coauthored for the National Conference on Tort Liability and Risk Management for Surface Transportation concluded that tort cases "invariably have to do with high speed," not street width.

Finally, for those ready to change, a few basic reminders:

The public interest requires safe, livable, and attractive streets that contribute to the urban fabric.

Streets should be designed to suit their function. Many streets, especially local ones, have purposes other than vehicular traffic. Some local residential streets should be designed for speeds of less than 20 m.p.h. Remember that the general population is aging, with the cohort over 85 growing fastest of all.

A hierarchical street network should have a rich variety of types, including bicycle, pedestrian, and transit routes.

Reid Ewing believes that the "overall system design has fallen into the cracks between the planning and engineering professions." The entire movement network should be considered, with connectivity given prominence.

Standards should be developed to enhance local streets' contributions to urban design. That means paying attention to "sense of enclosure" ratios (on residential streets, the distance between houses should be no more than 80 to 100 feet), landscaping, parking, setbacks, lot width to depth ratios, block length and perimeter maximums, materials, street furnitures, and signs.

A useful guide might be the "performance street" concept, which matches street types with adjacent land uses. Creating a street plan based on this model might seem a daunting task, but be assured that controlling scale (what's called "morphological zoning") can go a long way to ensuring the proper mix of urban elements.

Make the new standards available for infill and redevelopment, not just for new development. Where densification is a concern, maintain existing rights-of-way but narrow roadway width.

Streets should be designed in a collaborative, interdisciplinary process. Do a visual preference survey. Try workshops and charettes. Include your legal counsel. After construction, set up what Kulash calls a "robust, simple, and executable monitoring system."

Don't let cost stop you. We estimate that it will take $1.3 million to reconfigure Norwood Avenue, a 6,000-foot-long residential subcollector in north Boulder, as a 20-foot-wide street incorporating such traffic-calming measures as raised intersections, berms, a multipurpose path, and neckdowns (flared curbs constricting a street en-trance). It would take $2.3 million to build a typical 32-foot-wide street. The reconfiguration design has been approved by the city council and is now going through the capital improvements programming process.

Ideally, putting these ideas into effect will lead to a revival of street-centered small communities. Vaclav Havel, president of the Czech Republic, put it best in his 1992 book, *Summer Meditations*, "Villages and towns," he wrote, "will once again begin to have their own distinctive appearance, ... and the environment will become a source of quiet everyday pleasure for us all."

By planning our residential areas at a human scale, considering the needs of the most vulnerable among us, and relegating the automobile to its proper role, we can regain what we have lost.

CHAPTER 25

What West Palm Beach, Florida, Learned from the Shopping Malls

Steven Lagerfeld

Shopping with Robert Gibbs is like being shown around a museum of retailing by an eccentric curator. He mutters frequently, counting under his breath and pointing vaguely at store windows. He expounds enthusiastically upon foot-candles and price-point-to-aperture ratios. He is cast into gloom by what he calls internally illuminated signs.

Gibbs has the sort of occupation Anne Tyler might invent for a character in one of her novels. He is a retail consultant who travels the country telling towns and small cities how to survive and prosper by learning the lessons of a shopping mall. Trained as a landscape architect at the University of Michigan

at Ann Arbor, Gibbs worked for a dozen years as a retailing specialist in the service of strip-shopping-center and shopping-mall developers, studying, debating, and adjusting virtually everything that might affect a shopper's mood in the marketplace, from color schemes to the location of escalators. In a well-run mall, Gibbs says, even the benches are positioned so that the shopper at rest cannot help gazing at the wares offered in store windows. The overriding imperative is to lose no opportunity, no matter how small, to make a sale.

Gibbs walks down Clematis Street, the main shopping street in West Palm Beach, Florida, as if he were navigating a maze, seeming utterly distracted even

Originally published as "What Main Street Can Learn from the Mall," The Atlantic, Vol. 276, No. 5, November, 1997. Published by The Atlantic Monthly Company, Boston, Massachusetts. Reprinted with permission of the publisher and the author.

as he searches intently for clues to the street's secrets. At forty he still has something of a smirking manner of the high school wise guy. But on Clematis Street he is all business.

Gibbs is impressed that most of the trash cans and newspaper vending machines have been painted the same dark green, a fashionable hue now used in many malls. Even a pair of two-by-fours supporting a tree have been painted. "A little detail you would expect in mall management," Gibbs says approvingly.

At the corner of Clematis and Dixie Highway, one of the main intersections in town, a new gym has opened, its large plate-glass windows displaying its clientele to passing pedestrians and motorists. The gym is what Gibbs calls a "generator": the traffic it draws will help attract related businesses, such as restaurants, fast-food outlets, perhaps sporting-goods store, to the empty storefronts nearby.

The gym is also a brilliant piece of street theater, telling all who pass its windows that West Palm is young, hip, and attractive. It is not here by accident. Borrowing a page from shopping-mall management, the city's Downtown Development Authority and the City Center Partnership, an allied local nonprofit organization, have used loans and other incentives to manipulate the "tenant mix." They worked for four years to lure the gym to this important location. The DDA is a significant advantage to West Palm Beach, as is the energetic mayor, Nancy M. Graham. The city has attracted several plum projects in recent years, including a massive new county courthouse. In 1992 the city council approved a $12 million bond issue to renovate the downtown district. Other money was appropriated to convert Clematis from a one-way into a two-way street and to install new sidewalks, lights, and palm trees.

Half a block east of the gym, at 331 Clematis, Provident Jewelry and Loan offers more evidence of the city's ability to shape the street. A pawnshop that once lent a vaguely disreputable air to the neighborhood, Provident has been transformed with the aid of loans from the City Center Partnership. With a fresh coat of paint, a dapper awning, and a prim new sign that doesn't shout "pawnshop," it has become an upright citizen and an asset to Clematis Street. The Imperial Gallery, a frame shop, and The Last Resort, a Generation X clothing store, both opened up with loans and other help.

Elsewhere on Clematis a large old building is being carved up into smaller stores. To lend their operations a bit of local flavor, well-managed malls often create tiny low-rent spaces called "incubators" and recruit local entrepreneurs to set up shop; some of them will thrive and open bigger stores. West Palm Beach is doing the same thing.

There are reasons to be hopeful about West Palm Beach, and about other towns and cities that are willing to borrow intelligently from the lessons of the mall. For the first time in decades strong trends in the national retail market seem to be working in their favor. A reaction is setting in against the monotony and homogeneity of the shopping mall. People are spending less time in malls—an average of only an hour and a half to two hours a month this year, according to one source, as compared with three and a half hours a month in 1990—and few new malls are being built. Only four new regional malls (800,000 square feet or larger) opened in the United

States last year, as compared with twenty-seven in 1989.

Part of the explanation for this change is simply that suburban markets have become saturated, and part is that strip shopping centers, "big-box" retailers, and "power centers" that bring high-volume discounters together in one location are drawing customers away from the malls. But mall fatigue is a potent factor. In focus groups people tell Gibbs that they are tired of shopping in malls filled with the same stores that they can find everywhere else in the country. Many say they want to shop in downtowns, in quaint, one-of-a-kind stores. Gibbs does not have a monopoly on this intelligence. Retailers are already responding. Nordstrom has recently agreed to open a store in downtown Norfolk, Virginia. Even major discount retailers like Caldor and Kmart are feeling the lure of downtown markets. Kmart plans to open a store in Manhattan next year, in the historic Herald Square shopping district. "Signs of an urban boom can be found almost everywhere," the trade publication *Shopping Centers Today* reported last fall.

Gibbs came to West Palm Beach, a city of more than 70,000, two years ago, to work on a new master plan for the city with Andres Duany and Elizabeth Plater-Zyberk, the Miami-based pioneers of the New Urbanism. This small but influential movement among architects and urban planners proposes to revive nineteenth-century town-planning principles, using denser development and gridded street systems, among other things, as an antidote to suburban sprawl. Duany and Plater-Zyberk's greatest success so far has been the much-publicized new town of Seaside, a resort community in the Florida

panhandle. But Gibbs's enthusiasm for the New Urbanist cause and for downtowns in general doesn't stop him from working for the occasional shopping-mall company that seeks his services. And his own office, with its small staff, is located not in a gritty city but in the genteel town of Birmingham, Michigan, an affluent Detroit suburb.

What Gibbs contributes to complex cooperative projects like the one in West Palm Beach is a commercial sensibility unlike anything possessed by the urban planners and architects who usually design downtown-renewal efforts. Addressing audiences of such specialists, Gibbs takes a puckish delight in shocking them all with his view on conventional urban planning. He shows them slides of a generic "success" in street design and then points out, feature by feature, how the design actually hurts the town's businesses.

The shade trees and planter boxes? Lovely, he says, but they block shoppers' view of shop windows and signs. Those handsome groupings of benches and tables? They seem inviting until Gibbs points out that they often attract teenagers and other loiterers, who scare off shoppers. The elegant Victorian street-lamps, the expensive trash cans, and the distinctive granite paving stones—"so beautiful that people will stare at them as they walk by the storefronts," Gibbs says—are little more than money down the drain. Their costs must be amortized over many years, but long before they have been paid off (and before the town can afford to replace them) they will be old-fashioned, marking the entire street as out of date and out of step.

Gibbs sometimes clinches an argument by showing his audience slides of some of the world's most opulent shopping streets, including Palm Beach's Worth Avenue, which happens to be located about a mile (and a world) away from Clematis Street. The Worth Avenue slide reveals a pleasant but extremely plain street. It is lined with a row of palms and simple light poles. Its sidewalks, conspicuously, are mere concrete.

As Gibbs and I traverse Clematis Street over the course of two days, he pauses time and again to consider the textured sidewalk paving blocks that have been installed since his last visit. There is no question that they are attractive. But are they too porous to keep clean? Too fancy?

This is not the kind of question that planners and architects often ask themselves. They tend to see streets and sidewalks strictly as a civic realm, a social environment where people meet and interact, and they tend to favor the sorts of attractive sidewalks and streetscapes that seem to promote sociability. If they are not greatly concerned about the impact of their work on the welfare of haberdashers and stationers, that is not surprising. They belong to professions that are often at war with commercial interests.

Gibbs sees the street first as a commercial space. Nourish commerce, his implicit credo goes, and the people will come. A dirty street, a sidewalk spotted with old chewing gum and grime, is a turnoff for shoppers. And if people won't come downtown to shop, there simply won't be a civic realm.

Fear of crime is one of the things that keeps them away, and grimy sidewalks are one of many signs that hint at disorder, in Gibbs's view. Standing outside the gym at the corner of Clematis and Dixie Highway, he discourses at length on an untidy collection of

benches, tables, and chairs outside a café across the highway. This is civic space only in theory. In fact it poses a threat to civic existence. "Those benches make it look like this is a very difficult place to walk," he says, putting himself in the shoes of the average (that is, female) shopper. "You've got to squeeze between those benches. And if a teenager or some street person happens to be there, you would have to touch them, because you're so close together. That is like a sign saying DON'T ENTER."

Ironically, one of the forces working in favor of downtowns today is the erosion of the shopping malls' image as a safe haven from crime. Only a few years ago, Gibbs reminds me, it was rare to see uniformed security officers in malls, because the mere sight of a uniform was thought to be unsettling to shoppers. Today uniforms guards seem reassuring, and they can be seen in malls everywhere. Even janitors are equipped with thick, military-style belts and walkie-talkies. Parking lots are patrolled by security vehicles that proclaim their presence with roof-mounted flashing lights. The Palm Beach Mall, just a few miles from Clematis Street, is so notoriously locally as a dangerous place that all pretenses have been abandoned: the parking lot is studded with tall observation towers, making it resemble nothing so much as a prison yard.

Towns, Gibbs insists, must follow the malls' example in dealing with the public's fears. That means ensuring a visible police presence, removing or rearranging benches and other features that encourage loitering, and keeping the streets and sidewalks clean. Mall managers, ever inventive, are now improving the lighting in their parking lots. The norm for illumination was a footcandle or less just a few years ago, Gibbs says. Now it is closer to three footcandles. Many self-service gas stations, which must offer a reassuring prospect to lure passing motorists off the road, are now lit up like Hollywood sound stages. The lighting in West Palm Beach? Three quarters to one footcandle, Gibbs estimated.

A town's retail planning, Gibbs, says, should begin where a mall's does—far from the selling floors. A simple example of mall thinking is what Gibbs calls the "no-left-turn rule": Never locate a shopping center in a place where commuters will have to make a left turn to get in. People tend to shop on their way home from work, the thinking goes, and they are less likely to stop if it involves making a turn against traffic.

This is no idle observation. At one point in his career Gibbs traveled around the country as a member of a team evaluating sites for future shopping malls. Gibbs recalls that the opinion of the traffic consultant mattered most. He vetoed so many sites that he was called The Terminator.

There is a corollary for towns and strip shopping centers: coffee shops and doughnut stores ought to be located on the workbound side of a main road, grocery stores and other services on the homebound side. "Just one left turn will kill you," Gibbs says.

Mall merchandising begins in the parking lot. Gibbs points out that at the Gardens of the Palm Beaches, an upscale mall several miles from West Palm Beach, the plantings around the building and parking lots, with their lush, tightly trimmed shrubs, seem to suggest that shoppers are arriving at a special place, and that perhaps they are special as well. It's almost like having a door-

man. It's certainly a far cry from the feeling one gets in the rundown West Palm Beach parking lot where Gibbs and I parked.

Once, guiding me into a lavish urban mall called Georgetown Park in Washington, D.C., Gibbs was able to predict which way I would turn upon entering. Most casual shoppers who are not immediately bound for a specific store—which is to say most shoppers—travel counterclockwise. Nobody knows why, though it's reasonable to suppose that driving on the right-hand side of the road has something to do with it. A good mall designer will take special care to ensure that entering shoppers have a powerful unobstructed vista of storefronts to their right. Rarely will that vista run the length of the mall, however. It is a cardinal rule to keep shoppers' eyes on the merchandise at all times. Designers try to configure malls with enough twists and turns that the shopper looking ahead is constantly looking toward a wall of storefronts. Gibbs is so convinced of the importance of what he calls the "deflected view" that in laying out the main shopping street of a small new development in Novi, Michigan, he puts thirty-degree turns near its middle. Straight streets, he believes, are one of the biggest commercial handicaps in a town like West Palm Beach.

There are other rules. Clothing stores, for example, should never be located next to restaurants: for some reason the smell of food hurts clothing sales. In downtown areas clothing stores should never be located on the north side of a street: the colors of clothes displayed in a shop window with a southern exposure begin to fade within hours. Western exposures are bad for restaurants: the setting sun at dinner-time makes customers uncomfortable. Restaurants can prosper on side streets and in other less-desirable locations, because they usually do not rely heavily on drop-in business. They are destinations. Most retail stores count on drawing a lot of impulse shoppers, and thus need to be located in high-traffic areas.

Designers also know that the average shopper, strolling along at three or four feet per second, walks past a storefront in about eight seconds. That's how long a shop owner has to grab a consumer's attention with an arresting window display. Downtown merchants must live with the same eight-second rule, but they can also sell to passing motorists—and the window of opportunity for "merchandising to the car," as Gibbs puts it, is less than a second.

Sophisticated retailers use a variety of subliminal clues to attract shoppers. At Georgetown Park, Gibbs pointed out a high-priced stationery store that had created a window display featuring a small old wooden desk with a few pricey writing implements casually strewn about, including four ordinary-seeming lead pencils in a wooden box, priced at $215. The tableau, Gibbs informed me, was "lifestyling" par excellence—focusing the shopper's attention not on the goods themselves but on attractive things associated with them. Buy these outrageously expensive pencils, the display suggested, and you will have taken one more step toward a life of tweeds and contemplation in the English countryside.

The lifestyling message was amplified by the window designer's skillful exploitation of what is called the price-point-to-aperture ratio. The appealing desk-and-pencils tableau was framed inside the window, much as a picture is positioned inside a mat in a picture frame. In retailing the size of the aperture is often used to provide shoppers with clues about what is in the store. A relatively small enclosed space suggests high quality and prices to match. This is one reason why Tiffany & Co. displays its wares to passersby in tiny vaultlike spaces. Big windows and big displays generally suggest lower prices.

The Duany and Plater-Zyberk plan for West Palm Beach calls for a revitalized downtown core and also thousands of units of new housing in the surrounding area, now a depressing jumble of empty lots, old buildings, and gas stations. The dimensions of the challenge facing the city became clear to me after I drove through the area for the first time on heavily traveled Dixie Highway: I sped through the intersection with Clematis without realizing that it was the heart of downtown West Palm Beach, not just another cross street in the area's endless grid of semi-urban sprawl.

In the past the neglect of commerce by planners and architects was compounded by an inability to cope with the automobile. The car has generally been treated as an enemy, with disastrous results for downtown commerce. During the 1960s and 1970s, for example, there was a great vogue in planning circles for banning cars from downtown streets and creating pedestrian malls. The experiment was disastrous. Many downtown malls have since been ripped up, and the streets rebuilt for automotive traffic.

Surveying a small parking lot just off Clematis, Gibbs says that a conventional urban planner would waste no time converting it into a park, with benches, trees, and perhaps a fountain. "The shoppers will be happier if they have a place to sit and watch the fountain," he says, in disdainful deadpan imitation of a hypothetical planner's argument. In Gibbs's view, the problem is that people won't stop, park their cars, and get out to visit such a park. And if they don't do that, the merchants of West Palm Beach won't have an opportunity to sell them anything.

Slowly, however, towns are coming to grips with the car. At the intersection of Clematis and El Campeon Boulevard, Gibbs can barely make himself heard over the roar of heavy machinery. Even before he and his colleagues were called in to help draw up the new master plan, city officials had decided to reroute the traffic that flows over one of the Palm Beach bridges and around the outskirts of town onto an extended and widened El Campeon, recently renamed Quadrille. The goal, virtually unheard of in late-twentieth-century America, is to pump more cars into the downtown.

For Gibbs's purposes, not just any kind of traffic will do. Just east of that intersection Clematis Street is bisected by U.S. 1—which is actually two one-way roads when it passes through West Palm Beach. Cars and trucks speed by, creating a forbidding double moat that slashes through Clematis and discourages pedestrians from walking the length of the street.

The city's new master plan calls for a radical alteration of the traffic pattern. Both branches of U.S. 1 will be converted into two-way roads, with on-street parking, one lane in each direction, and a turning lane. Instead of flowing through town as quickly as water, traffic will slow to the speed of syrup. The idea is to transform this soulless thoroughfare into a vital city street.

As Gibbs sees it, Clematis Street is fighting the same problem that a lot of

other American main streets are: it doesn't have a purpose anymore. During the 1920s it connected the train station, on the west end of town, with the ferry to Palm Beach, on the east end. But after two bridges, on either side of town, began funneling traffic around Clematis, its fate was sealed. The Woolworth's, the McCrory's, and the Sears, Roebuck all continued to prosper for a while, but business inevitably followed the cars.

Historians analyzing the decline of America's towns and cities after the Second World War usually put most of the responsibility on the federal government's head. The interstate highway system and federal mortgage subsidies for single-family homes spurred suburban growth, the argument goes, and doomed the downtowns. In Gibbs's version of urban history, based on his travels, another force looms large: the highway bypass. As the number of cars on the road soared after the war, town merchants and residents sought relief from traffic-clogged streets. Their demands coincided with the interests of the state highway departments and traffic engineers, who wanted to keep building roads and whose highest professional goal was the unimpeded flow of cars. Routing highway traffic around the outskirts of town must have seemed the obvious thing to do. The downtowns thus unwittingly initiated their own march to a commercial grave.

Retailers flock to what Gibbs and other retailing specialists call a "main-main" intersection—the place where the two most heavily traveled roads in an area meet. Historically, towns grew up around main-mains. In one town after another across the country, the opening of a new bypass created a new main-main outside town. There, beginning in the 1950s, strip shopping centers began sprouting. Then came the interstate highways, creating where they crossed state highways or other interstates a new set of main-mains still farther from the old downtowns. It is usually at these new crossroads that one finds large regional shopping malls today.

Standing on the south side of Clematis under a hot Florida sun, Gibbs launches into an impassioned diagnosis—almost an autopsy—of a men's clothing store on the other side of the street, at No. 335. This touches on the matters that seem closest to his heart. Minutes before, he dragged me into the store almost against my will. Housed in an eight-year-old two-story building painted the color of putty, the store features a large blue umbrella awning overhung by a large internally illuminated white-plastic sign. The store's name appears in big letters of washed-out blue over the tag line MEN'S WEAR—SHOES. The sign seems to date from the 1950s or 1960s.

Inside, the store was everything I had feared—small, cramped, dark, and, in more ways than one, stuffy. Shoes and sport coats were displayed in closed glass case, and the store was dominated by a counter with cash register in the middle of the floor. The proprietor seemed to watch us suspiciously.

On the sidewalk Gibbs is almost angry. "You wouldn't have gone in there if I hadn't made you," he declares, "but he sells a lot of what you wear." He reels off a list of brand names he spotted in his expert visual frisking of the store: Corbin, Cole Haan, Allen-Edmonds, Bass, Sperry Top-Sider. These are "very fine names," Gibbs says, the kinds of brands that would interest affluent locals and tourists (not to mention visiting retail consultants and writers). But the store offers passersby barely a clue about what it has for sale.

Its most prominent signs should promote the brand names it carries, Gibbs says, to take advantage of the millions of dollars that big companies spend on advertising to shape perceptions of their products. And what would be good for this store would be good for West Palm Beach.

"People will see 'Cole Haan' and they will drive off the road," Gibbs explains. "They will say, 'I thought this was a dumpy area. If they sell Cole Haan, they can't be that bad.'"

The store could give itself an even bigger lift, according to Gibbs, by making use of a few rudimentary lifestyling gestures. To hear him tell it, lifestyling is the late-twentieth-century equivalent of the barber pole, announcing to shoppers what's for sale. It is ubiquitous in the mall but virtually nonexistent on Clematis Street and other American main streets. Its vocabulary is easily acquired. Simply placing a canoe paddle or a bicycle in the window of the men's store, Gibbs says, would telegraph several messages to passing shoppers, including the vital (and correct) information that it is selling clothes that fit what Gibbs classifies as "the L.L. Bean look."

Down the street, at Mac Fabrics, we count seven signs with the store's name on them, and none displaying brand names. "Brands are what give you credibility," Gibbs says. If he had his way, signs advertising brand names would hang from the imitation-antique light poles that line the street.

This, obviously, is not a sentimental view of the American town. Gibbs is not proposing to restore the cozy village of the popular imagination. Nor does he think that the town will ever eradicate the malls, Wal-Marts, power centers, and other commercial innovations of American retailing. The American shopper's expectations have by now been completely conditioned by malls and national advertisers. The shopper wants, at the very least, much more choice than the traditional town ever provided.

The same people who tell Gibbs in focus groups that they are tired of malls complain that many small towns are, well, too small. Why drive half an hour to browse through only a handful of stores? Gibbs's rule of thumb is that a town needs at least 200,000 square feet of retail space, about the same amount as in a small mall, to become what retailers call a destination—a place that people are willing to travel to.

And once they get to their destination, people don't really want to stop in old-fashioned small-town stores. Americans, in their time-honored way, want a variety of often contradictory things. They may like quaint, one-of-a-kind stores that seem to sell unique merchandise, but they also want the comfort and security of national brand names on the goods they buy, and they don't want to pay a lot for them.

Mall operators and national retailers are moving quickly to give people what they want, and Gibbs's message is that towns must do so too if they wish to survive and prosper. That still leaves plenty of room for individuality. Each town must build on its unique strengths and its unique markets. What can't be escaped, however, is the need for a conscious strategy for commercial survival.

Gibbs's prescriptions for the streets of West Palm Beach and of other American towns and small cities borrow so heavily from the mall that it becomes

difficult to see how, except for the absence of a roof over its streets, a place reconstructed along such lines would differ from a mall. It might be a town, but would it be a community?

When I ask him about this, Gibbs just shrugs his shoulders. He is not a philosopher-king. He does not pretend to know how to deliver an active civic life and a sense of community, but he believes that these things are impossible without a vital commercial life. That is something that he *can* help deliver.

He is not particularly worried that his prescriptions will lead to the homogenization of Main Street. The mall is a machine for shopping. In contrast, the pieces of the downtown shopping machine lie about unassembled, and in all likelihood they will never be put together in the way that they can be in a mall, with its single corporate owner. Main Street will always retain a certain redeeming randomness. But if it does not learn the ways of the shopping mall, it will not retain much economic vitality. People who care about cities, Gibbs says, should be outraged that mom-and-pop shoe-store owners renting space in a mall or a strip center enjoy the benefits of the latest thinking in retailing, while those who open for business downtown get virtually no help at all.

It is hard not to feel some trepidation about the world Robert Gibbs imagines. But it is also hard not to agree with him that commerce matters, even to the world his critics might prefer. The Greeks, after all, cherished their agora, but it was always first and foremost a place of business. It is probably true that community and civic spirit, like happiness and love, are often found when you're not looking—sometimes even when you're out shopping.

CHAPTER 26

Creative Infill Development Strategies in Buckland, Georgia

Jonathan D. Miller and Myron Orfield

"Battle Looms" blared a recent headline in the *Atlanta Journal Constitution*. Developers propose adding millions of square feet of office, retail, hotel, and residential space, but planners and residents say enormous problems, especially involving traffic, would ensue." The market at the center of the dispute is Buckhead, Atlanta's "uptown," probably the hottest and most dynamic urban center in Atlanta's swelling suburban agglomeration.

Twenty years ago, Buckhead was primarily an upscale residential area of single-family homes and two regional malls with some emerging office space, serving as a bedroom community for downtown, a 20-minute car commute away. Today, downtown Atlanta struggles without significant residential underpinnings, and areas like Buckhead thrive.

Until recently, real estate investors simply had characterized office markets as downtown or suburban. The so-called edge city entered the lexicon in the early 1990s to describe commercial centers like Buckhead that were becoming more attractive real estate markets at the expense of traditional downtowns. In fact, many observers had begun to discount downtown cores as skyscraper values plummeted and to tout the suburbs as the best places to invest.

Intuitively, such thinking makes considerable sense. After 40 years of

Originally published as "Suburbs in Flux," Urban Land, Vol. 57, No. 3, March, 1998. Published by the Urban Land Institute, 1025 Thomas Jefferson Street, N.W., Suite 500 West, Washington, D.C. 20007-5201. Reprinted with permission of the publisher.

interstate and subdivision construction, the United States has become a nation dominated by fragmented suburbs. In 1950, less than 25 percent of the country's population lived in suburban areas, whereas today more than 50 percent does. The country's fastest-growing metropolitan areas—Atlanta, Phoenix, Dallas—arguably are not real cities at all. They are suburban agglomerations, diffusions of residential culs-de-sac and horizontal development with no relation to the original urban cores that once anchored them. Following suit, the nation's suburban office stock now exceeds central business district space, and retailing is dominated by suburban malls and power centers.

As the mid–1990s real estate recovery takes hold, however, it has become increasingly clear that traditional cities like San Francisco, Chicago, Boston, and even New York remain investment bulwarks, while many suburban markets like Buckhead face increasingly difficult issues as they age, not all gracefully. In fact, the traditional urban cores offer attractive residential communities in relatively safe, multifaceted environments that are convenient to shopping and the workplace. As life becomes more complicated and time more constrained, people increasingly crave convenience.

The 24-Hour Paradigm

Commercial real estate investors should be increasingly concerned about the future of suburbs as the majority of their assets are invested in these markets. Which suburbs—and by extension which real estate markets—are better and why?

Successful real estate markets—whether urban or suburban—have similar characteristics that must be fostered to sustain their viability. These places—the so-called 24-hour markets—have the ingredients that attract people to live in or around them and provide the tax base that makes them better places to live. The essential principle behind the 24-hour paradigm is that people want to live near their workplace, and without strong residential fundamentals, commercial markets will fail. It follows that the best investment locations for real estate feature all of these elements:

Attractive upscale housing as well as nearby affordable housing for workers. CEOs and senior managers determine where their companies locate, and they want relative convenience as much or more than anyone else. Affordable housing is important too. If support staff has trouble getting to work, productivity will suffer.

Nearby shopping. Residents should be able to reach supermarkets, drugstores, and cleaners without struggling through traffic. Better yet, they should be able to walk. Optimally, retail has been integrated into master-planned, mixed-use developments. Every trip to a store should not be a major expedition.

Ample recreation and entertainment. People want a mix of parks, recreational trails, and golf courses along with restaurants, cineplexes, and cultural venues like museums and theaters. Again, they should not have to drive to them. In suburban areas, a nearby regional mall is more successful when it acts as a de facto town center.

Security. High crime ruins neighborhoods and surrounding commercial districts. Recent wholesale reductions in crime rates in big cities like New York have been a boon.

Good schools. A struggling school system spells trouble. Parents will flee before gambling their children's education and future.

Access to major transportation arteries. Downtowns without mass transportation networks are in bad shape because people will not spend the time to drive into them from increasingly far-flung suburbs. But suburbs without mass transportation are beginning to suffer too. Residential areas that do not depend totally on cars—where residents can walk or bicycle to recreation and essential shopping—will become more desirable as people grow increasingly intolerant of traffic. The more pedestrian friendly an area is, the better.

Diversified tax base. One-horse towns that depend on a single mall or a small group of businesses for commercial tax revenues are vulnerable when the mall fails or a major corporate tenant leaves town. The school system deteriorates and critical services like police and sanitation are reduced. Residential tax rates increase and people leave, extending the downward spiral.

Probably the two biggest issues threatening the stability of suburban markets and agglomerations, in particular, are automobile traffic congestion and fragmented patchwork government competing for limited resources.

The Growing Volume of Cars

Cars made suburbs possible. Today, however, they are beginning to make suburban life in some places almost impossible. Forty years ago, the car allowed

families to leave congested cities for a home in a suburban subdivision with space, light, a backyard, and a barbecue. The commute to work downtown was bearable for dad; turning lanes had not yet been invented; and mom stayed at home to take care of the house and the kids. In 1950, there were 50 million cars, one for every three Americans.

Today, ring roads and spaghetti junctions struggle to accommodate the growing number of cars—200 million and counting. That equates to four cars for every five people in the United States. Who lives in suburbia without a car? Since most suburban planning has been ad hoc, subdivision by subdivision, and retail/commercial strips have been zoned to be separate from residential areas, the only way to shop, get to work, or go anywhere is by car. That is the way it was meant to be. Many town planners and developers dispensed altogether with the idea of sidewalks. Today, more cars mean more roads, bigger parking lots, more traffic lights, and more frustration.

For owners of regional malls with anchor department stores and suburban office buildings, traffic congestion can be a killer. Time-pressed consumers are shopping closer to home, and often smaller retail is just more convenient. In addition, power center category killers and discounters offer value and wide selections. For many destination shoppers, visiting the nearby big box is better than roaming the less accessible mall. Some older regional centers in inner-ring suburbs, once on main thoroughfares, now find themselves relegated to aging secondary roads, while newer centers take advantage of prime access from more recently built highways in outer rings.

Office tenants increasingly search

for the building closest to the exit and entry ramps of an interstate. If employees can avoid traffic lights, it can mean a difference of hours in commuting every week. Ample parking, preferably decked or underground, is almost essential for suburban office buildings. Developments cut off from main arteries or inconvenient to restaurants and services are trouble for investors—tenants will tend to avoid them.

The biggest traffic-related problems involve the most attractive commercial markets in major suburban agglomerations, ones like Buckhead with first-class malls and prime office space, as well as hotels. Ironically, increasing commercial development could rock Buckhead's residential foundation as more cars are shoehorned into street networks that cannot handle the volume. Atlanta's subway system, MARTA, theoretically offers some relief but falls victim to suburban planners' dismissive approach to transit-oriented residential development.

For most subdivision dwellers in Atlanta agglomeration, the only way to get to MARTA is, not surprisingly, by car. If homes are near stations, typically residents are faced with streets without pedestrian walks and crossings at dangerous intersections. Even eight-lane Peachtree Road, the main north/south artery through central Atlanta into Buckhead, has only narrow, poorly maintained sidewalks.

It gets worse for workers headed for office parks at the Atlanta perimeter. Walkways leading from stations take a person only so far before ending in parking lots, at roadsides, or along landscaped lawns often soggy from rain or sprinklers. Finding one's way to and from the office can be an obstacle course.

While most subway systems in older, traditional cities were built to anticipate adjacent residential development, mass transportation networks in America's younger, car-dominated markets have been afterthoughts, imposed on areas that were not designed to use them effectively. The hub-and-spoke system of the classic 24-hour city will not work in Dallas or Phoenix, let alone Los Angeles. The diffusion of residents and commercial centers in agglomerations works against building an efficient, economical system. Unless workers can conduct their daily business in these commercial nodes without a car (i.e., on foot or by bus or train) mass transit will not work.

Live by the car, die by the car—residents in agglomerations grow frustrated with traffic jams and delays. "Traffic is getting worse ands worse," has become a familiar refrain. People try either to move closer to work or stretch the suburban envelope further, buying newer homes in outlying subdivisions not yet clogged to capacity.

Inefficiently Allocated Regional Resources

As metropolitan areas push the suburban envelope and people try to escape congestion and aging, early-generation suburban neighborhoods, regional resources are stretched and often inefficiently allocated. The impact on suburban areas is most apparent in older core and suburban ring cities in the Northeast and Midwest, but the consequences offer lessons for the ever-spreading suburban agglomerations in the South and West.

Contrary to popular belief, socioeconomic instability does not stop neatly at the city limits. Maturing suburbs are contracting big city ills other than congestion—aging housing stock, crime, and deteriorating school systems. For example, in Minneapolis more than 20 percent of children in nine of 11 metro, inner-suburban school districts were in the free lunch program, and those districts were gaining poor children faster than the city schools. The same pattern is occurring just outside Philadelphia.

Suburban rings encompassing once healthy middle-class neighborhoods to the south and west of Chicago are deteriorating rapidly, with higher crime rates than those found in the city. As urban problems leach into the close-in suburbs, families move away, if they can, leading to a downward spiral in the tax base reminiscent of the consequences of the exodus from inner-city areas in the 1960s and 1970s. Today, a drive through the empty malls and abandoned buildings of once-thriving suburban Harvey, Markham, and Ford Heights around Chicago recalls some of the worst inner-city neighborhoods. The economic consequences to property owners, both residential and commercial, have been devastating.

While some older suburbs find themselves struggling, the tax base and, not surprisingly, political clout are concentrated in more exclusive, lower-density areas that recall the original suburban ideal: the southwestern suburbs around Eden Prairie and Minnetonka in Minneapolis, the areas to the north and west of Chicago, and the King of Prussia area in Philadelphia. The same trends are occurring in other suburban agglomerations—the northern perimeters of Atlanta and North Dallas are highly favored residential areas. These

are the classic 24-hours suburban markets, attractive to commercial real estate investors.

Whether by design or not, many of these municipalities and towns are positioned to skim the cream from the metropolitan growth, while accepting few of the responsibilities. Typically their restrictive barriers to affordable housing and their emphasis on low-density development welcome upper-middle-class throngs in search of executive housing and businesses from core communities or struggling inner-ring suburbs. In the Chicago area, the more affluent northwest suburban quadrant, with only 20 percent of the region's residents, has garnered 80 percent of the job growth. Likewise, in the Twin Cities, Eden Prairie and Minnetonka together have the same commercial/industrial tax base as St. Paul—about $1.5 billion—but only one-third the residents and virtually no impoverished people.

As suburbs without affordable housing dominate regional job growth, a mismatch develops between where jobs are and where the people who need them live. Road systems are upgraded and expanded to serve these communities since cars are the only way to get to them, and congestion follows. Cars owned by people who cannot afford to live close to their workplace jam the regional roads. As long as most new jobs are created in communities without affordable housing and convenient mass transportation, traffic congestion will increase to unacceptable levels. Opened only two years ago, Georgia 400, the highway into Buckhead and other prime business districts north of Atlanta, has already reached traffic volumes predicted for 2006.

The further evolution of suburban

areas pushes the metropolitan envelope toward its exurban horizon, well beyond the more affluent districts. These budding subdivision tracts are magnets for blue-collar, middle-class families who long to escape the deteriorating inner-ring suburbs but cannot afford the better communities. Although many of these nascent communities aspire to attract major businesses and commercial development to support a diversified tax base, most are just too far out on the fringe to succeed.

This pattern of metropolitan polarization plays a cruel joke on families moving into the peripheral ring suburbs. As they flee the socioeconomic dislocations of the center city and inner suburban areas, they arrive in rapidly expanding school districts with small tax bases. The local governments, in turn, tend to cut corners on zoning and planning, allowing poorly conceived projects and chock-a-block development—anything to increase the tax base and balance the municipality's books. These areas will be ripe for early deterioration down the line. Meanwhile, people are moving farther away from the original urban cores and becoming more dependent on cars to get to work.

Although the affluent 24-hour suburban markets currently offer investors an advantage, over the long term, the entire suburban landscape is a treacherous investment environment. Older, inner-ring areas obviously are stressed, and some are in advanced stages of deterioration. The outermost ring of suburbs, meanwhile, raises questions about just how far metropolitan areas can go without a full complement of infrastructure and services—highways and sewers, in particular. A corporate campus built on a cow pasture in the early

1980s might have been a 45-minute drive from the airport or downtown. Today's cow pasture might be two hours or more away. Companies realize they can no longer attract the required workforce or support services when they move to the suburban fringes.

Regions with more comprehensive planning and less political infighting among fragmented jurisdictions for limited resources should provide for a stronger community fabric, more attractive lifestyles, and better long-term investment prospects. Studies show that when the incomes of central-city residents increased, incomes of suburban residents increased. The converse also was true: a decline in city incomes led to a decline in incomes among suburban dwellers. Also, metropolitan areas with smaller gaps between city and suburban incomes had the greatest job increases. The studies make sense. If New York or downtown Chicago failed, would their suburbs be far behind?

Banding Together

The absence of cooperation among local planners in adjoining suburban communities often creates a hodgepodge of retail strips and ugly commercial districts that must cannibalize each other to survive. Older regional malls recently have been prime victims of newer retail development in adjoining communities. The new development may create a substantial tax base for its municipality, but it comes at the expense of the neighboring municipality and can lead to a more general, areawide decline. In ten years, the municipality's mall may lose its customers to a newer center developed nearby.

Over time, communities that band together will strengthen the region and become more powerful magnets for real estate investors. Mass transportation strategies should be implemented to reduce car dependence and better unify regions. Districts and towns should coordinate well-conceived land use planning efforts. Providing pedestrian access from residential areas to nearby commercial districts should become more of a priority. Instead of abandoning struggling areas, creative infill strategies should be fostered to reestablish communities that offer 24-hour living—offices, shopping, and other commercial development integrated with residential uses, including affordable housing. Local governments must start paying attention to these issues or risk the consequences.

In general, mixed-use development—in which office, shopping, and commercial projects complement housing—will hold its value longer and stand the test of time better than single-use development. Investors and homeowners increasingly will seek out these communities. Unfortunately, many of our suburbs have been jerry-built for uncertain futures.

CHAPTER 27

Developing an Economic Incentives Ordinance in Cobb County, Georgia

J. Virgil Moon and *Tom Majors*

The Wall Street Journal called Cobb County, Georgia, "the hottest small business boom area in the country." Despite its acknowledged status as a business cradle and home to leading-edge firms, Cobb County has not taken its leadership position for granted. While the national economy suffered a downturn in recent years, Cobb County continued to be a mecca for business relocations. One of the nation's fastest-growing counties throughout the 1980s, the county still posts some impressive numbers. Among the most recent accomplishments checked off by local economic developers:

- $48 million convention center completed;
- 200 international companies located operations in Cobb County over the last decade;
- 303 percent increase in economic activity over the previous year;
- $136 million in new capital investment;
- 61 major construction projects, up from 39 one year earlier; and
- $402 million in total economic activity.

Originally published as "An Economic Incentives Ordinance in Cobb County, Georgia, Bears Fruit in a Big Way," Government Finance Review, *Vol. 10, No. 3, June, 1994. Published by the Government Finance Officers Association, 180 N. Michigan Ave., Suite 800, Chicago, Illinois 60601 (312-977-9700, fax 312-977-4806. e-mail GFR@gfoa.org). Annual subscription $30. Reprinted with permission of the publisher.*

To meet the competitive challenges posed by other areas, chamber, county and municipal leaders formed the Cobb Economic Coalition in October 1991, a collaborative effort on the part of government and business to promote positive economic growth. The coalition jointly commissioned a highly recognized business relocation firm to conduct a study of the county's strengths and weaknesses and to provide the county with a strategy to attract more businesses and do a better job of keeping those already in the county. This study, now serving as a blueprint for local leaders working to strengthen the county's competitive position, recommended that the county devise an incentive plan to attract more business to the county. It also identified those industries and businesses that would find locating in Cobb County a distinct advantage.

Attracting New Businesses

The new incentives ordinance, adopted in August 1993, established a mechanism for attracting new businesses to certain parts of the county through the negotiation or outright waiving of businesses licenses, building permits, water system development fees and other usual requirements. Depending on the number of employees in a prospective company, the impact could be as much as $50,000. In order to be eligible for incentives, prospective companies must offer at least 25 new jobs and an annual economic impact on the county of at least $500,000.

The mechanism involved the establishment of an Office of Economic Development. Working with an advisory committee of representatives of the Cobb Municipal Association, Cobb Chamber of Commerce and appointees of the five county commissioners, this office defines areas of the county where certain incentives are used to attract particular kinds of business and recommends the incentives to be offered a company relocating to the designated areas. The package includes incentives for both new development and special incentives for redevelopment of abandoned sites, recommendations defining eligibility criteria and duration of incentives, and determinations of eligible industries and particular areas of the county to be designated for offering the incentives. The overall criterion is that the incentives be paid back within a three- to five-year period. The offer then is made by the county manager and the chairman of the board of commissioners. Figure 1 displays characteristics of the various types of incentives.

Before the process to develop the ordinance could begin, a number of key elements had to be in place. First, attitudes had to be favorable to the proposition of the private and public sectors working together to achieve goals. These attitudes included a political leadership that was willing to be entrepreneurial and to take risks. Secondly, the county had to be ready to create and promote an image in order to sell itself as a product. It had to be willing to provide vigorous strategic planning and agreeable to fostering a working relationship between business and government.

The process to develop this ordinance started in November 1992, when two county commissioners requested, and the board unanimously agreed, to establish an Economic Development

Figure 1
Cobb County Publicly Adopted Development Incentives

Incentives	Eligibility Criteria	Range	Duration	Redevelopment Bonus
Impact fees	Yes—all	100%	Unlimited	N/A
Plan review fee	Yes—all	100%	Unlimited	N/A
Water system development fees	Yes—all	100%	Unlimited	N/A
Inventory tax	Yes—all	80% city— 100% county	Unlimited	N/A
Business license	Yes—> $1,000 fee	0–100%	3–5 years	Yes—by area
Property tax	Yes—awaiting state leg.	N/A	N/A	N/A
Sewer system development fees	Yes—> $10,000 fee base charge	100% financing	3–5 years	Yes—credit for prior capacity
Monthly wastewater user charges	Yes—meter size 6" or > credit base charge	100%	3 years	Yes—by area
Building permits	Yes—> $5,000 fee	0–100%	N/A	Yes—by area
Training	Yes—> 25 jobs	0–50% ($ available)	As $ available	Yes—by area

Threshold = three- to five-year payback to applicable funds

Incentives Task Force for the purpose of examining and recommending economic incentives to potentially new or expanding/existing businesses. The task force, comprising city, county and business leaders, worked for six months to frame recommendations that would serve as the basis for drafting an ordinance.

In the summer of 1993, public work sessions were held with the board, and the ordinance was drafted. Two public meetings were conducted to receive more citizen input before the board adopted the ordinance.

Provisions of the Ordinance

The incentives and conditions included in the ordinance and publicly advertised are described below.

Threshold. A threshold established by the ordinance provides for the payback of the offered incentives to the county within three years of the granting of the certificate of occupancy. The payback consists of future tax and/or fee payments rather than a direct cash repayment for the incentive.

Business License Waiver. A business license fee above $1,000 is waived for either all or part of the amount above $1,000. This may be granted for a period of three to five years, with a higher percent being waived for redevelopment.

Property Tax Abatement. A constitutional amendment and referendum will be required before the property tax abatement option may be offered.

Impact Fees. Fees as provided for by Georgia's Development Impact Fee legislation are not being charged by Cobb County in the areas of roads, parks, public safety and libraries.

Plan Review Fee. These fees are not being charged by Cobb County.

Sewer System Development Fee. Impact fees charged for capital components of the sewer system in excess of $10,000, will be financed over a three- to five-year period. If the total fee is between $10,000 and $20,000, the fee will be financed over a three-year period. If the total is greater than $20,000, the amount above $10,000 will be financed over a five-year period. Redevelopment will receive credits for capacity that existed prior to the redevelopment.

Water System Development Fees. Cobb County does not charge a development fee for water capacity.

Monthly Wastewater User Charges. If the new business is metered with a 6" meter or one of greater size, the monthly base charge will be waived for a period of three years.

Building Permits. Building permits, which are $4 per $1,000 of construction, will be waived totally or in part for the amount above $5,000, with a three- to five-year duration and redevelopment bonus by area.

Training. For firms training 25 or more workers, up to 50 percent of the training cost can be covered through locally administered Joint Training Part-

nership Act (JTPA) funds, based upon the availability of funds. An advantage is given for redevelopment.

Inventory Tax. This freeport tax exemption on inventory destined for out-of-state locations already is offered by the county at 100 percent of value and by the cities at 80 percent of value. The ordinance offers it on an indefinite basis.

The entire package of incentives is applicable on an industry-specific basis in particular, well-defined targeted areas of Cobb County. Figure 2 charts the incentives available by district for four types of development: manufacturing, distribution, office and retail. "Special project/major impact" in Figure 2 refers to a very large industry or headquarters operation which will have a significant impact on the Cobb County economy and will be given special consideration or incentives.

An important feature of Cobb County's policy is the offering of incentives to firms seeking to expand existing operations in Cobb County. A majority of employment growth historically comes from existing industry, not only in Cobb County but nationwide.

Publicly Adopted Incentives

the intense competition in the economic development field has resulted in businesses having a high level of awareness of incentives being offered by various jurisdictions. Today, virtually every meeting with an economic development prospect will involve, at the prospect's request, a discussion of available incentives. The feverish competition for the Mercedes-Benz Plant, awarded to Vance, Alabama, and the BMW plant, awarded to Greer, South Carolina, have

Figure 2
Cobb County Incentives Offered by District and By Industry

Area	Manufacturing		Distribution		Office		Retail
	New development	Redevelopment	New development	Redevelopment	New development	Redevelopment	Redevelopment
South Cobb	All*	All	All	All	All	All	All
North Cobb	All I-75 & Hwy 41	All I-75 & Hwy 41	All I-75 & Hwy 41	All I-75 & Hwy 41	All I-75, I-575 & Hwy 41	All I-75, I-575 & Hwy 41	All
East Cobb	None	None	None	None	None	All	All
West Cobb	All Old 41 & Hwy 41	All Old 41 & Hwy 41	All Old 41 & Hwy 41	All Old 41 & Hwy 41	All	All	All
Community improvement district	None	None	None	None	All	All	All
Special project/ major impact	All	All	All	All	All	All	All

*All—Entire package of incentives is applicable in that area.

been highly publicized. Incentives were a key, if not the most important factor in these decisions. The value of the incentives was reportedly high and some have questioned the wisdom of these offers and the extent of the behind-the-scenes commitments to these companies.

It is becoming increasingly clear that incentives are a necessary competitive tool and that a well-thought-out, publicly adopted policy has particular merit. With a publicly adopted incentives policy, the eligible industries and the value of the incentives are specified and open to public scrutiny and not subject to speculation about the appropriateness. The Cobb County incentives ordinance specifically requires that a cost-benefit analysis be done prior to offering the incentives so that citizens can be assured that there is a quick payback to the initial investment.

Perhaps more importantly, a publicly adopted policy is a signal to existing and potential new business that the county has a pro-business attitude and is willing to make an investment in reducing the start-up costs for business. Due to industrial competition, confidentiality is a key concern to business in the relocation or expansion process. The Cobb County ordinance empowers the chairman of the county commission and the county manager to respond quickly and confidentially to businesses in regard to the types of assistance the county may offer. With a standard policy, there is no need for individual and time-consuming deal making and no need to publicly expose the company because a full commission vote in a public meeting on each offer is not necessary.

For the practitioner of economic development, the incentives policy is a powerful sales tool that allows for the prospect's interest to be peaked and the other attributes of the county to be highlighted. For example, an excellent primary, secondary and college education system is one of Cobb County's selling points that can be showcased after the initial question regarding the availability of incentives is answered affirmatively. The incentives ordinance also allows the quick permitting and development process to be highlighted: In one case, although the county offered a lower value of incentives to a manufacturer than some of the competing jurisdictions, the speedy processing was the decisive factor, since a rapid move was required by the prospect.

For the citizens, since property tax abatement is not part of the policy, they can be assured that business will carry its share of the tax burden. The property tax rates of Cobb County are the lowest of the urbanized counties of the metro Atlanta area, which is a prime selling point. The property tax rates are so low that Cobb County will remain competitive even after property tax abatements are offered by the competition.

Bearing Fruit for the County

The incentives policy and ordinance bear primary responsibility for attracting or maintaining an estimated $500 million of economic impact to the county. Numerous manufacturers, distributors and headquarters operations have inquired about the announced incentives policy, and many have been successfully recruited to Cobb County or have expanded in Cobb County. A foreign manufacturer of printing presses was attracted to Cobb County and established its U.S. headquarters there. A domestic manufacturer of doors located in Cobb County. The Home Depot, already based in Cobb County, announced the expansion of its world headquarters, which will result in more than doubling its current level of employment from 1,800 to 5,000 employees and the construction of 1.5 million square feet of office space during the next five years.

As an example of how the ordinance is applied, the door manufacturer that recently located in Cobb County was the recipient of the following benefits: 1) the fee for building permits was capped at $5,000, saving the firm $7,000, and 2) the business license, capped at $1,000 for three years, saved the company $3,000 per year for three years. These concessions will easily be replaced by the first y ears' property tax collections, which amount to $45,000. The three-year payback criterion of the policy is readily met.

By today's standards, these are rather modest waivers of fees to offer as an investment by the county. Nonetheless, the publicly adopted incentives ordinance highlights the positive "business as usual" policy of the county, such as the lack of development impact fees, a fact that, previous to the ordinance process, was not emphasized as an incentive.

Strong competition almost requires that some incentives be offered to footloose industries in order to successfully recruit or retain them. No matter how well it is reasoned or constructed, economic development will not succeed without support, and the primary support must be in the grass roots of the community. Taxpayer concern over possibly giving away too much in agreements that are obscured from the public is a compelling argument for an openly formulated and adopted incentives ordinance such as Cobb County adopted in 1993. The policy has proven highly successful in attracting and maintaining firms in the county with, on net, a beneficial impact to the county government's revenues and the local economy.

CHAPTER 28

An Assessment of Economic Development Efforts in Rural Illinois Communities

Gerrit J. Knaap and *Alison Simon*

The last two decades witnessed a dramatic shift in approach to economic development. Whereas the federal government once led the charge to develop local and national economies, fiscal austerity, changing intergovernmental relations, and two consecutive conservative administrations relegated responsibility for economic development to local governments. As federal leadership declined, so also did local economies, forcing local governments to pursue economic development largely on their own. By the early 1980s, economic development became a leading implicit, if not explicit, function of local governments.

As economic development activity grew, so did academic research on economic development, most of which, however, focused on urban areas. Academic writing on urban economic development features three general perspectives (Stone, 1984). The first perspective, exemplified by Peterson (1981), praises local efforts to develop urban economies. According to Peterson, economic development activities clearly enhance the general welfare of urban residents and thus serve as an appropriate and class-neutral function of local government.

The second perspective is the more mainstream. Mainstream writers criti-

---

Originally published as "Economic Development in Rural Illinois Communities: A Critical Assessment," Journal of the Community Development Society, *Vol. 25, No. 1, 1994. Published by the Community Development Society, Milwaukee, Wisconsin. Reprinted with permission of the publisher.*

cize economic development programs for missing their targets and offer policy prescriptions for better economic development programming (Fosler, 1991; Blakely, 1989; Shaffer, 1989). Like Peterson, however, mainstream writers view economic development programs—when successful—as serving the general welfare of urban residents.

The third perspective is most critical. This perspective begins with the premise that local governments do not serve the public interests but instead serve identifiable private interests in society (Gottdiener, 1987). Economic development programs, from this perspective, generally serve the interests of capital but are shaped by conflict between capitalist and working classes (Fainstain et al., 1986; Friedland, 1982). As a result, economic development programs serve primarily the corporate growth machine (Molotch, 1976; Stone & Sanders, 1987; Squires, 1989) to the detriment of the working class (Mollenkopf, 1983; Swanstrom, 1985). According to writers with a critical perspective, politics in economic development matter, and politics in economic development are shaped by class conflict (Stone & Sanders, 1987).

In this chapter we offer a critical perspective on rural economic development based on case studies from rural Illinois communities. Following Gottdiener (1987), Fainstain et al. (1986) and others, we begin from the premise that economic development programs do not serve a generally defined public interest but tend to serve distinct private interests in society. Further, interests served by economic development are determined by those interests that sponsor economic development programs and participate in economic development

decision making. Finally, the structure of rural communities differs from the structure of urban communities in ways that cause differences in the nature of class conflict and thus differences in the practice of economic development.

The protocol was the same for the six community case studies. Summaries of findings in each rural Illinois community allow inferences about the practice of economic development in rural communities. The final section is a discussion of ways the structure of rural communities shapes the practice of rural economic development.

THE CASE STUDY PROTOCOL

Case studies of six communities in rural Illinois were funded by the Institute of Rural Affairs at Western Illinois University to provide examples of successful programs in rural economic development. Members of the research team included scholars at the University of Illinois at Urbana–Champaign, Illinois State University, and Western Illinois University. The research protocol for the case study research involved choosing communities active in economic development, examining economic development activities in those communities using a structured interview procedure, and drawing from the experience of active communities lessons for rural economic development.

The six communities were chosen from a list of communities identified by the Illinois Department of Commerce and Community Affairs (DCCA) as active in economic development. To gather information on these communities and their activities, a member of the research team conducted personal interviews with at least six representative individuals in each community, which were chosen to include representatives of local government, local businesses, local civic organizations, and other recognized community leaders. The interviews were designed to answer a distinct set of questions: What stimulated economic development activities? Who participated in the economic development effort? How as economic development pursued? What were the results of economic development activities? Care was taken to assure that each member of the research team used the same interview protocol. The findings and results were recently published as a monograph (Walzer, 1990).

Despite extensive efforts to maintain a standard interview protocol, the manner in which the case studies were conducted presents obvious difficulties and limitations for the purposes of this chapter. Because each of the communities was studied by a different person, the findings inevitably reflect the bias of the individuals conducting the research. However, utilizing information obtained by different people has advantages for the purpose of this paper as well. Because the case studies were not conducted by the same individuals, the case studies are not all tainted by the same interviewer bias. And because the research was conducted to identify examples of economic development success, the research was less likely to reveal critical elements of the process.

Six Case Studies

PROPHETSTOWN

Prophetstown (population 1,749) is located in Northwestern Illinois. The community provides services to the surrounding farm community in Whiteside County, but its economy is not inextricably dependent upon agriculture. Forty percent of Whiteside County residents are employed in manufacturing. Although there was no sense of impending crisis, the Prophetstown economy had noticeably weakened as both agriculture and manufacturing declined.

The impetus to take action was led by the mayor who, with a self-selected group of community leaders, formed the Prophetstown Economic Planning Commission (PEPCO). The PEPCO board included the mayor, a banker, the editor of the local newspaper, a real estate broker, a management consultant, an official of a local industry, a businessman with state political connections, and another community leader.

The PEPCO board met frequently to discuss economic development strategies. At several meetings, representatives of the Department of Commerce and Community Affairs (DCCA) provided information on state-sponsored economic development programs. The PEPCO board, however, opposed state intervention in local affairs and was loath to offer local tax concessions. Finally, one exasperated commissioner remarked: the only way we're going to attract a business to Prophetstown is to buy it. So they did.

To implement their plan to purchase a business, PEPCO formed Prophetstown Manufacturing Incorporated (PMI), a for-profit corporation able to sell stock. Selling stock in a new and unique corporation, however, presented problems. Meeting the requirements to sell stock by the Federal Securities and Exchange Commission and the Securities Division of Illinois Secretary of

State required considerable legal assistance. Some assistance was provided by local attorneys, but critical assistance was provided by the Illinois Secretary of State. With the assistance of the Secretary of State, the sale of stock was approved and more than $100,000 of stock was sold, 80 percent of which was sold to local residents.

After extensive market research by a paid consultant, PMI purchased Clear Creek Furniture, a furniture manufacturer, and relocated the company to Prophetstown in 1986. By 1990, Clear Creek Furniture employed ten full-time production workers, a half-time clerk and the two former owners as management consultants. Clear Creek Furniture made its first profits in 1990—$6,000 for a six-month period. With Clear Creek Furniture on solid footing, PMI is seeking to purchase other manufacturing concerns suited for Prophetstown, and is exploring the possibility of using state funds for further capitalization.

The experience of Prophetstown highlights certain features of innovative economic development programming. Creating a for-profit development organization required strong leadership by the mayor and substantial support by the local business community. Purchasing a manufacturing firm required capital contributions from local residents and technical support from state-level officials. Managing a risky and innovative program required a well-designed plan and experience in business management to make the program successful. Prophetstown met these requirements and received considerable notoriety (Thomas, 1988). However, Prophetstown's success was limited. Clear Creek Furniture took several years to turn a profit and at this writing employed only eleven residents.

Purchasing a firm through a community-sponsored economic development corporation was an innovative enterprise, but the benefits of such an enterprise relative to its cost were not large.

MOUNT STERLING

Mount Sterling (population 1,922) is the seat of Brown County in Western Illinois. The economy of Mount Sterling declined significantly during the past decade, particularly in the retail sector. Stores in Mount Sterling compete with Beardstown and Quincy, larger cities located nearby. With out-migration from the surrounding countryside, businesses in Mount Sterling became less competitive, and property values declined. Between 1980 and 1987, equalized assessed property values in Mount Sterling dropped by 12.7 percent. Steady declines in retailing and property values stimulated interest in economic development.

Economic development activities in Mount Sterling were led by a local banker, a retail store manager, a representative of the largest local employer, and a local resident employed outside the community. A business manager who had recently located to Mount Sterling noticed that the state government was seeking a site for a prison. Lacking local resources for economic development initiatives, the leaders focused on a single strategy: attracting the state prison to Mount Sterling.

Unlike traditional economic development activities, attracting a state prison requires the mobilization of political rather than economic resources. Thus, most development activities in Mount Sterling were directed towards generating political support for the project. The committee began at home, contacting by phone nearly every family in Brown County. Residents were informed that the prison would employ 400 workers, with a payroll of more than $10 million, and purchase $13 million in supplies. At a hearing conducted by the Department of Corrections, over 2,200 residents showed overwhelming support for the project. But in spite of the show of support, Mount Sterling was not selected by the Department of Corrections for a new prison. It was, however, placed on a list of six communities eligible for new prison in 1985.

For this new round of competition, Mount Sterling was well prepared. Once again the committee marshaled extensive public support at a local hearing, and delivered a message to the director of the Illinois Department of Corrections on the high school football field. The committee also enlisted the support of surrounding communities, the Illinois Department of Commerce and Community Affairs, the Illinois Department of Transportation, and the county board, which donated 80 acres of land for the construction site. The committee also lobbied state lawmakers, hosting a social on the state capitol grounds.

In 1985, the governor announced that a 750-bed medium security prison would locate in Mount Sterling. As the prison was constructed, income and employment in Mount Sterling grew. However, many prison employees were transferred from other institutions, and most prison supplies were purchased from outside the community. The growth in population created a shortage of homes in Mount Sterling, and many of the benefits of economic growth escaped the Brown County economy. But

Mount Sterling remains active in economic development. The committee regrouped as the Brown County Development Corporation, which is now pursuing a Community Development Action Grant for Mount Sterling's largest employer and is exploring new ways to alleviate the housing shortage.

The approach to economic development taken by Mount Sterling differs substantially from that taken by Prophetstown. Whereas Prophetstown shunned support from state government, Mount Sterling recruited a state prison. And whereas Clear Creek Furniture had at most a minor impact on the Prophetstown economy, the state prison created housing shortages in Mount Sterling. These differences illustrate both the limits of locally driven economic development programs and the potential consequences of externally driven programs.

BEARDSTOWN

Beardstown (population 5,270) is located in Cass County between Peoria and St. Louis on the Illinois River. Historically dependent upon agriculture and manufacturing, the Beardstown community suffered severe and rapid setbacks in the 1980s. First a bridge over the Illinois River closed for nearly a year, virtually isolating the community from its northern markets. As a result, several retail stores closed and downtown buildings were abandoned. Next the local Oscar Mayer plant closed, eliminating 780 jobs. As jobs and incomes declined, the city-owned hospital closed, terminating another 50 jobs, Finally, Bohn Heat Transfer closed, leaving the community with 250 fewer jobs and a seriously polluted industrial site.

Economic development activity began with the election of a new mayor in 1985. The new mayor brought extensive knowledge of state development programs based on previous in Springfield as a legislative assistance. The mayor convened a brainstorming session attended by business owners, labor leaders, bankers, and concerned citizens. The session set economic development priorities and established the mayor's office as the contact point for economic development activities. Recognizing the need for greater economic development efforts, the city council hired the mayor as a full-time economic development director—a rare hiring decision for a small community. With the support of long-time residents and the local office of the Central Illinois Public Service Corporation, the mayor immediately formulated an economic development plan.

Under the mayor's leadership, Beardstown adopted a multifaceted economic development program. First, Beardstown adopted several state-sponsored development programs, including a Tax Increment Finance (TIF) program and an Enterprise Zone. In the TIF district, located near a busy highway junction, increases in property tax and sales tax revenues become available for further local investments, such as infrastructure and loan subsidies. Wal-Mart, Hardee's and McDonald's located in Beardstown's TIF district, helping to generate over $130,000 for economic development in 1989. In the enterprise zone, created in 1986, businesses receive tax concessions for creating new jobs. By 1990, Beardstown's enterprise zone fostered nearly 1,600 jobs, resulting in a reduction of the unemployment rate in the enterprise zone of more than 2.5 percent.

Beardstown also recruited a replacement firm for the former Oscar Mayer plant—only six months after Oscar Mayer announced its closing. Although the new firm, Excel Inc., pays considerably lower wages than Oscar Mayer, the firm brought to Beardstown 400 jobs and expects to employ more than 1,200 workers.

Recently, with state support, Beardstown provided a lucrative incentive package to Rich Lumber Company, a long-time Beardstown firm. As a result, the firm expanded, and hired 80 new employees. Finally, Beardstown is looking to capitalize on its riverfront location. Recently, the Illinois legislature passed legislation permitting riverboat gambling. This legislation may create new opportunities for retail development along the Illinois River, opportunities Beardstown is currently exploring.

As in Prophetstown and Mount Sterling, economic development activities in Beardstown had strong leadership, provided primarily by the mayor. As in Mount Sterling, economic development was largely financed by external resources, provided by the state. Unlike Prophetstown and Mount Sterling, however, the focus of economic activities in Beardstown was diffuse. Rather than focusing on a specific firm or institution, Beardstown adopted a multifaceted development strategy. This strategy had the potential to benefit many new and existing firms in the community, thereby casting the potential benefits of economic development widely into the community. However, it is difficult for such strategies to demonstrate clear linkages between causes and effects.

PRINCETON

Princeton (population 7,197) is the county seat and largest city in Bureau County, locate din north-central Illinois. Princeton has an advantageous location on I-80, 20 miles west of the I-80/I-39 interchange. The Illinois River, 12 miles to the southeast, provides a natural waterway to northern and southern markets, and the Burlington-Northern Railroad serves Princeton with routes to the northeast and southwest. Accessibility made Princeton an attractive location for medium-sized industries, industries that kept the economy of Princeton relatively healthy and stable, at least until the early 1980s.

The 1980 recession affected Princeton like many other rural communities. Decline in the farm economy caused retail sales to slump and property values to fall. The regional office of Transamerica in Princeton closed, terminating 100 jobs. Soon thereafter, Pioneer Seeds announced the closing of its regional facility and suspended plans for a new seed processing plant. These events compelled Princeton leaders to action.

Economic development in Princeton was led by two individuals working with local bankers, business owners, and officials of the Chamber of Commerce. Until 1988, this group operated as a not-for-profit arm of the Chamber, entitled the Princeton Development Corporation (PDC). Since 1988, the PDC became an arm of the City of Princeton, and was renamed the Princeton Industrial Commission (PIC). Moving the organization from the Chamber to the City enabled the organization to offer regulatory concessions, to utilize city resources, and to coordinate with city planning.

While an arm of the Chamber of Commerce, the PDC gathered information and marketed the local community outside the region. The PDC also sought to develop an industrial park and to construct a speculative building for development purposes. The PDC failed to erect the speculative building, however, due to financial constraints. But with the cooperation of a local property owner, the PDC successfully completed two industrial parks which the PIC is now marketing to industrial prospects.

After aligning with the City, the PIC became eligible for financial assistance from city and state governments. As a result, the PIC now offers low interest loans to area firms seeking to expand. The first loan was made to the Harper-Hyman Company for new equipment, creating 50 jobs. The PIC also offers financial assistance for downtown redevelopment, for marketing, and for an industrial park. In 1986, the City of Princeton established an enterprise zone with several adjacent communities, in which 4 new and 11 existing firms have expanded. The enterprise zone represents a cooperative effort between neighboring communities in recognition of mutually beneficial regional economic development.

As in all the previous communities, economic development in Princeton was led by a select group, though the mayor was less prominent. As in Mount Sterling and in Beardstown, economic development activities in Princeton were diffuse, offering a wide variety of programs to a variety of industries.

The experience of Princeton highlights a different aspect of economic development programming: the choice of organizational structure. The Princeton Industrial Commission was able to accomplish many of its objectives—establishing an enterprise zone, providing state assistance to local firms, and offering regulatory concessions—only as an arm of city government. Economic development organizations can adopt a variety of forms—including for-profit corporations, not-for-profit corporations, departments of city government, and quasi-governmental commissions. The Princeton experience illustrates that particular organization forms are better suited to particular tasks.

SULLIVAN

Sullivan (population 4,354) serves as the seat of Moultrie County in east-central Illinois. The city is relatively isolated. The nearest interstate runs through Mattoon 17 miles to the east; the nearest river flows 100 miles to the northwest; and the nearest airport lies 30 miles to the northeast. Nevertheless the economy of Sullivan has remained remarkably healthy. Sullivan has felt the effects of decline in agriculture and has endured its share of plant closing. But Sullivan's largest employers—Illinois Masonic Homes and Brach's Candy—are cyclically resilient; thus there has been little sense of economic crisis.

In spite of Sullivan's economic health, residents of Sullivan have a long history of activism in economic development. For years the Chamber of Commerce has supported economic development and a county-wide economic development corporation was developed in the early 1980s. Recently, however, most economic development projects have been sponsored by city government and led by the mayor.

Although supported by local bankers and the business community, the mayor has been the prime actor in economic development for several years. In 1963 a former mayor lobbied the federal government to begin work on Lake Shelbyville, a man-made reservoir. Today Lake Shelbyville represents one of the largest water-recreation areas in Illinois. Although Lake Shelbyville provides Sullivan with only minimal direct economic benefits, the lake greatly enhances the quality of life in the region.

The current mayor was instrumental in obtaining a large incentive package from the Department of Commerce and Community Affairs (DCCA) to recruit the Tubular Products corporation into a recently abandoned manufacturing plant. The package included a $400,000 Community Development Assistance Program Grant to Sullivan to loan to Tubular Products. In addition, DCCA provided a $200,000 Build Illinois Small Business Development Loan directly to Tubular Products and a $107,000 grant to the local community college to train Tubular's employees. Sullivan provided five years of property tax abatement. In March 1987, Tubular Products employed 164 local residents; but in December 1989, the plant closed.

Other community members took the lead in a drive to save Sullivan's Theater on the Square. The Little Theater on the Square opened as an equity playhouse in the 1950s, the only one of its kind in Illinois south of Chicago. This quaint theater on Sullivan's main square hosted many big-name performers, including Bob Hope and Cary Grant, making Sullivan widely known as the "Home of the Little Theater on the Square." The theater suddenly closed, however, eight years ago, due to financial difficulties. Immediately a group named "Friends of the Little Theater" was formed to save the theater. The theater also received public support. The state provided a $100,000 Build Illinois Grant to improve the theater's physical structure. The City of Sullivan offered to match private contributions two-for-one, raising another $90,000. Today the theater once again draws attendance from throughout the Midwest.

More recently, the mayor of Sullivan was instrumental in the creation of the Sullivan TIF district, which attracted both a Hardee's and McDonald's restaurant. The proceeds from the TIF district have been used to finance infrastructure and housing improvements.

In sum, economic development in Sullivan was led by the mayor and financed in large part by state funds. The targets for development activities are broad, the instruments diverse. Economic development success in Sullivan is clearly mixed. Sullivan has difficulty overcoming its locational disadvantages, even with lucrative financial aid packages. Sullivan remains, however, an attractive place to live, and is able to capitalize on its quality of life.

MONTICELLO

Monticello (population 4,549) is the county seat and largest town in Piatt County, 30 miles southwest of Champaign and 30 miles northeast of Decatur in east central Illinois. Monticello has a history of affluence and today serves as a bedroom community for nearby cities.

Monticello's wealth arose from two sources: "millionaire" residents and the headquarters of Illinois Power and General Telephone. Illinois Power and General Telephone located headquarters in Monticello because Monticello residents were wealthy and property taxes

were low. Before the 1968 Illinois Constitutional Convention, corporations were required to pay property taxes only in the location of their headquarters, thus headquarters were located where property taxes were low. After 1968, corporations had to pay property taxes where their businesses were located. This ended the attractiveness of Monticello to statewide corporations; within five years the tax contributions of Illinois Power and General Telephone, which had formerly paid 86 percent of all property taxes, had been completely withdrawn. The decline continued when Sterling Drug closed its Monticello plant in 1982 and Americana Health Care moved its corporate office in 1983. These events for the first time created interest in economic development in Monticello.

Although recently becoming active in economic development, Monticello pursued economic development with less vigor and enthusiasm than many other rural communities. Three groups in Monticello were involved in economic development: the Chamber of Commerce, the City Council, and the Piatt County Economic Development Council. These groups, however, played only supporting roles and seldom initiated economic development programs. Leadership in economic development in Monticello was from local realtors, with the assistance of bankers, business leaders, and the mayor. This informal group met as necessary for economic development decision making.

The informal group made economic development decisions on three occasions. Between 1983 and 1985, Wal-Mart was considering Monticello as a location for a new store and sought support from the city council. Wal-Mart was opposed, however, by owners of a local department store and by drug stores concerned with competition from the national retailing chain. Since there was little local support for the Wal-Mart store, opposition from local businessmen convinced the city council to reject Wal-Mart's requests. At approximately the same time, a trust approached a Monticello realtor about developing a 76-acre tract for light industrial development. Shortly thereafter, the realtor was approached by the Ring Can Company about building a plant on the industrial land. With the assistance of the mayor, the president of the Chamber of Commerce, and local bankers, the realtor was able to package a deal which brought Ring Can to Monticello.

Currently, business leaders from Monticello are seeking a new firm to occupy the abandoned Sterling Drug building. A Japanese auto parts producer has expressed interest in the building. Illinois Power is leading the effort to attract this firm.

The experience in Monticello differed noticeably from the other communities. There were no strong individual leaders and no formal economic development organization. There was no economic development plan. Economic development activity in Monticello was led by those who stood to gain directly by economic development: realty and utility corporations. Monticello has not suffered economic disruption like the other communities in this study; therefore, Monticello had few of the necessary components in place for economic development.

Summary of Findings

THE STIMULUS FOR ACTION

Economic conditions in the six Illinois communities varied widely. Mount Sterling faced economic hardship while the Monticello economy remained reasonably healthy. All of the communities, however, suffered economic decline in recent years. Decreasing farm prices, depressed retail sales, and international competition in manufacturing caused plants to close in all six communities. In some cases the economy weakened severely in a short time; in others the economy stagnated over a longer period. Further, the vigor with which economic development was pursued appeared correlated with the depth to which economy fell. Mount Sterling and Beardstown seemed willing to support any form of economic development; Sullivan and Monticello appeared willing to support only those development opportunities that did not challenge the status quo or the quality of life.

The experience of these Illinois communities suggests that rural communities pursue economic development largely to mitigate the impacts of external economic forces. According to participants in the process, economic development programs were set in motion by falling property values, declining retail sales, and deteriorating tax revenues, not by rural poverty, unemployment, or falling wages. These reports support the proposition that rural communities pursue economic development to serve the joint interests of capital and the local state. Only one community conducted a community survey and none of the communities targeted economic development programs towards unemployed or underemployed local residents or specific low-income populations. Instead, the case studies suggest that economic restructuring at the national and international levels which adversely affect capital and the local state foster local programs to develop rural economies.

PARTICIPANTS IN DECISION MAKING

The number of participants in economic development activities and decision making in all the communities was small. Although Mount Sterling did elicit community-wide support for recruiting a prison, the effort was led by a four-person committee. In Prophetstown, Beardstown, and Sullivan, economic development was led by the mayor, with the support of a select few community leaders (see Walzer & Kapper, 1989, on mayoral leadership in economic development). The decision making group in all of the communities excluded explicit representation of labor and farming organizations. In general, the case studies portrayed an elitist model of economic development decision making (Sharp, 1990).

In all six communities, economic development was supported by the business community, but not necessarily every business. Firms in retailing, banking, realty and utilities were the most active supporters—especially those locally owned. These businesses were market oriented; their profitability depended on the growth of local markets. Input oriented firms—e.g., farmers and food processors—and firms nonlocally owned were less active but seldom opposed economic development. This weak segmentation of the business community rarely created a division within

capital over economic development issues, but did further narrow the decision making group. As a result, decisions in rural economic development were often made by the local head of state and representatives of locally owned and market-oriented business—that is, by the mayor and the merchants on the square.

INSTITUTIONAL FORM AND FINANCE

Economic development in five of the six communities was implemented by a formal economic development organization. In Princeton, Beardstown, and Sullivan, economic development programs were led and administered by municipal government. Municipal governments can offer tax and regulatory concessions which directly benefit business. Municipal governments can also finance economic development with general tax revenues, shifting costs to workers and residents. Municipal governments thus can serve class interests through economic development programming, and the case studies offer evidence that they do.

The second most common form of economic development organization was the not-for-profit corporation, such as a county-wide economic development organization or the chamber of commerce. These organizations often served marketing functions: gathering information, producing pamphlets, and serving as a liaison between the local community and DCCA. Although these not-for-profit organizations were limited in ability to shift costs, they were also insulated from community politics (see also Rubin, 1986, and Hill, 1984, on economic development organizations).

The case studies illustrated considerable variety in development finance. Only the PMI in Prophetstown used equity finance; all the others used voluntary contributions or tax dollars. In general, the greater the scope of the project, and the greater the need for financial resources, the greater the need for public support. Local contributions toward economic development projects, in economically depressed communities obviously were limited, even by banks and utility companies. For these reasons, all six communities relied on external sources to finance elements of their economic development programs. In most cases the State of Illinois provided grants and loans, in others the state offered tax concessions or contributions to tax-increment finance districts and enterprise zones. In Mount Sterling, the state located a prison and in Prophetstown sold 20 percent of the stock in PMI to residents outside the community. In general, when large sums of financial support were required, decision makers seemed more inclined to engage in building public support.

Economic Development Activities

Economic development activities differed widely across the six communities. The predominant form of economic development activity in the six communities was the recruitment of capital through tax concessions, land write-downs, and loan subsidies—even as evidence mounts that these programs are ineffective at raising wages, stimulating economic growth, or even attracting industry (Ross & Friedman, 1991; Bartik, 1991). The experience in Sullivan, where a large manufacturer was attracted by public subsidies only to leave at the threat of unionization, offered a vivid example of the risk involved in such policies.

Even when recruitment policies are successful, tax concessions and other business subsidies serve some interests at the expense of others (Harrison & Kanter, 1978). In fiscally constrained communities, business subsidies can come at the expense of other local services, especially schools. A school administrator in Sullivan made explicit reference to these costs in his comments opposing Sullivan's TIF district. Greater reliance on user fees for "extracurricular" activities, commented the administrator, enables only the children of the affluent to participate in such activities. The same logic holds for other public services as well (Badcock, 1984; Fasenfest, 1985; Feagin, 1983, Hartman, 1984).

The potential bias of the economic development programs was demonstrated as clearly by those programs that the six communities did not pursue as the programs the communities did pursue. None of the communities adopted a strategy focused on retraining workers to adopt to changing technologies. None of the communities attempted to replace firms leaving the community with worker-owned firms. None of the communities established cooperatives to help struggling farmers. And two of the communities rejected overtures from Wal-Mart—not for fear of low wages, but for fear of greater competition and lower profits for local merchants.

The Results of Development Programs

Finally, and perhaps most importantly, the economic development activities in the communities resulted in widely differing outcomes. Prophetstown, which initiated the most innovative and highly acclaimed economic development program, added 13 jobs. By attracting a state prison, Mount Sterling created many jobs but not necessarily for local residents. Housing costs in Mount Sterling rose, benefiting homeowners but costing renters. Princeton, Beardstown, and Sullivan attracted jobs using capital subsidies, tax abatement programs, and tax-revenue transfer programs. Most of these jobs, however, were low-paying service jobs, and most of the financing mechanisms reduced revenues for social programs. Finally, Monticello attracted a manufacturer but repelled a retailer.

The economic development program in each of the communities produced results; and often the results created jobs and economic growth. But the results in each community were mixed: growth required sacrifice that is unevenly spread. Businesses that sell in local markets benefit; displaced workers, renters, and taxpayers lose. The results of economic development in the rural communities can clearly benefit some segments of society but often at the expense of others.

Conclusion

The case studies offered insights into the practice of rural economic development. In general, the forces that stimulate economic development activity, the participants involved in decision making, the policies pursued, and the economic results of economic development activities in rural communities closely resembled the same forces in urban communities. Economic development is stimulated by external forces, adversely impacting local merchants and the property tax base. In response, an elite group of business and government leaders design and implement economic development programs through organization forms often insulated from community politics. The programs typically involve capital subsidies often at the expense of social programs. The programs in some cases generate jobs, but the jobs are low paying, and not always filled by local residents.

In rural economic development programs, the mayor is often more directly involved din economic development (Walzer & Kapper, 1989) than in urban programs. And more frequently than in urban areas, economic development programs in rural areas are administered directly by municipal government. Decisions are made by a smaller group of individuals (Moxley & Hannah, 1986). Programs are targeted to narrower objectives. Finally, resources more often comes from outside the community (Chicoine, 1988; Swinth & Alexander, 1990). Differences in economic development programs in rural areas differ in degree, not in kind, from urban economic development.

The difference between urban and rural areas stems from the fundamental difference in scale. The smaller scale of rural governments enables control of rural governments by a smaller group of community leaders. Further, the smaller scale of rural society eliminates the role of institutions in spawning community leaders. That is, community leaders are not typically leaders of large organizations such as national corporations and labor unions; instead they are groomed through informal networks within the rural upper class (Moxley & Hannah, 1986). This limits labor and minority access to economic development decision making.

Scale also influences the institutional form of economic development organizations in rural areas. Lack of size in most rural communities presents the creation of an organization focused exclusively on economic development at the municipal level (Walzer & Kapper, 1989). This leaves two options: adding economic development to the functions of municipal government or creating an organization for economic development for a larger geographic area such as a county or a multi-county region. Attaching economic development functions to municipal government can create political conflict between economic development and social programs (Harrison & Kanter, 1978). Increasing the geographic scope of the economic development organizations—e.g., into a county-wide or multi-county organization—can create political conflict over the focus of economic development programming (Wells, 1991; Henderson et al., 1992). The relative predominance of economic development administration by city governments suggests that it is easier to manage conflict between capital and labor in one community than to manage conflict between capital in different communities.

Finally, scale limits influence and access to resources. Whereas urban governments have access to bond markets, Community Development Block Grant entitlements, and sizable tax bases, rural governments do not. Thus rural governments are more reliant upon state government for economic development funding. Such reliance limits the scale, scope, and autonomy of rural developmental efforts.

In conclusion, economic development programs in rural areas exhibit many of the same characteristics as programs in urban areas. Economic development programs arise in response to economic restructuring at the national and international level. And economic development programs are managed by few for a few. But differences in scale between urban and rural areas cause differences in the practice of economic development. Lack of economic size increases the vulnerability of rural communities and limits their abilities to influence their own destines (Swinth & Alexander, 1990). Lack of bureaucratic scale removes institutional ladders to positions of rural leadership. These differences narrow both the goals and opportunity set of rural economic development decision makers. As a result, economic development programs in rural areas are even more constrained to the conditions imposed by external funding agents and thus narrowly focused on capital recruitment.

References

Badcock, B. 1984. *Unfairly Structured Cities.* Oxford, England: Basil Blackwell.

Bartik, T.J. 1991. *Who Benefits from State and Local Economic Development Policies?* Kalamazoo, MI: Upjohn Institute for Employment Research.

Blakely, E.J. 1989. New Federalism and rural America: Implications for local public economies. *Journal of the American Agricultural Association* 70(Dec.):1085–1090.

Fainstain, S., N. Fainstain, R. Child Hill, D. Judd, & M.P. Smith. 1986. *Restructuring the City.* New York, NY: Longman.

Fasenfest, D. 1985. Community politics and urban redevelopment. Presented at the 1985 Midwest Political Science Association.

Feagin, J. 1983. *The Urban Real Estate Game.* Englewood Cliffs, NJ: Prentice Hall.

Fosler, R.S. (ed.) 1991. *Local Economic Development: Strategies for a Changing Economy*. Washington, DC: Practical Management Series.

Friedland, R. 1982. *Power and Crisis in the City*. New York, NY: McMillan.

Gottdiener, M. 1987. *The Decline of Urban Politics*. San Francisco: Sage.

Harrison, B., & S. Kanter. 1978. The political economy of job-creation business incentives. *Journal of the American Planning Association* 44:424–435.

Hartman, C. 1984. *The Transformation of San Francisco*. Towata, NJ: Rowman & Allanheld.

Henderson, D., L. Tweeten, & M. Woods. 1992. A multi-community approach to community impacts: The case of the conservation reserve program. *Journal of the Community Development Society* 23(1):88–102.

Hill, R.C. 1984. Economic crisis and political response in the motor city. *Sunbelt-Snowbelt Urban Redevelopment and Regional Restructuring*. New York, NY: Oxford University Press.

Klemanski, J. 1989. Tax increment financing: Public funding for private economic development projects. *Policy Studies Journal* 17(3):657–671.

Mollenkopf, J. 1983. *The Contested City*. Princeton, NJ: Princeton University Press.

Molotch, H. 1976. The city as a growth machine. *American Journal of Sociology* 82(2):309–322.

Moxley, R.L., & T.S. Hannah. 1986. Individual participation patterns in community social action. *Journal of the Community Development Society* 17(2):1–23.

Peterson, P. 1981. *City Limits*. Chicago, IL: University of Chicago Press.

Ross, D., & R.E. Friedman. 1991. The emerging third wave: New economic development strategies, in R.S. Fosler (ed.), *Local Economic Development: Strategies for a Changing Economy*. Washington, DC: Practical Management Series.

Rubin, H. 1986. Local economic development organizations and the activities of small cities in encouraging economic growth. *Policy Studies Journal* 14(3):363–387.

Shaffer, R. 1989. *Community Economics: Economic Structure and Change in Smaller Communities*. Ames, IA: Iowa State University Press.

Sharp, E. 1990. *Urban Politics and Administration*. New York, NY: Longmann.

Squires, G.D. (ed.). 1989. *Unequal Partnerships: The Political Economy of Urban Redevelopment in Postwar America*. New Brunswick, NJ: Rutgers University Press.

Stone, C.N. 1984. City politics and economic development: Political economy perspectives. *Journal of Politics* 46:286–299.

Stone, C.N., & H.T. Sanders. 1987. *The Politics of Urban Development*. Lawrence, KS: University of Kansas Press.

Swanstrom, T. 1985. *The Crisis of Growth Politics*. Philadelphia, PA: Temple University Press.

Swinth, R., & A. Alexander. 1990. Power and dependence between the core and rural communities: Participating with actors in solving local problems. *Journal of the Community Development Society* 21(1):71–82.

Thomas, M.G. 1988. *Profiles in Rural Economic Development*. Kansas City, MO: Midwest Research Institute.

Walzer, N. 1990. *Economic Development in Small Illinois Communities*. Macomb, IL: Institute for Rural Affairs.

Walzer, N., & S. Kapper. 1989. *Issues and Concerns for Small City Officials in Illinois*. Macomb, IL: Institute for Rural Affairs.

Wells, Betty L. 1991. Building intercommunity cooperation. *Journal of the Community Development Society* 21(2):1–17.

CHAPTER 29

Public Plazas Bring New Life to Main Streets in Indiana, Texas, and Wisconsin

Chris Dimond

In the 1970s, a tangle of transportation problems prompted Lafayette, Ind., officials to begin planning for changes downtown. At the time, Amtrak trains ran down the middle of a central city street, requiring passengers to load and unload on the street, and the local bus station was situated on Lafayette's courthouse square, causing traffic delays and interfering with nearby business operations.

Officials decided to reposition the railroad tracks and create a junction using the city's historic train depot, which would have to be moved. The facility would not only serve as a trans-portation hub, but it also would stand as the centerpiece of a public plaza for Lafayette's 45,000 citizens.

In purpose, Lafayette's plans were similar to countless others in cities across the country. Driven by a desire to bring people—and dollars—downtown, local officials are implementing a variety of ideas to beautify their street-scapes, calm traffic and create pedestrian-friendly pathways and venues.

An Historic Hub

The Lafayette Railroad Relocation project included the 1902 Big Four

---

Originally published as "Made for Walkin'," American City & County, *Vol. 113, No. 8, July, 1998. Published by the Intertec Publishing Corporation, Atlanta, Georgia. Reprinted with permission of the publisher.*

Depot from the start. The building had served as an active railroad station for 70 years prior to its closing, and citizens wanted to preserve it as part of the city's heritage. The rails were relocated, and the depot was moved four blocks to a spot adjacent to the Wabash River near the heart of the city's downtown.

In 1996, the restoration was complete, and today the depot provides rail, inter-city and local bus service for more than 7,000 passengers per week. It also serves as the crossroads for pedestrian traffic traversing the historic John T. Myers Pedestrian Bridge, which joins Lafayette to West Lafayette.

As the depot underwent restoration, Lafayette began building James F. Riehle Plaza, an outdoor venue directly in front of the depot. Constructed of brick pavers and featuring extensive landscaping and a fountain, the plaza is a popular site for festivals, concerts, art fairs and receptions. A textured concrete wall on the east side screens the plaza from nearby trains and noise.

Since completion of the $7.8 million project, Lafayette residents have embraced the depot and plaza. New development, including retail establishments, restaurants, offices and housing, has sprung up within three blocks of the site. The project also has encouraged redevelopment in West Lafayette, across the Wabash River.

The railroad relocation was vital to business development in Lafayette, but it couldn't be done at the expense of the riverfront environment," says Liz Solberg, Lafayette's manager for the railroad relocation project. "We used the track relocation as an impetus for creating a vital, exciting civic resource."

"Driving" Development

Lafayette citizens are drawn downtown by the ambiance of the riverfront, open space and the retail surge created by the James F. Riehle Plaza. In Glendale, Wis., officials are creating a similar draw by implementing a new streetscape plan that incorporates pedestrian-friendly, unifying elements.

West Silver Spring Drive, a straight, 1-mile stretch of heavily traveled arterial, is lined with parking lanes and surrounded by vacant properties and underused land parcels. In its place, the city is constructing a gently curving roadway that will produce larger land parcels for office and retail development. The improvements will also slow traffic (which routinely exceeds the 35 mph speed limit by 10 to 15 mph) and remedy an accident-prone intersection.

Neighborhoods to the north and south of the new roadway will benefit from additional upgrades to the area, says Glendale City Administrator Richard Maslowski. "The neighborhoods will be united by the new configuration," he notes. "In addition to traffic being slowed, a number of new features will enhance [residents'] experiences."

For example, signal light intersections will increase from two to five; green spaces and pedestrian lighting will be added; and benches, bus shelters and rest areas will be installed. Overall, the city intends to produce a safe and inviting place for residents and visitors to stroll and shop.

The West Silver Spring Drive project will be completed this fall at a cost of $24 million. As it progresses, officials are ensuring that subsequent development will create a harmonious character for the area.

A landscaped entrance will open the west end of the project, and the city has established development guidelines that define acceptable architectural materials and building placement. For example, the guidelines specify that front entrances for commercial buildings must face the roadway. Side and rear entrances can be provided to enhance pedestrian access, but they must be less dominant visually than the front entrances.

Concrete Continuity

While Glendale is reconstructing a neighborhood to make it more attractive to new businesses and patrons, Waco, Texas, is using the streetscape concept to update its image citywide. The goal is to create an environment that offers downtown visitors easy access to an already-developed retail and entertainment base.

"Development came first in Waco," says Bill Falco, city planning director. "Rather than implementing the streetscape program to spur development, we were focused on enhancing the progress that was already being made.

"We have created a program that links Waco's various downtown areas," he explains. "People will be able to travel in a more friendly pedestrian environment between shops, restaurants, hotels, apartments and clubs."

The $4.1 million project kicked off two years ago, when Waco hosted a four-day design workshop in which city representatives, downtown business leaders and Baylor University shared ideas about the new streetscape. The city then analyzed primary vehicular and pedestrian linkages, development characteristics, existing sidewalks and other features.

Measuring 9,600 linear feet, the project incorporates lighting, furniture, paving, signage, landscaping and other features to help create an attractive and functional pedestrian environment. Work is under way, and residents already are seeing signs of transformation.

For example, as sidewalks are improved or replaced, they are inlaid with brick pavers and Texas stars that establish continuity yet provide some variation among the districts. Streetlights, trees and furniture have been installed, and the city has improved parking areas with the addition of pedestrian pathways and lighting.

Residents have responded favorably to the changes, as have developers. State and federal offices, hotels, loft apartments, restaurants and specialty shops have been added to Waco's downtown, and even more enhancements are in the works. For example, state symbols may be integrated into the sidewalk design and correlated to a map of key city sites. The city also is installing a bicycle/pedestrian trail along the Brazos River to connect with the downtown improvements.

Finally, Waco residents and visitors will have a new place to relax and play when the city celebrates the 150th anniversary of its founding in 2000. Heritage Plaza, which will connect the retail district to city hall, will be completed that year. Spanning 115,000 square feet, it will include fountains and shaded areas.

Waking the Waterfront

Balancing commerce with a sense of community is a recurring characteristic in local revitalization projects. Although new developments emphasize spaces that will entice commercial interests and the traffic they generate, they also incorporate elements that take the squeeze off pedestrians. As demonstrated in Lafayette, Glendale and Waco, such projects are changing the feel of downtown districts, ensuring that the public does not pass them by.

In Boston, officials are taking the pedestrian-friendly concept and extending it beyond the downtown perimeter to connect urban districts with some of the city's nearby natural resources. The City of Boston Beach Access Plans will improve public access to the beaches and parks along the Boston Harbor coastline, as well as to the harbor islands.

The plans are backed jointly by Massachusetts, Boston and the Boston Harbor Association. With them, the parties intend to reintroduce the vitality of the waterfront to Boston's urban neighborhoods.

Key elements of the plans include the Dorchester Project, which will connect and update pedestrian routes in the Dorchester Bay area, and the Long Island Project, which will open access to one of the harbor islands and create a new circulation route. Both projects emphasize convenience for pedestrians and cyclists.

The $5.2 million Dorchester Project comprises an area that is bordered by the University of Massachusetts to the north, an expressway to the west, Boston Harbor to the east and the Neponset River to the south. Existing pedestrian routes are disjointed and difficult to use, and the plan seeks to turn that around by connecting existing arteries and by introducing consistent design elements and signage.

When completed (a target date is not available), the Dorchester Project will provide a critical ink in Boston's HarborWalk, which was initiated in 1986. Extending from east Boston through Dorchester to the Neponset River and Greenway, HarborWalk eventually will connect 43 miles of public and private space via a network of continuous walkways and green spaces.

Along with the Long Island Project, the Dorchester Project ties into "Back to the Beaches," a $30 million program to develop and restore 8.5 miles of urban shoreline and harbor beaches. Launched in 1993 by the city, Back to the Beaches is a long-term project, like Boston's other beach-related ventures.

"The Boston Harbor waterfront is one of the city's most valuable recreation, cultural and educational resources," says Lorraine Downey, director of Boston's Environment Department. "Boston's Beach Access Plans are an important component of HarborWalk and the Back to the Beaches programs. Together, these projects are providing access to and linking miles of open space along Boston Harbor."

Similar to the Dorchester Project, phase 1 of the $8 million Long Island Project specifies enhancements to existing infrastructure. It focuses on a 214-acre island that is physically connected to Boston's mainland but closed to the public. The project will open access to the island, which offers spectacular view of the city and Boston Harbor.

Additional phases for the Long Island Project call for design and construction of new facilities to create an extensive circulation route along the island's shoreline. As in Dorchester, consistent design elements and signage are included in the plans, as are connections with Boston's transportation network. Overall, the project is intended to create a direct, efficient intermodal transportation system and to strengthen recreational and cultural possibilities for the region.

There is no single way to revitalize downtowns; successful projects have included everything from streetscaping to reconfigurations of existing districts. However, cities across the country appear to be focusing on a need for pedestrian-friendly elements that create a sense of convenience, safety and community. And in doing so, they are stretching the old definitions of redevelopment and changing the urban landscape.

CHAPTER 30

Establishing a Main Street Through Architecture in Columbus, Indiana

Robert Campbell

You know something's going to be different when you see the big billboard on the interstate. You're driving south toward Columbus, Ind., from Indianapolis, where your plane landed. The billboard blares:

WORLD RENOWNED ARCHITECTURE
FREE SAMPLE 22 MILES AHEAD

Later, when you turn off I-65 to head into Columbus, you find yourself passing beneath the arch of a red bridge, a bridge as bold and bright as the gate to a Zen temple. You learn this arch was designed by Jean Muller, a Swiss engineer headquartered in Paris.

The folks in Columbus call it "the front door."

Columbus, it's clear, is a town that pays attention to architecture. In this city of 35,000—no more people than jam Fenway Park in my hometown of Boston—and in its surrounding Bartholomew County, there are at least 60 buildings, plus a few parks and monuments, designed by nationally or internationally known architects. For any fan of architecture, the roll call is impressive: Eliel and Eero Saarinen, I.M. Pei, Kevin Roche, Cesar Pelli, Charles Gwathmey, Harry Weese, Edward Larrabee Barnes, Robert A.M. Stern,

Originally published as "Modernism Meets Main Street," Preservation, Vol. 50, No. 5, September/October, 1998. Published by the National Trust for Historic Preservation, Washington, D.C. Reprinted with permission of the publisher and author.

Eliot Noyes, Aldo Giurgola, Richard Meier, Thom Mayne, the firm of Hardy Holzman Pfeiffer, and many more.

There's a source for Columbus' obsession with architecture. For more than 40 years now, a local businessman, J. Irwin Miller, and his Fortune 500 company, Cummins Engine, have taken it upon themselves to improve the town's architecture. Cummins and other Miller interests not only build buildings themselves. They also help select the architects for almost all the new public buildings in town. And for those public buildings, they pay the architects' fees and expenses.

I have been sent here to answer a couple of questions. After four decades, what's been the impact of all that so-called good design? Is Columbus a scattered world's fair of self-regarding ego trips? Or do the buildings add up to something more?

After wandering the town for two days and talking to lots of people then and later, I came to two conclusions. First, yes, the Columbus architecture program has been an incredible boon to the city and its county. Second, if Columbus is the measure, it's going to take more than architecture to rescue the American small town from decline.

Whatever conclusions you reach, Columbus is certainly worth a visit. If you enjoy town life, you'll probably do what I did: ignore the Holiday Inn and its clones out near the interstate and come downtown to stay, instead, at the Columbus Inn at Fifth and Franklin streets. Possibly the world's largest bed-and-breakfast, the inn fills an 1895, Romanesque Revival building that was originally the city hall. It's a few steps from the center of everything.

You'll probably begin your visit at the visitors center, cater-cornered from the inn. Unlike other visitors centers, Columbus' is almost entirely devoted to architecture. During my visit, it was offering a major exhibit on the work of Harry Weese, a Chicago architect who designed many of the early buildings under the Columbus architecture program. There were also displays on the meaning of architectural terms, on the architecture of Florence and Rome, and on the 16th-century Italian architect Andrea Palladio. A small theater offers a film on the town, its history, and, of course, its architecture. An architectural bus tour leaves regularly; you can choose the one-hour or the two-hour version.

J. Irwin Miller, who started all this, is 89 now. The running of the architecture program has largely been taken over by a son, Will Miller. Will heads one of the family companies, Irwin Financial, but he admits he spends a quarter to a third of his time on pro bono work—"because that's how the family wanted it." Miller talks about the program in his office, which is housed in a magical building, designed by the Pritzker Prize–winning Connecticut architect Kevin Roche, with etched glass walls that resemble lightly drifting snow.

"We've made architecture something to think and talk about," he says. He explains how the program works. The Cummins Engine Foundation maintains a list of about 30 leading American architects. It's a secret list; if you're an architect, you may not even know you're on it. The foundation deliberately keeps the process "shrouded in mystery," says Miller, to discourage architects from lobbying for consideration. Frequent consultation with distinguished older architects, deans of architecture schools, and critics helps keep the list up to date. Since Will took over, there's been a serious effort to refresh it with younger names. When the city or county needs a new public building—a school, a fire station, a city hall—the foundation picks five or so architects off the list, people it thinks would be appropriate. It suggests those names to the client—the school board, fire department, county library, or whomever. The client picks the architect it likes best. From then on, the only role of the foundation is to reimburse the client for the architect's fees and expenses.

Will Miller emphasizes there's more to Columbus than architecture. "That's only about 20 to 25 percent of the giving of the foundation. Architecture is one piece of the puzzle. We've got community identity, pride, a sense of place. There's a healthy aspiration level. There's the ethic of self-help of the Midwest, nurtured by a series of leaders over time, of whom my father is one. We can accomplish what normally only a bigger city could do. Our county of 65,000 has the cultural life of a city of 250,000. We have, for example, an excellent symphony orchestra."

I hint that a visitor might not suspect this richness of cultural life from a walk through the largely deserted downtown. He admits the problem.

"We've got to keep the pedestrian experience alive," Miller says. "I don't know how you make a city out of parking lots."

Later, over lunch, I meet J. Irwin Miller himself. At 89, he's impossible to one-up. I tell him I first saw his name when his face appeared on the October 1967 cover of *Esquire* magazine. The article was entitled: "Is It Too Late for a Man of Honesty, High Purpose and Intelligence to Be Elected President of the United States in 1968?" I remember thinking, I tell him, "Who the hell is J. Irwin Miller?" He replies equably, "That's a question I often ask myself." Miller, I learned from that old article, besides being a master businessman, reads Greek and Latin, plays a Stradivarius, was the first layman ever elected president of the National Council of Churches, and helped organize the August 1963 March on Washington at which Martin Luther King, Jr., delivered his "I have a dream" speech.

He talks about the accidental way in which the architecture program began. "At Yale around 1930 the only thing we were interested in was architecture. Yale was building its traditional colleges, but we undergraduates knew about the modern architecture in Europe. I'd followed the [1922 competition for a new *Tribune* building] in Chicago, where Eliel Saarinen, the Finnish architect, finished second with a modern design. I was a fan of that. So a few years later, when my family was involved in building First Christian Church here, I wanted him. He'd come to the United States to head Cranbrook School near Detroit. At first he said that as the son of a Lutheran, he didn't do churches because they'd become too fancy. I went to see him and told him ours was a congregation of simple external signs and a rich inner life. It's been said that Frank Lloyd Wright was also interviewed for the job, but he wasn't. Saarinen said, 'You go tell your mother I'll do the building.' At first people hooted at the design—'Why can't you do a church that looks like a church?'"

That was the first Miller involvement in architecture, around 1940. The program as it exists today began 15 years later, when Bartholomew County realized it would have to build an elementary school a year for the baby-boom generation. The first, says Will Miller, was terrible. The school board then came to Cummins Engine Foundation for help. The foundation suggested Harry Weese, and the company underwrote his fee. Weese designed a small gem, the Schmitt School. After that, the school board went to Cummins for almost every school, and the architecture program, which nobody ever planned, was under way. "The first team of outside advisers," says J. Irwin Miller, "were Douglas Haskell, the editor of *Architectural Forum*, Pietro Belluschi, dean of the architecture school at MIT, and Eero Saarinen [Eliel's son], who was probably my best friend."

Over time, the program became codified, but it's still pretty informal. New York City architect Deborah Berke remembers the phone ringing one day. Will Miller was on the line. "My understanding is he's made a million phone calls, and if your name came up often enough, he'd call you to interview you over the phone," she says. Six months later, she was designing a branch library. Kevin Roche, who not only designed several Columbus buildings but also served as an adviser, says he'd get calls asking him to suggest an architect for a particular new building. "I never knew who else they'd called, and I never knew how they made the final selection," he says.

Not everyone, it should be noted, loves the program. Recently there occurred a minor revolt at Cummins, led by stockholders who thought the company should spend more on dividends and less on good works. And you hear mutterings in the town about elitism, about the Millers trying to run every-

thing. But those are minor dissonances in a general chord of public approval.

Enough about the process. We're here to look. What's Columbus really like? First of all, among all those buildings, only a few qualify as remarkable works of architecture.

The best is still Eliel Saarinen's First Christian Church. No architect I spoke with failed to give it first place. First Christian is modernism at its best: logical in its order and orientation, bold in its shapes and spaces, but still in touch with the crafts tradition. Photographs don't do justice to the magic of its perfectly balanced yet asymmetrical architecture, especially in the main sanctuary. But there's more than the sanctuary; First Christian fills a whole city block. Wings containing offices, classrooms, and a daycare center branch out from the sanctuary to frame elegant courtyards.

One of these wings is particularly successful: Raised a story above the ground, it's a bridge that allows the lawn to flow beneath it in the modern manner, while indoors its corridors are illumined with south-facing glass. Unfortunately, it's necessary here to ring the preservation alarm. A minister with a growing congregation plans to double the width of this wing, thus destroying all those elegant corridors, and—worse still—fill the open space beneath with new construction. Most buildings only become more interesting as change layers up over time, but a few are so perfect you don't mess with them. First Christian is one. And since the church owns a parking lot across the street, why try to expand on the old site? Isn't crossing the street part of the neighborliness of small towns? Isn't that how you generate community life?

Probably the second most remarkable design isn't architecture; it's the landscaped gardens around J. Irwin Miller's own house in a pleasant neighborhood a mile or so north of downtown. The house—one of a very few by Eero Saarinen, well known for Dulles Airport near Washington and many other buildings—is a gem in itself. But the landscape, by Dan Kiley of Vermont, who has done a lot of work in Columbus, is a true masterpiece—not, alas, open to the public. Among other winners are *The Republic* building (1971), home of the town's newspaper and one of the most elegant modern glass boxes ever conceived, by the late Chicago architect Myron Goldsmith; and Eero Saarinen's Irwin Union Bank and Trust (1954), including its addition by Kevin Roche (1973), where Will Miller has his office. The younger Saarinen also did a much-admired church, North Christian, but it's perhaps too theatrical, in the mode of Saarinen works like the TWA terminal at JFK Airport in New York. Also strong are two of the newest additions, the Veterans Memorial in the main town square, by Thompson and Rose of Boston, where the carved quotations from soldiers' letters home bring you to tears; and Mill Race Park, by Michael Van Valkenburgh, also of Boston, a relaxed, pleasantly varied large park next door to downtown. The park isn't helped much by garish pavilions designed by Stanley Saitowitz of San Francisco, including an observation tower that's a nostalgic revival of the gritty industrial architecture of a bygone era—although in fairness, Saitowitz's grandstand is elegant.

So there's plenty for the architecture buff to see. And there are less visible virtues, such as the fact that Columbus has jump-started the careers of a lot of good architects ("the chance to work in Columbus made my career," says Van Valkenburgh, who's done several projects there). But do these gems add up to anything larger than their individual selves? Not usually. They're pretty much scattered, like raisins in a pudding. They reinforce each other in only a couple of places, of which the best, always photographed as the iconic view of Columbus, is a plaza where I.M. Pei's main library looks past a Henry Moore sculpture toward First Christian Church.

Do the buildings, on the other hand, destroy the genius loci of Columbus? Is this an example of globalization, in which the special character of a place is violated by the inrush of outside fashions? Will Columbus eventually become Anywhere? I don't think so. For the most part, the new buildings don't feel as if they've landed from Mars. Modernism is sometimes castigated as an international style that ignores local scale and context, and that's often a fair rap. But in Columbus, the architects have usually looked around and found ways to be good neighbors. "I did a less aggressive, less industrial looking building than I might have done elsewhere," says Deborah Berke of her new branch library in the neighboring community of Hope. "This building's *nice*." On the other hand, nobody's done any stage-set revivals of the past, either.

Finally, the key question: Does the architecture program nurture community life? I wish I could say so. But Columbus's main street, called Washington, is pretty lifeless, although not so bad as many of America's boarded-up Main Streets. And in the whole city you can't get a good meal, as far as I could tell. I asked one knowledgeable resident for the best restaurant; he thought for a moment and then suggested the name of a private country club. Another recommended what turned out to be a chain restaurant with galvanized-steel peanut buckets and galvanized-steel partitions: a nostalgic, theme-park nod to the industrial past, a lowbrow clone of that high-style viewing tower in Mill Race Park. Along Washington, there's been a lot of cute renovation of Victorians, but hardly anybody (except tourists like me) ever seems to be on the sidewalks, and the few real stores are pretty much empty. Editor Harry McCawley of *The Republic* tells me the owners aren't renovating to make money; they just want to feel, he says, "I'm part of something here." That's great, yes—as at Disney— it can lead to a Main Street that is a representation of the past, not the real vital thing. If you define Main Street as the place where the action is, then the real ones in Columbus are elsewhere: National Road in the north (they used to call National the bypass, but now it's the center) and Route 46 to the west, a car-culture fast-food strip a former mayor calls Mayonnaise Mile. Mayonnaise Mile leads to Tipton Lakes, a brand-new, picture-book house-and-garden suburb where bicyclists and joggers snake among streams, lakes, and mostly hideous phony-traditional houses: a kind of Hallmark card version of paradise, terminally boring to me, but obviously a marketing success.

I try some of these questions on Will Miller. Doesn't Tipton Lakes (a development with which he was involved) suck life out of downtown? As always, his answer is interesting. He points out that Columbus developed at a confluence of rivers and streams, from which flatboats once traveled as far as New Orleans. Downtown grew up next to those streams. But they occupy a floodplain that can't be built on. (Mill Race Park is in the floodplain.) So downtown Columbus isn't a center; it is, in fact, at the extreme southwest corner of the city, bordered by floodplain at its south and west. By putting Tipton Lakes on the other side of the floodplain, developers hoped to recenter the downtown. It's an idea that may look better on a map than in reality. I find it hard to see how a suburban sprawl development is going to help the downtown.

Two other, more disastrous attempts have been made, over the years, to invigorate Washington Street. The first, in 1974, was designed by Cesar Pelli and is called the Commons. Occupying a full block at the lower end of Washington, it's a shopping mall sheathed in dark solar glass, a sort of black hole in the city. The Commons violates every commonsense principle of marketing you can think of. You can't see what's for sale through the black glass, so there's nothing to lure you in. If you do go inside, you find yourself in an intimidatingly huge volume of empty public space, surrounded by a few small shops and restaurants, along with commercially unrentable space that's used for things like two art galleries (one closed much of the time), a friendship association with a Japanese sister city, and a branch outlet for government licenses. There's nowhere near enough critical mass of activity to hold your interest or make you want to return. Like other urban malls of its era, the Commons is a misguided attempt to bring a suburban idea downtown. All you get is a bad mall and a damaged Main Street. The Commons is kept on life support

by means of an endless series of pro-
grammed activities, everything from
concerts to aerobic calisthenics.

The other, less forgivable mistake is
the Cummins Engine corporate headquarters designed in 1983 by Kevin
Roche. It's only a block off Washington
and brings 700 office workers to the center of town, workers who should be out
lunching, strolling, and socializing with
other townsfolk. Instead, the Cummins
building turns its handsomely landscaped backside to the town, and the
employee entrance faces onto a parking
lot that in turn fronts a highway and the
floodplain. Still worse, Cummins installed a company cafeteria to make sure
nobody ever needed to go outside.
"When I go there, I never recognize
anyone," reports a long-time Columbus
observer. "You never meet those people
anywhere else."

I harbor a bias: that the function of
towns is to bring people together as a
community, to introduce them to one
another so they can develop a life rich in
experience. Life is impoverished when
we feel we know the stars of our favorite
sitcoms better than we know our neighbors.

Columbus has done wonders. But
maybe the focus is still a little off. "We're
still in the mode of saving retail downtown," says Will Miller. "We've done a
C-plus to B-minus job." I'd argue he has
the cart before the horse. What downtown needs is people living and working
there. Some kind of retail will follow
them, but it isn't going to bring them
there. What if Cummins found a way
to encourage its younger employees to
live above the Washington Street stores?
What if it closed that headquarters cafeteria?

Why would you want to live above

the store, you ask? Well, you can forget
the commute, you can walk to work, you
can enjoy restaurants and entertainment
without a car trek, you can save a lot of
money, you can enjoy the social and cultural buzz of a living town. Ask anyone
who's inhabited such a place. A Columbus woman remembers how, way back
around World War II, her family and
many others used to come downtown to
Washington Street in the evenings. To
eat, I ask? No, she says, just to sit on the
fender of the car or stroll the sidewalks,
talking to everyone. She remembers it
with affection.

Some of the latest initiatives aim
at this kind of community life, but
they're half measures. There's attention
to what Will Miller calls "ligaments"—
connective tissue, such as new bike,
roller-blade, and hiking trails that will
link the city's parks. Even at that bold
bridge "front door" interchange out at
the interstate, room was left for such
trails to thread through the concrete and
steel. There's been attention, too, to
streetscape in the form of tree plantings
and patterned paving, sometimes including bricks with donors' names en-
graved on them. A graphics program is
being tested to help visitors by dividing
the city into five color-coded districts,
with coordinated directional signs.

There's admirable local patriotism
in much of this activity. But some of it
may be missing the point. The last thing
Columbus needs is more aesthetic fine
tuning. Washington Street is already too
tame. What it's desperately lacking is a
sense of irrepressible life busting out.

"Retail is the obvious answer to
pedestrian traffic," says Miller. But there
were cities filled with pedestrians before
the age of the retail consumer, which
began only with the department stores

of the late 19th century. Samuel Johnson rarely went shopping in 18th-century London. Florence in the Renaissance did not offer a retail experience (although it certainly does today). If major retail isn't going to return to downtown—and I don't see why it should—does that mean the end of city life? Is that really all there was?

Columbus poses what may be the key question for the city of the 21st century. How do you make a city center that isn't dependent on consumerism? How do you recapture the intensely rich cultural and social life of cities, without a blitz of shopping?

Only a few miles away, I stopped at Franklin, a similar town that hasn't had the benefit of anything like Columbus'

architecture program. I wanted to compare. This town's courthouse square, which obviously had once been magnificent, was now occupied largely by antique malls. The town was selling its image while its life was disappearing, as if you were peddling your dying grandmother's jewels. Columbus could become an upscale version of that. It could turn into a painted mask of itself: a theme park of architecture and a theme park of Main Street America. Or it could reinvent the American small town. Oddly enough, so far as I can find out, no other patron has tried to emulate the great achievement of the Millers anywhere else in America. It's still Columbus' ball game to win or lose. I wouldn't bet against this town.

CHAPTER 31

Preserving Main Street in Madison, Indiana

Bradley Skelcher

Nothing won is lost:
Every good deed, nobly done,
Will repay the cost.
Leave to Heaven, in humble trust,
All you will to do;
But, if you succeed, you must
Paddle your own canoe.
        Sarah Bolton, 1814–1893

Although Sarah Bolton of Madison, Indiana, wrote this poem in the mid–19th century, it remains relevant today and exemplifies the spirit of the Main Street Pilot Project. This historic preservation and economic rehabilitation program allows local citizens to control their community's destiny without government interference. Using a grassroots approach, the Main Street Project developed a plan enabling small cities to "paddle their own canoes."

The project was born amid the fes-tivities of the 1976 bicentennial celebration. The event generated widespread interest to learn about the nation's heritage and then to celebrate it. Many of the celebrations were community-based. But, when citizens began looking at their own communities' history, they discovered that they were losing part of their local heritage—the historic buildings lining Main Street. In response to pleas for assistance to reverse this trend, Mary C. Means, director of Chicago's Midwest Regional Office of the National Trust for Historic Preservation, created the Main Street Project.

Two years later, Means had received financial support from private and public foundations. She assembled a staff of preservation consultants and advisers and then chose three pilot cities in need of downtown restoration: Gales-

Originally published as "Preserving Main Street in the Heartland: The Main Street Pilot Project in Madison, Indiana," Small Town, Vol. 22, No. 2, September/October, 1991. Published by the Small Towns Institute, Ellensburg, Washington. Reprinted with permission of the publisher.

burg, Illinois; Hot Springs, South Dakota; and Madison, Indiana. While many previous historic preservation efforts often included residential houses, the Main Street Project focused on the city's central business district, or Main Street. Together, Means and her staff sought to demonstrate that preservation produces economic benefits for downtown businesses, as well as improves the entire community's quality of life.

Early Preservationists in Madison, Indiana

In 1977, the National Trust chose Madison, a small city located on the banks of the Ohio River in southeast Indiana, as a pilot city. The trust concluded that Madison exemplified a city in the mid-position of its population requirements (5,000 to 60,000 people). And, the city contained a relatively stable population along with a sound business base and the potential for growth. Most importantly, Madison featured historically significant architecture.

The city has had a long-established commitment to preservation. Since the early 1960s, John Windle, founder and president of Historic Madison, Incorporated (HMI) and member of the National Trust's Board of Advisors, had promoted historic preservation. The efforts of Windle and HMI safeguarded many of Madison's Italianate and Federal architectural styles and cast-iron storefronts. Now, virtually the entire city is on the National Register of Historic Places, including almost every structure within the central business district.

In 1972, a key player in the Madison story, Tom Moriarity, first visited the town as a member of the Historic American Building Survey. The team surveyed the town's Federal-style riverfront buildings. Moriarity's work impressed Windle and he offered him a position as executive director of HMI in order to utilize his skills in promoting and supervising the town's preservation activities. Moriarity was impressed with the town's historic architecture and accepted the offer. Later, the National Trust hired Moriarity as its first Main Street Project Manager in Madison.

Unveiling Madison's Historic Past

During 1976, the National Trust took a special interest in Madison and the community's preservation. Things began to happen. Windle secured a National Register of Historic Places grant to restore the Schroeder Saddle Tree Factory for use as an industrial museum. Moriarity convinced the owners of the Steinhardt-Hanson building to replace its modern sign with a flush-mounted and more historically accurate one. In the process, the owners uncovered the original storefront, finding it virtually intact. Moriarity then convinced the owners to restore the facade.

Moriarity saw this as an opportunity to inspire other downtown building owners to consider historic preservation. And, the event inspired the National Trust to send a film crew to record the storefront restoration in a film titled, "What Is Preservation?" and feature Madison in its magazine, *Historic Preservation*.

The combination of the building restoration and the bicentennial celebration provided inspiration for Madison's historic preservationists. Citizens formed a grassroots group, Save the Neighborhood, to stop new business encroachment on the town's historic residential areas. Another group, led by Moriarity, organized Preserve Our Fountain, a campaign to restore Madison's cast-iron Broadway Fountain. The group collected over $85,000 from private citizens and the city of Madison. Nearby Hanover College sponsored a lecture by Leopold Adler II concerning preservation activities in Savannah, Georgia—efforts which partially inspired the Main Street Project.

In all, Madison appeared to be the most promising community in the competition to become a pilot city. The town's citizens and officials showed strong commitment to historic preservation. The city had the organizational and administrative ability to handle complex projects. Basically, all that Madison needed involved guidance with design changes in order to enhance the historic qualities of the central business district architecture.

Madison's Historic Building Stock

Virtually all of the buildings in Madison's downtown had remained stable and unaltered over the decades. Nonetheless, during the 1950s and 1960s, some owners remodeled their buildings with aluminum false fronts and hung new signs to attract auto-oriented customers. Luckily, the cast-iron storefronts remained intact underneath, making the preservationists' job much easier. The buildings' major problems involved maintenance (such as paint) and the replacement of various building components.

In June, 1977, the National Trust hired three consulting firms to assist in Madison's preservation. Chicago's Shlaes & Company provided an economic analyst and a plan to improve the retail market. Foran and Greer, a firm from Akron, Ohio, was hired as a promotional adviser. Miller, Whiry, and Lee, Incorporated, from Louisville, Kentucky, surveyed Madison's design problems. The firms worked closely with Moriarity, Historic Madison, Incorporated and the downtown merchants.

Growth Threatens the Downtown

Since the 1950s, Madison had experienced steady economic and population growth stemming from the expansion of the electric power industry along the Ohio River. The Indiana and Kentucky Electric Corporation spurred part of the growth when it built a power plant north of town in the 1950s. In the 1970s, the Indiana Power Company began construction of the nearby Marble Hill Nuclear Power Plant, employing over 2,000 construction workers.

Consultants warned that this increased economic activity might harm the historic district by stimulating movements to remodel and modernize the buildings. And, since the downtown lay along the waterfront and had limited space, people feared that potential developers might demolish old buildings in order to replace them with new, more spacious ones. This type of quick development posed a real threat to the welfare of the downtown building stock.

A major problem for downtown businesses involved the district's lack of space. To the north and south, the Ohio River and the surrounding hills blocked expansion. West and east expansion space was also limited: To reach the central business district, shoppers must negotiate a treacherous descent of 800 feet from the surrounding bluffs. Therefore, retail and service businesses had begun to locate along the hilltop area overlooking the old downtown. The hilltop was simply easier for shoppers to access. It also allowed for expansion.

As in many other cities, the downtown merchants faced challenges from the new commercial strip development. Merchants there formed the Hilltop Business and Professional Association and demanded an extension of city services. Pressed for funds, municipal officials took maintenance money away from Main Street needs to pay for the expanded services.

Meanwhile, the central business district's infrastructure had already deteriorated due to inadequate funds. The city had neglected to repair sidewalks and streets and had not replaced the water system since the 1860s. The downtown also had parking problems and space limitations. But, the new hilltop development made funds even more scarce.

Historic Buildings as Shopping Promotion Strategies

Ironically, the hilltop development had a bittersweet effect on the downtown. While it threatened downtown's retail market, it also helped preserve the building stock from modernization since the retail expansion occurred elsewhere. Now business owners needed to find ways to increase trade and available retail space and make the downtown more attractive—without endangering the architecture. The consultants advised that solutions should include minimal intrusions on and the adaptive reuse of existing buildings. They suggested engaging in aggressive marketing and promotional strategies using the Victorian-era architecture as a theme.

In October, 1977, promotional advisers Richard Foran and William Greer outlined suggestions for downtown businesses to jointly promote the upcoming Christmas season and develop thematic window display designs. Enlisting the services of Susan Jackson Keig, a Chicago-based graphic artist, Foran and Greer showed examples of shopping bags which highlighted a Charles Dickens theme of "The Spirit of Christmas Past" to promote the shopping area's historical aspects. Foran and Greer said these promotions would offset the advertising costs and show downtown unity. They advised merchants to find ways to entertain customers and extend shopping hours. Furthermore, they directed merchants to begin publishing catalogues for direct mail orders.

Moriarity and Historic Madison used these recommendations to initiate joint promotions for the Christmas season. The downtown merchants organized a Christmas doorway competition with a multicultural theme. Moriarity urged the merchants to research and recreate Victorian-era decorations. And, the Madison *Courier* newspaper published information about traditional Yule decorations.

The promotional scheme was a success. It both increased sales and showed downtown merchants the benefits of cooperative activities. With renewed enthusiasm, merchants anxiously awaited the release of the final reports on Madison's problems and potentials from the economic and design consultants.

Hilltop District Again Hinders the Main Street Effort

In 1978, Shlaes & Company released its market investigation results. This report became Madison's Main Street Project economic plan. The town had captured close to two-thirds of all sales in its larger secondary area, which extended into Kentucky. The report concluded that Madison is a central place for southeast Indiana due to the town's preexisting retail business concentration and mix of available goods and services.

Even though Madison had a long-established retail market, the consultants warned merchants not to stay passive. Automobile-equipped shoppers do not have to trade with Madison stores, especially if expansion elsewhere provides them with better alternatives.

Adjoining market areas, however, are not the main competitors of Madison's central business district. It is the hilltop strip development which competes with downtown. For example, Sears had transferred its operations to the hilltop area to locate near higher volumes of automobile traffic. Much of Madison's retail sales reputation is due to the volume of trade on the hilltop commercial strip. The Shlaes report cautioned downtown merchants not to fight the new development but to cope with it by making their own stores more appealing.

In the meantime, the report advised the city to formulate guidelines for future growth. It said Madison needed to encourage less dispersion of shopping facilities and regulate lot sizes to encourage more concentrated development. This would also provide the hilltop with more efficient municipal services. And, the report said that potential small lot investors considering the hilltop area might also investigate the small space availability in the downtown district.

Adaptive Reuse Increases Downtown Space

Virtually the only way for merchants to increase the amount of available space in the concentrated central business district was to utilize upper floor space. Much of the downtown buildings' second floors had been neglected or left undeveloped. The economic report recommended that building owners consider adaptive reuse of their second and third floors to increase space. This, they said, is especially attractive to professional tenants desiring offices near the county government and to older citizens looking for convenient apartments with easy access to services and retail spaces.

In addition, the hilltop shopping area only offers convenience items and does not provide merchandise for upper-income consumers. By upgrading their inventory to meet these demands, downtown merchants could attract these consumers. Also, changing merchandising techniques, utilizing joint promotions and extending store hours would enable downtown merchants to attract the higher income groups. The report suggested that the Madison Business and

Professional Association should take the lead in promoting these ideas among downtown merchants.

Modern Demands with Traditional Values

The downtown's major attraction is its architecture, which, the report stressed, reflects traditional retailing values. Changing traditional merchandise to meet modern demands without losing quality and the personal contact between customer and merchant often presents the store owner with a challenge. The report suggested the downtown should offer a mix of modern merchandise, such as current clothing designs, with traditional wares, such as collectibles and antiques. This, combined with the buildings' restored appearance, would express an inviting mix of modern and traditional merchandising values.

To draw people from outside the area, Madison needed to promote the entire town's historic qualities. Shlaes & Company recommended engaging in a market strategy that incorporated historic home tours by community service groups to draw interested customers into the downtown. Merchants, with the assistance of HMI, could provide information and promote a sense of intrigue about the city's history.

The report also criticized merchants for not exploiting the benefits of special events, which already drew large numbers of people, like the chautauqua of arts, the weekly farmers' market and the annual speedboat regatta. Merchants also complained that inadequate parking facilities posed a major problem for people attending these events and kept regular clients from shopping downtown. Parking problems also inconvenienced regular clients year round. However, the report contended that parking was not the main problem. Downtown merchants do not service their clients like the hilltop businesses. For example, unlike the downtown merchants, the hilltop district maintained expanded and uniform hours. People are willing to forgo expansive parking lots if they receive personal customer service.

Committee Demands Conformance to Historic Architecture

By the end of the project, the downtown had not implemented most of the Shlaes & Company's suggested strategies. But, merchants did follow suggestions on how to enhance their buildings as a marketing tool, even though Miller, Whiry and Lee's first report on design enhancement proved unsatisfactory.

This initial report was the project's most disappointing aspect. The consultant presented its downtown design plan to the Madison Steering Committee in late 1978. However, the committee found the designs unsympathetic and too modernistic. In response, the National Trust demanded that the firm produce a more compatible design that better fit the city's historic fabric.

With the aid of Moriarity and HMI, the consultants developed a design plan and submitted it to the steering committee in February, 1979. This sought to reestablish the historical bonds between the downtown and the Ohio River. The designers wanted to reunite the central business district's architecture with the city's original purpose—Ohio River trade.

To accomplish this, the plan suggested a blend of old and new designs. It also recommended installing sidewalk furniture and planters, improving streets and sidewalks, and planting trees and shrubbery to screen parking lots and provide sun protection for customers. The plan called for removing false storefronts to reveal the hidden Italianate features of massive cornices, decorative window caps and cast-iron storefronts. Once revealed, the historic buildings would illustrate both architectural continuity and a connection with the past.

Grand Plans for the Historic Riverfront Park

Beginning with the Broadway Foundation Esplanade, the consultants designed a park blueprint which would visually connect the downtown to the riverfront. Flagpoles with the Main Street Project logo would accentuate the building's uniform cornice lines. Proposed sidewalk improvements included bas-relief sculptures of important local figures, such as town founder John Paul, and important events in the city's past. The designers planned to use old paving bricks to blend with modern materials—a technique which would reinforce the downtown's commitment to both the past and the future. They hoped to replace modern outside lighting with reproductions of historic streetlights. The plan also called for burying overhead utility lines to provide aesthetic and historic continuity. The designers believed the riverfront park would evolve into a symbolic entrance and welcoming point

for the bridge entry across the Ohio River.

The Reality: Skepticism and High Costs

Delays and high estimated costs produced skepticism and reluctance among Madison merchants. As a result, very little of the plan was completed by the end of the Main Street Project. However, the city of Madison did complete the Broadway Fountain Esplanade, portions of the riverfront park and a parking lot renovation.

And, individual building improvements produced positive results for the entire city. Moriarity chose to focus efforts on individual building preservation to demonstrate to owners the associated economic benefits before encouraging the pursuit of the designer's more costly projects. To do this, he built coalitions among business organizations and governments in order to lead and publicize the project. He worked with people like John Galvin, president of the Madison Business and Professional Association; Dottie Reinhardt, former president; and Harold Gossman of the chamber of commerce. With their help, Moriarity successfully convinced merchants of preservation's economic and historic validity.

Local Leader Spurs the Project Onward

Project Leader Tom Moriarity held seats on several other agencies in addition to HMI and the Main Street Project. This participation helped him secure $650,000 for elderly housing from the Department of Housing and Urban Development. Moriarity (as a member of the Madison Housing Authority) then persuaded other members to locate the elderly housing in existing downtown structures. He successfully argued that this would bolster the downtown economy and demonstrate adaptive reuse of old buildings.

In addition, Moriarity worked with the city of Madison and Public Service of Indiana to bury utility cables and install footings for them. He then secured another Housing and Urban Development grant for $21,000 to revise the city's 1960 comprehensive plan. And, he developed an innovative idea which used revenue sharing funds to pay the $11,000 fee required by the National Trust to enter into the Main Street Project.

Moriarity used the success of the Steinhardt-Hanson Building's renovation to catapult the Main Street Project into the forefront of the community's consciousness. Virtually all merchants joined in the restoration effort in varying degrees. Many replaced nonconforming signs with flush-mounted signs and painted their buildings to make them historically authentic. An NBC crew filmed the removal of a thrift store sign as the owner replaced it with a more accurate one. Several storeowners removed aluminum false fronts to expose the cast iron underneath.

To resolve the downtown's space problems, Moriarity campaigned for upper story renovations. He convinced building owners Harold and Susie Nowling and Bula Keeton to renovate their upper floors into apartments. Moriarity also sought investors to develop new apartments through the adaptive reuse of the vacant Meese Building.

And, when one firm filed bankruptcy, he found a replacement business—relieving a panic-stricken group of merchants.

Funding Proves to Be a Major Obstacle to Rehabilitation

For larger projects, merchants often needed to obtain additional financial support through low-interest loans. Moriarity attempted to negotiate with local banks to provide a loan pool at 7 percent interest. This would enable Madison to attract outside investors and continue its preservation efforts. however, this was a problem.

In actuality, Madison banks offered very little financial support. For example, although Moriarity found outside investors to purchase the vacant Meese Building, they could not secure local financial support. And, with no local support, they couldn't obtain money from outside financial institutions.

Since the banks provided little local funding, financial assistance had to be solicited from other entities. Moriarity helped secure an Urban Development Action Grant and a matching grant from the Heritage Conservation and Recreation Service to help develop Madison's riverfront.

However, the lack of local financial support remained a major obstacle to realizing the owners' renovation projects. Moriarity was forced to depend mainly on cash awards provided by the National Trust and other preservation agencies in order to induce owners to continue their efforts. For example, he used a $1,500 National Trust award to assist the Koehler Buildings owners in purchasing paint.

Despite scarce funding, the visual

appearance of the downtown was transformed by the end of the Main Street Project, and it was done primarily by private initiative. Moriarity's efforts leveraged $10 of private investment to every $1 in project costs.

Assessments Prove the Project's Overall Success

The Main Street Project was truly a grassroots movement in Madison. Even with low fund availability, the private investment and the building owners' hard work produced remarkable results. With more assistance, they could have achieved even greater results.

Two representatives from Heritage Canada's newly organized Canadian Main Street Program visited Madison in 1980 to offer their observations and summarize the project. John J. Stewart, director of the Canadian Program, said the project was "so successful that you don't see the success of it—and that's the success of it. It makes the most of the town's existing fabric."

Without the project, Madison wouldn't appear the way it does today. Prior to the program, grass grew between the unrepaired sidewalk cracks. The downtown was in a confused, deteriorated state with decayed buildings and cluttered signs trying to entice an increasingly reduced number of customers. The Main Street Project offered guidance to improve the city's appearance.

In terms of economic development, unfortunately, the project failed to produce much growth. Yet, unlike the unfortunate experience of fellow Main Street pilot city, Galesburg, Illinois (recounted in the July-August, 1990, issue

of *Small Town*), it did help stabilize Madison's economy. Retailers did not lose much ground. The project even slowed the movement of retail establishments to the hilltop area (though the trend continued in that direction).

Madison Paddles Its Canoe in the Wake of the Project

Above all, the Main Street Project instilled an awareness of historic preservation—though much of this credit is due to Historic Madison, Incorporated, and Moriarity's charismatic leadership, as well as the volunteers' efforts. However, Madison's program may have relied too much on Moriarity and the volunteers since, when he left, he had cultivated no leaders to take his place.

When preservationists hoped to move beyond voluntary action by persuading the city council to pass a restrictive historic preservation ordinance in 1981, the community split between advocates of individual rights and community design. The strong opposition even equated the ordinance with oppressive laws in the Soviet Union.

The ordinance included items like paint color restrictions, mandatory facade restoration, roof design and the planting of historically compatible shrubbery. Most importantly, the ordinance also required a mandatory review of all proposed demolition projects. Opponents argued that the ordinance placed too many restrictions on private property rights. Preservationists contended that the community had a right to protect its historic and architecturally valuable resources.

Opposition to the ordinance was strong, even among some original Main

Street Project members. Had Moriarity and the Main Street administrators cultivated new leadership in Madison before departing, the town's battle over the 1981 preservation ordinance might not have been so bitter.

Despite the conflict, the Main Street Project made citizens aware of Madison's architectural heritage—an accomplishment which is not only important for Madison, but for the entire nation. The pilot project even fostered a Main Street movement in Canada. All this was accomplished by the grassroots efforts of volunteers attempting to "paddle their own canoe" to increase the quality of life, better their economy and preserve the historical value of the places they call home.

CHAPTER 32

Dealing with a Volume Chain Store in Carroll, Iowa

Jerry Knox

When a major national volume chain store moves into a small town, there is cause for both excitement and alarm. Small towns face difficulties when dealing with a large national chain wishing to locate in or adjacent to the community. However, one small town (Carroll, Iowa, population 9,579 in 1990) successfully guided Wal-Mart, a major national chain store, into the town's central business district, where community leaders believed it would complement previous downtown development efforts. An examination of Carroll's experience can help other communities finding themselves facing a similar situation.

Carroll, Iowa's Downtown

During the late 1960s, Carroll took advantage of then-available federal urban renewal funds to redevelop its existing business core. The approach taken was somewhat novel for a community of its size and for that time. Rather than use a clearance and redevelopment approach, local leaders decided that they could best strengthen the central business district by converting the existing building stock into a downtown shopping center or mall. They accomplished this by retaining the outward appearance of the two primary square blocks comprising the bulk of the city's retail activity and building interior connections through them.

Originally published as "Dealing with a Volume Chain Store: Carroll, Iowa, Guides Development and Protects Its Downtown," Small Town, Vol. 22, No. 2, September/October, 1991. Published by the Small Towns Institute, Ellensburg, Washington. Reprinted with permission of the publisher.

As a result, shoppers can enter a store and find themselves in a mall-like setting which permits passage from one business to another via a central corridor with connections to all shops within the complex. The two square blocks represent the downtown's primary retail building mass; once shoppers are inside the area, interior access to all of the establishments is provided.

The downtown mall represents a significant financial, economic and political commitment to remaining a strong retail central city core. It shows a high level of understanding about a strong downtown's function in preserving a healthy community. In addition, the recent financial investment in the central business district underscored the need to keep the downtown robust in order to protect that investment.

The National Chain Store Arrives

Wal-Mart expressed strong interest in locating in or adjacent to Carroll. This, of course, generated a number of local discussions concerning the desirability (and inevitability) of a major chain locating in town.

Coincidentally, the city council and planning commission invited a graduate planning class from the Community and Regional Planning Department at Iowa State University to come to town and provide planning and design advice for the downtown. When the class discovered the imminent prospect of a national chain store locating in Carroll, members immediately examined the siting aspects in detail. The class's conclusions reinforced community leaders' belief that a

downtown location was preferable to the more typical outlying one.

The class argued that a downtown location would complement existing businesses, while a location away from downtown would compete with the efforts already expended in developing the interior mall approach. Initially, civic leaders suggested that Wal-Mart be given land within the general downtown area, but separated from the two-block interior mall by a large parking lot. Additional analysis by the ISU graduate class led to the suggestion that having the large parking lot located between two retail centers was a better alternative than accepting a traditional chain store location on the outskirts of town, but that the parking lot also represented an unnecessary barrier. Accordingly, the class strongly recommended that the community leaders guide Wal-Mart into a location either directly adjacent to or integrated with the existing mall.

The city did have cleared land available for development, thanks to a local urban renewal project. A large tract on the outskirts of the central business district was available at fair market value. Although owners had cleared this land with no idea that the national chain would be a prospective buyer, the community had decided that it needed retail/office expansion.

Why Is a Strong Downtown Important?

The class helped underscore for the community the importance of a strong downtown city core. Several reasons are that the downtown:

- is the activity center of the city,
- is the retail and financial center,
- is a major employment center,
- is accessible to all areas of the city, and
- represents a major investment in infrastructure, and Carroll's infrastructure (especially roads and parking) is specifically designed to serve downtown.

Helped in part by the graduate class's planning and design advice, the town convinced Wal-Mart to accept the city center location *and* agree to build the new store to complement the existing mall. As importantly, the community convinced itself that such a move was desirable to protect and enhance its investment in the central business district *and* that it is possible to stand fast and force a national chain to recognize local goals.

Carroll entered into negotiation with Wal-Mart officials. As a result, the city agreed to share the costs of water main and storm drainage improvements. Because Carroll needed these improvements anyway, the city easily rationalized the expenditures. On the other hand, Carroll persuaded Wal-Mart to pay for 50 percent of the cost of a large new parking lot, with the agreement that everyone, not just Wal-Mart customers, could use it. In addition, the city obtained a grant from the Iowa Department of Transportation to finance additional traffic signals needed to help smooth and regulate traffic flow.

Carroll's Advantages

Several reasons explain Carroll's ability to deal with a national volume chain on a more or less equal footing. First, the community had made major investments in the downtown, and business and government leaders alike understood and supported maintaining the investment. Then, Carroll had a high degree of community consciousness or agreement. This is not to suggest that citizens don't debate community issues. To the contrary, previous debates concerning the advisability of proceeding with the downtown renewal project informed the public and community leadership about the need to protect its previous investments.

Carroll has a long history of strong community leadership. It was (and is) known as a town that can make things happen, especially with economic development.

Finally, design consultation was available from an outside "expert," and the community leadership availed itself of that expertise. In sum, Carroll had downtown development plans, a new major retail chain store fit within the scope of the plans, and both the city and the developer were willing to negotiate.

Options

Communities have three main options when a national volume chain expresses interest in opening a store. The first approach is "business as usual" where the community merely lets the process play out as it will by treating the case as a normal land use decision. This option works better, of course, where the community has a highly defined redevelopment or rezoning process and a professional staff to oversee the process. The obvious disadvantage is that the city is in a reactive rather than proactive stance. If the location of the new major retailer is crucial to overall retail and service business health, this option does not offer much help in guiding the new business to an optimal site.

A second option is to treat the location as a private market decision. So long as there is a willing buyer and a willing seller, and the zoning is appropriate, the city stance is merely that of an interested bystander. To be sure, the zoning is crucial, but, because most American towns vastly overzone land for commercial uses, zoning is typically not an issue. This has the same disadvantages as the first option. However, much less city staff involvement is needed or expected. In fact, this approach works without a professional staff.

The third option—that one chosen by Carroll—is for the community to define community goals and work to meet both community and developer objectives. This puts the city in a proactive stance.

Lessons, Strategies, Cautions

There are advantages to working *with* the developer to meet city objectives—although this implies a willingness to compromise. It is essential that community goals, and the supporting reasons for these goals, are clearly defined and understood. If a downtown location is favored, zoning—plus other incentives—can guide new development there. Land, or assistance in acquiring land, will be needed. In addition, it is essential that the city and county synchronize land use policies. It does little good for the city to expend efforts to guide development into the central business district if the county will permit the same development on the unincorporated outskirts of town. In Carroll's case, an intergovernmental agreement with Carroll County permits the city to exercise extraterritorial zoning control.

From the city's perspective, it is important to keep the city in control of the process. It is almost a certainty that the development process will take longer than expected. The developer will want a "fast track" approach. But, unforeseen events can sidetrack the process. If unanticipated surprises occur, the city has a responsibility to its business community and citizens at large to prudently investigate the change's probable impact before proceeding. Of course, the city should perform such additional investigations expeditiously so as not to unduly delay the process.

In a January, 1991, telephone conversation, Carroll's city administrator, Mike Johnson, offered suggestions based on his experiences regarding the implementation of large projects. He said that adequate staffing is needed in order to efficiently and effectively address the development process when undertaking a large project. In particular, a city needs an attorney with land development experience, a good financial adviser and an experienced planner. It doesn't matter whether the staff is in-house or consultants. This type of expertise is essential and the people must have freedom from any current or ongoing duties in order to react quickly to changing situations.

If a city has clearly articulated development goals for the central business district, and if the community at large generally understands and shares these goals, it can reap substantial advantages to actively working with large national volume chains or mass merchandisers who express interest in coming to town. Carroll's businesspeople and merchants found it advantageous to negotiate with Wal-Mart in order to pursue city goals. Other towns facing similar prospects can use Carroll's experience.

The wisdom of Carroll's decision to retain and strengthen a strong city core is borne out by a recent (August, 1991) announcement. K-Mart, Payless Shoe Source, Fashion Bug, Burger King and Hy-Vee (a major Iowa-based food store) have all decided to build in Carroll's central business district.

CHAPTER 33

Building Community Through Strategic Planning in McPherson County, Kansas

David E. Proctor and *Leah E. White*

In 1990, the Kansas State Legislature adopted a three-year program of community strategic planning grants that provided funds to county-wide and multi-county economic development entities (Ott & Tatarko, 1992). Legislators believed it important for Kansas counties to assume responsibility for planning and development so as to strategically position themselves within the rural, state, national, and international economies. The goal of these strategic plans was to strengthen and expand local and regional economic development efforts, thereby maximizing chances for county stability, growth, and long-term survival. According to Section 3 of House Bill 2603, the Community Strategic Planning Assistance Act, the purpose was to:

a. build and enhance economic development capacity at the local and regional levels;

b. develop and sustain long-term commitments for local development efforts;

c. encourage broad-based local and multi-county development strategies that build on local strengths and to

Originally published as "Building Community Through Strategic Planning: A Case Study of McPherson County, Kansas," Journal of the Community Development Society, *Vol. 27, No. 2, 1996. Published by the Community Development Society, Milwaukee, Wisconsin. Reprinted with permission of the publisher.*

complement and reinforce statewide economic development strategy;

d. maximize state investments in economic development through more efficient implementation of limited resources.

The strategic planning sessions also became, however, moments in which the rural culture reflected upon itself. Consistent with other strategic planning experiences (see Bryson & Roering, 1987; Kaufman & Jacobs, 1987), county citizens spoke of their visions for the future, their strengths, weaknesses, opportunities, and threats. Rural Kansas told of their history and dreams, their needs and goals. Interestingly, however, these strategic planning participants also worked to build community during these sessions. Bellah et al. define community as

> a group of people who are different yet interdependent, who are bound together by mutual responsibilities arising out of a common history, a history which they have not simply chosen to be a part of but which they are nonetheless responsible for carrying on (1987, p. 246).

During the strategic planning process in McPherson County, Kansas, two conceptions of community were articulated: one focusing on the county as community, another viewing individual towns and population groups as the locus of community. By the end of the strategic planning process, the county view of community emerged as the preeminent perspective.

To fully explore this case, this chapter will: (1) provide a brief context of McPherson County, (2) detail the method of data collection and analysis, (3) present the results of the analysis by

detailing the argument structure of the two positions on community, and (4) offer some conclusions drawn from this study as well as implications for community development.

A Case Study of Community Building

STUDY AREA

McPherson County, named in honor of Civil War General John Birdseye McPherson, is located in south central Kansas. The county is approximately 190 miles southwest of Kansas City, 450 miles east of Denver, and 60 miles north of Wichita. The county is thirty miles wide and thirty miles long, about the size of Rhode Island. The county is very rural, encompassing nine communities: Lindsborg, Roxbury, Canton, Galva, Inman, Moundridge, McPherson, Marquette, and Windom. Approximately 27,000 people live in McPherson County with nearly half that population residing in McPherson, its largest city. The county ranks among the top ten Kansas counties in number of farms and total acres harvested (Docking Institute, 1992, p. 22). The population of this rural county, as in many Kansas counties, is aging. In 1980, the median age was nearly 32 and by 1990, almost 35 (p. 1). Per Capita personal income in McPherson County averaged just over $17,000 in 1991 (p. 21).

Method

Communication scholars explore various types of discourse to examine the process of community-building, including mythic language (Malinowski, 1948), ideological language (Procter, 1991), fantasy themes (Bormann, 1985), and narratives (Langellier, 1989; Fisher, 1992). In the current study, communication from a variety of sources was examined, and from that communication, narrative structures of community-building were discerned. Walter Fisher, professor of communication at the University of Southern California, explained that, "Communities are co-constituted through communication transactions in which participants co-author a story that has coherence and fidelity for the life that one would lead" (Fisher, 1992, p. 214). These co-authored stories create common bonds and identity in citizens by constructing a common knowledge base, expressing and instilling values, and motivating action for groups of people (Fisher, 1992; Langellier, 1989; Lewis, 1987; Peterson, 1991).

Data Collection: Most data were collected at seven monthly strategic planning sessions. Each meeting was approximately two and one half hours long. The meetings were held at a variety of locations in McPherson County, including a hotel conference center, a public grade school, a local bank, a Lutheran church, a college library, and an American Legion hall. An average of fifty people attended each meeting. Participants represented a wide variety of ages, occupations, incomes and opinions. Two researchers attended the meetings as participant observers. One served as a meeting facilitator and the other as a meeting recorder.

Each meeting was audiotaped. Strategic planning participants would organize in small groups around tables. Researchers randomly selected two of these tables for each meeting and recorded the interaction at those tables. Participants were told that the meetings would be audiotaped so that the facilitators received an accurate record of what transpired at each meeting. Additional communication data were collected from comment in a county-wide survey, newspaper reports of the meetings, and from informal discussions with several county residents.

Data Analysis: After collecting the communication, grounded theory—"the discovery of theory from data" (Glaser & Strauss, 1967)—was selected as the method for data analysis. The initial coding began by "breaking down ... an observation, a sentence, a paragraph and giving each discrete incident, idea, or event a name, something that stands for or represents a phenomenon" (Strauss & Corbin, 1990, p. 63). For the current study, individual sentences represented the unit of analysis for initial coding. This step of analysis revealed twenty-seven different initial codes which viewed community as county and twenty-one initial codes which articulated community as individual town or population group (Table 1). The second step was to group these initial codes to recognize linkages and identify attitudes, causes, and motivation. The following narrative, delivered by a farmer at one of the strategic planning meetings, illustrates the coding process.

> I've been trying to get the EPA to come out here and live with me for about a month now (*Initial Code: EPA/government agency*). I want them to understand what it's really all about (*Initial Code: lack of understanding*). They're out here mandating for us, but they don't have to live out here (*Initial Code: unfair mandates*). We're all gonna go hungry someday because of all the rules and regulations of the

EPA (*Initial Code: harmful and excessive regulations*).

From this narrative and these initial codes, a focused code was created and labeled *Government agencies are perceived negatively*. After completing the initial and focused coding process, researchers engaged in theoretical sampling, or the process of collecting and analyzing additional data in order to check and refine the identified categories (Glaser & Strauss, 1967). Specifically, after all data were collected, ten percent of the data pool was set aside and examined only after all the initial categories and focused categories were identified. This step seeks to (and did) verify that the identified categories accurately and exhaustively represent the data (Glaser & Strauss, 1967). Once all data were coded and theoretically sampled, analysis was conducted to organize focused codes into overarching community-building narratives. This grouping revealed two general and competing narratives differing in basic knowledge, value structure, and proposed actions. In the following section, the argument structure of each narrative is outlined, then each element of the overarching narrative is illustrated through the words of the strategic planning participants.

Results

Two competing community narratives were articulated in McPherson County during the strategic planning process. One narrative constructed community as encompassing the entire county (Table 2). This narrative (1) contrasted strengths of McPherson County with surrounding counties, (2) stressed the interdependence of the entire county and the importance of cooperation and broad vision, and (3) warned of the threats to McPherson County and the strategic planning process. In a competing narrative, community was located within groups and individual towns of the county (Table 3). This narrative (1) urged protecting the unique characteristics of specific towns and groups within the county, (2) emphasized the importance of individualism, and (3) warned listeners of threats to individualism existing in the county.

COUNTY-WIDE NARRATIVE

Those county citizens who supported a vision of a county-wide community spoke highly of the county as a whole rather than of focusing on individual towns. These citizens spoke favorably of the "county's leadership," "the progressive nature of the county," and the county's ability to "address industrial prospects, their individual problems and idiosyncrasies and make positive moves to address those issues." These citizens contrasted the strengths of McPherson County with weaknesses of other counties. One banker contrasted McPherson County farming with that of surrounding counties:

> I used to be in the bank in Herington and you drive into Dickinson County and Morris County and northern Marion County and you'd see farmstead after farmstead that was vacant and you just don't really see that out in McPherson County. Farming here is strong.

In another comparative narrative, a CPA highlighted McPherson County's ability to deal with prospective industry. He contended that,

Table 1
Perceptions of Community in McPherson County:
Initial Codes for Communication Analysis

Initial Codes Constructing Community as County

- joint projects
- cooperation
- sharing
- working together
- county-wide issues
- broadness of scope
- interested citizens
- involved citizens
- lack of separation
- participation
- need for integration
- interdependence
- unity
- uniqueness causes problems

- diverse representation
- county economic strength
- county farming strength
- long range planning
- planning beyond specific issues
- General McPherson as county symbol
- inclusiveness
- equitable
- threat of losing faith
- threat of competing interests
- threat of pessimism
- broadness of vision
- knowledge/understanding of county

Initial Codes Constructing Community as Individual Town and Population Groups

- locally-owned
- local control
- uniqueness
- county harms localities
- separation
- possessiveness
- protectionist
- isolationist
- self-sufficiency
- self-reliant
- negative perception of government agencies (EPA, County Commission, City Commission, Universities)

- individual interests/needs
- individual talents
- lack of involvement
- lack of understanding of county
- entrepreneurship
- rivalries
- self-serving
- unfair government mandates
- threat of loss of freedom
- threat of loss of uniqueness

There's a lot of counties that don't have the abilities, the economics, and the mechanisms to address prospective industries that are coming into the county. They come into our county and we say, "O.K., this is what your problem is, we'll address it. You tell us what you need and we'll fix it, we'll find it." We've got those abilities, we've got the mechanisms in place to do it, we've got the economics, we've got the money to do it.

Diversity and uniqueness were also discussed as strengths of the entire county.

A vice president at a local college stated, "We have populations that represent a variety of ethnic and cultural backgrounds and we celebrate that. Communities that generate positive public interest from the state, from the national and the entire world. We are drawing attention to ourselves and we are proud of it."

Citizens who promoted a county-wide vision of community talked of the county's interdependence. One participant told the story from the perspective of the small towns.

Table 2
Elements of County-Wide Community Narrative

Contrasted Strengths of McPherson County with Surrounding Counties

- Economic strength
- Diversity as strength
- County leadership as strength
- Farming as strength

Stressed Importance of Interdependence, Cooperation, and Broad Vision

- Issues are county-wide
- The more one community gains, the more everyone gains
- Total county involvement needed
- Working together = survival

Warned of Threats to County Community

- Negative attitudes
- Lack of participation
- Competing interests, including parochialism, outside economic entities

Table 3
Elements of Individualistic Community Narrative

Urged Protection of Unique Characteristics of Individual Towns and Groups

- Allegiance not to McPherson County, but to local town or group
- Competing interests acknowledged as fact of life
- County gains perceived at expense of localities
- Specific towns/ethnic cultures need to be preserved and protected

Emphasized Importance of Individualism

- Entrepreneurship
- Volunteerism
- Neighbors helping neighbors
- Self-reliance

Warned of Threats to Individualism

- Big government/government issues
- Outsiders (big business, university officials)
- County-wide attitude

Being from Canton and Galva, we realize we're going to be bedroom communities for McPherson. So we feel the more McPherson gains, the more people they can draw, that's going to benefit communities that surround McPherson.

Another county citizen spoke of the significance of interdependence for the entire county.

To tell you the truth, McPherson as a city, whether you realize it or not, cannot get along without the rural people. Any more than the rural people can get along without the city. When the farmers hurt, they don't know it, but everybody hurts. There's just no way. And I'd like to see a unity where you don't think of yourself as a rural person, you think of yourself as a county person. And you work together. And if we work together, that's how we survive.

Because of their interdependence, citizens argued it was important to cooperate and participate in joint projects. They believed this would help deal with a variety of issues and would benefit the various communities and ultimately the county as a whole. A business owner explained:

> I was born and raised in McPherson and it's time that we stop thinking about McPherson and Canton and Moundridge and Marquette. For economic development, for youth, for education we need to be thinking McPherson County, if not a little larger area.... We can recruit business, we can train people and promote tourism or whatever that helps the whole county.

Thus, this group of citizens argued it was important for all people to participate in the planning process and stressed the need for a "dedicated effort in the macro of this effort," "to see this in a broader scope of the community-wide being a county-wide effort." These county citizens wanted a county vision that was "not necessarily trying to maintain or expand at the expense of someone else, but that we try very hard to be fair and open-minded so that everyone can be a net winner." These citizens stressed the need to maintain "cooperative spirits in terms of communities helping other communities."

Finally, these citizens warned of threats that could derail the county's strategic planning and ultimately hurt the county as a whole. This narrative identified such threats as negative attitudes, lack of participation, and competing interests. One woman lamented that "people don't get involved unless there's something that's gonna smash their toe. And then they'll be there." Another woman from Inman told this story about the threat of negative attitudes,

> Well, if you have a group of people who are all for something, it doesn't take very long and one person can make the whole group feel like what they're doing is not worthwhile or they can't do it or just a negative attitude. It's a threat. It's a threat to growth, to getting the job done.

A banker warned of another type of negative attitude—defeatism.

> Do you think the fact the group is smaller is the fact that maybe some people ... I don't mean to be critical here at all ... but maybe sometimes people go into something real "gung ho" and when they see what it is all about they lost faith.... And I wonder if maybe some people perhaps almost see this as a lost cause. And if we see it as that, then truly we have already lost.

A final threat to building community identified in this narrative was competing interests. County citizens spoke of such competing interests as emphasizing individual towns rather than the county as a whole, one segment of the population being singled out for help rather than the entire county. As one citizen stated, "I feel that McPherson County as a whole is a pretty good place to live. Just like any other place in the U.S., we take each other for granted, have certain cliques of people who do not go outside of their clique. I would hope that we can all work together for the benefit of everyone, not just a few."

INDIVIDUALIST NARRATIVE

This conception of community was organized by an overarching belief in individualism. This was a narrative characterized by a focus on the interests of individuals, specific communities and groups within the county over the interests of the entire county. For example, instead of venerating the entire county, these citizens celebrated individuals, specific groups and communities, including the Mennonite population, farmers and entrepreneurs. The key for each of these groups was that they possessed qualities characteristic of individualism—perseverance, pride, willingness to work hard, and a desire to help other sin the county. For example, Mennonites "tend to establish deep roots. And if there is ever a tragedy or need, they're the first ones there and they're very willing to help." This narrative also celebrated entrepreneurs. For example, a female participant offered this story:

> My dad is from a very small community, about 500 people. They decided they wanted to have a medical clinic in their community, and after, what, ten years, they finally got one built. They had to recruit a physician and recruit people to fill it up. And after, what, two years, they finally got a physician and now they have a full clinic and he's looking for another physician to help him. So, you know, it took a long time and a lot of hard work, but it happened.

This success story came not because of county effort or government help, but the energy of citizens in one town. In addition to celebrating individuals and specific groups of people, this narrative also valued specific communities and their interests and needs over the county at large. Embedded in this discussion was the issue of protecting what existed in the individual communities. As one participant pointed out, "Well, there's your comments about a county-wide library system, but you know, I think we are the last Carnegie library in the state. We don't want to give that up at any cost." A banker from Canton spoke frequently and eloquently about this issue. He explained why protectionism was so important:

> We've lost so much, so to speak, and we are so fearful that we are going to lose more that now we're clinging to what little we have left and we are becoming so protectionist. In our thought process, we say to hell with everybody else, what is mine is mine and I'm going to put my big arms around it and I'm not going to let go.

The perception was not of independence, of cooperation or working together, but rather of a win-lose relationship. Participants talked of "not feeling a part of McPherson County," and "looking out for their own yards first." Statements representing this narrative argued that "some of the [suggestions for county-wide cooperation] would be a detraction or subtraction from elements within the local communities," that some suggestions for county-wide cooperation were based on "the assumption that smaller communities perhaps will, for lack of saying it better, wither on the vine and not see growth." Finally, this narrative also identified threats to their way of life. Threats in this narrative came mainly from government and big business. Government and big business were viewed as villains because they were "out-of-touch," "uncaring," and "self-serving." In one narrative, a farmer talked of his frustrations with the government and its insensitivity concerning local environmental conditions:

> Well, you can talk about cutting trees. I got myself in trouble with the tree huggers back in D.C. I cut maybe a thousand hedge trees a year, but now I'm screwing up the environment. I've been trying to get the EPA to come down here and live with me for a month. See what it's all about. I want them to understand. They're out here mandating us, but don't know nothing about what's going on.

Besides government, this narrative constructed big business as a threat because it was perceived as self-serving and not caring about local communities. Several stories were offered about cities where big business was very disruptive. One man talked about a business in Hays, where a company "at one time, employed 1,100 workers, then downsized to around 600 people, then all of [a] sudden closed the plant." Another participant recalled Hutchinson, "where Cessna had 3,000 people working and now they've cut back to 500." A local banker summarized this fear using the banking industry as an example:

> I think there is a tendency sometimes for the large metropolitan banks when they come in and purchase a local institution to not be quite as concerned about whether we go quite as far out on the limb, so to speak, to support local efforts and opportunities.

Conclusions

In their discussions, one group of McPherson citizens articulated a rhetoric which urged the planning participants to think of their community as one which encompassed the whole of the county. Others in McPherson County endeavored to identify community within the framework of the individual towns and population groups. While it was difficult to precisely chart the process in which the county-community rhetoric emerged over the individual-community rhetoric, there were indicators that this, in fact, did occur. Initially, the report which emerged from the strategic planning sessions promoted county-wide projects. Examples included creating a pipeline/aqueduct system to provide a potable water supply to the county; creating a county-wide economic development consultant position; conducting a survey of businesses in McPherson and surrounding counties; improving lines of communication among county businesses; establishing a county business-incubator program; developing a videotape production to promote McPherson County's economic development and tourism potential; creating a county-wide recruitment enhancement network for physicians, nurse practitioners and other health-care providers; enhancing county-wide recycling programs; and establishing a county-wide information clearinghouse (McPherson County Assembly, 1992). Each of these action steps promoted the good of the entire county over the needs of a specific town or population group and is premised on the concepts of interdependence and cooperation articulated by the group supporting a county-wide perspective on community. These actions, approved by the McPherson County Assembly for Strategic Planning and the McPherson County Commission, moved the county toward a larger sense of community. Indeed, only one individual community project (construction of a swimming pool in Inman, Ks.) made the final list of proposed actions (McPherson County Assembly, 1992). Second, evidence of success of the county-wide perspective also came from post-session survey information in which participants indicated that the number one benefit they received from the strategic planning meetings was "increased cooperation and bonding among communities within the county" (Kansas Department of Commerce and Housing, 1992).

Why did the county-wide perspective of community prevail over the more individualistic community perspective? Essentially, we believe that those citizens urging a county-wide view were more successful in constructing community because they articulated a rhetoric of civic responsibility. This rhetoric created the interdependence, mutual responsibilities, and common history that Bellah et al. argue is fundamental to community. Thus, their rhetoric naturally let to the county-wide perspective of community. Theses participants created this rhetoric through the communication of definition, value, and group communication.

Professor of communication studies David Zarefsky writes, "Since the meaning of a situation is not intrinsically given, it must be chosen. By selecting which symbols indicate a situation, people define what it means" (1986, p. 3). Indeed, as the participants defined the situation, they worked to construct the scope of community as "the county" rather than "the town" in their planning process. The enabling legislation, for example, argued that the purpose of the legislation was to "encourage broad-based local and multi-county development strategies" and it directed funds to "county-wide and multi-county economic development entities" (Ott & Tatarko, 1992).

McPherson County participants also defined the process from a county perspective. The county-wide perspective admonished participants to think no longer of the individual communities, but think in terms of the county at large. In fact, the county-wide group's language subsumed many of the concerns of the individualist perspective. For example, the county-wide group recognized the uniqueness of the Mennonite population, the Swedish population, and the diversity of the small towns, but defined that uniqueness as a strength of the entire county. Thus, many of the concerns of the individualist perspective were obviated by the rhetoric of the county-wide group.

The county-wide group also emphasized more universal and general values. Citizens in this group stressed "unity" and "interdependence," while citizens advocating the individualist narrative promoted the more narrow values of "protectionism" and "looking out for their own yards first." These values then translated into different action steps. The more broad-based group supported actions which would touch the entire county, while the individualist group advocated projects which would enhance a specific community, such as building a swimming pool in Inman and renovating the Opera House in McPherson. Most participants could find some benefit in county-wide projects and thus, as the strategic planning group worked together, they came to support projects based on group benefit rather than individual town benefit.

In addition to definition and value communication, group communication also helped explain the dominance of the county-wide perspective. Ryan argues that in a group situation, "individual interests are 'welded together' into a higher form of group consciousness." He further explained that this type of bonding "typically occurs among individuals experiencing a common crisis" and that this "increases their propensity for shared collective action" (1994, p. 12). In fact, strategic planning in McPherson County was often described in the crisis language of survival. One participant pondered, "I wonder if maybe some people perhaps almost see this as a lost cause. And if we see it as that, then truly we have already lost," while another participant argued that, "if we work together, that's how we survive." Indeed, most individualist narratives came from a survey residents completed on their own, while in the small group meetings of the strategic planning sessions, most narratives supported the vision of a county-wide community.

Celeste Condit, professor of speech communication, contends that "there is a tendency of public argument, *because of its very nature*, to favor those values, stories, and descriptions directed at the most universal audience present" (1987, p. 1; emphasis Condit). In this strategic planning situation, the more general audience supported a county-wide community rather than individual towns or populations groups as community boundaries.

IMPLICATIONS FOR COMMUNITY DEVELOPMENT

Strategic planning sessions such as those held in McPherson County and around Kansas are vehicles which improve the health of rural communities. Dr. Leonard Duhl argues that a healthy community exhibits the following characteristics:

- A common sense of community, including its history and values that are strengthened by a network of leaders,
- People and community groups who feel empowered and have a sense of control,
- An absence of divided turf, conflict, and polarization,
- Structures where people from diverse groups can come together to work out decisions about community,
- Leadership that functions both from the top down and the bottom up, and
- Effective channels for networking, communication and cooperation among those who live and lead there (1993, pp. 87–112).

The strategic planning in McPherson County addressed, in some way, each of these characteristics. Histories and values were often discussed. A clearer sense of community emerged from the meetings. People from all social and economic stations discussed their concerns, identified issues needing attention, and helped formulate plans of action to address those issues. Certainly, there was some conflict and turf protection in the meetings, but the strategic planning sessions provided a structure in which these differences of opinion could be addressed. The strategic planning meetings helped to empower county citizens and provide a channel for networking, communication, and cooperation.

Perhaps in the end, public-sector strategic planning is not only an "effort to define organizational mission, translate that mission into strategic goals, and implement these goals programmatically" (Baum, 1994, p. 251), but also a way to build a sense of cooperation and community.

References

Baum, Howell S. 1994. Community and consensus: Reality and fantasy in planning. *Journal of Planning Education and Research* 13:251–262.

Bellah, Robert N., Richard Madsen, William M. Sullivan, Ann Swidler and Steven M. Tipton. 1987. *Individualism and Commitment in American Life*. New York: Harper and Row.

Bormann, Ernest G. 1985. *The Force of Fantasy: Restoring the American Dream*. Carbondale: Southern Illinois University Press.

Bryson, J.M., & W.D. Roering. 1987. Applying private-sector strategic planing in the public sector. *Journal of the American Planning Association* 53(1):9–22.

Condit, Celeste M. 1987. Democracy and civil rights: The universalizing influence of public argumentation. *Communication Monographs* 54(1):1–18.

The Docking Institute of Public Affairs. 1992. *A Profile of McPherson County: An Internal and External Environmental Analysis*. Hays, KS: Fort Hays State University.

Duhl, Leonard J. 1993. *The Social Entrepreneurship of Change*. New York: Pace University Press.

Fisher, Walter F. 1992. Narration, reason and community. In R.H. Brown (ed.), *Writing the Social Text*. New York: Aldine De Gruyter.

Glaser, Barney G., & Anselm L. Strauss. 1967. *The Discovery of Grounded Theory: Strategies for Qualitative Research*. New York: Aldine De Gruyter.

Kansas Department of Commerce and Housing. 1992. *Community Strategic Planning Assistance*. Report to The Joint Committee on Economic Development. July 16.

Kaufman, J.L., & H.M. Jacobs. 1987. A public planning perspective on strategic planning. *Journal of the American Planning Association* 53(1):23–33.

Langellier, Kristin M. 1989. Personal narratives: Perspectives on theory and research. *Text and Performance Quarterly* 9:243–277.

Lewis, William F. 1987. Telling America's story: Narrative form and the Reagan presidency. *Quarterly Journal of Speech* 73:280–302.

Malinowski, Bronislaw. 1948. *Magic, Science and Religion and Other Essays*. Garden City, N.Y.: Doubleday.

McPherson County Assembly for Strategic Planning. 1992. *Options for McPherson County's Future: A Strategic Plan.*

Ott, Gina M., & Beth Tatarko. 1992. *Kansas Community Strategic Plans*. Topeka, KS: Kansas, Inc.

Peterson, Tarla R. 1991. Telling the farmers story: Competing responses to soil conservation rhetoric. *Quarterly Journal of Speech* 77:289–308.

Procter, David E. 1991. *Enacting Political Culture: Rhetorical Transformations of Liberty Weekend 1986*. New York: Praeger.

Ryan, Vernon D. 1994. Community development and the ever elusive "collectivity." *Journal of the Community Development Society* 25(1):5–19.

Strauss, Anselm, & J. Corbin. 1990. *Basics of Qualitative Research: Grounded Theory Procedures and Techniques*. Newbury Park, CA: Sage.

Zarefsky, David. 1986. *President Johnson's War on Poverty: Rhetoric and History*. University, AL: The University of Alabama Press.

CHAPTER 34

Using Specialty Retail for Economic Survival in Ponchatoula, Louisiana

Manon Pavy and Fritz Wagner

The viability of a small town's main street gives a good indication of the overall health of the community. Ponchatoula, Louisiana (population 5,000), located in a rural area an hour's drive north of New Orleans, demonstrates this truism. In the mid–1980s, residents saw a downtown that had gradually deteriorated over the years and was virtually deserted. In order to assure Ponchatoula's economic survival, the community came together to focus on redeveloping the central business district with an emphasis on specialty retail while retaining the small businesses that had traditionally serviced the community.

The Decline of the Downtown

Ponchatoula's economy is based on local agricultural production. The town is located in an area where strawberries are harvested for delivery throughout the United States and it has dubbed itself the "Strawberry Capital of the World." Every April, it hosts the annual Strawberry Festival. In the past, the small businesses that occupied the downtown formed the town's commercial base. During the mid–1980s, however, a serious decline in the economy, mirroring the depressed economy of the entire state of Louisiana, threatened the downtown's stability.

Other factors also contributed to

Originally published as "Focusing the Old Downtown on Specialty Retail for Economic Survival," Small Town, Vol. 24, No. 3, November/December, 1993. Published by the Small Towns Institute, Ellensburg, Washington. Reprinted with permission of the publisher.

the downtown's decline. The expansion of Highway 22 from two to five lanes created a series of detrimental changes. Louisiana Route 22 cuts through the center of Ponchatoula's retail district and a two-block-long portion of it (named Pine Street) is considered Ponchatoula's main street. The widening project lagged for four years and created serious access problems for downtown stores.

The state expanded Highway 22 to create better access to Interstate 55. The highway intersects Interstate 55 in an area west of Ponchatoula's downtown. While the expansion promised an improvement in the region's transportation network, it also threatened the viability of Ponchatoula's main street as an economic center. Residential growth occurred at the west end of town as a response to the highway improvement project. In turn, commercial development, primarily national and regional retail outlets and strip malls, emerged to serve the area's new population. A leading example of this trend involved the construction of a large shopping mall in Hammond, a city four miles west from Ponchatoula.

The highway project triggered a shift away from the downtown's previous function as the center of the community. Competition from outlying large retail outlets together with the obstruction of shopping due to the road construction, led to a dramatic loss of business for downtown merchants who operated small businesses. Consequently, six years ago, 80 percent of the buildings in Ponchatoula's downtown lay empty.

The deterioration of the downtown soon became a symbol of Ponchatoula's overall problems. During the late 1980s, downtown Ponchatoula was threatened when a private company made offers to buy up the entire area. A factory outlet developer expressed interested in buying all of the buildings on Pine Street in order to develop factory outlet stores under unified management, in lieu of building a new shopping mall. The possible loss of the town's economic independence through single ownership and the harsh reality presented by the vacant downtown buildings spurred the business community to take action. In January, 1989, owners of downtown real estate formed the Property Owners' Association in order to fight community decline.

Ponchatoula's downtown revitalization occurred because of community teamwork that reflected a long-standing tradition of self help. An early example of the community's initiative involved the conversion, in 1973, of Ponchatoula's historic train depot into The Country Market. Townspeople saved the railroad station from being sold to out-of-town interests by forming a nonprofit corporation which then developed and submitted a successful bid that allowed it to purchase the station.[1]

The Country Market has a strong local emphasis, selling only handmade, homemade or homegrown goods. A volunteer board governs the market, scrutinizing receipts and disbursements and monitoring the quality and type of merchandise sold. Vendors rent booths from the nonprofit corporation in order to showcase their products. They are responsible for managing their own booths and also take turns minding each other's when necessary. The market has no paid employees and its support staff, the manager and assistant manager, receive free booth space as compensation for their work. Booth rents pay for the market's maintenance and operating expenses. The nonprofit corporation manages its own booth which sells commercial products, such as cookbooks, t-shirts and souvenirs, to provide additional financial support. The booth's revenue, along with the rent money, also pays for the market's publicity.

The success of The County Market rests on its nonprofit status, which allows it to offer space to local vendors at low rates. It has also played an invaluable role as a model for community involvement.[2]

The Advent of the Property Owners' Association

The Property Owners' Association followed The Country Market's group participation model when it developed its strategy for revitalizing the downtown. Downtown property owners agreed to make rules by majority rule and act in unison in developing and maintaining a revitalization strategy.

The Property Owners' Association, from the outset, decided to make the revitalization of Pine Street its primary goal. Members, for example, supported the siting of a downtown retail outlet to generate new business. The association made an early decision, however, to target a large part of Pine Street as a specialty retail site for a cluster of antique stores.

In 1968, the National Register of Historic Places had officially designated Ponchatoula's downtown as a registered historic district. The association believed that an antique theme could capitalize on the designation, as well as the quaint, nostalgic feel of downtown Ponchatoula.

Ponchatoula already had a toehold in the antique market through the weekly Ponchatoula Auction. Conducted every Saturday night, this is the largest antique auction in the South. The Country Market's success in antique sales also proved the viability of this theme. An antique booth had operated in the Market for one-and-a-half years and this store served as an incubator for the Property Owners' Association's Antique City concept.

Practical physical considerations influenced the choice of the Antique City theme for Ponchatoula. The sale of antiques would require little or no repair to the inside of the buildings. Restaurant development, for instance, would pose problems, as the downtown buildings did not meet fire safety standards for such enterprises.

An antique specialty theme also seemed to be a realistic choice in terms of its regional appeal. Antique sales would not compete with the specializations of neighboring areas. Nearby Hammond, for example, attracted tourists because of its major university and the variety of its retail shopping areas. Amite, a town located twenty miles away, had a thriving bed-and-breakfast industry which could compliment rather than compete with Ponchatoula's tourist trade.

The Property Owners' Association relies on volunteer contributions from its members and their adherence to specific contract terms. Owners of downtown real estate are required to rent space at "bottom" prices and to follow standard lease and standard sales agreements. They also agree to limit rent increases to no more than 5 percent per year.

As an investment toward revitalizing the downtown, each property owner is required to make an annual donation to the Property Owners' Fund that matches one month's rent for each rentable space. The merchant who rents the property is also required to make an annual contribution that equals one month's rent. If the property owner and the merchant are the same, only one contribution is required. For instance, on space that rents for $250 per month, both the owner and the merchant must make an annual payment of $250, for a total of $500. Money donated from real estate transactions also supplement the fund. On a lease with a traditional 10 percent commission, for example, the agent receives a 7 percent commission, while 3 percent is targeted for the Property Owners' Fund. The Country Market provides a single yearly contribution of $300.

The revenue is used to promote Ponchatoula as "America's Antique City." It supports a year-round marketing campaign promoting the community's economic development. The effort consists of locally and nationally distributed advertisements, billboards and fliers.

Ponchatoula's Success

Today, six years after the start of the initiative, the Property Owners' Association has 29 members, represents 29 buildings and has a budget of $22,000. The downtown area is now 100 percent occupied. As a sign of the new pride that property owners have in the district, many have financed renovations on their buildings on an individual basis. By supporting the specialty retail theme for the downtown and contributing to the Property Owners' Fund, owners hope to

create and maintain profitable investments.

On March 11, 1991, the town celebrated Antique City's success, represented by sales of a million dollar's worth of merchandise since its inauguration, by hosting a block party at the community center. Downtown sales have increased greatly since the inception of Antique City. Total gross revenue from the downtown antique stores came to $231,000 in 1989. In 1992, it rose to $2.3 million. Focusing the downtown toward specialty retail has boosted the overall economy on Ponchatoula, as well. City sales tax collections have increased more than 10 percent over the past three years and, in 1991, revenues reached $810,000.[3]

The success of the Antique City theme depended on the shared goals and values of Ponchatoula's business community. The philosophy behind the enterprise has been described as spread the wealth. The stores complement one another, with each having its own specialization, such as crafts or quilts. Merchants trade information freely and wholeheartedly support each other's efforts.

While the owners of downtown property are responsible for the Antique City initiative, the further development of the retail shopping theme depends on continued cooperation between the downtown merchants—not all of whom own their businesses—and property owners. This seems to be occurring. Participation in the Property Owners' Fund is now 100 percent of both the property owners and those leasing the buildings. The ongoing participation of all of the merchants in the overall marketing strategy for Antique City is necessary for maintaining the vitality of the project.

While Ponchatoula's downtown re-vitalization is notable for its large volunteer base, it is also a gamble that stakes itself on the continuing interest and support of the community. For example, the Property Owners' Association does not mandate participation in the association when downtown property is sold. Thus, its future depends on the enthusiastic participation of new property owners and their dedication to continuing the Antique City concept.

The creation of a specialty retail focus for Ponchatoula's downtown has resulted in a tourist industry that supports traditional retail shopping in Ponchatoula's downtown. Apart from the new antique stores, a variety of small businesses provide service to Ponchatoula residents, as well as to tourists. The majority of these, except for the restaurants, are representative of the functions of the old downtown and are survivors of the competition from the nearby mall developments. A variety of professional businesses that provide services to the general community are also located on Pine Street and they include finance companies, law offices, real estate companies, insurance companies and medical professionals.

The central business office is also the site of a number of traditional downtown businesses. They include a barbershop, drugstore, laundromat, beauty shop, shoe repair store and the hardware store, called the "Feed and Seed Store." The viability of these stores is aided by the pedestrian traffic and the revenue provided by Antique City. The traditional stores, in turn, help to maintain the viability of Ponchatoula's local economy apart from the tourist trade. Waiting lists for apartments on Pine Street

also attest to the downtown's appeal to local residents.

Ponchatoula's continued economic development depends on an ongoing marketing campaign to draw attention to the new specialty focus of its downtown. The Property Owners' Association promotes Ponchatoula as a Mecca for antique lovers and as the site of numerous special events. For example, the town hosts the Louisiana Antique Festival in the Spring, and, in 1992, Great American Automobiles held its ninth annual antique car rally in Ponchatoula.

To bolster the Antique City concept, the town has capitalized on its historic identity. A local paint company, wanting to join the community spirit bandwagon, contacted the Property Owners' Association and donated paint to revamp the faded colors of Pine Street. For authenticity, the colors follow guidelines developed from an historic preservation study done for New Orleans that featured the period of 1920 through 1930.

The downtown business community made Antique City viable in less than a year from its inception. From the outset, the campaign to save the downtown has been characterized by its volunteer nature and the determination of the community to save itself by itself. No outside marketing experts were hired and the original antique mall project received no federal or state funds. As a result, the town has greater autonomy in dealing with its problems and potentials.

The local chamber of commerce estimates that an average of 1,000 people per day visit Ponchatoula on the weekends.[4] The arrival of such large numbers of visitors has created problems. The most obvious one, at this stage, is that of congestion. To address this, the city used state and federal commuter project funds to purchase three blocks of land near the business district in order to establish a parking lot. This has eased most of the parking problems during weekends.

While parking has been problematic, the sheer volume of the new people has stressed the local infrastructure. For example, the Property Owners' Association failed to foresee the impact of large numbers of people on the sidewalks and did not anticipate the need to accommodate tour buses and to provide public rest rooms. Since these new pressures have surfaced, the Property Owners' Association plans to identify grant opportunities and hopefully secure funds to help adapt Ponchatoula's infrastructure to meet the needs of the scores of people who now visit downtown.

Through careful management and planning, Ponchatoula's community leaders hope to retain the small town atmosphere that makes the community so appealing while integrating a thriving tourist industry into the old downtown. Plans to bolster the Antique City concept in the years to come include expanding and upgrading the selection of merchandise in the specialty stores.

The efforts of Ponchatoula's downtown business community to revitalize its main street will require a constant balancing act to maintain the integrity of the old downtown. The economic success achieved thus far, however, can serve as an example of how a small town can refocus the economy of its downtown in order to ensure the district's economic survival.

Notes

1. Fritz Wagner, "Ponchatoula's Country Market: The Re-Use of a Railroad Station," *Small Town*, Vol. 7, No. 9, March, 1977, pp. 11–14.

2. Wagner.

3. Bob Warren, "Louisiana. Town Rings Up a Thriving Antiques Business," *The New Orleans Times-Picayune*, February 9, 1992.

4. Warren.

CHAPTER 35

Revitalizing the Old Mill Town of Maynard, Massachusetts

John Mullin

Virtually every planner I know has visited some part of New England as a tourist, student, or participant in a professional meeting. Invariably, the visitors recall with pleasure Boston's idiosyncrasies (its crooked streets and compactness, even its residents' driving habits); the vast beaches of Cape Cod; the tidy villages nestled in the hillsides of rural Vermont—model towns for many of today's new urbanists.

Those who are about to subsidize their children's higher education often combine business with a side trip to one of the region's unique college towns—Hanover, New Hampshire, for instance, or Northampton, Massachusetts.

But there's another, more utilitarian New England attraction that gets less attention: the mill towns. The villages and cities that grew up along such rivers as the Androscoggin, Deerfield, Merrimac, Nashua, Housatonic, and Blackstone were the first centers of industrial power in the U.S. Jane Jacobs summed up their importance in *The Economy of Cities*:

"In the nineteenth century," she wrote, "saws and axes made in New England cleared the forests of Ohio; New England ploughs broke the prairie sod; New England scales weighed wheat and meat in Texas; New England serge clothed businessmen in San Francisco; New England cutlery skinned hides to be tanned in Milwaukee and sliced

Originally published as "Mill Town Roots," Planning, Vol. 64, No. 3, March, 1998. Published by the American Planning Association, 122 South Michigan Avenue, Suite 1600, Chicago, Illinois 60603-6107. Reprinted with permission of the publisher.

323

apples to be dried in Missouri; New England whale oil lit lamps across the continent; New England blankets warmed children by night and New England textbooks preached at them by day; New England guns armed the troops; and New England dies, lathes, looms, forges, presses, and screwdrivers outfitted factories far and wide."

Downward Slide

By the beginning of this century, faced with competition from other regions, the mill towns had lost their competitive edge. They gradually entered into a decline that in some cases persists to this day. There are plenty of examples of such "losers" in the isolated areas along the banks of the Quinebaug River in Connecticut, the Kennebec River in Maine, and the Shetucket River in Rhode Island.

Some communities were able to adapt. Villages like Peacedale, Rhode Island, have attracted a variety of small businesses to their mill complexes. The larger industrial town of Dalton, Massachusetts, has continued to succeed as a paper producer, and in Clinton, Massachusetts, the Nypro Corporation, a plastics manufacturer, has revitalized an old factory complex. The small city of Lowell survived in part by becoming the nation's first national park with an industrial theme.

The mill towns have always struggled. From the beginning, they depended on the vagaries of water flow. If the flow of the river was slow in late summer, production would come to a halt. If the owners' financial condition was unstable, the machines stopped. And, of course, there was always competition, even from within. How, for instance, could the mill villages compete with the efficiencies and technological advances found in the larger industrial cities such as Lowell, Lawrence, and Chicopee?

The downhill slide hastened after World War I. Mill owners had to look farther afield for raw materials and spend more to transport finished products. More important, the skills of southern workers had dramatically improved. Health regulations and labor reforms in New England added new costs to production while companies scrambled to keep pace with technological and infrastructure advances.

World War II and the Korean War temporarily bolstered the market for New England products, but by the 1950s, the mill communities were clearly failing. Industrial analysts and planners alike saw little hope for these depressed—and depressing—communities.

Miracles Don't Last

In the 1960s, a miracle occurred, at least a temporary one. Even as factories closed all over the region, entrepreneurs began spotting the empty buildings as a resource. A new set of industries began to replace those that had closed or relocated. Stimulated by inventions, innovations, and licenses acquired from and by the region's universities, laboratories, and research and development centers, new companies emerged, enticed by the mill towns' inexpensive space and available labor.

At the same time, the region's service industries began to realize that there could be substantial cost savings if they were to locate in these old structures. And finally, planners, industrial development officials, and historic preservationists began to realize the potential of the old mill buildings, which were even beginning to develop a kind of cachet.

One building that caught the eye of investors was the behemoth Assabet Mill in Maynard, Massachusetts, just west of Boston. Built in the 1840s, the mill complex had been expanded to over a million square feet by 1952, when it was closed by the American Woolen Company.

Thanks in part to the efforts of town officials, the old woolen mill gradually began to fill up with some of the growing industries that were emerging in the Greater Boston area. The new users included plastics and paper companies, millworking operations, warehousing firms, printers, and stereo manufacturers. A major coup was the attraction of the Digital Equipment Corporation.

By the early 1960s, the mill was virtually fully occupied and the town had become relatively prosperous. In a strange turn of events, Digital continued to grow and grow until, by the 1970s, the mill was again occupied by one company, and Maynard was once again dominated by one industry.

But then came a new bust. By the late 1980s, as the Massachusetts computer boom declined and the severe recession of 1989-90 struck, Digital consolidated its operations. The company closed its Maynard operation in 1990 and sold the mill. Four years later, the new owners began to market the structure and expect to fill it, once again, over the next three years.

Winners and Losers

The Maynard story is not unique. The same sequence of boom-bust-recovery takes place in all six New England states. At times the sequence occurs rapidly, while at other times it happens painfully slow.

Three types of mill communities can be clearly noted: There are those that continue to struggle, those that are performing quite well, and those with promise.

The strugglers are isolated. They do not have easy access to modern highways, they don't have modern telecommunications, and in some cases they lack water or sewer capacity. They also have a history of attempting to keep industries that are destined to leave anyway.

Some of the most vivid examples can be seen in the mill towns along the Mohawk Trail in West Central Massachusetts. Once proud centers of furniture, cutlery, and precision tool manufacturing, these towns have not for the most part been able to attract or develop new growth industries.

It is these towns where a cycle of despair has set in and where state statistics on high school dropouts, unemployment, teenage crime, and children needing medical help show the depths of the troubles they face. The mills remain, the people remain, but the jobs are gone. Pockets of such mill villages can be found in all six New England states.

Meanwhile, the good performers continue to grow and attract (and shed) new industries on a regular basis. Most noticeable are the communities clustered around the plastics center of Leominster, Massachusetts. Firms throughout this region have slowly and steadily shifted their focus from low-end products (e.g., plastic forks) to sophisticated high-value products such as night visioning devices. They have also placed high value on research and development and have even created a plastics museum. The firms (and even the museum) are located in old, revitalized structures.

As for the communities that show promise, there are too many to name. In my consulting work I have noted a significant growth in requests for proposals concerning the revitalization of old mills throughout the six-state region. As the economy continues to boom and industrial land becomes scarce, firms are looking at these mill communities with renewed interest.

Some Lessons

The experiences of these towns is not confined to New England. The American landscape is littered with old mining towns, railroad towns, and factory towns that have lost their reason for being. Many of these towns, because they developed much later than the New England mill communities, may be undergoing changes for only the first time.

These are some of the things planners in such communities should keep in mind.

- Don't count on an industry staying put. Planners should focus more on the structure than the occupant. Everyone gets excited when IBM or Mercedes comes to town, but what happens when the high-end company leaves and is replaced by "Average Warehousing, Inc."? Make sure that enough in-

dustrially zoned land is available for a variety of companies.

- Preserve what should be preserved. Work with the owners of empty mills to make sure that the structures are minimally heated and protected from vandals. Once water damage or frost buckling occurs, the expense of renovation increases dramatically.

- Recognize that not all structures are worth saving. Selective demolition can create open space, eliminate the most blighted buildings, and allow the best structures to be seen—a key marketing feature. Our rule of thumb is that 10 percent of New England's vacant mills are economically recoverable.

- Make sure that regulatory problems are addressed. Few of these structures comply with the Americans with Disabilities Act, OSHA standards for elevators, floodplain standards, and local zoning and building code ordinances. As long as such problems remain, there will be little incentive to revitalize the structures. Some of the problems cannot be overcome (i.e., the mills are often within 15 feet of a frequently flooding river). However, local zoning, ADA, and OSHA issues can be resolved.

- Work through a public-private partnership. Grants from the Economic Development Administration may be obtained through local and county planning agencies or state economic assistance agencies.

- There must be tax relief. Too often, communities see the mills simply as a source of property tax revenue. They are reluctant to provide abatements or to lower a structure's assessed value. That approach may be shortsighted. Tax abatements and tax increment financing programs are frequently key to stimulating revitalization.

- Target your marketing. In New England, industrial marketers are rarely able to attract firms from distant regions. It is generally best to identify firms that are expanding in your region and to develop packages that will attract them to the community.

- Move quickly after a firm leaves the mill. Any industrial occupant is better than none. An occupant will at least maintain the building. Moving quickly is also a way to make sure that the community's skilled workers stay put.

- Most important, commit to a long-term strategy. The recovery of mill towns is almost always slow, incremental, and complex. Nonetheless, it is worth the effort.

Predictions

The future of these communities is quite mixed. Those that are close to the region's major economic engines (metropolitan Boston, Worcester, Providence, Springfield, Portland, Nashua) are likely to do well because there is a steady demand for inexpensive space. With long-term economic strategies, tactical grant writing, regulatory assistance, infrastructure improvements, and a public-private partnership, I am confident that the mill towns within commuting distance will survive.

Those that have cachet will also recover. For example, the mill communities located in the Blackstone and Quinebaug river valleys are now part of federally designated heritage corridors and will be the beneficiaries of direct and indirect federal assistance. Further, they have the good fortune of being located along newly improved state and interstate highways.

I am less optimistic about the small and isolated communities that are well beyond an easy commute to metropolitan areas and that have not benefited from tourism. It is here that planners' skills will be most tested.

But there's reason for optimism. These small mill communities are indelibly a part of our national psyche and our heritage. They were envisioned as the answer to Blake's "dark Satanic mills" and Dickens's "Coketown." And in many cases, they fulfilled their mission. The motto on the town seal of Thetford, Vermont, summarizes the ideals of these towns: "Scenic Beauty–Industry–Agriculture." They are indeed special places.

CHAPTER 36

Evaluating Main Street in Corning, New York

Bert Winterbottom

Over the past quarter of a century, most local governments, large and small, have undertaken planning for their downtowns. Many localities have been successful, while others have written plans that have languished on the shelf.

Using a report card to assist in the planning process if an approach particularly well suited to the needs of small and medium-sized communities. This kind of objective, outside review can confirm success, verify and refine development objectives, foster mid-course corrections in plans and programs, and reenergize public and private leadership.

What Is a Report Card Assessment?

Report cards traditionally have been used to measure the progress of students in educational systems. In the school-and-student relationship, the criteria used to gauge performance are fairly formal and rigid. A major objective is to share with the student his or her progress at a particular point and to identify areas in which performance can be enhanced.

Slightly modified, the traditional report card approach to measuring progress and making mid-course adjustments has a valid application to downtown revitalization projects and organizations. The report card assessment often is a critical component of the

Originally published as "Maybe Your Downtown Needs a Report Card," Public Management, Vol. 79, No. 6, June, 1997. Published by the International City/County Management Association, Washington, D.C. Reprinted with permission of the publisher.

traditional process of strategic planning. It is sometimes called a strategic assessment, strategic audit, status report, or peer review. Whatever it is called, a report card can be an important management tool for public officials, elected leaders, and private organizations concerned with a community's downtown.

The report card process is short-term and strategic. It focuses on current issues and problems, as well as accomplishments.

The process includes four, relatively brief steps: (1) listening/recording/learning, (2) processing, (3) sharing, and (4) taking action. The purpose of this chapter is to demonstrate that report cards can encourage change by identifying opportunities, solving problems, and producing sharply focused recommendations for planning and action.

Report Card Case Studies

Localities that have approached downtown planning using the report card process include Corning, New York, with two report cards in the past six years; Pueblo, Colorado; Macon, Georgia; and Greenville, South Carolina.

The objective set by each locality varies from that of a report card making mid-course corrections and reenergizing community leadership (Corning); to confirmation by peer review of a major plan before implementing it (Pueblo); to a status report designed to confirm community, public, and private leadership support for a planning initiative (Macon); to a more complex and comprehensive strategic assessment (Greenville).

The costs for these products have ranged from just under $10,000 for a simple report card assessment, to $25,000 for a more sophisticated strategic planning process.

Corning, New York: First Report Card

Corning's first report card was prepared in May 1990 and completed in July of the same year.

Corning is a small town with a population of approximately 12,000 located in the sparsely populated Southern tier region of the state of New York. While the area has seen relatively little growth, it is headquarters to Corning, Inc., and the home of the Corning Glass Center, New York's third largest tourist attraction.

In 1990, Corning Intown Futures, Inc., the public/private organization responsible for downtown planning in Corning, decided to undertake a report card assessment. The community had successfully implemented the Intown I plan in 1982 and created the more ambitious Intown II plan in 1988.

The community was enthusiastic about the 1988 plan and implemented a great deal of it between 1988 and 1990. In 1990, however, malaise set in. The public and private leaders were tired, and there was frustration over where priorities lay and what should be next on the implementation agenda. The concept of a report card appealed to those who wanted to conduct a candid evaluation of Corning's new and revised priorities.

The first report card was prepared over a six-week period at a cost of just under $10,000. The final product, a brief report, contained four sections: plan implementation progress, current development issues, high-priority issues, and input for the Intown Corning Action Agenda.

The report card gave the community high marks for implementing 12 major projects in the 1988 plan, plus an additional $18.7 million in other intown projects not included in the plan, for a total of $63.1 million. In spite of the remarkable implementation success of the Intown II plan, there was concern about the future and what should be done next.

The assessment identified 39 issues under five broad headings: leadership, public fiscal policy and management, public services and facilities, property and development, and tourism. The 39 issues were reduced to nine specific recommendations as input for the Intown Corning Action Agenda.

Since 1990, four recommendations as described here, have been acted upon with dramatic results.

Public Fiscal Policy and Management Strategy. A recommendation to develop a fiscal policy and management strategy led to the appointment of a private sector task force to evaluate policy and management needs. The task force report persuaded Corning's city council that it needed to adopt the council-manager form of government, and Corning's first city manager, Suzanne Kennedy, was appointed in June 1995.

A Visionary New Look at Tourism Development. It was recommended that the Corning Glass Center be enhanced as an attraction of national and international significance. A regional tourism strategy was prepared, and in 1995, Corning, Inc., invested $50 in the project.

Graphic Identification Package. Such a package, when it has been implemented, will give image and design guidance for informational and directional signage leading to and around Corning.

Short-Term Parking Strategy. The report card suggested that meters on Market Street be removed and that two hours of free parking be enforced. So far, the council has mandated the two hours of free parking, with appropriate enforcement.

Corning's Second Report Card

While a great deal of progress had been made since the 1990 assessment, the board of Intown Futures again felt the need to refocus, and a second assessment was begun in March 1996 and finished in May 1996.

A number of negative changes had occurred, including a modest downturn in the economy; corporate changes and downsizing at Corning, Inc.; and the introduction of almost 600,000 square feet of new, big-box retail space near a mall 12 miles away.

At the same time, Corning, Inc., was making plans for revitalizing and expanding its Glass Center to include a reconfiguration of its retail offerings. Intown Market Street merchants viewed this idea as potentially harming their businesses, so growing dissension arose between the merchants and the Glass Center.

The board of Intown Futures decided that the second report card assessment would differ from the first in that it would be more diagnostic. It would try to look carefully at the underlying causes of the decline on Market

Street and would make recommendations for addressing these issues.

Scope of Work

Modeled after the first report card, the second one involved a careful review of reports, plans, and newspaper articles published before a site visit, which, along with a three-day work session, included a walking tour of the Intown neighborhood and informal discussions with retailers and others. The final product was an 18-page report with sections on progress made since 1990; a situation analysis; the current Intown Futures agenda; "The Challenge of April 2000: A New Agenda"; and "Action Agenda: Next Steps."

Findings and Recommendations

The period of 1991 to 1996 saw 29 major projects implemented in the city and 20 in the Intown area, with the 20 Intown projects alone representing an investment of just over $69 million in five years. Another measure of success was an assessment of the high-priority issues identified in the 1990 report card. Five high-priority issues had been dealt with aggressively; four had been partially addressed; and five had not been dealt with at all.

Overall, the community rated high in its ability to deal with implementation. The report card, however, suggested that one major challenge facing the community was not project-oriented: the perceived loss of the community spirit, cooperation, communication, and civic will that had always been a part of Corning.

Counterbalancing the negative findings was the announced revitalization plan for investing approximately $60 million over five years in the Corning Glass Center, to result in a grand opening in April 2000. The report card begged one question. In April 2000, the eyes of the world would be on Corning, New York. Would it be ready to welcome visitors to Corning and to reap the promotional and economic benefits of international publicity and guests from around the world?

The 1996 report card called for an action plan whose specific steps included convening in-town stakeholder leaders (action completed); creating and empowering a Corning Action 2000 Task Force (action completed); starting an immediate action program involving nine high-priority initiatives (several initiatives are just beginning); and working on an Intown III planning process (action in progress).

The report card roused new interest in Intown Corning. It helped city officials and citizens to get organized and become focused on the action agenda. In four months, the community became reenergized and is working to achieve both short- and long-term initiatives designed to make Corning a model for other localities.

Peer Review for Downtown Pueblo, Colorado

Standing 40 miles south of Colorado Springs, Pueblo is a community of 100,000 with a traditional manufacturing economy. Tourism is being looked upon as a means of diversifying the economy and building on the strengths of the historic downtown.

A peer review process undertaken in November 1994 and presented in January 1995 had as its goal to provide a critical, objective, and outside review of the work undertaken in planning for tourism development. While the review considered all of the downtown, the focus was on the proposed historic Arkansas Riverwalk Project (HARP), a bold effort designed to create an unusual and authentic place in the heart of downtown Pueblo by reopening the river channel running through it.

The process involved a review of resource materials provided by the city; 18 leadership interviews conducted during a three-day site visit; downtown planning and tourism briefings; and the preparation of a brief report summarizing the key findings, conclusions, and recommendations of the peer review process. A SWOT analysis listed the strengths, weaknesses, opportunities, and threats facing downtown Pueblo.

The key finding of the peer review was that Pueblo had undertaken a valid planning process for HARP. The review recommended that the project should be carried to the next phase, with detailed development plans designed to build a great public environment and a chance for substantial private, urban development.

Other recommendations suggested that the project deal for the downtown hotel and civic conference center be consummated and the project built in a timely fashion, with all supporting infrastructure required to make it a success. Completion of the Union Avenue Historic District also was endorsed, as well as a number of secondary recommendations intended to bring about a concentration and critical mass, to encourage residents to use the downtown, and to enhance the overall image of the downtown.

In 1995, a referendum was held on a $12.85 million bond issue for implementing the river project. The referendum passed by a favorable margin, and the project now is under way, with completion scheduled for April 1998. The convention center should open in May 1997, and a hotel project has been approved and will begin construction in April 1997.

Downtown Macon, Georgia

Macon, located in central Georgia approximately 80 miles south of Atlanta, has a population of 106,000. The executive director of The Peyton Anderson Foundation, a local philanthropic trust, was concerned about the future of Macon's downtown. The foundation was called upon to support and fund projects in the downtown, but the director could not see how individual projects would work together. She believed that there was a need for an overall downtown plan.

The status report process conducted in July 1996 involved a three-day site visit to evaluate the situation, to interview local public and private leaders, and to prepare a brief status report. The consultant team returned in 30 days to present the findings to a group of downtown stakeholders. Following are some of the more important findings:

- The Ocmulgee River represents a tremendous, untapped resource in Macon's downtown that needs to be explored.
- The Medical Center of Central Georgia is a major employment

and economic force in the downtown and can play a big role in the future of the area.

- Downtown has other strengths to build on: a compact structure with many historic and architecturally significant buildings, a growing employment base, and attractive boulevard parks.

During the status report process, a group of public and private leaders decided to start a new organization to coordinate the downtown initiative and to call that organization the NewTown Macon Board. The group reviewed the status report, and three recommendations for action were implemented:

1. Create a new "umbrella" organization to direct and coordinate downtown planning and action.

2. Undertake an economic development strategy and plan for the downtown.

3. Take on an immediate action project early in the process.

Downtown Greenville, South Carolina

Greenville is located in the economically dynamic Piedmont Crescent region of the Carolinas. During the past decade, Greenville has developed one of America's most successful downtown Main Streets.

The regeneration process began in 1982 with the development of the Greenville Hyatt Regency Hotel and Convention Center at the northern end of Main Street. At about the same time, two new corporate office buildings were built nearby. In 1991, the Peace Per-

forming Arts Center was developed on a historic site at the southern end of Main Street, on the Reedy River.

In recent years, the northern blocks of Main Street have seen a resurgence of retail activity and a proliferation of high-quality restaurants, pubs, microbreweries, and entertainment venues. Most recently, the city has developed a new West End Market Place that provides retail, food, beverage, and entertainment outlets. And finally, a 17,000-seat arena is under construction.

As City Manager Audrey Watts observed, "There was a need to carefully assess recent progress, assure that we were doing the right things, and maintain the momentum in the years ahead."

The Greenville report card process was budgeted at approximately $25,000. It included a detailed site assessment, backed up with approximately 25 leadership interviews and the preparation of a comprehensive report card giving specific recommendations as to the next steps required to keep downtown revitalization on a successful track.

The report card process identified "21 Challenges and Strategies for the 21st Century," with some of the more important challenges being:

- Developing downtown Greenville's new and enhanced "personality."
- Preparing a downtown master plan.
- Realizing that downtown housing is an essential ingredient of success.
- Proving that retail uses can work in the downtown.

The report card concluded with recommendations and an action agenda. Two key recommendations were (1) to adopt the "Challenges and Strategies for the 21st Century" as the high-priority program to be implemented during the next five years, and (2) to use the report card as a vehicle for building an enhanced working relationship between public and private downtown stakeholders.

Experience Gained

Some insights into the report card assessment process have been garnered through the case studies presented in this article and other studies prepared by the author.

Overall, the report card process is a quick, relatively inexpensive way to assess progress, or the lack of it, objectively; to make mid-course program and investment corrections; to create a new

focus; to energize leadership; and to set new planning and implementation agendas. It also is an objective means of testing ideas, confirming plans before implementation, and providing a comfortable level of peer review.

But the local government must need this kind of assessment, and a legitimate purpose must be identified. The process can be called almost anything, as long as its purpose is clear. Some local governments need a report card, while others may need a strategic assessment, strategic audit, status report, or peer review.

The process should be brief (four to five weeks), intensive, inclusive, reasoned, unbiased, and honest. Finally, any report card is most useful when acted upon in a timely fashion.

CHAPTER 37

Rebuilding Downtown in Grand Forks, North Dakota

Diane Suchman

Even for the hardy and resilient citizens of Grand Forks, North Dakota, 1997 was a tough year. Located at the eastern edge of North Dakota, Grand Forks is home to hard-working Midwesterners who pride themselves on their ability to thrive despite the city's long, harsh winters. The winter of 1996-1997 was extraordinary, however, even by Grand Forks's standards. It lashed the city with record storm after record storm, piling up a total of nearly 100 inches of snow. Spring brought more blizzards, followed by rapid warming and heavy rains. The rains and melting snow caused the rivers to swell and surge. When the Red River rose to 55 feet above sea level (more than double

the 26-foot flood level), it broke through its earthen dike. Water flowed freely over the city, until more than two-thirds of Grand Forks was under water and nearly all the city's 50,000 citizens had to evacuate their homes. The city water system was contaminated, and the sewage treatment plant had to be shut down.

Downtown Grand Forks, which is adjacent to the river bank, was especially hard hit. Streets, basements, and the first floors of all buildings were awash with sewage-fouled floodwater, mud, and debris. Fires raged in 11 downtown buildings during the flood, wreaking further destruction. Torrents of water also flooded homes in adjacent neighborhoods and

Originally published as "Rebuilding Downtown Grand Forks," Urban Land, *Vol. 57, No. 2, February, 1998. Published by the Urban Land Institute, 1025 Thomas Jefferson Street, N.W., Suite 500 West, Washington, D.C. Reprinted with permission of the publisher.*

flowed over and beyond the city, across the plains of North Dakota.

When the floodwaters finally receded, the city, under the leadership of Mayor Patricia Owens, began the arduous job of cleaning up and rebuilding. U.S. Secretary of Housing and Urban Development (HUD) Andrew Cuomo moved immediately to help and pledged $171 million in aid to the city. As part of its assistance effort, HUD offered the city the services of a ULI advisory services panel, which visited Grand Forks last September.

Re-Imagining Downtown

The city of Grand Forks began to consider how to organize its recovery effort by taking a hard look at its downtown. Even before the devastating flood, downtown Grand Forks, like many U.S. cities, had begun to evolve from being the region's primary office and retail center to being its residential, governmental, and educational center. Over the past 20 years, changes in retail development and spending patterns had resulted in the movement of many stores and services to suburban locations, particularly after a regional mall was built in the southwestern part of the city. Many downtown businesses had been replaced by professional services and entertainment uses, while other storefronts remained vacant. In an attempt to compete with the shopping mall and other retail outfits, an indoor shopping center, City Center Mall, had been developed downtown by closing a street and connecting buildings on either side with a roofed enclosure.

Since the flood, many of the businesses that had remained downtown have relocated, have closed completely, or are in temporary space and have no definite plans for permanent relocation. Although government offices and schools are expected to rebuild in their existing downtown locations, the future of many of the retailers and professional service firms is uncertain.

The flood therefore has presented the city and its citizens with an opportunity to ask basic questions about the role and function of downtown. Some people believed the downtown core was obsolete and that perhaps the city should not devote resources to rebuilding it. Others felt that the downtown should be redeveloped, not simply as it was before, but in a way that reflects today's changed market realities.

With this in mind, the city's charge to the ULI panel was to determine, in the light of current market conditions and trends, what role downtown Grand Forks should play in the regional economy and to suggest rebuilding strategies that would enable it to fulfill that role. A great deal of useful planning work was done before the panel's arrival, including preparation of a report issued by Grand Forks' Re-Imagining Downtown Committee, a plan known as the River Forks plan, an interim business program, and more. In preparing its recommendations, the panel reviewed these reports, briefing materials prepared by the city, and information gleaned from interviews with more than 100 individuals.

Envisioning a New Heart for Grand Forks

The ULI panel advised that downtown Grand Forks be redeveloped in a way that asserts its historic role as the symbolic, physical, and functional "heart" of the region. To that end, the panel envisioned the city core as an exciting gathering place, with restaurants, specialty shops, entertainment, and festivals; public open space along the river; governmental, educational, and financial offices; and housing that offers easy access to downtown amenities, and, when possible, views of the river. The proposal also included a traditional town square that would serve as the main public space and focal point for the entire community.

The panel found that downtown Grand Forks has an essentially strong and stable economy founded on agriculture, retail trade, wholesale distribution, aerospace technology, and education. Key economic forces include the University of North Dakota, which has 13,000 students, faculty, and staff, and nearby Grand Forks Air Force Base, which employs 12,500 people. The city also functions as a metropolitan service center and provides retail stores and services to a 17-county area of 210,000 people in eastern North Dakota and western Minnesota.

The city's urban core seems to have many strengths on which to build. From a financial point of view, millions of public dollars have been invested in buildings, infrastructure, and community facilities downtown, which include a central high school, the city hall, the county courthouse and administrative offices, public safety offices, and a federal building. There also has been significant private sector investment. Despite the flood, underground utilities are in reasonably good condition. There is little crime, and the city is considered safe. The central business district is surrounded by generally stable and well preserved neighborhoods. In addition, downtown Grand Forks has remained a viable and affordable residential location. Before the flood, multifamily housing downtown served the needs of the elderly and university students. These generally affordable units were typically fully occupied, and waiting lists were common.

Downtown Grand Forks remains the geographic center of the metropolitan area and is one of the most accessible points in the entire region. The downtown area is small and well defined, with a grid street system that creates an urban scale and character that is unique in the Grand Forks metro area. The proximity of city and county government offices downtown provides an opportunity for the two systems to work together and employ a large, stable population of workers who represent a potential market for other business activity downtown. In addition, there is significant unmet demand for both replacement and new development in all segments of downtown real estate: residential, office, entertainment, public sector, and hotel uses.

The city also embodies the heritage of Grand Forks, with a collection of historic buildings that is admired throughout the West. Although it lacks a defined physical and social focal point, the downtown area—and particularly the riverbank—continues to serve as the gathering place for citywide community celebrations. Little riverfront infrastructure is in place, however, and little effort has been expended to capitalize on the river as one of the city's major assets and gathering spots.

Containing—and Celebrating—the River

The panel proposed a conceptual land use plan for downtown Grand Forks that includes a flood protection system; creation of exciting public spaces along the river, including a traditional town square; clustering of land uses by development type; and streetscape and infrastructure improvements.

The first order of business was to recommend ways to contain and celebrate the river. To make the area safe from future flooding, the panel, after consulting with the U.S. Army Corps of Engineers, advised creating a flood wall, part of which would be architecturally integrated into the historic buildings parallel to the river along the east side of Third Street, thereby preserving both sides of that street. All major streets would pass through the wall, allowing physical and visual access to the river. Movable flood gates would secure open passages during periods of flooding. The gates also would present opportunities for public art to mark and enhance the entrances to the river. At the same time, the panel suggested both making the river more efficient in its hydraulic flow and enhancing its value as an aesthetic and recreational amenity by creating a weir, an underwater dam, that would raise and widen the river's surface area. To accommodate the wider flow of water, reconstructing approaches to bridges would enable water to flow beneath them.

According to the panel, the river is the key to establishing a sense of place in downtown Grand Forks. To realize its value, the cities of Grand Forks and East Grand Forks were encouraged to work together to create a bistate Red River Park that would feature a landscaped esplanade anchored by the proposed town square, which is located at what is now City Center Mall. The town square would serve as a formal "living room" for civic and cultural events, provide a balcony overlook to the river basin, and be the point of transition from the flood wall to the park. The park would include regraded shorelines landscaped with natural flora, pedestrian promenades, hard-surface hiking and jogging paths, and, at the upper reaches of the floodway, baseball and football fields. Marinas, bicycle paths, and other amenities also could be included.

Repositioning Downtown

Next, clustering development downtown into three districts was recommended. Each cluster would emphasize a particular type of land use: a residential, retail, and entertainment district in the few blocks near and overlooking the river and the proposed town square; a financial district that would provide a first-class, high-profile home for financial institutions and professional service firms; and two government and educational centers that would build on existing clusters of public uses flanking the proposed financial center location. The activity centers would be connected by street-level retail activity, upper-floor apartments, and civic amenities such as street trees, lighting, paving, sculpture, fountains, and banners. Initial development would be concentrated within a five-block area to create a compact, walkable environment that would be attractive to downtown residents, workers, and visitors.

To reposition downtown Grand

Forks so that its market potential would be maximized, the panel recommended that the city embrace the strategic elements of the nationally recognized Main Street Program of the National Trust for Historic Preservation, which consist of economic restructuring, through a business retention and recruitment program; organization, enabling downtown businesses to collaborate; design guidelines and assistance that emphasize historic preservation; and marketing strategies that present downtown as a unit to both investors and consumers. To encourage historic preservation, the city was urged to support retention of cultural landmarks and to work with the Historic Preservation Commission to develop a reuse strategy for individual historic buildings.

The panel suggested that the existing River Forks Commission (RFC) assume responsibility for marketing and promoting downtown, river-related events, and the region, using its delegated legal powers. RFC would also be responsible for developing the bistate Red River Park and ensuring good communication between Grand Forks and East Grand Forks. Also advised was that an autonomous public/private subcommittee of RFC, to be known as the Downtown Development Committee (DDC), be established to create and implement the plans and budget for rebuilding downtown Grand Forks.

Progress in rebuilding downtown Grand Forks was thought to require public/private partnerships. The panel suggested that the DDC encourage a stronger private sector role by preparing and marketing "packaged" development opportunities for desired projects when appropriate.

Both short-term and longer-term strategies to revitalize the downtown area were recommended. Short-term projects include completing demolition of unusable structures; clearing, grading, and seeding lots as an interim measure to prepare them for development; creating a skating rink/farmers market; engaging a historic preservation consultant to prepare site-specific development proposals; and rehabilitating existing housing in key areas. As an important early but highly visible step in establishing confidence and investment momentum downtown, the panel suggested that the city take the first step toward creating the recommended financial center downtown by negotiating an equitable and mutually beneficial lease with First National Bank and interested attorneys and accountants as soon as possible. Longer-term projects include developing site-specific plans for infill and new housing, assembling sites for strategic development, addressing zoning and other regulatory issues, hiring a director of development, and preparing a detailed infrastructure improvement plan budget.

Since most market-rate downtown projects initially will not pencil out financially without some public funding, the panel recommended that the city allocate $50 to $70 million of its community development block grant (CDBG) allocation for the rebuilding of downtown and outlined various ways that the city could leverage its investment. The use of public funds would be essential for stimulating both initial revitalization projects and private investment, and it should be viewed as an investment that will pay future dividends to the entire community.

Taking a Regional View

The panel also looked across the river. East Grand Forks is about to complete its own ambitious comprehensive redevelopment plan, and the community's leadership is prepared to make a significant investment to implement it. In its final comments, the panel stressed that its suggestions for Grand Forks and the proposed plans for East Grand Forks are complementary, interdependent, and mutually reinforcing, and it urged the two cities to work closely together in implementing their downtown redevelopment plans.

Much of what the citizens of Grand Forks are proud of in their downtown was built by an earlier generation at the turn of the century. In about two years, there will be a new source of pride, based on what *this* generation gives to the future citizens of Grand Forks and East Grand Forks.

CHAPTER 38

Suburbs Working Together in Cleveland Heights, Ohio

Rob Gurwitt

It's not that Ken Montlack is bitter, or even especially angry. But from his perch on the city council in Cleveland Heights, Ohio, he has been watching his town struggle to maintain its housing standards and fix its roads and keep its apartments filled and spruce up the facades of tottering commercial strips, and he confesses himself vexed.

Cleveland Heights, which sits just to the east of the city whose name it bears, was once one of the crown jewels in the ring of suburbs that immediately surround Cleveland. If you lived on Cleveland's east side, it was one of the places that you dreamed of moving to someday. Now, although it is still a respected-enough address, it is just like older suburbs everywhere, striving to keep up appearances as money and people leapfrog outward in search of greener surroundings, better schools and more space. Montlack has come to the depressing conclusion that, try as it might to remain attractive, Cleveland Heights is heading for failure.

He isn't worried just because Cleveland Heights' housing stock is old, the lots small and the space for new development gone, although all of this is true. What irritates him is that when he looks around, he sees all the external cards stacked against his town.

Federal and state subsidies for communities trying to stave off decay? "The government's policies have been that if you want monies, you must be slummy and blighty," he says. "If your

Originally published as "The Quest for Common Ground," Governing, *Vol. 11, No. 9, June, 1998. Published by the Congressional Quarterly, Inc., Washington, D.C. Reprinted with permission of the publisher and the author.*

central city looks like Hiroshima, *then* they'll give you money." Road maintenance? Don't even get him started on the Ohio Department of Transportation and its priorities. "You can't reform ODOT," he says wearily, "you can only drive a stake through its heart." Zoning in the rich outer suburbs? "If you have no poor people, then you've eliminated your social costs while increasing your tax base, and you've stuck the cities and inner suburbs with the job of taking care of them. You can't really take on the outer ring's restrictive zoning," he admits. "All you can do," and he says this with a friendly smile, "is make their life miserable."

Well, maybe not *miserable*. Cleveland's booming outer suburbs seem to be doing quite well for themselves at the moment, and some of them barely acknowledge that places like Cleveland Heights exist. But can they be made a bit nervous, their confidence shaken a bit? They can, and Ken Montlack is dedicating much of his energy to doing it.

About two years ago, he and other elected officials from Cleveland's older, inner-ring communities—upper-end towns such as Shaker Heights and Lakewood, blue-collar towns such as Euclid and Garfield Heights—began meeting monthly to compare notes and see if, in combination, they could begin rewriting some of the rules of the metropolitan economic and political game. They named themselves the "First Suburbs Consortium," complete with letterhead and a set of advisers, including Cleveland State University Professor Tom Bier, who is the best known analyst of local development trends.

So far, the group's tangible victories have been modest: an agreement with HUD that the federal agency will no longer foreclose on inner-ring properties and then let them deteriorate; a compromise on a state highway-widening proposal out on the suburban fringe; better inner-ring representation on boards that make regional spending decisions. The First Suburbs have been busy, but no one, least of all the politicians who belong to their coalition, would argue that they have become metropolitan power brokers. Even the city of Cleveland itself, which clearly has some interests in common with its older suburbs, has for the most part remained aloof from their efforts, although City Council President Jay Westbrook does send a representative to the consortium's meetings.

Yet, there is also no doubt that the First Suburbs have begun to unsettle the region's politics, and it is no stretch at all to suggest that, over the next few years, they will unsettle it a good deal more. That is because they are zeroing in on the issue of suburban sprawl, and in Cleveland, as in a growing number of places all over the country, sprawl is the issue around which the politics of regional development is being remade.

From Chicago to St. Louis to Philadelphia, and in Maryland, Michigan and California, coalitions are taking shape that would have been unthinkable a few years ago—between central cities and their close-in suburbs; among inner-ring communities whose officials have for decades ignored each other; between communities in the metropolitan core and rural officials concerned about the loss of farmland.

These developments are being propelled by a growing conviction that, as Paul Oyaski, the mayor of Euclid, puts it, "there is a direct cause-and-effect relationship between outer-belt strength and inner-belt weakness." Oyaski, Montlack and their allies believe central cities and older suburbs are unfairly burdened by policies at every level that steer resources to new development rather than redevelopment, with congestion and rising taxes the ultimate result. They are winning converts, giving the debate over regional growth and decline a heft it has never had before.

"I'm sensing that this issue means something to people all across the state," says Gene Krebs, a conservative Republican from a rural district who has emerged as the most forceful proponent of farmland preservation in the Ohio House. "It's urban sprawl in the cities, farmland preservation in rural counties, and in the suburbs it's that it used to take 45 minutes to drive home from work, and now it takes an hour and 45 minutes."

For years, there have been only two real examples of regional approaches to the sprawl issue: the decades-old tax-base sharing system around Minneapolis and St. Paul, which was designed to get at the fiscal inequities that evolve when one community develops much faster than another, and the urban growth boundary and elected metropolitan board in Portland, Oregon. Now, not only are there a passel of approaches being discussed, from statewide growth management plans to targeted infrastructure investment to giving more teeth to regional planning bodies, but a fundamental strategic split is developing, between those who favor a direct confrontation with the outer edge over who gets more resources and those who believe that only regional cooperation will ultimately benefit both core and outer communities.

What is indisputable is that, as the stunning rates of outer suburban growth continue unabated, ferment on these matters is growing. In the year since Maryland passed its "smart growth" initiative, directing state infrastructure funding largely to older areas, more than half the states in the country have gotten in touch with its planning office. Chattanooga, Tennessee, recently decided—after much public debate—to shift a chunk of its regional transportation funding away from exurban road expansion toward downtown road repair. The St. Louis region is embroiled in a bitter debate over whether to build a bridge over the Missouri River from St. Louis County to fast-growing St. Charles County. And in Fresno, California, an unprecedented coalition of farming interests, homebuilders and business leaders, fed up with governmental inaction, has just called on the county to promote compact, rather than sprawling, development patterns.

"What we're seeing," says Bruce Katz, who directs the Brookings Institution's Center on Urban and Metropolitan Policy, "is a sort of in-out movement built around equity, and an out-in movement built around the preservation of open space or farmland. One or the other might arise first or have more weight in a given region, but what is striking is that this stuff wasn't even on the map two years ago."

Not everyone realizes it, but any discussion of regional "growth" in the Cleveland area obscures the fundamental point: The area is not gaining people, it is just shuffling them around. While each of the four counties that fringe Cleveland and its inner suburbs grew in population by as much as 50 percent between 1970 and 1994, the five-county region as a whole actually declined slightly. During those years, Cleveland lost 34 percent of its residents, and the inner suburbs were not far behind: Euclid saw a 26 percent drop, Garfield Heights 25 percent, Lakewood 19 percent, Shaker Heights 16 percent.

The dynamics of metropolitan dispersal are complex, and there are those who argue that cities and inner suburbs are victims only of the marketplace and their own shortcomings—that what is at work is not urban "sprawl" but urban "choice," as homebuyers and employers opt for better schools, lower crime, better housing values, lower taxes and an escape from the density and decay afflicting the metropolitan core. By focusing on regional imbalance, the argument goes, urban activists are sidestepping their own responsibility for failing to address crime, education and other problems head-on.

But these arguments do not strike much of a chord with officials like Ken Montlack, who for years have been engaged in a determined battle to stave off decay. They have raised taxes to support their schools, they have subsidized homebuyers, they have refurbished storefronts, they have given tax breaks to retailers tempted to move out, they have bought up commercial strips and sold them cheap to developers, they have given loans and grants to employers, they have even launched public relations campaigns to appeal to young families. But the thrust of all this is unmistakable: It is upkeep, not development. "We realize we have to be aggressive and proactive to retain people and grow jobs," says Madeline Cain, the mayor of Lakewood, which sits on Lake Michigan just to the west of Cleveland.

"At the same time, we see millions and millions being drawn from our citizens and being used to provide incentives for people not only to flee the inner suburbs but Cuyahoga County."

It's not just that money that might have gone to already-developed communities is being spent on new development; it's that public policy *encourages* new development. As Cleveland State's Tom Bier argues, public policies made at all levels of government "have made it more expensive to redevelop than to build on farms. Government has structured the marketplace by deciding where the road goes, by how it zones, by where money for water and sewer lines gets spent."

The example he likes to use is a recent federal grant to build a new road in one of the suburbs beyond the Cuyahoga County line, designed to open 200 acres for new industrial development. That grant was an outright gift. A few months before that, the state established a loan fund to promote the development of "brownfields"—vacant, usually polluted industrial land in the inner ring. Communities will have to pay it back, with interest. "Here's public money saying that it is good and proper to give money away for the development of farmland," Bier points out, "but that it is somehow tainted to give it away for brownfields. This is the mindset."

State and local spending on water and sewer lines, state funding of new schools, state-subsidized enterprise zones and economic development policies all shape the way development happens. So, too, do less obvious things, such as federal housing policy. The way the inner-ring leaders see it, Washington has been holding them to the most rigorous standards of social equity, while placing little or no pressure on the outer suburbs, which have been able to avoid involvement in social issues altogether. "The inner-ring suburbs, every one of them has been responsible in terms of open housing, accepting housing for the mentally retarded and the like, and we see no pressure on other communities to do the same," says Madeline Cain.

But what galls Cain and her colleagues most is the extent to which road spending on the periphery is subsidized by urban tax dollars. New roads, and especially new highway interchanges, open up new areas for development, or at least promote it. In Ohio, much of this construction is paid for through gas-tax money, the bulk of which, Euclid's Paul Oyaski argues, comes from cities and older communities. "When Strongsville, out at the edge of Cuyahoga County, puts in a new mall, that's a local zoning decisions," he says. "So why the hell should the people of Ohio subsidize building interchanges for it? They put in industrial parks and shopping mall sand then come to ODOT for these improvements, but that money is generated in the densely populated areas of Cuyahoga County. We're subsidizing building yuppie enclaves, and we can't afford to fix our sewers."

The best demonstration of what these arguments can do is on display in Minnesota, where Myron Orfield, a Democratic state representative from Minneapolis, has built a bipartisan coalition of legislators from the central cities and older and poorer suburbs aimed at redressing the regional imbalance. Three years ago, Orfield's forces pushed through legislation to give the Twin Cities Metropolitan Council, the board that oversees regional development and transportation, more leverage in deciding where roads and sewer improvements might go. More recently, they have been pushing to have the members of the council elected rather than appointed by the governor—a move that would give the whole regional movement more political weight. The coalition has passed bills extending the reach of the region's tax-base sharing system, requiring newer suburbs to accept far more affordable housing units than they now do, and refiguring the area's entire land-use planning structure. All have been vetoed by Republican Governor Arne Carlson, and blocked from becoming law. But the issues reemerge in every legislative session, and this is Carlson's last year in office.

Similar political constellations have been appearing elsewhere, although in more piecemeal fashion. In Illinois last year, a group of urban and inner-suburban legislators—backed by a heavy lobbying effort from a network of churches in Chicago and its suburbs—worked with Republican Governor Jim Edgar to shift reliance for school funding out of property taxes and onto the state treasury; they succeeded in the House, but failed in the Senate. In Missouri, a group of St. Louis and St. Louis County legislators introduced a measure last year to create an urban growth boundary modeled on Portland's; it died in committee. This year, they are trying a different approach. They are pushing to allow the region's metropolitan planning organization, the East-West Gateway Coordinating Council—until now largely restricted to transportation planning—to begin addressing sprawl.

Meanwhile, in Michigan, a new, determinedly bipartisan Urban Caucus has formed in the legislature, inspired in no small part by Orfield and David

Rusk, the former mayor of Albuquerque who has also become a national analyst of urban decline. The group has been meeting to look closely at state policies affecting urban disinvestment and sprawl, and is in the process of drawing up a legislative package for next year.

One of the Michigan caucus's most active members is a Republican named Bill Bobier, who represents a district just below Traverse City, in the heart of Michigan's fruit belt. He is the group's only rural member, and his presence hints at the potential strength that urban anti-sprawl forces may be able to built statewide by allying with farmland preservationists. Most new suburban subdivisions, after all, are built in the countryside, and these days, more often than not, they are built on what had been productive farmland. Michigan lost 854,000 acres of farmland between 1982 and 1992—roughly 10 acres an hour—and Bobier and many of his constituents are alarmed.

"Once a year," he says, "I meet with the same group of apple growers from my district, and it's always a freewheeling couple of hours—about deer and deer damage, pesticide management, stuff like that. But the last time, half the discussion was about land use and farmland preservation. It's clear these guys are really worried about the future now. They're seeing subdivisions and homes built where previously they could spray or grow whatever they wanted. Well, somewhere along the way it became apparent to me that the problems of urban sprawl—and the problems of rural areas that come with that—were really the result of the fact that we were suffering this urban degradation. It was clear to me that you aren't going to save the

countryside or preserve farmland without saving the cities."

He's got company. The Michigan Farm Bureau has decided that sprawl and farmland preservation are among its most important issues, and in April it sent off two busloads of farmers, local officials, planning commission members, real estate brokers, business people and state legislators to tour parts of Maryland and Pennsylvania and study local farmland preservation and growth-control initiatives.

In Ohio, a farmland preservation task force appointed last year by Republican Governor George V. Voinovich rapidly came to the conclusion that urban sprawl and disinvestment in core urban areas were a crucial piece of what they were looking at—to the apparent discomfort of Voinovich and his proxy on the panel, Lieutenant Governor Nancy Hollister. An initial proposal by members of the task force to mandate regional planning for Ohio was, after much politicking, watered down to a suggestion that counties consider undertaking planning on their own. "This was a *farmland* task force, and we didn't want to get bogged down in trying to have a full-blown discussion of urban issues," explains Howard Wise, Hollister's executive assistant.

This is, of course, the difficulty with tackling sprawl. It's controversial. Fast-growing areas, struggling to deal with the people and businesses that are flocking in, *need* new roads, water and sewer systems, new schools and industrial parks and office complexes. They do not have much sympathy for suggestions that government money get channeled into areas that are not growing. As Tom Bier says, "The most emotional battleground in America is race, and the second most emotional is development and where it's located and why. It's a political power struggle that involves allocating resources. So someone is going to have to give up something to meet anyone else's agenda, and they're not going to give it up with a smile."

That is why, among the national figures who have been grappling with sprawl and its consequences, there is some division over how to proceed. Orfield and Rusk argue bluntly that core communities will be able to redevelop only if money and attention are redirected inward and the social costs of dealing with poverty are directed outward. And they don't think the outer suburbs will go along with such a program unless they are forced to do so by a show of superior political strength. "I just have not seen instances in this country," Rusk argues, "where voluntary agreements among local governments have produced significant compacts."

But some of the local leaders who are forced to deal with these issues believe Rusk and Orfield are playing a dangerous game. "Organizing it the way they think you should," says Curtis Johnson, who heads the Twin Cities' Metropolitan Council, "is the political equivalent of shooting at the bear in the forest. If you fail to take him down with that first show, you're gone.... These fast-growing suburbs have lots of political clout. Which is why I think we're a lot better off building bridges than throwing bombs. This is a good time to sue for peace rather than pursue war."

In its own way, the First Suburbs Consortium is mulling this question over as well. To be sure, no one expects Ohio even to discuss anything like tax-base sharing—"Frankly," says one consortium member, "Myron's message

bombs here." But the First Suburbs *are* trying to develop political clout. "I want the policy makers to know we're out there," says Madeline Cain, "and when it comes to economic development legislation, transportation legislation and tax legislation, I want them to be cognizant of what impact those initiatives will have on fully developed, aging cities."

At the moment, this mostly involves small but significant steps. A study of the boards that affect Cuyahoga County growth—such as the local body that hands out state infrastructure money—revealed that the inner suburbs were unrepresented. "We dropped the ball on that one," says Cain. Now she, Oyaski and Pat Mearns, the mayor of Shaker Heights, sit on the most important regional boards.

The First Suburbs have a lot of sorting out to do as they try to figure out where to go. There is, for instance, the knotty question of their relations with Cleveland. On the one hand, the city's gradual revival has been a boon to many of the neighboring communities. On the other hand, some mayors are now worried that the city's free trade zone, its empowerment zone and its economic rebuilding in general could steal businesses from them just as surely as the outer suburbs are stealing it with their green land and infrastructure subsidies. "I fear we are being squeezed, and are last in the grand scheme of things," says Cain.

There is also the tricky business of whether to expand the coalition into the range of suburbs just beyond the inner ring. Some of the towns that thought of themselves as outer suburbia just a few years ago are now seeing employers and residents pick up and move still further into the hinterland. They are beginning to feel some of the same pressures as Lakewood and Euclid and Cleveland Heights. But too heavy an emphasis on urban issues could drive them into the political arms of the outer ring. "If you're at a disadvantage to the inner suburbs because they're building political power, and to the outlying areas because they've got cheaper land costs, cheaper labor costs and tax subsidies, then your communities are in danger," says John Jelepis, the mayor of Bay Village, two towns beyond Lakewood. "So I don't think it would take too long to make 15 calls to the outer-ring communities and have a consortium there."

If this vision of warring rings that pushes some of those who are sympathetic to the First Suburbs group to argue that ultimately, the only answer lies in strong regional cooperation that takes in the entire metropolitan area. One who feels this way is Sara Pavlovicz, a county commissioner in Medina County, who is worried by Medina's untrammeled growth. "You have communities," she says, "that are literally stealing businesses and people back and forth. We're duplicating infrastructure, we're duplicating roads, we're spending money on expansion, but it's not good, true economic development. This region needs to act as a region if we're going to actually *attract* growth."

Ken Montlack, from his inner-ring vantage point in Cleveland Heights, listens to arguments like that and finds them interesting, but premature. If communities such as his are to survive, he believes, they need to build power now, not wait for anyone to share it with them. "I believe in regionalism," he says. "Believe me, I want to reach the Promised Land. But around here, you don't do it by just having Jesus in your heart. You've got to do it through political organizing. You've got to have a roomful of registered voters to get people focused. All it is, is just good old class warfare."

CHAPTER 39

Developing a Downtown Design Assistance Program in Pullman, Washington

Barbara Ryder and *Kelsey Gray*

The concept of recycling applies to far more than empty beer cans and old clothes. The term can and does apply to the revival of currently run-down commercial buildings in the downtown districts that once served as the cornerstones of communities.

Reviving the downtown Pullman, Washington, business district is a task being approached through a partnership among the downtown businesses, the Pullman City Council, Washington State University and several civic groups—the Pullman Main Street Program has coordinated their joint and individual efforts.

Following is a case study of the process used by the Pullman Main Street Program's Design Committee to create an assistance program to guide design choices made by downtown business owners. The process is now well on its way to creating visual improvements in downtown Pullman.

The techniques and design materials that the committee used may be quite useful to other communities endeavoring to improve the appearance of their downtown.

From Small Town, *Vol. 18, No. 5, March/April, 1988. Published by the Small Towns Institute, Ellensburg, Washington. Reprinted with permission of the publisher.*

The National Main Street Program

The National Main Street Center, sponsored by the National Trust for Historic Preservation, is a technical reference center created to stimulate small town economic growth within the context of historic preservation. Following a three-year pilot program initiated in 1977, the trust established the permanent Main Street center in 1980 in response to growing concern that traditional preservation did not suit many older commercial districts. Today, a network of Main Street cities spreads across the United States. In addition, scores of individual towns have established their own Main Street–type programs based on the center's approach to revitalization.

Pullman was selected as a Main Street City in 1984 by a Washington State Steering Committee composed of representatives from a variety of state organizations. Along with this designation came a certain degree of status, access to current information and technical assistance and a combination of hope and skepticism from downtown business interests. Of course, the mere fact of selection to special status does not guarantee a successful downtown rejuvenation; the responsibility for creating beneficial change rests with the citizens of each individual city.

Demographic and Economic Conditions in Pullman

Pullman, located in Whitman County in eastern Washington at the Idaho border, is the home of Washington State University (WSU), the state's land-grant university and one of two major research institutions in the state. Its Main Street Program has benefited both directly and indirectly from access to the human resources and technical aid provided by the proximity to WSU.

Pullman's population, including students, is approximately 22,250. Of that total, 15,230 are university students. Most Pullman residents live there in order to attend classes at WSU, serve the institution's employment needs or work in support service activities generated by the university's enrollment. Only one other county in the entire United States has a greater percentage of the total employment working at one institution or business.

WSU students are an inherently transient clientele, and the great majority lack ties to town or to the downtown district. Long-time residents are the mainstays of the district and tend to shop downtown for specific items such as gifts and restaurant services. The four banks located in the central business district also draw considerable local traffic. Residents who bank in Pullman tend to shop in the nearby stores and become personally acquainted with the merchants. The store owners say that the local residents are loyal customers.

The student population is not nearly as lucrative a market as the downtown merchants would like because of competition from two shopping malls located ten miles to the east, across the state border in Moscow, Idaho. Many people, such as a majority of WSU students, grew up in suburban settings and have developed shopping habits based on a familiarity with suburban malls. Consequently, they are very willing to drive to Moscow to continue to shop in a familiar environment. These students travel to the malls even though the area offers no intercity transit system, and despite the fact that much of the same merchandise is available at competitive prices in downtown Pullman.

When merchants lose sales to the malls, the city of Pullman loses sales tax revenues. The exact amount of the loss is not known because of recent changes in downtown Pullman and the opening of another shopping area on the southern outskirts of the town; however, estimates of the loss to Idaho range from 23 percent to 48 percent of potential gross sales.

Today, downtown Pullman is developing a marketing strategy based on a frank assessment of the qualities that comprise the downtown's assets and which the commercial strips and malls lack. The downtown offers proximity to the university, the pleasant visual appearance of the downtown buildings, their historic nature and the ambiance of a marketplace created by the variety of shops, window displays and restaurants. The strategy recognizes that, while storefront rehabilitation can enhance a business' appearance, improving sales also requires a combination of efforts involving interior design, selection and display merchandise, advertising and financial management.

Pullman has entered the third year of its Main Street Program and visual changes have started to occur. Three improvement projects are complete and banners have been purchased and hung along downtown streets. The efforts of several energetic individuals and the community's willingness to support aesthetic enhancement made these improvements possible. An atmosphere of change is developing through an active partnership between the downtown business owners, Washington State University, civic groups and the city of Pullman.

The Structure of the Pullman Main Street Program

The Main Street Program's manager is the organization's only paid staff person. A steering committee provides the necessary organizational structure and develops policy while three other volunteer committee report to it and represent elements of the Main Street approach: promotion, design and economic restructuring. Skilled, hardworking volunteers willing to serve on committees are important to any successful Main Street city and Pullman has a solid base of these through active community organizations such as Rotary, Kiwanis, Campfire, Scouting, the Civic Trust and others.

One of the Main Street Program's volunteer committees, the Pullman Main Street Design Committee, was formed to advise business owners about design problems and to develop possible solutions. The committee is currently devising a design assistance program and gathering support materials and it is expected that the efforts will create positive visual changes in the downtown.

The committee has a loose organizational structure. The volunteers elect a chairperson. Regular meetings are held and a formal agenda and recorded minutes are used to help keep the members organized, focused and on-task. Often members form small subcommittees to carry out specific jobs more efficiently.

The way the design committee has recruited and employed volunteers has been important to its success in developing a design assistance program. It has recruited people it has identified as having important skills in specific areas such as business, planning, law, architecture, landscape architecture and community development. Since 1984, the design committee has completed a number of projects. It has compiled a document detailing design guidelines, conducted a needs assessment, organized a self-help design seminar and recruited WSU architecture and interior design students in order to produce conceptual drawings for business owners interested in having their establishments become Main Street Program demonstration projects.

The Value of Design Assistance

The goal of a successful downtown design assistance program is to enable the businesses to design the marketplace so that the downtown can stand on its own merits by offering customers quality businesses and an attractive atmosphere. This type of program does not attempt to redesign whole blocks or entire downtowns; instead, it acts as a broker of information and resources that serves private citizens, contractors, merchants, commercial property owners and all who have a stake in creating a prosperous community. Development of a design assistance program is essentially the art of devising and implementing a course of action which will lead to an effective educational and resource referral program. It is a restorative process which requires continued involvement as the process evolves.

Facade design is a critical element for any effort to improve business in a downtown district. Visual improve-ments to storefronts are often undertaken by property owners operating either new enterprises or who maintain established businesses and recognize the need to upgrade or update the business district's physical appearance. Owners virtually always renovate their buildings in the hope of stimulating economic activity.

Unfortunately, however, even the most well-intentioned business owner can make inappropriate design choices in an attempt to "modernize" and create a new commercial image. The resulting appearance sometimes actually detracts from the business instead of achieving the desired result of creating an image that attracts customers and contributes to the appearance of the downtown district as a whole. Therefore, basic information about design must be available to store owners so that they can make well-considered, appropriate decisions about design improvements.

In an ideal world, business owners would take time to thoroughly research and evaluate the appropriate choices when planning to improve the visual image of their particular business. However, most avoid this process as it can be both time-consuming and require expertise far beyond that of common experience and general business training.

According to Ronald Fleming, president of the Townscape Institute in Cambridge, Massachusetts: "In our work with downtown planners, merchants, architects and property owners, five factors are significant in evaluating a storefront renovation project: (1) The sensibilities of the owner and his commitment to the renovation project. (2) The construction and design quality of the original facade. (3) The size of the budget. (4) The resources available, including design advice, materials and skilled artisans. (5) The relationship between owner and tenant."[1] When renovation work is planned, these five factors must be carefully considered. The analysis may reveal hidden opportunities or discover constraints not initially known.

According to Scott Gerloff, director of the National Main Street Center, "Too many times, towns hope that one single thing will save downtown—a new building, urban renewal... Because downtowns developed in stages, it makes sense that they return to life in a similar fashion."[2] This incremental perspective is important to consider when planning for economic and visual changes in a downtown business district.

Development of a Design Assistance Program for Pullman

During its first two years, the design committee developed a series of drafts of design guidelines for Pullman's downtown revitalization. The committee proposals used commonly accepted design principles originally compiled by the National Trust for Historic Preservation, and then applied by the National Main Street Program.

The design committee then expressed concern about how to persuade the downtown business community to agree to and implement the guidelines. Pullman business owners have chosen to be self-employed and independent. They seem to prefer the life provided by private business and find personal satisfaction in being their own bosses and operating on their own schedules. This quality of independence is the strength upon which they individually draw for success, but it can also create a barrier against achieving coordinated downtown improvement. Committee members believed that it was important for the business owners to decide which guidelines they thought would be useful and which ought to be followed.

Also, before developing Pullman's design assistance program, the design committee needed to know which economic and design issues business and property owners believed faced the downtown. It also was important to know what specific design information and assistance the business people needed. The committee wanted to identify the sense of "place" that had been ingrained in the buildings during the history of the town and define the question: "What makes Pullman, Pullman?"

The Survey

To answer that question, the committee developed a two-part survey. Community volunteers, university students and staff personnel and business owners conducted the poll and each interviewed three business owners and three people shopping in the area. The interviewers assured confidentiality to the respondents in order to encourage candor and the interview gave people a wide range of opportunities to provide information on their perceptions of the Pullman business district.

The first part of the survey involved a visual response assessment which registered respondent reactions to visual aspects of the downtown and documented their subjective impressions about its aesthetic qualities. The tool used to solicit the visually-oriented responses was a photomontage prepared by merging photographs of the downtown building front elevations in order to create a panoramic view of the buildings along the street. The survey included photocopies of panoramas on both sides of each street. Survey responses were written and sketched directly onto the panoramas. This format enabled the store owners and their customers to directly comment about their building, about neighboring buildings and about the structures in view across the street.

The second part of the survey consisted of standard questionnaires. Two slightly different questionnaires were developed. The form for business owners asked about the kinds of building improvements they had made in the past, about changes they anticipated making in the future and about their interest in having their building become a demonstration project. The form for the customers asked for their reactions to past building improvements and about what changes were still needed. The questionnaires asked both groups if they believed that a central rehabilitation theme would be good for Pullman, what they thought it would take to upgrade and change the downtown and which factors should be included in the design guidelines.

The survey served several purposes. First, the process of gathering the data proved as important as the data itself. People can indeed become motivated to consider new behaviors if they are made part of the process of planning change. And, over one hundred people took part in the survey process. Consciousness about design was raised simply by asking people for their opinions about what

they wanted for the downtown, and what they disliked about the status quo. An added benefit involved an increase in the level of communication between the business people, the volunteers and Main Street Design Committee members. The survey process also helped to advertise an upcoming design seminar sponsored by the Washington State Main Street Office, the Pullman Design Committee and the Pullman Civic Trust, a local civic group. Each person interviewed received an invitation to the seminar and was asked to invite anyone else who would be interested.

In the spring of 1987, twenty-six volunteers were recruited and trained to conduct the survey interviews. Then, business owners were randomly chosen to be interviewed. The committee used random sampling because of time limitations and the need to keep both the volunteers' assignments and amount of raw data manageable.

At the beginning of the volunteers' training session, the surveys were distributed to them and they received both verbal and written instructions about how to conduct the survey. They then practiced by interviewing each other in order to become familiar with the questionnaire. The trainees' responses were included in the final survey results. Then, the volunteers dispersed to conduct their interviews. Once the surveys had been completed and collected (the effort generated a 63 percent response rate), the responses were grouped by question, dictated into a tape recorder and transcribed. Design committee members read the transcript and they made note of repeated similar responses about building features, issues and preferences.

The Demonstration Projects

During the survey interviews, four business owners indicated that they intended to make some changes to their buildings during the next year. Therefore, the design committee designated their buildings as demonstration projects. To show their commitment to making the design improvements, the owners of each of the four businesses and the Main Street Program drew up contracts which required the owner to pay a $50 down payment to the Main Street Program for design assistance. A local attorney who is a design committee member drew up and donated the contract form. It states that if, during the next year, the owner uses the reviewed designs to make approved building improvements valued at $500 or more, the $50 will be refunded. And, if the changes are not made, the down payment becomes a donation to the Main Street Program.

The design committee also arranged for architecture and interior design students from WSU to be assigned to each business. The students received college credit to work with the business owners and they generated conceptual drawings for design committee review. The Pullman Main Street Economic Restructuring Committee then agreed to help the business owners devise a strategy for financing the proposed improvements.

The Consultant and the Seminar

At this pint in the process, Pullman area residents had provided most of the input toward the development of a design assistance program. The design committee then decided that an outside perspective would be useful and informative, especially if it took into account what other communities had accomplished and how they managed the projects. An outside consultant could review the proposed design guidelines, critique the designs for the demonstration projects and offer suggestions about how the city planning and building department could help with promoting the design guidelines.

The Pullman Main Street Program then asked for a $5,000 grant from the state Main Street office to fund the consultant. The proposal, submitted in January of 1987, was funded, and the program used the monies to pay the consultant fees, the survey costs, expenses for holding an informational seminar and for further development of the design guidelines.

The committee contacted Nore Winter, a Denver architect and urban-design specialist, and he agreed to a one-day visit to Pullman to help the design committee accomplish the tasks it had identified. Before conducting an evening seminar, he spent the day touring downtown Pullman, talking with business owners, reviewing guidelines and meeting with city officials.

At the beginning of the night's seminar, the design committee presented the survey results to the participants. Members showed slides of the city blocks and gave a summary of the interviews. Then, participants each received a listing of all of the individual responses to the survey, so that they could read the data at their convenience. Releasing the complete responses allowed people to compare their comments to those of others, and it also provided them with an opportunity to discern similarities and trends and to focus their attention on fundamental design issues affecting the downtown. Because the survey and seminar process had been design to encourage involvement, the business owners received both the survey results and seminar discussion with enthusiasm.

During the seminar, Winter commented on the survey results and gave a slide presentation featuring examples of successful and unsuccessful renovation projects in other communities. He made specific suggestions about Pullman and related his observations and suggestions to accepted principles of commercial architectural design. In the final portion of the seminar, WSU students presented a report on the demonstration projects. Their conceptual drawings were also displayed and they provided a vision of possible improvements that generated much interest in the downtown's future.

The Program to Date

Of course, the design assistance process' tangible results will be realized in the future, but prospects for success appear good. As a first step, the design committee will continue to give direction and information to the owners of the demonstration projects in order to encourage their completion. Members are also looking forward to planning additional projects once other merchants see the economic benefits of the demonstrations. It is not expected that every business owner will make changes, but the process of actual change has started. One of the first results is a new spirit of communication between building own-

ers and tenants. Shop owners, for example, who were once reluctant to ask their landlords to make improvements for fear of increased rents are now starting to focus on how rehabilitation provides added potential for attracting business.

The Pullman Main Street Steering Committee has now adopted and published the completed design guidelines and made them available to business owners and the general public. Also, the Main Street staff is compiling a resource directory that lists local contractors, designers, sign makers, painters, awning makers and other artisans. This will be made available to property and business owners who will need to rely on the technical expertise of local professionals in order to conduct remodeling projects.

The entire process has helped build hope in the revitalization of downtown Pullman. Multiple benefits will continue to come from involving the community, WSU and the downtown business owners in upgrading and recycling downtown Pullman's business district. With increased communication, improved morale, better programming and the greater availability of technical expertise and information, an improved business climate for downtown Pullman is indeed possible.

Notes

1. Ronald L. Fleming, "Why Merchants Renovate Storefronts," *Home Again*, Spring, 1984, pp. 20–21.
2. D.A. Fryxell, "Before You Can Sell Main Street, Main Street Must Be Sold on Itself," *Friendly Exchange*, Winter, 1985, p. 13.

Figure 1
Survey Questionnaire for Business Person

Survey of Design Preferences for Downtown Pullman, Washington

First, we want you to look at your street, its buildings, landscaping and storefronts. We have a picture of the street for you to mark on.

Q-1. As you look at your building, what do you notice that is attractive? (Please mark your comments on the picture.)

Q-2. What, if anything, don't you like, or would like to change about your building? (Please make comments on the picture.)

Now look at the entire street.

Q-3. Please note on the picture what you especially like and what you do not like. Include the buildings, colors, signs, landscaping and things you can see along the street (sidewalks, crosswalks, benches, etc.).

Q-4. In the past few years, what improvements have you made to your building/business?

Q-5. Within the next two years what improvements do you anticipate that you will need to make to your building? (Include everything from minor changes to major construction.)

Design improvements for a central business district have been shown to significantly improve the profit margin of downtown businesses. A Central Theme for the downtown has been suggested for Pullman.

Q-6. Do you believe a Central Theme would be good for Pullman?
_____ Yes _____ No

Q-7. If so, what do you feel could be done to motivate other business people in Pullman to upgrade and change the downtown building facades (storefronts)?

Q-8. In order for this to work there must be a concerted effort. How much would you be willing to spend to accomplish this?

On April 13th, the Pullman Main Street Design Committee and the Pullman Civic Trust are sponsoring a workshop at 6:30 P.M. The location will be announced later. At the workshop the results of the survey will be presented. There will be an opportunity to learn about design assistance and to participate in developing guidelines for Pullman. It is very important that all central business district business owners be present.

Q-9. What do you want as a product or outcome from this meeting?

The Main Street Design Program is looking for demonstration projects. This means that the Design Committee will work with you to advise you on revitalizing your building as well as give you community-wide publicity and recognition for your business and your participation with the Main Street Program.

Q-10. Would you like to be a demonstration project?

Q-11. If so, when would you like to start working with the committee?

Name: _____

Business: _____

Address: _____

_____

Phone Number: _____

Figure 2
Survey Questionnaire for Customer

Survey of Design Preferences for Downtown Pullman, Washington

First, we want you to look at the street facing you, its buildings, landscaping, and storefronts. We have a picture of the street for you to mark on.

Q-1. As you look at the building across the street, what do you notice that you consider to be attractive? (Please make your comments on the picture.)

Q-2. What, if anything, don't you like, or would like to change about this building? (Please make comments on the picture.)

Now look at the entire street.

Q-3. Please note on the picture what you especially like and what you do not like. Include the buildings, colors, signs, landscaping, etc. you see along the street (sidewalks, crosswalks, benches, etc.).

Q-4. In the past few years, what improvements have you noticed and liked in the central business district?

Q-5. Within the next two years, what further improvements do you think should be made in the central business district? (Include everything from minor changes to major construction.)

Q-6. The Main Street Design Committee is considering developing a design guidelines book to be used by main street businesses. What should be included in this book? (Please rank the items in the list below in their order of importance for inclusion in the proposed book, beginning with 1 for the **most** important.

_____ a.   Color recommendations
_____ b.   Texture/Materials recommendations
_____ c.   Scale suggestions
_____ d.   Signs
_____ e.   Entrances (front and rear)
_____ f.   Windows
_____ g.   Awnings
_____ h.   Doors
_____ i.   Lighting
_____ j.   Display

Q-7. Is there anything we've missed in this list, that you think should be included in this book?

Design improvements for a central business district have been shown to significantly improve the profit margin of downtown businesses. A Central Theme for the downtown has been suggested for Pullman.

Q-8. Do you believe a Central Theme would be good for Pullman?
_____ Yes   _____ No

Q-9. If so, what do you feel could be done to motivate business people in Pullman to upgrade and change the downtown building facades (storefronts)?

Q-10. In order for this to work there must be a concerted effort. Would you support businesses engaged in such a project?
_____ Yes   _____ No

(continued on page 359)

Figure 2, continued

On April 13th, the Pullman Main Street Design Committee and the Pullman Civic Trust are sponsoring a workshop at 6:30 P.M. The location will be announced later. At the workshop the results of the survey will be presented. There will be an opportunity to learn about design assistance and to participate in developing guidelines for Pullman.

Name: _____

Address: _____

Phone Number: _____

PART V
Conclusion

CHAPTER 40

Rethinking Local Economic Development

Nancy Stark and *Hamilton Brown*

When *Harvesting Hometown Jobs* was first published by the National Center for Small Communities, it hit a responsive chord. Echoing throughout the nation's small and rural communities were earnest concerns and desires for economic development:

"The young people are leaving our town. Graduates can't stay to start families because there are few good jobs. We need more employment opportunities for our young people."

"The economic recovery hasn't arrived in our town. Several businesses have closed or cut back. Some of us are skilled in manufacturing or other jobs that no longer exist. We need new business activity."

"Our community is still principally agricultural. But farming alone can no longer substantially support the town.

We need to vary our local economy and offer more off-farm employment opportunities."

"Residents are demanding new and better local services, but raising the needed revenue through property tax increases is not an option. We need an alternative strategy for expanding the local tax base."

"The quality of life in our community is special. We want to preserve it. And it's an important asset in encouraging economic development."

"If we don't plan for our own economic future, it may be planned for us— maybe not to our liking."

These same worries and goals are voiced loud and clear today. Active citizens, local government leaders, and business entrepreneurs are striving— perhaps harder than ever—to expand

From Chapter 1 of Harvesting Hometown Jobs, *1997. Published by the National Center for Small Communities, Washington, D.C. Reprinted with permission of the publisher.*

local revenues; to retain and/or create local, permanent jobs. Meanwhile, the conditions and circumstances governing economic development have shifted; communities explore greater economic opportunity on the one hand, yet face more pressured competition on the other.

Here are some of the pluses and minuses that small town economic development leaders must consider on the threshold of the 21st century:

- *Globalization* invites firms to compete in the larger marketplace through exporting, but it also places undue strain on domestic wages. Businesses seeking low-cost labor pools may relocate operations to distant countries where wages can be one-tenth of the average U.S. pay. Abundant land, affordable labor costs, and a strong work ethic are no longer the sole claim of rural areas and the southern U.S.
- *Technological advances* can minimize the distance penalty endured by rural areas, permitting entrepreneurs to set up business nearly anywhere. However, new jobs and income gravitate toward communities that have instituted the necessary telecommunications infrastructure, and made its access affordable.
- *Demographic changes* have inspired a rural rebound. As reported in *American Demographics*, "three in four non-metropolitan counties gained population between 1990 and 1994, a stunning reversal following a decade of rural decline." But, that growth is uneven and potentially problematic. As a

rule, the poorest and most remote counties in the U.S. do not experience this in-migration from disgruntled urbanites, or new settlements of retirees. Meanwhile, areas of rapid growth struggle to provide the higher levels of service demanded by more residents, yet still maintain a rural quality of life.
- *Intense economic competition* is forcing businesses to downscale operations, demanding more from fewer employees. However, this restructuring and downsizing create new opportunities for contracting our or spinning off operations to startup firms, potentially enhancing local entrepreneurial opportunity. Also, as the competition for business recruitment intensifies, there are fewer companies to attract and many businesses are far smaller than they used to be.
- *Recent welfare reforms* are moving more able-bodied recipients toward employment. While most Americans applaud these policy transformations, the transition from welfare to meaningful work is not easily made. Few decent-paying, entry level jobs are available, especially in rural towns and inner cities. Many of the rural poor already work, but because their wages are insufficient to support a family, federal assistance is still necessary.

What impact do these changing conditions and circumstances—globalization, technological advances, demographic shifts, downsizing and productivity campaigns, and welfare reform—have on small town economic development? How must a community's pursuit of jobs and income adjust as a result of these changes? The answers to these questions both encourage and trouble many local leaders. While these shifts expose fresh possibilities for economic development, they also make the task of creating, retaining, expanding and attracting jobs more formidable.

Rethink economic development before your community embarks on strategic planning or visioning, and in advance of launching specific job creation strategies, as described in the chapters that follow. Seeing economic development in a different light can enable your community to compete more favorably in today's evolving economy and set a path toward prosperity.

Build Community Capacity First, and Economic Development Will Follow

Robert Putnam, professor of government at Harvard University, recently ignited a public discussion about community capacity building drawing on his research of civic engagement and economic development both in Italy and the United States. Putnam discovered that communities in North-Central Italy did not become civic because they were strong economically. They became strong economically because they were civic—because they had generated what Putnam calls "social capital," evidenced by a rich network of community organizations and vibrant citizen involvement. These prosperous Italian communities developed community capacity first, and economic development soon followed.

The idea that community building should precede job creation runs counter to the way most places practice economic development. A plan to transform the vacant industrial building into a business incubator usually incites more immediate activity than a proposal to fortify the leadership skills of citizens volunteers. Of course, concrete projects are an important rallying measure, but long-time community worker Helen Lewis agrees with Putnam's findings about social capital and prosperity: communities that take the time to grow capacity among its people and organizations are empowered to achieve much more economically. Lewis has seen how ongoing, skill-building workshops can bring forth new, powerful leaders who initiate and persevere with worthwhile economic development projects.

How do we know community capacity building when we see it? A group of seasoned rural development practitioners recently explored this question and, in the process, identified eight outcomes of community capacity building. The group—the Community Capacity Building Learning Cluster—has been assembled by The Aspen Institute's Rural Economic Policy Program to strengthen the practice and tools of community capacity building. The eight outcomes of community capacity building are described in detail in *Measuring Community Capacity: A Workbook-in-Progress for Rural Communities*, published by The Aspen Institute, Washington, D.C.

The group suggests that by concentrating on these eight outcomes, or goals, a community strengthens its overall capacity and, with time, builds a solid foundation for economic development. The eight outcomes are:

1. Expanded diverse but inclusive, citizen participation.
2. Expanded leadership base.
3. Strengthened individual skills.
4. Widely shared understanding and vision.
5. Strategic community agenda.
6. Consistent, tangible progress toward goals.
7. More effective community organizations and institutions.
8. Better resource utilization by the community.

View the Community as a System for Harvesting Hometown Jobs

No single economic development idea creates and sustains a growing, wealth-generating economy. Rather than searching for the magic lamp—the one initiative that promises increased jobs and income; the one program that brought economic success to a nearby town—regard the community or region as a system for economic development, and make the system work effectively.

Viewing problems and devising remedies systematically is the heart of systems thinking, a theory and approach largely attributed to W. Edwards Deming, an international business consultant. When Deming advised Japanese industrialists in the 1950s, he urged them to view their nation as a system; this philosophy has meaning for communities as well.

This call to think and act as a system was sounded at an entrepreneurship conference convened by the Tennessee Valley Authority's Rural Studies Program, and several other organizations.

Participants considered why efforts to foster more dynamic economic development have largely failed, and concluded: "Unfortunately, many of these initiatives have tended to attack the problem from a particular perspective such as training, technological support, capital and so on. It is clear, however, that building an entrepreneurial economy rests not with one or two factors... Success lies in an approach that is integrated and systemic."

The power behind system thinking is that community leaders come to view their community and its problems as a whole, rather than focus on singular events or conditions. Peter Senge, author of several books about systems thinking, explains the value of seeing the systems that control events: "When we fail to grasp the systemic source of problems, we are left to 'push on' symptoms rather than eliminate underlying causes." Community leaders put it even more simply: "When we continually ask 'why' a local problem exists, we gradually reveal the real causes of our troubles. Asking 'why' over and over again is like unpeeling an onion. It enables us to understand and deal with the underlying roots of local problems, rather than 'bandaiding' the symptoms."

When communities focus on symptoms rather than systemic problems, economic development takes a misguided path: high-priced consultants aggressively market the town's new vision, although only a few citizens have participated in the planning process; a revolving loan fund is established to meet the capital needs of new firms, although what entrepreneurs really lack are basic management and accounting skills; and, industrial parks, built for unsecured tenants, become empty pastures with costly water, sewer and electrical hook-ups.

Consider How Community Development Decisions Affect Everyone

Often, the process and outcomes of development are inequitable. The community doesn't necessarily intend to treat one person differently than another, but it happens anyway. Key players orchestrate activities, while others stand in the background. Economic and social benefits flow to some individuals, but not to others.

It isn't always possible for everyone in a community to share equally in its well-being, but equity is a very important consideration. "Where there is equity, [community development] decisions are based on fairness, and everyone—regardless of race, income, sex, age or disability—has opportunity and is treated with dignity," explains the Mountain Association for Community Economic Development (MACED) in *Communities by Choice: Economy, Ecology, Equity.*

An example of equitable community development is Tupelo, Mississippi, located just east of the nation's Delta. When Tupelo's economy was spiraling downward in 1936, George McLean, the owner and publisher of the local newspaper, set forth a 10-year plan with a bold mission: to improve the quality of life in Lee County for all of its people.

McLean believed that every citizen was a vital resource. Despite widespread segregation in the 1940s, people of all color joined as partners in the new county-wide Community Development Foundation (CDF). McLean called for total desegregation in 1946 and saw the city's schools and swimming pools transform into places that welcomed all.

Deep regard for equity appeared in Tupelo's bottom-up economic development strategy. McLean rejected the idea that economic benefits "trickle down" to those most in need. Instead, he focused the CDF on projects that could raise the incomes of poor people from the outset. For many years, this novel approach generated increased long-term profits for the county's farmers, industrial laborers, furniture manufacturers, health care employees and others. By treating people with fairness and dignity, Tupelo experienced impressive economic and social gains that remain today.

Strive for Family Wage Jobs

For decades, community leaders nationwide paid scant attention to the wages promised to newly hired workers. Economic developers dangled tax incentives to entice new companies to town, regardless of the skills that those businesses required or the wages that they paid. A job was a job, and developers simply counted them as such.

But now we understand that not all jobs are created equal. Some are permanent jobs, paying more than $10 an hour and supplying a range of benefits. Others are temporary or part-time jobs, paying the minimum wage and offering no benefits. In many small communities and rural areas, the good jobs are scarce, and they require training that many workers lack. While there is an abundance of low-skill, low-pay jobs, the wide gap between jobs that pay and those that don't is persistent and tough to narrow.

Structural changes and the shift from a manufacturing to a service economy have diminished median real wages for full-time male workers from $34,048 in 1973 to $30,407 in 1993. For those without a college education, the contrast is even more severe. In 1979, college-educated men earned 40 percent more than the average high school graduate. Today, the gap has nearly doubled, with college-educated men earning 75 percent more. The implications of these somber figures for economic development are clear.

In response, public schools, community colleges and state universities must teach students the skills they need to compete in a higher-skilled economy. Schools can design effective and innovative education and training programs through partnerships with business and industry.

Community leaders must get assurances that the wages to be paid by assisted businesses are adequate. Legally enforceable contracts between a firm receiving tax abatements and the local government offering such financial incentives should specify not only the number of jobs created, but also the wages they pay, the benefits, and the standard of living they support. Similar commitments can be spelled out in agreements governing revolving loan funds, business incubators, and other economic development programs.

Forge Partnerships with Neighboring Communities, for Collaboration and Peer Learning

For decades, many small towns have acted as though brick walls encased their boundaries. Old rivalries stemming from annexation battles, business recruitment failures of years past, or even sports competitions, prevented one town from consulting or collaborating with its neighbor. But, in today's competitive economy "going it alone" can be a recipe for failure. Rethinking economic development means altering deep-seated patterns of behavior, and actively cultivating partnership opportunities with nearby communities.

Several states are experimenting with programs to encourage collaboration and peer learning among neighboring communities. The Nebraska Community Builders Program organizes clusters of communities to examine the strengths, weaknesses, opportunities and threats of their region; and envision a different future. The program is based on the belief that the best answers to a town's economic renewal can be found not in the state's capitol or a consultant's office, but in neighboring small communities. The Idaho Rural Development Council recently established the Community Exchange Peer Fund to provide up to $250, in travel reimbursement, to enable volunteer community groups to visit and learn from each other's successes. Other states encourage, or even require, communities to cooperate with neighboring towns when submitting proposals or other ideas for funding.

Seeded throughout *Harvesting Hometown Jobs* are examples of why and how collaborative economic development brings forth more lasting results than a small community can achieve on its own. Chapter 8, *Creating Small Business Partnerships*, published by the National League of Cities, examines this issue in greater detail.

Be a Smart Consumer of Outside Resources

Communities that are most effective at harvesting hometown jobs have learned how to be smart consumers of technical resources. Despite shifting conditions and circumstances governing economic development, numerous no-cost or low-cost resource providers exist.

Possible nearby sources of assistance include: the local chamber of commerce, regional planning or economic development district, community development corporation, utility company or cooperative; also, a Small Business Development Center; Extension Service or Forest Service office of the U.S. Department of Agriculture; community college; area banks and civic organizations; downtown merchants association; local telephone company, real estate company; local news media; and retired business executives and private consultants.

Assistance can also come from organizations and agencies located outside the region, including: the state government department of economic and community development/commerce; state government agriculture department; state rural development council, historic society, and association of local governments; state library, college or land grant university; community foundation; federal government offices of the Economic Development Administration and Small Business Administration; state office of the chamber of commerce; regional center for rural development; national community and economic development organizations; and private foundations and corporations interested in furthering economic development.

"The idea of being a smart consumer of outside technical resources doesn't come naturally to most community leaders," explains Heartland Center for Leadership Development's Co-Director, Vicki Luther. The Heartland Center, based in Lincoln, Neb., encourages citizens to be intelligent and satisfied consumers of community development resources, by structuring the community's requests for outside assistance. Citizens should find out specifically what assistance the helping agency or organization provides, just as a smart homeowner would find out what services a contractor furnishes before beginning a project. Leaders must also know exactly what the community needs or wants, just as a smart shopper would know exactly what he or she wants before phoning a mail order catalog company.

Finally, citizens must be very clear about the results or impacts the community expects from engaging outside help. Rural Development Initiatives (RDI), a nonprofit community development organization serving rural Oregon, has experimented with memorandums of understanding (MOUs) to spell out the scope of work, roles and responsibilities, time frame, and quantity of services of any project involving itself and a rural community. The MOU details exactly what each party will do for and with each other, and has helped to clarify partners' responsibilities and monitor progress. When arranging for services from an outside organization or agency for your community, consider how an MOU or contractual letter might help assure satisfaction.

CHAPTER 41

When to Use
Incentives

Kurt Hahn

Increasingly, municipal governments are being asked to join states and utilities to provide incentives to attract business or to retain existing business. The incentive may take a variety of forms, but among the most common forms of incentive are the following:

1) **Expedited or preferential processing.** Commonly known as fast-track processing, this technique typically involves prioritizing a desired job and/or revenue-producing project's review ahead of others, as well as coordinating regulatory approvals between departments or agencies so as to speed the processing.

2) **Loan of public assets such as land, building or equipment to business for private purposes.** Sometimes an industrial development authority, re-

development agency, or even a municipal electric utility will provide bridge financing to attract a job- or revenue-producing project. More common, however, is the provision of conduit private activity bond or industrial development bond financing to the enterprise.

3) **Grant of public funds to business for private purposes.** Direct gift of taxpayer funds is prohibited in most states; however, provision of tax rebates and advance payment of some leases for parking facilities or grants for historic preservation or aesthetic improvements, such as building facades or landscaping, often are permitted.

4) **Loan of public funds to business for public purposes.** Too often ignored is the provision of loans to finance a development's required infrastructure

Originally published as "When and When Not to Use Incentives to Attract Business or to Retain Existing Businesses," Government Finance Review, *Vol. 12, No. 3, June, 1996. Published by the Government Finance Officers Association, 180 N. Michigan Avenue, Suite 800, Chicago, Illinois 60601 (312-977-9700, fax 312-977-4806, e-mail GFR@gfoa.org). Annual subscription $30. Reprinted with permission of the publisher.*

or fees. This technique, when not adversely affecting the municipality's cash flow, can frequently be realized with an interest rate exceeding both investment earnings and bond financing. This can provide a win-win situation for the developer and municipality.

5) **Grant of public funds to business for public purposes.** Many redevelopment agencies or municipalities will provide grants for required infrastructure when a project achieves a positive utility outcome or positive municipal revenue impact.

6) **Lease or sale of public land at below-market rates.** A typical redevelopment strategy is to acquire and/or assemble land using tax increment financing and then sell or lease it at a price that will allow the desired development to be successful.

7) **Legally permissible waiver or deferral of fees.** This technique is always fraught with political problems. Many developers planning a project which they know the city wants will ask for the waiver or deferral of city fees. Some cities have adopted policies to provide partial or whole city-free waivers or deferral, if a development meets specific criteria, and then substitute redevelopment agency or utility money in the city's treasury to offset the waiver. In many states, performance-based deferrals designed to provide the developer time to build up the business are legal.

8) **Provision of services at public expense (e.g., architectural planning or expediting).** A new incentive that frequently is also a win-win for developer and the city is to provide the developer, at the city's expense, an outside expediter who knows the city's processes as well as the developer's needs.

9) **Special utility rates.** In an at-mosphere of increasing utility deregulation, new businesses will seek or be offered special rates based on incremental added cost to the utility or through discounting the rates for an initial two- or three-year period.

Legal Constraints

The Internal Revenue Code regulates the use of tax-exempt bond proceeds for private purposes, while federal statutes govern the use of federal funds or the reuse of Urban Development Action Grant (UDAG) or Community Development Block Grant (CDBG) monies. Many states impose a variety of legal constraints on incentives, the most typical of which are "gift of public funds" statutes which preclude fee waivers or cash gifts to a private business under a variety of circumstances. Additionally, many states in their redevelopment laws limit public acquisition of real estate and subsequent price write-downs in resale. Many state development fee statutes have equity provisions between business and residential development which indirectly limit fee waivers in either area unless fully funded from a third source, such as an industrial development authority, a redevelopment agency, or the state.

Locally adopted investment policies or state statutes adopted since the Orange County bankruptcy may further limit the use of public funds for incentives. Finance directors and city attorneys need to be involved in incentive negotiations to assure their legality.

What Is a Desirable Incentive?

In the broadest possible terms, a desirable incentive is one that is financially profitable to the city and its redevelopment or industrial development agency and produces jobs. Profit can be defined in this case as net revenues from the project exceeding the cost of incentives plus recurring costs and providing municipal services. Another criterion for a desirable incentive is that it does not immediately create a charge of unequal treatment of businesses in similar circumstances. Lastly, a desirable incentive should be one that causes an investment or relocation that would not have otherwise happened.

In determining whether an incentive is a positive one or not, a finance director should be prepared to produce a discounted proforma indicating the public investments and tax or utility revenues generated to determine the payback period and compare current values of each. The public investments should include not only incentives but recurring costs to provide services including, if applicable, utility services.

Sound incentives can be secured loans to developers in which the city is assured of full repayment with interest equal to or above the rate of the city's investment pool. Many cities will finance utility-related infrastructure or developer/capacity fees and add loan payments to utility bills. Another example is a grant/loan that positions the city as an equity partner in the development and provides for loan repayment with interest and/or participation in the income flow of the development. Typically used in many UDAG projects, this approach is increasingly employed when local incentives are sought by the developer. Similarly, a positive incentive can be a land sale or lease that gives to the city a downstream share of a project income flow and recovers the city's investment in the site. Others are those in which the city or redevelopment agency recovers in new revenues the cost of the incentive plus a significant net gain for the community in jobs and revenues.

There is nothing wrong with a city making a good investment. The challenge often is to have the courage to ask for something in return for an incentive. Most entrepreneurs do not react unkindly to an entrepreneurial approach by the city.

What Is an Undesirable Incentive?

First, undesirable incentives are those that look bad to the public. They can create the appearance of unequal treatment of similar businesses under similar circumstances. Secondly, they also can be activities that cause or offer the potential for litigation, such as a developer fee rebate or sales tax exemption. Thirdly, an incentive is unwarranted when the recipient would have come to the community regardless of the incentive. Lastly, an incentive is not a positive one if it is likely to cause a future budget or cash-flow problem for the city.

No finance director should be bashful when it comes to preparing a confidential report for the city manager or legislative body 1) indemnifying specific cases or prospective cases where there could be the charge that unequal treatment was provided, 2) analyzing the financial ramifications if similar incentives were provided generally, and 3) pointing out potentials for litigation based on gifts of public funds. If, in the view of the finance officer, a business will come to the city absent incentives or if future budgets will be adversely affected, the finance officer should so advise the city manager loudly and clearly.

Undesirable incentives take many forms, but the most typical is one in which virtually all new revenues generated by a project are returned to the developer, which has been the case in a variety of "big box" transactions. Another case is the use of incentives in bidding wars to relocate an existing business, in some cases from a nearby municipality. Still other examples are a grant or loan to business which would have come to the town without an incentive, a retroactive incentive, or a tax rebate incentive to every business in town just to create the image of a business-friendly locality.

If cities should eventually be denied the option to use tax-exempt private activity bonds as a tool for economic development, it will be because of abuses, typically involving assistance to developments that would have happened without the incentive. Not only

the federal government but many state legislatures as well are reacting negatively and in some cases punitively in response to the perception that many incentive transactions are a waste of tax resources and do not achieve a public purpose. The role of finance officials is to make sure every incentive can be defended.

Conclusion

The pressures associated with economic development are substantial. Frequently the elected official is invited to the negotiating table before the finance director is. Jobs sometimes can take priority over balancing the city budget. The challenge to the finance director is to pre-educate the city council, then ensure that he/she is at the table. This calls for horse sense and close consultation with the city attorney. The approach to incentives should be entrepreneurial: the city is seeking to make money. While portraying a pro-business attitude, dollars on the table for the city is by far the most important approach to successful incentive negotiations.

CHAPTER 42

Ten Myths About Downtown Revitalization

Dolores P. Palma

Since the first suburban shopping malls opened their doors, communities all across the country have been concerned with revitalizing their downtowns. Today, a large body of knowledge has been developed—the "dos and don'ts" of the trade—that can be used to guide local downtown revitalization efforts.

This body of knowledge includes myths about downtown revitalization as well as "secrets of success." The ten most common downtown revitalization myths—and the seven secrets of downtown success—are discussed below.

Myth 1—If We Build It, They Will Come

This has become known as the "Field of Dreams Approach" to downtown enhancement. It centers on the belief that a community only needs to undertake physical improvements for customers and investors to flock to downtown.

Over the last 20 to 30 years, many communities have proven this to be a myth. They have done so by implementing massive physical improvement projects that usually include new sidewalks, landscaping, street trees, planters, benches, facade improvements, etc.

From Western City, *Vol. LXX, No. 6, June, 1994. Published by the League of California Cities, Sacramento, California. Reprinted with permission of the publisher. For information about subscribing, please call 916-658-8223 or visit the magazine's website at www.westerncity.com. Subscription information is also available by calling 1-800-572-5720 and asking for document #45.*

Thinking that their work was done, these communities then sat back and waited for customers and investors to return to downtown. Unfortunately, these communities learned that physical improvements, made on a grand scale and made in isolation, do not result in renewed downtown vitality.

Downtown and City Hall leaders in Robbinsdale, Minnesota, learned the truth—that *minimalist* public improvements which are combined with *economic* improvements yield downtown success. Mayor Joy Robb and the City Council of Robbinsdale spearheaded making downtown revitalization a priority in their community. The city's elected officials acted as the catalyst for revitalization by having a comprehensive downtown streetscape project designed and implemented along West Broadway. In April of this year, the city was presented with a Merit Award for the project from the Minnesota Chapter of the American Society of Landscape Architects. The streetscape project also won broad approval from the community. In a recent survey of area residents, 87 percent of those who had seen the newly completed streetscape improvements found them attractive. But Robb and city council members knew that streetscape improvements alone—a physically driven approach—would not revitalize downtown. Instead, the city and downtown business community worked together to take a market driven approach by completing a downtown market analysis and a downtown business plan, which is being implemented by a newly formed partnership of city hall and downtowners. In fact, the entire downtown enhancement effort must be *market-driven* to serve customers and users, rather than physically driven, in order to succeed.

Myth 2—If We Demolish It, They Will Come

This is the flip side of Myth #1 and is known as the "Urban Renewal Approach" to downtown revitalization. This myth holds that, if old buildings are torn down and land is cleared, developers will flock to downtown. And, unfortunately, there are communities all across the country that still have vacant downtown land which was cleared in the 1960s and 1970s as part of this revitalization approach.

Since the days of the federal Urban Renewal program, community leaders have learned that clearance does not attract developers to a downtown whose market is weak. Since that time, communities also have learned that structurally sound old buildings—no matter how run-down they might look at the time—can become a tremendous draw if they are renovated and their architectural character is preserved. In fact, older restored structures constitute the most valuable commercial real estate in this country today.

In Peabody, Kansas (population 1410), downtown leaders have learned the truth: If we save and rehabilitate our older commercial buildings, tenants and customers are more likely to come. With help from the Kansas Main Street Program, Peabody completed a market analysis for its downtown as part of a comprehensive enhancement program which also included having downtown listed in the National Register of Historic Places. By implementing an intensive business recruitment and building preservation effort over the last four years, Peabody's downtown went from a total of eleven retail businesses in 38,400 feet to 21 retail businesses occupying

61,000 square feet of space, a 91 percent increase in retail businesses and a 59 percent increase in occupied retail square footage.

Myth 3—If We Complete One Major Project, They Will Come

This is the "Silver Bullet Approach" to downtown revitalization. It holds that if a community identifies and implements one key, major project then "everything will take care of itself." Examples of communities that pursued the Silver Bullet Approach are those that built downtown convention centers, festival marketplaces, parking structures, or pedestrian malls—*in isolation*. Unfortunately, these communities learned the hard way that there is no silver bullet. Instead, successful downtown revitalization requires a multi-faceted effort that addresses all of a downtown's key issues.

In Thousand Oaks, California, a private-public partnership is forming to spearhead a multi-faceted downtown enhancement program. The program, based on a shared community vision of what downtown should be like by the year 2000, addresses all of downtown's key issues and opportunities, instead of taking a silver bullet approach.

Myth 4—If We Can't Get a Department Store to Come Back to Downtown, Downtown Will Never Be Healthy Again

This is known as the "Traditional Anchor Approach" to downtown revi-

talization. It is true that—except for tremendously healthy downtowns—the chances of attracting a major, national department store to downtown are very slim. However, this fact does not dictate that a downtown can no longer be healthy. Instead, the most successful downtowns today are those that have redefined the concept of "downtown anchors."

All across the country, downtowns are embracing new anchors. These include cultural facilities, government complexes, entertainment facilities, tourist draws, housing units, professional office buildings, and specialty retail shops. And, communities are finding that by promoting and leveraging these anchors, their downtowns can experience renewed vitality, without a traditional department store anchor.

Elko, Nevada, named the best small town in America by Norman Crampton, author of *The Best 100 Small Towns in America* in 1993, has for years had non-traditional anchors in its downtown in the form of casinos. More recently, a new anchor has opened in downtown Elko. This is the Western Folklife Center, whose exhibits attract local residents and visitors all year long, and which has become known as the headquarters of the annual Cowboy Poetry Gathering.

Myth 5—We Can't Get a Department Store to Locate Downtown, So Downtown Can No Longer Support Any Kind of Retail Trade

This is the "Big Retail or No Retail Approach" to downtown revitalization.

Again, it is true that the chances of recruiting a major, national department store to most downtowns today are slim. It is also true that few downtowns today can be considered to be *primarily* retail centers. However, these truths alone do not prove that a downtown cannot support a degree of retail trade.

In fact, many downtown professionals would argue that, by definition, a healthy downtown is one that contains some degree of retail activity. This belief holds that it is retail trade that brings pedestrians to downtown's sidewalks and, therefore, gives downtown a look of activity and health. Therefore, no matter how healthy a downtown's economy actually is, without some degree of retail trade a downtown will *look* dead. That is why most, if not all, downtown revitalization programs operating in this country today contain a retail retention component. And, many of these downtown programs have been successful in strengthening, and increasing, their downtown's retail base.

In Monroe, North Carolina, downtowners and community residents alike have seen this myth dispelled by young, energetic entrepreneurs who are operating specialty retail businesses in their downtown, retail businesses that are successful because they have defined their target customers and cater to the needs of those customers. A graphic example of this is a men's apparel shop called Neil Glenn, Ltd., long a part of downtown in Monroe, North Carolina. The shop recently was purchased from its retiring owner by a young entrepreneurial couple. Being customer driven, the new owners decided to target downtown attorneys, banks and business owners—a built-in, daily market—as their prime customers. This meant "retooling"

the shop's merchandise from general men's wear to apparel specifically for businessmen. And, the owners realized that to truly cater to these customers, retooling must involve the services that make it easy for busy businessmen to shop at Neil Glenn—opening the shop for a customer before or after regular store hours by request, special ordering for customers, tailoring, etc. Because of their entrepreneurial and customer-driven approach to retailing, Neil Glenn's new owners are proving that specialty retailers can grow and thrive in downtown, long after the traditional downtown department stores are gone.

Myth 6 — Competition Is Bad Business

This is the "Head-in-the-Sand Approach" to revitalization. The commercial districts—both old and new—that are the most successful in this country today are those in which similar and compatible businesses are located side by side in convenient groupings. There is example after example in this country of commercial districts which have proven that the clustering of compatible businesses is actually very good for business.

Rather than providing dangerous competition, the clustering of businesses expands and magnifies the market that the cluster—and each of the businesses in it—can hope to draw. This multiplier effect occurs because a cluster of businesses is more appealing to a customer—in terms of convenience and variety—than is a single, stand-alone business. Therefore, customers have a tendency to come to the clustered businesses in larger numbers, and to spend more dollars once in these clusters, than they would at a single, destination business.

Progressive small business owners in Old Town Alexandria, Virginia, have proven this myth is false by taking the initiative themselves to create several business clusters. One of these clusters, which is about three blocks long, includes a variety of home furnishing businesses—where customers can find everything from traditional rug and lamp stores to shops that offer creative home accessories, design services, and "art f/x."

In Pomona, California, private sector investors formed an antiques cluster. This is comprised of many antique vendors, located side by side, who draw customers from a great distance because of their number and variety.

Myth 7—For Downtown to Be Successful, Downtown's Retail Businesses Must Keep Uniform Business Hours

During the last several years, many downtowns across the country have included, as part of their revitalization efforts, attempts to standardize the hours of operation kept by downtown retailers. This is known as the "Let's Pretend We're a Mall Approach" to downtown revitalization. Given the independent nature of downtown business owners, and the large number of business owners in any downtown, this approach has failed dismally.

Recognizing that a single set of uniform business hours is difficult to achieve in a downtown, and *possibly not advantageous to the district's retailers* as a whole, the most successful downtown

enhancement programs today are promoting "market-driven business hours." With this approach, retail businesses keep hours that best meet the needs of their targeted customers. By doing this, and by coordinating their hours of operation with each other, these businesses are able to accommodate and share customers.

In addition, many downtown small business owners are finding that keeping hours that are convenient for customers often means shifting to *different* hours rather than keeping *longer hours*.

In the Old Town Alexandria home furnishings cluster mentioned above, the owner of Art and Soul—a specialty retail shop offering original, high-quality art and craft items for the home—moved to smarter hours shortly after opening in Old Town. Art and Soul's original weekday hours of 10 A.M. to 6 P.M. were changed to 11 A.M. to 7 P.M., because their owner noticed:

- The hour from 10 A.M. to 11 A.M. was the slowest business time on weekdays.
- Many area tourists were on the sidewalks after 6 P.M., returning to their Alexandria hotels after a day of sightseeing.
- Both tourists and local residents heavily frequent Old Town's popular restaurants and window shop on their way to dinner.
- And, several of the shop's customers mentioned they find it difficult to get to the shop after work by 6 P.M.

By opening the same *number* of hours, but shifting to customer driven hours, Art and Soul enjoys the increased patronage of both visitors and residents of the area.

Myth 8—We Have to Be as Lenient as Possible with Developers or They Won't Do Business in Our Community

and

Myth 9—We Have to Be as Tough as Possible with Developers or They'll Take Advantage of Us

These are the twin "Play Dead or Play Hard Ball" revitalization myths. Over the last fifteen years, both of these myths have been proven false by communities all across the country. It has been proven that developers *will* do business in communities that demand quality projects and that take steps to ensure they obtain such projects. In fact, many developers *prefer* to do business in communities that demand quality projects and seek out such communities—because they know their investments will be protected in these communities.

It has also been proven that communities that are unreasonably stringent and demanding of developers will cause developers to locate their projects elsewhere. In that sense, these communities are successful in making sure that the development community does not take advantage of them! However, this attitude also makes them successful in *not attracting* quality developers and quality projects to their communities.

The communities that have been most successful in obtaining quality development projects in their older commercial districts are those where a partnership has been formed between the community, the city government and local developers. These efforts are commonly known as public-private partnerships. They can be highly successful in creating quality projects for the community and economically successful projects for the developer. The essential ingredient for making the partnership a success if one of attitude. All parties in the partnership must agree to cooperate so that a quality project—and one that is mutually beneficial—results.

Myth 10—If We Had More Parking, They Would Come!

This is the "Let's Find a Scapegoat Approach" to downtown revitalization. This myth holds that all of downtown's ills stem from a lack of parking. Those who believe in this myth claim that customers have left downtown for shopping malls because malls offer customers seas and seas of parking which is often (but not always) free. Therefore, the reasoning goes, "we need more parking"—this change will make downtown's businesses competitive with the malls and will make customers return to downtown.

Unfortunately, communities that have gone to great expense in creating downtown parking lots and decks, *without making other needed improvements in their downtowns*, have learned the fallacy of this myth. The new parking facilities remain as empty as our downtown stores. In fact, many of the more progressive downtown leaders across the country now say "we need to *create* a parking problem in our downtown" because this will mean that downtown stores are busy.

In fact, in the vast majority of downtowns where there is a parking problem, it is one of parking management rather than one of parking supply. This means that the number of parking spaces available is adequate. However, customers are having difficulty finding a parking spot because:

- Downtown employees and business owners are parking in spaces that are nearest to businesses and that should be reserved for their customers and clients; and
- Downtown's public parking lots are often not clearly marked.

This problem can be resolved through better management and identification of the existing parking supply and does not typically warrant creating additional parking spaces.

At the forefront of a nationwide trend, The City of Millville, New Jersey, recently improved and signed several small downtown public parking lots, making a vast dent in the issue of downtown parking.

Downtown programs which have been most successful in re-attracting customers and clients are those where business owners *differentiate* their businesses and give customers and clients a compelling reason to patronize that business. Successful downtown business owners have found that if they offer what customers and clients want (a specialized product, an exceptional service, a unique atmosphere, etc.), make sure customers know that this is being offered, and make existing parking convenient for their customers, then the issue of downtown parking often becomes irrelevant.

Lastly, the seven simple secrets to downtown success, which can assist in your revitalization efforts, are highlighted below.

Secret 1: Form Partnerships — Between the business sector, the public sector, civic organizations, and community residents. The most successful downtowns are those where these sectors come together, make decisions together, and each carry their weight to reinvest and reinvent their downtown. None of these sectors can or should do it alone.

Secret 2: Know Your Vision — Define and aggressively pursue a shared community vision of success. Waiting until the handwriting is on the wall, and then reacting to it, is the old way of doing business. The new, more successful way of revitalizing downtown is to define a clear vision of where you want your downtown to go — a vision that is realistic and that is shared by the business community, the local government and the citizens of the community — and then aggressively pursuing that vision.

Secret 3: Be Market-Driven — Market analysis is THE critical first step for success in revitalizing your downtown; it's a tool without which downtown cannot succeed. The Field of Dreams Approach is out. Instead, the successful approach is much more business oriented — know who your customers are, who your *potential* customers are, what they want today, what they will want tomorrow — and provide those things. And, be flexible to keep up with the customer's changing needs and desires. This market knowledge must drive all downtown improvement actions — all of the private sector's business decisions and the public sector's governance decisions — including how to market the downtown, what business hours to keep, what types of streetscape improvements to make, etc.

Secret 4: Create and Use a Busi-

ness **Plan**—Businesses that operate according to a business plan are more successful than those that don't—and the same is true for business districts. Based on your shared community vision and a realistic market analysis, the downtown partnership must identify—and implement—an aggressive course of action.

Secret 5: Dare to Be Different—Downtown must create, carve out, and become known for a particular niche in the market place. Downtown can't out-mall the mall AND it can't out-discount the discounters. However, the malls and the discounters can't out-downtown downtown. The most successful downtowns accentuate their uniqueness to make downtown stand out from the competition in the minds of its customers.

Secret 6: Focus—Concentrate limited resources in well-defined focus areas. Downtown leaders have learned from experience that resources are too scarce to be able to successfully tackle all of a downtown's ills at once. And, our downtown areas are often too large to enhance all in one bite. Therefore, clumping downtown into focus areas has proven to be the road to success. This allows results to become more visible more quickly. And, nothing breeds success like visible results.

Secret 7: Know the Indispensable Five M's—*Management* of downtown like a business; *marketing* campaigns for downtown and its businesses; *maintenance* of downtown's private and public property; *market-knowledge* to create a niche for downtown; and *money* for ongoing, quality downtown management and enhancement. While our downtowns should not try to compete head-on with shopping malls, they should learn and use these essential management techniques.

CHAPTER 43

Community Agendas for the Future: A Corporate View

Nancy Williams

The 1980s was a decade of economic turmoil that affected every community. Jobs shifted from the Snowbelt to the Sunbelt; foreign imports forced cuts in American industry; and businesses merged, downsized and consolidated to become more competitive.

Communities tried to react to a fluid national economic environment that required short-term mitigation efforts and far-reaching structural changes at the same time. Most were unprepared, and during the decade, learned valuable lessons in the need for strategic planning and reassessment of business-as-usual programs.

How did the economic develop-

ment professional fare during this period? Reflecting community situations, about the same—mostly unprepared. Some were forced to overhaul virtually all aspects of their day-to-day operations. Many experienced dramatic changes in the scope and magnitude of their activities. Some were left in a dilemma of what to do and how to heighten their sophistication to keep pace with neighboring and regional actions. Few, if any, escaped the challenges of the decade, which included foreign competition, new technology, demographic changes, employment restructuring, environmental and growth management and the globalization of the U.S. economy.

Originally published as "Community Agenda for the 1990s: A Corporate View," Economic Development Review, *Vol. 9, No. 3, Summer, 1991. Published by the American Economic Development Council (AEDC), 9801 W. Higgins Road, Suite 540, Rosemont, Illinois 60018 (847-692-9944, website www.aedc.org, e-mail aedc@interaccess.com). Reprinted with permission of the publisher.*

The 1980s was perhaps the most significant decade in terms of community survival and economic development response. Vision, vigor, ingenuity and increased professionalism were keys to a community's successful transition. the breadth and depth of programs and the management of an ever broadening array of issues were keys to an economic development organization's success. Today most communities realize that the stakes are higher and the pursuit of economic stability is dependent on managing change and shifting priorities when circumstances dictate.

The 1990s

The new decade of the 1990s is already upon us and so far, is no less challenging. The U.S. has recognized and accepted its roles in the global economy, yet continues to seek stability and competitive positioning for its industrial and business base.

Community leaders, now setting their agendas for the '90s, are more mindful of the dynamic changes of the '80s, and are resolved to address these needs with a clearer understanding of the issues, and most assuredly, with more proactive measures. The emergence of the strategic planning process during the '80s made a lasting contribution and served to focus diverse resources, viewpoints and organizations on a common set of goals and objectives. As well, communities are now more prepared to implement sophisticated business management and research techniques to support these plans.

Community Agenda for the 1990s

One assurance we have about the 1990s is that there will be no way to avoid the difficult decisions of allocating limited and diverse resources to ensure that communities effectively compete in a global environment.

What communities will also have to accept is that the challenge will be the same for the private sector. Downsizing, merging and consolidating will be continuing themes for corporations in this decade. Businesses will be making the hard financial decisions to compete globally, nationally and locally. They will also be making hard decisions about priorities and resources for community initiatives.

Will these goals be mutually exclusive? Or is it possible for communities and businesses to find a path that guides both to realize their course in the growing global market?

Through strategic economic development, communities, businesses and other players can unite to build a sound agenda and foundation to meet these challenges.

The first step in that process for GTE Telephone Operations was the need to better understand what was important to communities and how that might affect the company's own business objectives, as well as the allocation of company resources to support communities.

To support customers in 40 states and over 9000 communities, GTE recently utilized the survey technique as a means of better planning the strategic direction of its community involvement. While not a new approach, the company had never employed this process on a national scale that could provide a broader perspective and context in which to plan and budget,.

GTE commissioned a benchmark survey last year of 900 community leaders across America in search of answers to questions about community needs, issues and programs.

Nationally and in each of the four regions, the GTE National Community Economic Development survey explored five subject areas and the relationships among them:

- community issues
- community economic development
- corporate role in the community
- global competitiveness, and
- role of telecommunications in community economic development.

What are the issues most important to communities? Do they differ by community size or locations? Are community economic development programs solving these problems? What do communities want from the private sector?

In addition to serving its own strategic planning process, GTE believes the information gathered can also benefit communities. The following summary is provided to community leaders, such as economic development practitioners, with the hope that it can lend a focus for strategic planning, economic development, and other priority programs in this decade.

National Overview

Jobs is the leading concern of community leaders across the nation. Elementary/secondary education, economic development and the quality of life are other issues dominating their thinking as well.

The survey respondents showed a remarkable consistency nationally when asked to identify the most important issues facing their communities. When asked for their top-of-mind thoughts (unaided questions), jobs and elementary/secondary education were the most frequently mentioned, with 33 and 32 percent, respectively. They strongly linked the two, saying quality jobs are the result of quality education.

Economic development placed third on the unaided list, with 24 percent saying it was the most important issue. The majority of participants believe the primary role of economic development is to create, retain and improve jobs. This linkage further emphasized the concern for jobs, and, when grouped, (jobs/employment and economic development) it gives a more prominent ranking of 57 percent.

Next were housing (19 percent) and substance abuse (15 percent). Other issues identified were the environment, transportation, crime, taxes, quality of life (defined as housing, health care and culture), growth management, the underprivileged, national political issues, water supply and job training.

Perhaps the most significant finding of the survey is the linkages among the top issues. While employment is the paramount concern, respondents acknowledged that education in combination with economic development is crucial to job creation, retention and attraction.

This alliance is evident in both aided and unaided responses. Since survey results varied only slightly between these questions, the linkage between the top three issues suggests a clear community agenda for the 1990s.

Community Economic Development

This section first asked participants to define "community economic development." The majority said it meant economic growth, improved employment opportunities and a higher quality of life. These definitions were most often given, either alone or in combination.

When asked about 11 specific economic development activities, elementary/secondary education again was most frequently rated as extremely important (75 percent). Business retention and expansion closely followed (73 percent).

Those surveyed were generally satisfied with their local development programs, although their responses indicated room for improvement. Almost half (46 percent) believe their communities are addressing the important issues. With participants holding community leadership positions, they may have helped establish (or were active in) the community economic development programs they were asked to evaluate.

Rural and Urban Comparisons

Although the top issues remain the same in rural and urban areas, their rankings shift and percentage points vary. Jobs and economic development reached higher percentage ratings in rural areas, reflecting concerns about

loss of jobs, plant closings, small town decay and decline of small farm operations. Education K–12 ranked third (26 percent) in the rural areas, not as high a priority as in the urban areas. Community survival emerged as a concern expressed by rural leaders, which was not echoed by their counterparts in urban communities.

When asked about specific economic development programs (not shown), rural community leaders rated elementary/secondary education tops and placed greater importance on it than urban participants. Also, rural leaders favored more financing and new business ventures assistance, pointing to needs generated by rural decline in the 1980s. Finally, the role of telecommunications in community economic development was rated very important by more rural leaders than urban leaders.

Regional Overview

Although regional attitudes generally paralleled national findings, some significant differences exist. This was likely because of the vastness and diversity of GTE's operations, encompassing the Sunbelt as well as the Snowbelt, rural and urban areas, growing and declining communities.

(See end notes for a listing of states by region.)

NORTH REGION

Survey results from this region best parallel the national findings by listing jobs, elementary/secondary education and economic development as their top-of-mind concerns. When asked the question, unaided by examples, the North participants were emphatic about jobs (45 percent) as the most important community issue. This high level of concern distinguished the North region from the other three in the importance it placed on jobs.

Although not shown here, the North gave higher education and job training far greater ratings than the other regions. Due to its industrial restructuring in the 1980s, it may have recognized the regional need for labor to make a transition from factory worker and farmer. Northerners also were concerned about the quality and affordability of housing.

SOUTH REGION

The South called for a more extensive economic development program than any other region, with emphasis placed on elementary/secondary education, jobs and traditional economic development. Southerners see economic development as a means to solve major community problems.

According to the survey, the three most important top-of-mind (unaided) issues were elementary/secondary education, jobs/employment and economic development.

Education also led the way for community economic development activities with 82 percent of the South's participants citing it as extremely important. Southerners regard their school systems as inadequate and see education K–12 as crucial to job creation and retention.

Southerners trailed only Westerners in their concern about growth management, with most of these responses emanating from Florida. They also expressed concern about the need to improve deteriorating physical infrastructures, especially highways. Finally, the South gave telecommunications higher ratings both as a form of infrastructure and for its role in economic development.

SOUTHWEST REGION

The Southwest looked at its needs from a different perspective. Most of the region (GTE areas) is underdeveloped or rural, but it has a few pockets of intense metropolitan development, mostly in Texas. Either way, leaders wanted more economic growth, new jobs and business diversification.

Economic development was a consistent top issue in Southwestern responses, followed closely by jobs and elementary/secondary education. They also see a strong connection among the three. The focus of participants' answers was on economic survival, a by-product of the oil industry recession.

When rating community economic development activities, business retention/expansion and elementary/secondary education scored closely (78 and 76 percent, respectively) with business attraction a nearby third (72 percent).

Although Southwesterners had an overriding concern about economic development, they also voiced concern about substance abuse and crime more than any other region on the aided questions.

WEST REGION

Although not always markedly, the West departed the most from the norm with its responses. The West was the region least concerned about economic development and the most concerned when it came to growth management and the environment which they saw as linked. Quality of life was another consistent issue, especially as it related to affordable housing.

When asked unaided to name the most common community issues, housing topped the West's list (31 percent) followed by elementary/secondary education (29 percent) and jobs (23 percent). Transportation emerged as an issue more in the West than any other region.

Westerners rated quality of life higher than any other region. Much of its importance can be attributed to spiraling housing costs (at the time of the survey), but the high rating could also be attributed to respondents' concern for culture and health care issues in this same category.

On the environment issue, the West region had the deepest concerns about their natural resources of land, water and air. Transportation was a key concern, more so in West locations than other regions. It was the second ranked concern among twelve specific issues in the Pacific Northwest (urban Washington and Oregon) and a key issue in the Los Angeles metroplex.

The Corporate Role in the Community

This survey investigated the most effective and important role business can play that is beneficial to the community as well as the company. Sixty percent of the participants agreed that business should have a strong role in community economic development.

Participants were vocal in their call for top, talented business executives as volunteers. Government officials especially noted the difficulty of recruiting the "best and brightest" executives. The "token" company representative does not always meet specific requirements, especially in addressing the longer-term community needs. Community leaders called for business volunteers with problem-solving skills, such as strategic planning, training and finance.

The Role of Telecommunications

While telecommunications is an important factor in economic development, community leaders nationwide said they see other issues as more immediately pressing. Seventy-two percent indicated it was extremely or somewhat important; 24 percent cited it as not important or somewhat unimportant.

However, the survey revealed that many community leaders were unsure of telecommunications' role in community economic development or saw the technology in limited terms. They did not always see it in the broader context of reducing historical, geographic, time and capacity constraints by making information and communications more accessible, interactive (voice, data and video) and portable. Those who saw the importance of telecommunications in community economic development said its impact would be realized in the coming years.

Global Competitiveness

More than half of the participants (53 percent) said that competing in the global economy was extremely important. Twenty percent did not see it as important. Without further research, no conclusions can be drawn about this issue. However, there were two notable findings. Small, rural communities often listed global competitiveness as a lower priority, because it is removed from what they see as their communities' more immediate concerns. And, community leaders who rated global competitiveness as more important were also more likely to value the importance of telecommunications.

Summary

The findings of the GTE National Community Economic Development survey reflect the widespread economic shuffling that grassroots America experienced during the past decade. Jobs, education and economic development have become the links of a chain critical to a community's economic health, according to its leaders. From state to state, rural area to urban area, leaders nationwide were consistent in their views. And they were consistent in emphasizing that the well-being of one is critical to the well-being of the others.

These relationships send an important signal to companies like GTE whose own economic health mirrors that of the communities it serves. Our missions are compatible—to achieve sound economic foundations to be competitive and productive in the global market. Achieving this mission requires that the company implement programs in partnership with local, state and other strategic development allies.

When linked to priority needs and issues, corporate participation enables communities to more efficiently and effectively focus on solutions. The survey data also gives GTE and other corporations a means to benchmark and measure their progress toward building a better economic climate and a higher quality of life for communities.

GTE, as a national provider of telecommunications, takes that process one step further. Community infrastructures, once defined as roads, sewers, water and power, now include more advanced telecommunications. Linked to community and national competitiveness, enhanced telecommunications, such as high speed data transmissions, video conferencing and fiber optics, that may appear to be a luxury today will be vital to every community sometime this decade.

Contributing technological solutions for community economic development and competitiveness is an important priority for GTE. Leaders who recognize the economic advantages offered by telecommunications will find their communities better positioned to meet the challenges of the 1990s.

ABOUT THE SURVEY

The GTE National Community Economic Development Survey was a nationwide telephone survey of 900 leaders from 29 states and some 350 communities in GTE's operating areas. Those surveyed included representatives of private industry, government, school systems and colleges, non-profit organizations and special interest groups. The list targeted specific people as well as titles or positions likely to have influence in their respective communities. Eighty-five percent of the respondents described themselves as civically active.

The survey was conducted in August, September, and October, 1990. The overall margin of error was 3.9 percent.

The states within the regions described in this chapter:

Southwest Region: Arkansas, New Mexico, Oklahoma, Texas

South Region: Alabama, Florida, Georgia, Kentucky, North Carolina, South Carolina, Tennessee, Virginia, West Virginia

North Region: Illinois, Indiana, Iowa, Michigan, Minnesota, Missouri, Nebraska, Ohio, Pennsylvania, Wisconsin

West Region: California, Idaho, Hawaii, Montana, Oregon, Washington.

CHAPTER 44

Working Together: Cities and Suburbs

Larry C. Ledebur and William R. Barnes

There is a strong economic justification for addressing the needs of central cities and for cooperation among cities and suburbs to meet the mutual economic needs of their local economic region. It can be found in the strong and consistent relationship between changes in central city incomes and changes in suburban incomes. For every one dollar increase in central city household incomes, suburban household incomes increase by $1.12.

In each of the 25 metropolitan areas with the most rapidly growing suburbs, measured by changes in median household income, central city incomes also increased over the 1979–1979 period. No suburbs in this high growth set experienced income growth without corresponding growth in their central city. This evidence indicates that cities and suburbs are interdependent. Their fates and fortunes are intertwined. Further, the evidence suggests that this interdependence of city and suburbs is becoming stronger, rather than diminishing.

This documentation of the significant relationship between cities and their suburbs is critical to the debate about whether suburbs can prosper and succeed, regardless of the fortunes of their central cities. This finding, however, should not be surprising. Cities and their suburbs are not two distinct economies. They are a single economy, highly interdependent with their fortunes inextricably intertwined.

These local economic regions are key to federal efforts to "grow the national economy." Federal efforts to "jump start" the economy through a short-run

Reprinted with permission from All in It Together: Cities, Suburbs and Local Economic Regions, *February, 1993.* Published by the National League of Cities, Washington, D.C.

stimulus package, as well as long term efforts to increase national productivity and investment must target these local concentrations of economic activities and sources of productivity growth.

The debate over the shape of national economic program should also recognize the diversity of circumstances and performance of these local economic regions. The breadth and depth of variations in performance of these economies, make it less likely that uniform national economic policies, administered as if there was a single national economy, will suffice as a "national program for economic growth." There is a wide range of variation on most measures; this study presents the variation in median household income, employment change, and unemployment.

This range of diversity strongly suggests that federal policies should be sensitive to these differences.

The findings of this study suggest looking at the U.S. economy as a common market of local economic regions rather than as a huge but undifferentiated "national economy." In turn, this view indicates several directions in which federal policy should develop.

- Federal economic policy should aim at improving the condition and performance of the local economic regions.
- Federal economic policy should address the variety among these local economic regions as to their circumstances and needs.
- Federal economic policy should seek to diminish city/suburb disparities within the local economic regions.

Interdependence of Cities and Suburbs

The 1990 Census provides a new focus on the critical issue of the relationship between central cities and suburbs in the United States.[1] The debate is most severely formulated in terms of whether suburbs can prosper and succeed, regardless of the fate and fortunes of their central city; or whether the prosperity of cities and suburbs are intertwined and interdependent.

This issue is critical. In the State of the Union speech President Clinton declared, "We are all in it together." If cities and suburbs are "in it together," a strong *economic* justification can be made for addressing the needs of central cities and cooperation among cities and suburbs to meet the mutual economic needs of their metropolitan area. If, on the other hand, the fate of cities and suburbs are not economically intertwined, the case for addressing the problems of central cities must be made in terms of social equity and avoidance of the longer term costs of failure to address these problems. In the current politics of the nation, the economic argument appears to be more compelling than the call for social equity.

The recently available 1990 median household income data provide new opportunities to test the hypothesis that the economic futures of cities and suburbs are interdependent.[2]

- If cities and suburbs are economically independent, rather than interdependent, then changes in suburban incomes and central city incomes should not be related or move together. A plot of these relationships will appear randomly scattered.

- If there is some degree of interdependence, changes in suburban incomes would be related to changes in central incomes and vice versa. A plot of these relationship, the scattergram, will cluster in a clear and discernible pattern.

This is clear evidence of a strong and consistent relationship between changes in central city incomes and changes in suburban incomes. The interpretation of this relationship is as follows. For every one dollar increase in central city income, suburban incomes increase by $1.12. Conversely, for every increase of $1.12 in suburban income, central city income increases by one dollar. The relationship does not imply causation, i.e., that change in one causes the change in the other. Rather, the relationship is mutual, interactive, and interdependent. This evidence strongly suggests that the economic fate and fortunes of cities and suburbs are inextricably intertwined.

Where suburban incomes are increasing, central city incomes are increasing. Conversely, where central city incomes are decreasing, suburban incomes are decreasing. Tables 1 and 2 present detailed data on these patterns of change. Table 1 focuses on the 25 largest metropolitan areas in which suburban incomes increased most rapidly between 1980 and 1990. Table 2 deals with the 18 largest metropolitan areas in which suburban incomes declined over this period.

In high growth areas, suburbs and central cities grew together. Table 1 shows that in each of the 25 metropolitan areas with the most rapidly grow-

ing suburbs, measured by absolute and percentage gains in median household income, central city incomes also increased over the 1979–1989 period. In other words, in the high growth set of metropolitan areas, no suburbs experienced income growth without corresponding growth in their central city. This also means that no central city in this high growth sample experienced income growth in the absence of suburban growth. In all but one (San Diego) of the 25 metropolitan areas, the absolute gains in suburbs exceed those in their central cities. In 10 of these metropolitan areas, however, the rate of central city income growth exceeded that of their suburbs.

The interdependence between suburbs and their cities is also apparent for suburban areas experiencing income decline. Over the 10 year period, suburbs in 18 of the 78 largest metropolitan areas experienced declines in real median household incomes (see table 2). In all but four of these, central city incomes also declined. In only one of these four did the decline in suburban income exceed one percent (Salt Lake City: −4.7 percent). The corresponding increases in central city incomes were also relatively small, ranging between one and four percent.

Of the remaining 35 metropolitan areas (not presented in the two tables above), all experienced suburban income growth. Central city median household income grew in 25 and declined in 10. In the overall sample of 78 metropolitan areas, therefore, suburban incomes grew in 60 and declined in 18. Central city incomes grew in 54 and declined in 24 (31 percent). The direction of change in suburban and central city household incomes was the same in all but 14 of these metropolitan areas (18 percent).

Table 1
Metropolitan Areas with Rapidly Growing Suburbs
Change in Median Household Income, 1979–1989

		Suburbs		Central City	
		Absolute	*Percent*	*Absolute*	*Percent*
1	Bridgeport-Stamford-Norwalk-Danbury, CT NCMA ·	$12,519	26.1	$9,196	29.8
2	Oxnard-Ventura, CA PMSA	$10,995	28.2	$8,095	26.4
3	New York, NY PMSA	$10,395	26.3	$6,464	27.7
4	San Jose, CA PMSA	$10,096	25.1	$7,620·	19.7
5	Boston-Lawrence-Salem-Lowell-Brockton, MA	$ 9,083	26.3	$7,087	32.2
6	Middlesex-Somerset-Hunterdon, ' NJ PMSA	$ 8,906	21.4	$4,639	19.6
7	Newark, NJ PMSA	$ 8,669	22.9	$4,592	26.9
8	Hartford-New Britain-Middletown-Bristol, CT NECMA	$ 8,650	22.8	$4,790	19.4
9	Bergen-Passaic, NJ PMSA	$ 8,433	21.7	$6,729	33.3
10	Anaheim-Santa Ana, CA PMSA	$ 8,372	21.0	$4,817	14.8
11	New Haven-Waterbury-Meriden, CT NECMA	$ 8,286	23.2	$6,010	25.4
12	Washington, DC-MD-VA MSA	$ 7,315	17.1	$3,396	12.4
13	San Francisco, CA PMSA	$ 7,237·	18.2	$6,663·	24.9
14	Worcester-Fitchburg-Leominster, MA NECMA ·	$ 7,234	22.7	$5,306	21.7
15	Oakland, CA PMSA	$ 6,687	18.2	$3,862	16.6
16	San Diego, CA MSA	$ 5,914	19.7	$6,021	21.8
17	Philadelphia, PA-NJ PMSA	$ 5,880·	16.7	$2,401	10.8
18	Raleigh-Durham, NC MSA	$ 5,672	18.4	$4,756	18.5
19	Honolulu, HI MSA ·	$ 5,593	14.7	$3,644	10.9
20	Los Angeles–Long Beach, CA PMSA	$ 5,351	16.4	$4,586	17.3
21	Providence-Pawtucket-Woodstock, MA NECMA	$ 5,301	17.5	$3,472	16.9
22	Riverside–San Bernardino, CA PMSA	$ 5,238	18.3	$3,293	12.0
23	Baltimore, MD MSA	$ 4,838	12.9	$2,445	11.3
24	West Palm Beach–Boca Raton-Delray Beach, MSA	$ 4,586	16.4	$3.950	14.0
25	Albany-Schenectady-Troy, NY MSA	$ 4,562	14.7	$3,297	15.6

Furthermore, the strength of the relationship between cities and their suburbs appears to be increasing rather than declining. In 1979, the relationship between central city and suburban median household incomes was quite weak.[3] Ten years later, in 1989, this relationship had become stronger and more apparent. In other words, the degree of economic interdependence, as measured by income levels, increased over the decade.

Growing the Economies

While the documentation of the positive relationship between suburban

Table 2
Metropolitan Areas with Suburbs
Experiencing Income Declines
Change in Median Household Income, 1979–1989

		Suburbs		Central City	
		Absolute	Percent	Absolute	Percent
1	Fresno, CA MSA	($ 9)	0.0	$600	2.5
2	Cincinnati, OH-KY-IN PMSA	($ 24)	−0.1	($363)	−1.7
3	Portland, OR PMSA	($ 204)	−0.6	$669	2.7
4	Las Vegas, NV MSA	($ 281)	−0.9	$1,139	3.9
5	Kansas City, MO-KS MSA	($ 314)	−0.9	($554)	−2.1
6	Buffalo, NY PMSA	($ 743)	−2.2	($1,063)	−5.4
7	Tucson, AZ MSA	($ 755)	−2.3	($2,001)	−8.4
8	Detroit, MI PMSA	($ 969)	−2.4	($4,830)	−20.5
9	Tulsa, OK MSA	($1,005)	−3.4	($2,737)	−9.6
10	Louisville, KY-IN MSA	($1,050)	−3.3	($552)	−2.7
11	Oklahoma City, OK MSA	($1,327)	−4.5	($1,079)	−4.0
12	Denver, CO PMSA	($1,347)	−3.5	($1,038)	−4.0
13	Cleveland, OH PMSA	($1,380)	−3.7	($2,878)	−13.9
14	Salt Lake City–Ogden, UT MSA	($1,628)	−4.7	$224	1.0
15	Akron, OH PMSA	($1,765)	−5.0	($2,510)	−10.1
16	Pittsburgh, PA PMSA	($3,418)	−10.8	($1,859)	−8.2
17	Houston, TX PMSA	($4,667)	−11.0	($4,886)	−15.7
18	New Orleans, LA MSA	($4,913)	−14.7	($1,442)	−7.2

and city household incomes is important, it should not be surprising. A city and its suburbs are not two distinct economies. They are a single regional economy, highly interdependent, with their fortunes intertwined. Given this interdependence in the regional economy, it would be surprising, indeed, if changes in city and suburban incomes were not highly interrelated. *The fate of the local economic region will dictate the fortunes of both cities and suburbs.*

Previous *Economic Reports* examined the relationships between local economic regions and the disparities between central cities and suburbs. We found that in metropolitan areas where disparity (as measured by per capita income) is high, total employment growth is lower than in metropolitan areas

where disparity is lower.[4] This analysis did not find a direction relationship between the disparity and indicators of suburban economic performance. Rather, the relationship is between the city/suburb disparity and the performance of the overall local economic region.

Disparities between cities and suburbs are sharp. Some became increasingly distinct between 1980 and 1990.

- The rate of increase in employed residents was four times greater in suburbs than in cities over this decade.
- By 1990, the ratio of employed persons living in central cities to those in suburbs was .54, compared to .61 in 1980.

- Unemployment rates in 1990 were significantly greater in cities than in their suburbs (disparity ratio = 1.7).
- The percent of persons in poverty was more than two and a half times greater in central cities (disparity ratio = 2.4).
- The proportion of residents with high school degrees in cities was 83 percent of that of the suburbs, and the proportion of college graduates is 59 percent.

In policy terms, it appears that diminishing these disparities will strengthen the overall local economic region upon which both central city and suburb depend.

The local economic regions are not bounded by government jurisdictional lines. These local economic regions comprise city, suburb, and often nearby rural areas. Taken all together with the linkages among them, the U.S. common market of these local economic regions constitute the "national economy."

The performance of these local region economies will be crucial to the success of federal economic policies. Federal efforts to "jump start" the economy through a short-run stimulus package, as well as long term efforts to increase national productivity and investment, will inevitably target these concentrations of economic activities and sources of productivity growth. "Growing the economy" means stimulating growth in the nation's local economic regions. This essential reality should not be ignored as the President and Congress work to reach consensus on a new national economic program.

This debate over the shape of the national economic program should also recognize the diversity of circumstances and performance of these local economic regions. The breadth and depth of diversity across the many local economic regions—described in the next section—make it less likely that uniform national economic policies, administered as if there was a single national economy, will suffice as a "national program for economic growth." Effective federal policies to "grow the economy" must recognize the importance of local economies to prospects for national growth; those policies must also be sensitive to the differences among the local economies.

Variations Among Local Economic Regions

Too often, national averages underlie federal policy and program decisions. Data, however, indicate a wide range of variation around these national averages across local economic regions. When federal policy and program decisions are driven by these national averages, therefore, the variety of circumstances and needs in local economies are ignored.

The degree of variation in the performance of local economic regions is easily demonstrated. This study examined median household incomes, employment growth and unemployment rates across the 50 largest metropolitan areas in 1990. These figures also identified the comparable national levels. These data clearly demonstrate the extent of the variation around the national average measures that underlie federal policy and program decisions.

In 1989 median household income was $30,056 in the nation. Median household incomes in these 50 largest metropolitan areas ranged from a high of $46,848 to a low of $24,442, a difference of $22,406.

Eight metropolitan areas fell below the national average and 42 were above. Of these higher incomes metropolitan areas, 18 exceed the national average by more than $5,000, 10 by $10,000 or more, and five by $15,000 or more. The range of variation in metropolitan median household incomes, therefore, is significant, and the national averages mask the extent of this variation. This diversity of metropolitan income performance is not related to metropolitan size, at least within the 50 largest metropolitan areas examined in figure 3.

Metropolitan areas also exhibit significant variations in rates of employment growth. Among the 50 largest metropolitan areas, the rate of employment growth between 1980 and 1990 ranged from a high of 43.5 percent to a low of −1.4 percent.

The national average growth rate over this period was 18.2 percent. Twenty-six of the 50 large metropolitan areas had growth rates in excess of the national average. Of these, 10 had rates in excess of 30 percent over the 10 year period, and 10 experienced a less than 10 percent rate of growth. The rate of growth in employment was negative in three of the areas.

The unemployment rate is a primary measure of the performance of the national economy and its constituent local economic regions. In 1990, the national rate of unemployment averaged 6.3 percent. Again, the range in unemployment rates across the 50 metropolitan areas is wide, from a high of 9.2 to a low of 3.7.

The majority of these metropoli-

tan areas (29) experienced unemployment rates below the national average, but the remaining 21 had rates in excess of the national mean. Again, there appears to be no consistent relationship between urban size and unemployment performance.

Almost all measures of economic performance reveal similar patterns of variation across local economic regions. The breadth and depth of these patterns of variations indicate that there is a need for federal policies to be sensitive to the diversity of local economic regions and their unique circumstances and needs.

Some Implications for Federal Policy

The findings of this study suggest looking at the U.S. economy as a common market of local economic regions rather than as a huge but undifferentiated "national economy." In turn, this view indicates several directions in which federal policy should develop.

- Federal economic policy should aim at improving the condition and performance of the local economic regions.

  For example, the importance of infrastructure and of education and training for workers must be related to each local economic region. Also, a stimulus for job creation will work best if it is targeted and delivered locally where it is needed.
- Federal economic policy should address the variety among these local economic regions as to their circumstances and needs.

For example, an investment tax credit can be structured with an incentive for investment in local economies that need it and can use it best. Analysis of the presence and absence of this and other prerequisites for economic growth should be focused on the local economic regions.

- Federal economic policy should seek to diminish city/suburb disparities within the local economic regions.

    For example, redlining by providers of mortgages or insurance undercuts the ability of some areas to contribute to the development of the local economic region. Also, efforts to overcome the spatial mismatch of job openings and people seeking jobs will strengthen overall performance of the local economy.

(80 minus Nassau-Suffolk, NY PMSA and Monmouth-Ocean, NJ PMSA for which no central city is identified either in the name or by the Census Bureau). The size ranking was based on total population tabulated in the 1990 Census of Population and Housing. This ranking was performed on Primary Metropolitan Statistical Areas (PMSAs), Metropolitan Statistical Areas (MSAs) and New England County Metropolitan Areas (NECMAs). Central cities are defined as those in the name of the metropolitan area, rather than multiple central cities in the areas by the Census Bureau. When no central city was in the title, the city or cities identified by the Census Bureau was used. In the case of the Kansas City, MO-KS MSA, both Kansas City, MO, and Kansas City, KS, were used. 1980 Metropolitan Areas were reconstructed based on 1990 geographical definitions. Counties were added to, or subtracted from, the 1980 SMSAs, and the variables were retabulated. 1980 Central Cities were also based on the 1990 definitions.

2. For the analyses that follow, 1979 median household incomes were adjusted to 1989 dollars.

3. The R^2, a measure of the percent of the variation explained, was a very low .07. On the 1989 data, the R^2 was .310.

4. *City Distress, Metropolitan Disparities, and Economic Growth.* Combined Revised Edition, NLC, September 1992.

Notes

1. The information in this study is based on the largest 78 metropolitan areas in 1990

APPENDIX

Resource Organizations

General Resource Organizations

American Planning Association
122 South Michigan Avenue
Suite 1600
Chicago, IL 60603
Phone: 312-431-9100
Fax: 312-431-9985
Internet: http://www.planning.org

The Aspen Institute
Rural Economic Policy Program
1333 New Hampshire Avenue, NW
Suite 1070
Washington, DC 20036
Phone: 202-736-5804
Fax: 202-467-0790
Internet: http://www.aspeninst.org/
  rural/

Asset-Based Community Development Institute
Institute for Policy Research
Northwestern University

2040 Sheridan Road
Evanston, IL 60208-4100
Phone: 847-491-3518
Fax: 847-491-9916
Internet: http://www.nwu.edu/IPR/
  abcd.html

Center for Compatible Economic Development
7 East Market Street
Suite 210
Leesburg, VA 20176
Phone: 703-779-1728
Fax: 703-779-1746
Email: ecodev@cced.org

The Center for Rural Affairs
Box 406
Walthill, NE 68067
Phone: 402-846-5428
Fax: 402-846-5420
Internet: http://www.cfra.org

Community Development Society International

Originally published as "Resource Organizations for Small Town Economic Development," Harvesting Hometown Jobs, 1997. *Published by the National Center for Small Communities, Washington, D.C. Reprinted with permission of the publisher.*

1123 North Water Street
Milwaukee, WI 53202
Phone: 414-276-7106
Fax: 414-276-7704
Internet: http://www.infoanalytic.
   com/cds/

Corporation for Enterprise Develop-
   ment
777 North Capitol Street, NE
Suite 410
Washington, DC 20002
Phone: 202-408-9788
Fax: 202-408-9793
Internet: http://www.cfed.org

The Foundation Center
   79 Fifth Avenue
New York, NY 10003-3076
Phone: 212-620-4230
Fax: 212-691-1828
Internet: http://fdncenter.org/

Heartland Center for Leadership
   Development
941 O Street, NW
Suite 818
Lincoln, NE 68508
Phone: 800-927-1115
Fax: 402-474-7672
Internet: http://www.4w.com/
   heartland/

Kellogg Collection for Rural
   Development Resources
Heartland Center for Leadership
   Development
941 O Street, NW
Suite 818
Lincoln, NE 68508
Phone: 800-927-1115
Fax: 402-474-7672
Internet: http://www.unl.edu/kellogg/
   index.html

National Association of Counties
Joint Center for Sustainable
   Communities
440 First Street, NW
Washington, DC 20001-2080
Phone: 202-393-6226
Fax: 202-393-2630
Internet: http://www.naco.org

National Association of Development
   Organizations
444 North Capitol Street, NW
Suite 630
Washington, DC 20001
Phone: 202-624-7806
Fax: 202-624-8813
Internet: http://www.nado.org

National Association of Regional
   Councils
1700 K Street, NW
Suite 1300
Washington, DC 20006
Phone: 202-457-0710
Fax: 202-296-9352
Internet: http://narc.org/narc

National Association of State
   Development Agencies
750 First Street, NE
Suite 710
Washington, DC 20002
Phone: 202-898-1302
Fax: 202-898-1312
Internet: http://www.ids.net/nasda

National Association of Towns and
   Townships
444 North Capitol Street, NW
Suite 294
Washington, DC 20001
Phone: 202-624-3500
Fax: 202-624-3554
Internet: http://www.natat.org

National Center for Small
  Communities
444 North Capitol Street, NW
Suite 294
Washington, DC 20001
Phone: 202-624-3500
Fax: 202-624-3554
Internet: http://www.natat.org

National Main Street Center
National Trust for Historic
  Preservation
1785 Massachusetts Avenue, NW
Washington, DC 20036
Phone: 202-588-6219
Fax: 202-588-6050
Internet: http://www.nthp.org

National Rural Electric Cooperative
  Association
Community and Economic
  Development
4301 Wilson Boulevard
Arlington, VA 22203
Phone: 703-907-5813
Fax: 703-907-5531
Internet: http://www.nreca.org

Rocky Mountain Institute
Economic Renewal Program
1739 Snowmass Creek Road
Snowmass, CO 81654
Phone: 970-927-3807
Fax: 970-927-4510
Internet: http://www.rmi.org

Yellow Wood Associates
95 South Main Street
St. Albans, VT 05478
Phone: 802-524-6141
Fax: 802-524-6643
Internet:
  http://www.together.net/~yellow

Business Attraction Resource Organizations

American Economic Development
  Council
9801 West Higgins Road
Suite 540
Rosemont, IL 60018
847-692-9944

National Council for Urban Economic
  Development
1730 K Street, NW
Suite 700
Washington, DC 20006
202-223-4735

Business Retention and Expansion Resource Organizations

Business Retention and Expansion International (BREI)
    BREI supports the retention and expansion of existing businesses and industry as a primary economic development strategy. The association pursues this mission by facilitating research, instruction, publications, meetings and other activities. BREI's website provides an annotated bibliography of business retention and expansion literature, as well as information about the association's annual meeting, research network, newsletter and certification programs. [The association does not maintain an office.]
Internet: http://www.brei.org

Appalachian Center for Economic
  Networks (ACENet)
94 North Columbus Road
Athens, OH 45701
614-593-5451

National Institute of Standards and
  Technology
State Technology Extension Program
Building 221, Room 343
Gaithersburg, MD 20899
301-975-3086

Entrepreneurship Resource Organizations

Ewing Marion Kauffman Foundation
Center for Entrepreneurial Leadership
4900 Oak Street
Kansas City, MO 64112
800-489-4900

Cognetics
(David Birch and Associates)
100 Cambridge Park Drive
Cambridge, MA 02140
617-661-0300

National Business Incubation
  Association
20 East Circle Drive
Suite 190
Athens, OH 45701
614-593-4331

National Community Reinvestment
  Coalition
733 15th Street
Suite 540
Washington, DC 20005
202-628-8866

Center for the New West
Denver Center
600 World Trade Center
1625 Broadway
Denver, CO 80202
303-572-5400

REAL Enterprises
115 Market Street
Suite 320
Durham, NC 27701
919-688-7325

Self-Employment Learning Project
The Aspen Institute
1333 New Hampshire Avenue, NW
Suite 1070
Washington, DC 20036
202-736-5821

National Development Council
211 East 4th
Covington, KY 41011
606-291-0220

First Nations Development Institute
The Stores Building
11917 Main Street
Fredericksburg, VA 22408
703-371-5615

Rural Community College Initiative
MDC
P.O. Box 17268
Chapel Hill, NC 27514
919-968-4531

Tourism and Retirement Development Resource Organizations

National Association of State Development Agencies
National Conference of Tourism Development
750 First Street, NE
Suite 710
Washington, DC 20002
202-898-1302

Travel Industry Association of
  America
1100 New York Avenue, NW
Suite 450
Washington, DC 20005
202-408-8422
Internet: http://www.tia.org

Tourism Industries
U.S. Department of Commerce
Room 1860
14th and Constitution Ave., NW
Washington, DC 20230
202-482-2404
Internet: http://tinet.ita.doc.gov

Rural Resources Online

A website providing a comprehensive
listing and linkage to many other
online resources on a variety of rural
issues. RRO provides access to most
U.S. Department of Agriculture
programs including the Extension
Service, Empowerment Zone/En-

terprise Communities Program,
Rural Information Center (a clearinghouse on grant opportunities,
foundations, publications, etc.), National Rural Development Partnership and State Rural Development
Councils, and four regional rural development centers serving the nation. Access on the Internet at:
http://www.rurdev.usda.gov/nrdp/
rural.htm.

Additional Resources

Please visit the National Center for
Small Communities' website at
http://www.natat.org. The site is
shared with the National Association of Towns and Townships. It
provides linkages to many helpful
governmental information sources
and rural development organizations, including several of the organizations listed above.

Annotated Bibliography

Ady, R.M., "Emerging Trends in Economic Development," *Economic Development Review*, Summer 1987, page 7.

This is a brief survey of the most current and significant trends in economic development. It provides a good, and fairly inclusive, introduction to the major influences on the field of economic development and the field's possible future directions. The author advocates a proactive role for city officials in economic development; he encourages them to learn as much as they can about contemporary manufacturing, unions, international markets, and new technologies in order to prepare their cities for a prosperous future.

Albrandt, R.S. and deAngelis, J.P. "Local Options for Economic Development," *Economic Development Quarterly*, Vol. 1, No. 1, February 1987, page 41.

The authors detail alternative strategies to industrial recruitment. They strongly favor a regional economic development approach. These strategies were used in a once-heavily industrialized region of Pennsylvania by a new organization, the Steel Valley Authority. The activities of the Authority, which has the power of eminent domain to take abandoned plants and also to issue revenue bonds, are explained here.

Alexander, L. (Ed.), *Downtown Improvement Districts: Creating Money and Power for Downtown Action*, New York, N.Y.: Downtown Research & Development Center, 1989.

During recent recessionary times, the movement to form more downtown improvement districts has become popular throughout the country. Twenty-five case studies are interspersed with narrative description on the powers of a downtown development authority, how referenda work, what ills a downtown improvement district can reasonably be expected to correct. The downtown improvement district is now an accepted way to tackle the problems of downtown and economic development, but new ways of approaching the district concept are introduced by this book.

Alexander, L. (Ed.), *How Downtowns Organize for Results: 24 Case Studies*, New York, N.Y.: Downtown Research & Development Center. 1987.

Examining economic development and downtown rehabilitation, this work concentrates on larger cities and the structure of the organization and planning efforts they utilized. The case studies are organized according to the lesson they teach and the

---

Reprinted with permission from Small City Economic Development, *1991. Published by the National League of Cities, Washington, D.C.*

major focus of the development plan. Each case study is well written and guides the reader through most of the highlights of the formation of the city organization, as well as describing the organizational structure used in its pure, theoretical state.

Armentrout & Associates, *The Small Business Retention, Expansion and Recruitment Project*, Washington, D.C., National Trust for Historic Preservation, 1987.

Using the Main Street program to retain and develop small businesses has been a successful approach for many small cities. This book not only explains the Main Street Program in a more sophisticated way than some other publications, but it also considers the role of retention and expansion within the context of a city's economic development program. The author includes case studies of some of the older Main Street projects throughout the country.

Arndt, H.W., *Economic Development: The History of an Idea*, University of Chicago Press, 1988.

An international approach to the history of economic development is taken by this book. Tying seemingly dissimilar cultures, for instance, nineteenth century India and the modern U.S., economic development clarifies the struggles of the field to forge its own identity, and explains how economic development and economics diverge.

Bartsch, C., Kessler, A.S. (Eds.) *Revitalizing Small Town America: State and Federal Initiatives for Economic Development*, Northeast-Midwest Institute, Center for Regional Policy, 1989.

This is a text with two identities: the first half is a case study approach to state economic development programs; the second half is a reference-work approach to federal economic development programs. *Revitalizing Small Town America's* Introduction provides a good analysis of the goals and history of economic development and its current impediments in today's economic climate. The book is particularly useful for identifying emerging trends and the most

highly effective economic development programs.

Bingham, R., E. Hill, S. White (Eds.), 1990, *Financing Economic Development: An Institutional Response*, Newbury Park, Ca.: Sage Library of Social Research.

Technical, detailed information about the difficult subject of financing is presented in a clear and usable form here. The book consists of eighteen chapters written by economists, professors of business administration, tax experts, lawyers with an expertise in constitutional law, and city officials. The chapter on Tax Increment Financing (by Paetsch and Dahlstrom; a professor and a city Planning Director) gives one of the most complete and straightforward descriptions to be found in the secondary literature on the subject.

Blakely, E., *Planning Local Economic Development: Theory and Practice*, Newbury Park, Ca.: Sage Library of Social Research, 1989.

Sophisticated and experienced economic development organizers or scholars of the field are most likely to benefit from this book. Planning Local Economic Development takes an international perspective on the field, and it is nearly all-inclusive in terms of coverage of its subject matter, but the author (Chair of the Department of City and Regional Planning at U.C. Berkeley) assumes more than scanty knowledge of the subject. A fine glossary in the book helps the neophyte who is curious about the deeper policy and economics questions involved in development, but is probably not enough to help the totally inexperienced reader get a lot out of the book.

Branch, M.C., *Regional Planning: Introduction and Explanation*, Praeger, New York, 1988.

Planning is often thought of as a local and highly specialized undertaking. This book corrects that impression, and provides a well-written and thoroughly researched overview of the regional impacts and implications of many types of planning for different settings—urban, military, economic, environmental. It is written from a business/management point of view and is intended for the city official or urban planning student.

Burrows, T. (Ed.), *A Survey of Zoning Definitions*, American Planning Association, Chicago, Illinois, Planning Advisory Service, Report Number 421, 1989.

In simple and straightforward language, this pamphlet explains the most significant terms needed to understand zoning. It includes drawings and photographs that sometimes are so apt that they could substitute for the written definition. Since many of the definitions comes from one or more city statutes, the cities of origin are identified at the end of each definition. This glossary is not highly technical but it will provide a good, general guide particularly useful for those new to the downtown development process.

California Department of Commerce, *California Business Retention and Expansion Program*, Office of Local Economic Adjustment, Sacramento, 1988.

Not many city officials are experts in business retention and expansion programs; this book guides the city official, or other individual new to economic development. How to plan for business retention, its theory, how it fits in with an overall economic development plan, and how to assess the progress of a retention and expansion program are all spelled out clearly in this book. While written by the California Department of Commerce for California cities, very little of the information applies only to that state, and city officials from around the country will find valuable information in it.

Cloar, J.A., *Centralized Retail Management: New Strategies for Downtown*, Urban Land Institute, Washington, D.C., 1991.

Using management and organizational principles developed by shopping centers, cities can rejuvenate central business districts. This book recognizes that often cosmetic changes, for instance streetscaping efforts, don't work on long-neglected downtown shopping districts. The pilot CRM programs in four cities show that the use of shopping center management principles involves a strong public-private organization, a community consensus in favor of change, and cooperation by property owners. The pilot programs also show that size of the city does not appear to have a significant impact on whether the program is a success.

Coleman, W.G., *State and Local Government and Public-Private Partnerships*, Greenwood Press, New York, 1989.

This book draws together a wide range of research, including Rand Corporation studies on urban affairs. It introduces the reader to the myriad of political, legal, social, and economic issues involved in public-private partnerships. The author is candid about the limitations of public-private approaches, especially in difficult areas like pollution control that involve local economics, public policy, and emotionally charged citizens. Tips on avoiding problems and observations on how to organize public-private partnerships are some of the most useful parts of the book.

Council of State Community Affairs Agencies, *Incubator Training Manual*, Washington, D.C., 1988.

Written for trainers in a formal program, this manual provides an organizational framework for a three day seminar on incubators. It has a competent introduction to incubators, what they do, who should be in them, and what they can do for a community. Also included are articles and actual copies of newsletters related to different aspects of incubators, for instance, articles on what makes a good entrepreneur. The manual is well organized and clearly written and can be used profitably by anyone starting an incubator or trying to get an existing one to work better.

Farr, C.A. (Ed.) *Shaping the Local Economy*, ICMA, Washington, D.C., 1984.

The formation of public-private organizations to manage and implement successful economic development programs is the focus of this work. The essays are reprints of articles that appeared previously in other periodicals, but they are nonetheless informative. Two sections have the most material: "Successful Local Programs," and "Public Sector Intervention in the Marketplace."

Favero, P., and Heasley, D.K., *Cooperative Extension and New Alliances for Rural Economic Development: Five Case Studies*, University Park, PA, Northeast Regional Center for Rural Development, 1989.

The five communities examined here are geographically dispersed throughout the country and present a variety of economic development models and situations. Each case study is only about five pages long, well-organized, and each is followed by a good bibliography for those interested in researching similar issues.

Federal Reserve Bank of Philadelphia, *Resources for Revitalization*, Philadelphia, PA, 1991.

Written for banks interested in community reinvestment, *Resources* could also be an invaluable tool for local officials learning about how to obtain bank funding for their economic development or housing programs. More than 100 community development programs in Pennsylvania, New Jersey and Delaware are profiled in this looseleaf book. The categories of programs include affordable housing, small business development, and general community development.

Fosler, R.S. (Ed.), *Local Economic Development: Strategies for a Changing Economy*, International City Management Association, 1991.

Intended as "an overview of a rapidly changing field and detailed treatment of selected topics that local leaders should know about," this small book contains a lot of insightful commentary by renowned experts. The two introductory chapters open the world of economics to the neophyte: "The Changed World Economy" by Peter Drucker and "The Meaning of Local Economic Development, by Edward Blakely. The additional chapters on economic development organizations and on evaluating

economic development programs are especially thought provoking and educational.

Flaccavento, A., "Making the Connection Between Values and Community Development Strategies," *Small Town*, Vol. 19, No. 1, July-August 1988, page 22.

The story of the progress of community development in Central Appalachia is interwoven with the story of the personal growth of the community developer in this article. Self-examination and coming to grips with one's cultural prejudices are important steps before an outsider undertakes leadership of an economic development program. This article points out some of the areas to explore and how to assess the match between the community and the outside economic development expert.

Fleming, C., "A Tale of Two Towns: Using Tourism to Revitalize Iowa's Small Communities," *Small Town*, Vol. 12, no. 2, September-October 1988, page 22.

Written by the Coordinator of the Iowa Community Betterment Program for the Iowa Department of Economic Development, this short article conveys a great deal of information about how a tourism effort was mounted in two villages. It details the hurdles and the successes, how government and citizens contributed to the efforts, as well as funds spent on the programs.

Friedman, R., Schweke, W., *Expanding the Opportunity to Produce: Revitalizing the American Economy Through New Enterprise Development*, The Corporation for Enterprise Development, Washington, D.C., 1981.

Essays by well-known political figures, media economic commentators, and economic development experts are collected in this "policy reader," clearly intended for a general reader audience. The book is divided into four parts: (1) The Role of New Enterprise Development in Economic Revitalization: An Overview; (2) The Context of New Enterprise Initiatives; (3) Financing New Economic Development; and (4) Critical Elements of Enterprise Development. They provide a fresh perspective on the possibilities for the American economy in the future.

General Accounting Office, *A Glossary of Terms Used in the Federal Budget Process and Related Accounting, Economic, and Tax Terms*, Washington, D.C., 1981.

For those lacking a basic knowledge of economics, this dictionary will be a sound, general introduction to the vocabulary of the field. Its definitions are well-written and clear; they are detailed but don't presume any prior knowledge on the part of the reader. The reader who was totally unfamiliar with this field might not know under which category to find a word, but since the book is relatively modest in size, finding words is quick and easy.

Glissen, L., 1984, *Main Street: Open for Business*, Washington, D.C., National Trust for Historic Preservation.

The Main Street Program has been successful in salvaging the economy of small city downtowns. This short book traces the history of the Main Street Program, its first successes, and describes the underlying philosophy of the program. Its assessments are honest, but the focus of the book is on Main Street programs that worked; any that might have failed are not described. The authors admit that none of the city's central business districts ever achieved the level of retail business they had in their prime, but merchants and residents were all happy with what Main Street did for them.

Grossman, J., "Regional Public-Private Partnerships: Forging the Future," *Economic Development Quarterly*, Vol. 1, No. 1, February 1987, page 52.

Focusing on the success of an older public-private organization, The Economic Development Council of Northeastern Pennsylvania, this article explains the regional economic crises the organization faced and shows the strengths of the regional approach. The article discusses the long history of the organization, its revolving loan funds, and its numerous programs to promote international trade, and to benefit the environment in its long-industrialized region.

Harlow, L.F. (Ed.), *Servants of All: Professional Management of City Government*, Brigham Young University Press, Provo, Utah, 1981.

Veteran city managers, and other city administrative employees, have written 100 essays on the everyday problems of local government. The range of subjects covered is extremely wide—from the philosophy of politics to how the family of a city manager copes with a new city. The section "Economic Development" contains four good introductory essays, "What Do You Do When Your City Goes Bust?", "Stop Growth!", "The Most Interesting Mayor I Never Met" (a city manager recounts the 1906 term of a notorious mayor), and "Where's Your Proof?" (an account of failed redevelopment in a moderate sized city). The Appendix with charts explaining different kinds of city governments does a good job of exposing the strengths and weaknesses of each form.

Heilbroner, R., Thurow, L., *Five Economic Challenges*, Prentice-Hall, Englewood Cliffs, N.J., 1981.

For the city official who never took Introductory Economics, this book helps to fill in some of the gaps. The five challenges and their political underpinnings—inflation, recession, big government, the falling dollar, and the energy crisis—are discussed in layman's terms by experts. The authors note in the introduction, "Just as a good mechanic can teach a lot about how a car works without subjecting his listeners to a lecture on compression ratios, so a good teacher of economics should be able to explain a lot without subjecting his audience to long, technical explanations."

Henderson, D., and Hines, F., "Increases in Rural Income May Not Help Small-town Retailers," *Rural Development Perspectives*, Vol. 6, Issue 3, June–September, 1990.

Ten rural counties in Minnesota between 1979 and 1986 were the subject of examination for this article. In agriculturally dominated small towns, retailing accounted for about 20 percent of wages. However, when consumers had more money to spend they tended to divide their spending between stores in larger and smaller towns. When personal income falls, in both manufacturing and agricultural towns, consumers tend to spend more in closer, small town stores and restaurants.

Hester, R., "Inspiring Community Action: A Basic Small Town, Do-It-Yourself Approach," *Small Town*, Vol. 19, No. 1, July-August 1988, page 16.

In a systematic yet entertaining way, this article highlights the necessary ingredients for successful community organizing. The approach could be applied to organizing for nearly any activity. The article emphasizes the necessity of maintaining a balance between leadership and community participation. This short and practical essay will be useful for nearly all city officials and employees who want to open the lines of communications with their community and ensure the success of a program.

Hoppe, R., and Ghelfi, L., "Nonmetro Areas Depend on Transfers," *Rural Development Perspectives*, Vol. 6, Issue 2, February–May 1990, page 22.

Transfer payments mean retirement, disability, public assistance, unemployment, medical benefits, or veteran's benefits. An example of such a payment would be Social Security payments. From 1969 to 1987, the percentage of rural income from such sources rose from 11.6 to 18.7 percent. In 1987 when transfer payments accounted for 18.7 percent of non-metro income, it accounted for 13.7 percent of metropolitan area income. The article points out that while such payments can act as a buffer against economic downturns, they also make local economies particularly vulnerable to changes in federal spending on such programs.

International City Management Association, *Taking Charge: How Communities Are Planning Their Futures*, Washington, D.C., 1988.

This is an ICMA "Special Report," whose intended audience is elected officials. It is a straightforward, nuts and bolts book on

group dynamics, leadership, and community organizing. Particularly noteworthy is the chapter, "Building Consensus," which discusses different ways of creating and strengthening a community's consensus, and both the long term and short term implications for the city of varying approaches.

International City Management Association. *The Entrepreneur in Local Government*. Washington, D.C., 1983.

Using business as a model for city government is hardly a new idea, but this book takes a systematic approach to the subject. A selection of essays written mostly by city managers, and state officials, this book gracefully points out the underpinnings and prerequisites of good leadership. The book is easy to read and understand with many charts, graphs, and outlines of difficult subjects.

International City Management Association, *Small Cities and Counties: A Guide to Managing Services*, Washington, D.C., 1984.

City department heads are the intended audience for this book, which evolved out of ICMA's "Small Cities Management Training Program." However, the book could also be useful for elected officials or new city employees. It is a general introduction to city government and includes a full discussion of organizational issues, service delivery problems, and design questions. The chapter on economic development is divided into five areas: (1) economic development policy decisions, (2) information and analysis, (3) resources, (4) implementation, (5) evaluation.

International City Management Association, *Achieving Economic Development Success: Tools That Work*, Washington, D.C., 1991.

Recognizing from the outset that local government is not the only, or even the dominant, force for economic development success, this work emphasizes public/private and private actors that have provided the impetus for economic improvement. The study discusses economic development in both small and large cities and includes good appendices including a Tax Increment Financing regulation and a sample Site Inventory Form.

John, D., *Shifting Responsibilities: Federalism in Economic Development*, National Governor's Association, Washington, D.C., 1987.

A good background piece on the role of the federal government versus local government in economic development policy, this book also traces the history of city economic development successes and failures during the past twenty years. The author advocates enhancing exports, better targeting of federal resources, and a deemphasis on industrial recruitment, among other strategies for bettering the economy of U.S. cities.

Kenyon, J.B., "From Central Business District to Central Social District: The Revitalization of the Small Georgia City," *Small Town*, Vol. 19, No. 5, March-April, 1989.

The relation between historic preservation and economic development in several small cities in Georgia's Main Street Program is the focus of this article. The discussion of the cities and their history, economic problems, and social environment is insightful. The progress of cities is compared and their constraints in attempting economic development programs is examined intelligently.

Killian, M., and Parker, T., "Higher Education No Panacea for Weak Rural Economies," *Rural Development Perspectives*, Vol. 7., Issue 1, October–January 1991, page 2.

The myth that a more educated population is highly correlated with a better economy is debunked in this article. Other studies holding that education and economic strength are linked have been geographically limited, while the one in this article studied the relationship between education and economics in cities throughout the country. More significant predictors of a healthy economy than education seem to be: (1) the local mix of industry, (2) the demands of those industries for a population possessing not only certain educational characteristics but also having particular work experience, and (3) the cost of local labor.

Lamm, W.O., *Special Improvement Districts in Colorado*, Denver, Colorado Municipal League, 1991.

Any city contemplating a special improvement district could profit from this book; its applicability is not limited to the state of Colorado. This handbook discusses the state constitutional requirements, organization of a district, and highly technical issues such as the issuance of special assessment bonds and how to handle challenges by property owners. Included are sample city statutes from around the state as well as a copy of the regulation authorizing special improvement districts for the state.

Lawton, R. (Ed.), *The Rise and Fall of Great Cities*, Belhaven Press, London, 1989.

The role of technology, demographics and even disease, have been largely discounted as forces in western history. This book emphasizes those forces that have been neglected and provides a new perspective on the progress of cities throughout time. The book concentrates on Western European cities, particularly British cities, but the authors approach their subject in a broad fashion and attempt to teach lessons applicable to all cities.

Lenzi, R.C., and Murray, B.H. (Eds.) *Downtown Revitalization and Small City Development*, North Central Regional Center for Rural Development, Iowa State University, 1987.

This is a collection of the speeches presented at a conference on Downtown Revitalization and Small City Development at University of Wisconsin, Madison, April 13–15, 1987. The presentations were made by professors, city officials, and economic development researchers from associations. City officials will find new information based on concrete examples particularly in the chapters "Implementation and Financing" and "Evaluation and Ongoing Planning."

Levy, J.M. "What Local Economic Developers Actually Do," *American Planning Association Journal*, Spring 1990, p. 153.

Lonsdale, R., and Seyler, H.L., *Nonmetropolitan Industrialization*, V.H. Winston, Washington, D.C., 1979.

Essays by agricultural economists, sociologists, statisticians and others constitute this book. The essays concentrate on the American experience with industrialization, but data on Europe and Asia are used for the sake of comparison. Much of the information is technical and specific, but the presentation is never statistical or in any way inaccessible to the general reader.

Monkkonen, E.H., *America Becomes Urban: The Development of U.S. Cities and Towns 1780–1980*, University of California Press, Berkeley, 1988.

While well-researched and scholarly, this work is easy to understand. It is most valuable for its insights into the development of the modern American city. The author has a sophisticated understanding of sociology, criminology, law, political science, and the use of statistical analysis, but never writes in a lofty or wholly theoretical manner. Interesting photographs and prints from the nineteenth century help break up the text and contribute to the reader's appreciation of the impact of the past upon the present.

Morley, D., Proudfoot, S., Burns, T. (Eds.) *Making Cities Work: The Dynamics of Urban Innovation*, Westview Press, Boulder, Colorado, 1980.

This is a collection of essays, most of which were originally oral presentations at the York University Urban Innovation Conference in Canada. While the conference took place in Canada, the subject of the vast majority of the essays is urban problems in the United States. Most of the authors are sociologists who approach their subjects from a broad, theoretical perspective. The essays deal with a variety of issues such as the environment, crime, and the process of innovation.

National Council for Urban Economic Development, *Coordinated Urban Economic Development*, Washington, D.C., 1978.

Twenty-two case studies form the basis of this book which analyzes economic development strategies used by large cities. The thoroughly researched chapters focus on key issues such as development financing and coordination of manpower and economic development. While some of the information on federal sources of funding is old, the information about how programs actually worked is invaluable.

National Council for Urban Economic Development, *Establishing and Operating Private Sector Development Organizations*, Washington, D.C., 1984.

Twelve private development organizations from around the country are examined in this book's case studies. Though somewhat outdated in terms of available federal aid programs, the case studies provide solid information about how the organizations were founded and developed, as well as insights into the results each organization achieved. The book's summary chapter, "Ingredients for Success," has practical advice, in succinct form, for anyone trying to make a private development organization more effective.

National League of Cities, *The Local Official's Guide to the Community Reinvestment Act*, Washington, D.C., 1991.

Significant changes in 1990 make the Community Reinvestment Act stronger. CRA now creates a broader number of opportunities for economic development in cities. This short book explains the history and goals of CRA and how it works in practice. Twenty case studies from large, small, and medium sized cities around the country round out the description and evaluation of CRA's applicability to cities.

National League of Cities, *Tools and Targets: The Mechanics of City Economic Development*, Washington, D.C., 1987.

This book summarizes the results of an NLC economic survey of 322 large and small cities. Tools include infrastructure improvements, the provision of venture capital funds; the objectives of these tools are the targets. *Tools and Targets* is a detailed examination of the mechanics of a wide range of economic development strategies cities have taken.

National League of Cities Working Paper, *The Visible Hand: Major Issues in City Economic Policy*, Washington, D.C., 1987.

How do successful economic development programs come about? What city government environments are most likely to lead to significant economic development? These questions are some of the major ones addressed by *The Visible Hand*. Policy examinations are based on an NLC survey of 322 cities throughout the country. The book's title derives from Adam Smith's observation that "an invisible hand" guides economic forces in a market economy.

National League of Cities, *Financing Infrastructure: Innovations at the Local Level*, Washington, D.C., 1987.

In an era of diminishing federal aid, cities increasingly bear the burden of financing infrastructure. This book describes financing techniques such as special financing districts, exactions, public-private partnerships, and the creation of independent public corporations to operate public works. The twenty-four case studies flesh out these financing arrangements, their benefits and limitations.

National League of Cities, *Economic Development: What Works at the Local Level*, Washington, D.C., 1988.

This is the companion volume to the present *Small City Economic Development* book. Thirty-one case studies of large cities are used to detail the basics of economic development and how the most popular strategies work in practice. The emphasis of the book is providing a useful guidebook for the city official with little knowledge of economic development.

National League of Cities, *Small Business Partnerships*, Washington, D.C., 1989.

Robust small businesses create jobs, keep a small city stable, and are a fast-growing sector of the national economy. Their fragility, especially in their incipient stages, is a cause of concern for city officials. The varying roles city government can play to encourage the development of small business are described in this book. Six case studies show how mostly large cities approached the problem of small business development, but the examples can readily be applied in the small city context.

National Park Service, *Respectful Rehabilitation: Answers to Your Questions About Old Buildings*, Washington, D.C., Preservation Press, 1982.

While aimed at homeowners or merchants, city officials or downtown managers could also profit from the straightforward answers to questions about preservation contained in this book. In the process of answering commonly asked questions, the history of American architecture is detailed. The main benefit of the book, however, is its step by step instructions on how to actually repair and rehabilitate old buildings.

Parker, T., "Nonmetro Job Growth Lags Its Apparent Potential," *Rural Development Perspectives*, Vol. 7, Issue 1, October–January 1991, page 15.

Between 1969 and 1979, job growth in rural areas was slightly ahead of job growth in metropolitan areas; job growth in rural areas lagged significantly between 1979 and 1987, but then sprang ahead, although minimally, between 1987 and 1988. The author postulates a "rural factor" that holds down the expansion of jobs in non-metro areas. The components of the "rural factor" include isolation, distance from metropolitan areas, small size, as well as other differences between metropolitan and rural areas that can be accounted for only by a regional analysis.

Paumier, C., *Designing the Successful Downtown*, Urban Land Institute, Washington, D.C., 1988.

Emphasizing concrete examples of successful urban design, this book for the lay person provides a comprehensive, but uncomplicated to understand, guide to downtown redevelopment. The writer is sensitive to the political and financial hurdles to urban renovation, and the advice and observation are all practical. The book discusses urban design in cities of all sizes around the country.

Peltz, M., and Weiss, M., "State and Local Government Roles in Industrial Innovation," *Journal of the American Planning Association*, Vol. 50, No. 3, Summer 1984, page 270.

Encouraging high-tech business to relocate in one's community or to expand there, has become an extremely popular development tactic. This article suggests three major ways to enhance high-technology business: (1) start by coming up with consistent policy objectives that will serve to bring together various programs, (2) focus only on specific programs that fit well within those objectives and the community, (3) the major objective in adopting such a program should always be to diversify the local industry/technology/employment base of the economy.

Porter, P.R., and Sweet, D.C. (Eds.), *Rebuilding America's Cities: Roads to Recovery*, Rutgers University Press, New Brunswick, New Jersey, 1984.

The history of successful and unsuccessful attempts to revitalize larger cities is the substance of this collection of essays. While most of the authors are professors, the tone of the book is neither intimidating nor academic, it provides a rich introduction to the basic methods of downtown redevelopment and the major characters in the past who played a significant role in city planning and urban affairs. The essays were first oral presentations at The Cities' Congress on Roads to Recovery, organized by Cleveland State University's College of Urban Affairs.

PTI, *Business Location Decisions and Cities*, Public Technology, Inc., Washington, D.C., 1983.

What are the most important factors in making the decision about where to locate a business and how can local government

make its city more attractive to business are the main themes of this book. The author is attuned to the different locational needs of specific businesses, but emphasizes the city's point of view. Case studies are included which explain how location decisions worked in practice.

Ramati, R., *How to Save Your Own Street*, Garden City, New York, Doubleday, 1981.

Equally applicable to small villages and large cities, this book was a joint effort of the City of New York and its Urban Design Group. Ramati was Director of the Urban Design Group for 16 years and currently serves on the New York Arts Commission. The book is focused on the nuts and bolts of downtown revitalization, but takes a broad, often historical, perspective of that task. It is written in a lucid and lively style, and is filled with photographs, charts, blueprints, and other architectural drawings.

Redstone, L. (Ed.), *The New Downtowns: Rebuilding Business Districts*, New York, McGraw-Hill Book Company, 1976.

Pedestrian malls, streetscaping, and esthetically pleasing infrastructure repairs are often used, but not as often understood in the context of regional and city development. This book places development of a central business district in a wider context. It contains about 100 case studies of recent downtown development projects around the world, from Buffalo to Kuwait City. The federal financing programs described by the book are for the most part history now, but the design concepts and the outcomes of downtown development are still fresh.

Reed, B.J., and Paulsen, D., "Small Towns Lack Capacity for Successful Development Efforts," *Rural Development Perspective*, Vol. 6, Issue 3, June–September 1990, page 26.

This article is based on a study of 135 small towns in Nebraska. City officials were sent a questionnaire that posed questions about specific economic development activities, leadership pool, availability of people with skills and knowledge, and financial resources of the town. The survey results showed that despite great need, small cities do not have a necessary critical mass of people to carry out development programs, particularly those requiring competing for grant funding.

Rutter, L., *The Essential Community: Local Government in the Year 2000*, International City Management Association, Washington, D.C., 1980.

Written for city managers, elected officials, and citizens, this book hopes to "clarify choices so that we can enhance the communities of tomorrow." The Essential Community introduces the World Future Society and discusses some of the forces that will shape urban policy in the near future. One of the appendices, "Five Scenarios for the Year 2000," is especially useful. It consists of five charts comparing various types of communities' approaches and reactions to critical issues they are likely to face soon.

Schiffman, I., *Alternative Techniques for Managing Growth*, Institute of Governmental Affairs, University of California at Berkeley, 1990.

Massive population growth in California has forced city planners and city officials to devise often creative ways to control development. This book is written by a professor, but is not pedantic or weighty. It provides a clear guide to twenty-six strategies successfully employed by cities in California, along with an assessment of how they worked, and references for continued research on each strategy.

Schmenner, R.W., *Making Business Location Decisions*, Prentice-Hall, Englewood Cliffs, New Jersey, 1991.

Aimed at the business executive or owner rather than city officials, this book could still be useful for economic development coordinators and others who want to understand the business point of view. The book includes a short (10-page) chapter, "Helping Industry Locate New Capacity: Advice to States and Localities." The most significant portion of the book is given over to the planning process, value clarification, and how to fit the decision about location into an overall business plan.

Smilor, R.W., Kozmetsky, G., and Gibson, D. (Eds.), *Creating the Technopolis: Linking Technology Commercialization and Economic Development*, Cambridge, MA, Ballinger Publishing Co., 1988.

This is a specialized book written by experts, but anyone involved in retention or expansion or attraction of a high-tech firm will profit from reading some of the essays in the book. The chapters on international technology companies are written by overseas city managers, professors, and industry officials. Part II on "The U.S. Experience" provides a wealth of insights into how various communities in this country have profited through high technology. The U.S. articles are detailed and astute about the demographics and long-term economic implications of high-tech businesses.

Solomon, A.P. (Ed.), *The Prospective City: Economic, Population, Energy, and Environmental Developments*, Cambridge, Massachusetts, The MIT Press, 1980.

To many readers this may seem merely like a book suitable for an introductory college-level course in political science or urban affairs course. *The Prospective City*, however, contains a fine group of thought-provoking articles, and would benefit anyone involved in municipal affairs. Most of the articles were originally offered at a conference on urban growth at MIT. The articles on economic development avoid broad, sweeping generalizations, and are not heavily statistical or technical; they are well-written and thoroughly researched, emphasizing concrete experience over theoretical data.

Spreigeren, P.D., *Urban Design: The Architecture of Towns and Cities*, New York, McGraw-Hill, 1965.

By clearly tracing the history of urban design, this book provides a broad perspective on the interaction of urban design and the political, social, and economic life of the city. *Urban Design* is particularly useful for its insights on improving transportation while enhancing the appearance of an urban area.

Stark, J., Morton, L., Reisdorph, D., Thornton, L., *Industrial Parks: A Step by Step Guide*, Midwest Research Institute, 1988.

Beginning with "Park Development and Utilization Checklist," this book takes a functional approach to industrial parks and how they work. Relatively little space is devoted to whether an industrial park is appropriate for one's community, so this is more a book for those who have already decided it is for them. However, the authors emphasize that "Developing an industrial park is not a quick fix for a sluggish economy." The book is an excellent guide to organizing the development of such a park and assessing the progress of development.

Starr, Paul. *The Limits of Privatization*, Economic Development Institute, Washington, D.C., 1988

Not a politically conservative treatise, this brief essay attempts to show the set of circumstances in which privatization is the best option. The author suggests, "The choice is not public or private but which of the many possible mixed public-private structures works best." The subjects include privatization of public schools, national parks, water works, fire departments, public transportation, infrastructure, and other traditionally government activities.

Sultan, P., and Harrick, E., "Labor 'Climate': Perspectives on Labor in an Economic Development Program," *Economic Development Review*, Summer, 1987, page 10.

The contribution of labor to U.S. economic competitiveness as well as local economic growth is the subject of this essay. The authors have not performed any new research for this article but their perspective on the subject is informed by knowledge of a diverse group of subjects: psychology, sociology, labor statistics, business administration, and the study of negotiation, which cuts across subject-matter lines. Their observations are often very good and they are couched in terms a layman can easily understand.

Tyler, N., "Evaluating the Health of Downtowns: A Survey of Small Michigan Communities," *Small Town*, Vol. 20, No. 2, September-October 1989, page 4.

Eight Michigan towns with populations ranging from 5,000 to 10,000 were studied for this published version of a doctoral dissertation in Architecture and Urban Planning at University of Michigan. Downtown business owners, city officials, and other individuals were interviewed and given a questionnaire on the city's current, past, and future physical, economic, social, and political conditions. The existence of a planning proposal, good downtown organizations, building rehabilitation, and streetscaping were all mentioned as the top factors in improving downtowns by those interviewed.

United States Conference of Mayors, *Tapping Federal Laboratories and Universities to Improve Local Economies: The Role of the Mayor and City Government*, Washington, D.C., 1988.

Case studies of economic development in large cities plus good charts on the interaction of city government and business make this an excellent introduction to economic development for the city official. A functional approach for city officials is adopted by *Tapping Federal Laboratories*; the booklet suggests concrete actions mayors and other city officials can take to improve the economic climate of their city. In addition to federal labs and universities, the local economic development programs of the Small Business Administration are highlighted and fully described in the booklet.

Urban Land Institute, *Downtown Development Handbook*, Washington, D.C., 1980.

Emphasizing the process of downtown development rather than the end result, this is a "how to" guide for the city official, city planner, or economic development director. The *Handbook* covers the real estate market, project initiation and implementation, site acquisition, as well as other basics. The appendices are especially useful sample contracts, ordinances, leasing agreements, and other actual documents for all the fundamentals are included.

White, N., *The Architecture Book*, New York, Alfred A. Knopf, 1976.

Those interested in downtown development or redevelopment but unfamiliar with architectural styles, or the theories behind urban development, will benefit from this lengthy dictionary. It is extremely comprehensive, beginning with a biography of the Finnish Architect Alvar Aalto and ending with a definition of "Zoophorus," "Early Greek cartoons; bas-relief animals in procession on a frieze; most famous at the Parthenon (but on anyone else's frieze as well)."

Young, R.C., and Francis, J.D., "Who Helps Small Manufacturing Firms Get Started?" *Small Town*, Vol. 6, Issue 1, October 1989.

More than half of the new small manufacturers surveyed in this article received financial support from local, state, or federal government. Valuable information on finances, management practices, and the distinctions between high and low tech manufacturers are included in this article. The article is based on a study of 123 small manufacturers in rural, south, central New York state.

About the Contributors

Affiliations are as of the time the articles were written.

James M. Banovetz, Professor of Political Science and Public Administration, and Director of the Division of Public Administration, Northern Illinois University, De Kalb, Illinois.

William R. Barnes, Director of the Center for Research and Program Development, National League of Cities, Washington, D.C.

Philip Benowitz, Partner, Deloitte & Touche, Parsippany, New Jersey.

Hamilton Brown, Director of Training & Technical Assistance, National Center for Small Communities, Washington, D.C.

Robert Campbell, Contributing Editor, *Preservation*, National Trust for Historic Preservation, Washington, D.C.

James Carras, President, Carras Associates, Boston, Massachusetts.

Chris Dimond, Vice President and National Director of Urban Design and Planning, HNTB Corporation, Kansas City, Missouri.

Drew A. Dolan, Assistant Professor of Public Administration and Urban Affairs, Department of Urban Affairs and Geography, Wright State University, Dayton, Ohio.

John W. Dorsett, Principal, Walker Parking Consultants, Indianapolis, Indiana.

Cheryl Farr, Office Director, West Coast Region, International City/County Management Association, Washington, D.C.

John M. Fernandez, Director of Information Services, Department of Community Planning and Development, City of Boulder, Boulder, Colorado.

Al Gobar, President, Alfred Gobar Associates, Placentia, California.

Kelsey Gray, Organization Specialist, Cooperative Extension, Washington State University, Pullman, Washington.

John E. Greuling, Executive Director, Chamber of Commerce and Economic Development, Bloomington-Normal Area, Bloomington, Indiana.

Rob Gurwitt, Correspondent, *Governing*, Congressional Quarterly, Inc., Washington, D.C.

Kurt Hahn, Director, Department of Financial and Economic Services, City of Healdsburg, Healdsburg, California.

Gerrit J. Knaap, Associate Professor, Department of Urban and Regional Planning, University of Illinois, Urbana, Illinois.

Jerry Knox, Associate Professor, Department of Community and Regional Planning, Iowa State University, Ames, Iowa.

419

Warren Kriesel, Assistant Professor, Agricultural and Applied Economics, University of Georgia, Athens, Georgia.

Steven Lagerfeld, Deputy Editor, *The Wilson Quarterly*, Woodrow Wilson International Center, Washington, D.C.

Larry C. Ledebur, Director, Center for Urban Affairs, Wayne State University, Detroit, Michigan.

Kathleen Les, Principal, Les-Thomas Associates, Sacramento, California, and Downtown Coordinator, City of Davis, Davis, California.

Charles Lockwood, Author, Los Angeles, California.

Tom Majors, Office of Economic Development, Cobb County, Marietta, Georgia.

Deborah M. Markley, Rural Development Economist and Private Consultant, West Lafayette, Indiana.

Edward M. Marshall, President, Marshall & Associates, Inc., Washington, D.C.

Virginia M. Mayer, Senior Staff Associate and Manager of the Economic Development Program, National League of Cities, Washington, D.C.

Kevin T. McNamara, Assistant Professor and Rural Development Economist, Department of Agricultural Economics, Purdue University, West Lafayette, Indiana.

Jonathan D. Miller, Senior Vice President, Equitable Real Estate Investment Management, Inc., Minneapolis/St. Paul, Minnesota.

J. Virgil Moon, Director of Finance/Comptroller, Cobb County, Marietta, Georgia.

John Mullen, Professor, Department of Landscape Architecture and Regional Planning, University of Massachusetts, Amherst, Massachusetts.

Pat Noyes, State Coordinator, California Main Street Program, Sacramento, California.

Myron Orfield, Adjunct Professor, School of Law, University of Minnesota, Minneapolis, St. Paul, Minnesota.

Dolores P. Palma, President, HyettPalma Inc., Alexandria, Virginia.

Manon Pavy, Research Assistant, College of Urban and Public Affairs, University of New Orleans, New Orleans, Louisiana.

Adam J. Prager, Senior Manager, Deloitte & Touche, Chicago, Illinois.

David E. Proctor, Associate Professor and Head, Department of Speech, Kansas State University, Manhattan, Kansas.

Barbara Ryder, Associate Professor, Department of Horticulture and Landscape Architecture, Washington State University, Pullman, Washington.

Marina Sampanes, Senior Associate, Carras Associates, Boston, Massachusetts.

Robert Schein, Senior Manager, Deloitte & Touche, Parsippany, New Jersey.

Ron Shaffer, Professor of Agricultural Economics, University of Wisconsin, Madison, Wisconsin.

Alison Simon, Doctoral Student, Department of Urban and Regional Planning, University of Illinois, Urbana, Illinois.

Bradley Skelcher, Associate Professor, Department of History and Political Science, Delaware State College, Dover, Delaware.

Kennedy Smith, Program Manager, Communications and Education, National Main Street Center, National Trust for Historic Preservation, Washington, D.C.

Nancy Stark, Director of Community & Economic Development, National Center for Small Communities, Washington, D.C.

Diane Suchman, Project Director, Grand Forks Panel, Urban Land Institute, Washington, D.C.

John W. Swain, Assistant Professor, Department of Political Science, University of Alabama, Tuscaloosa, Alabama.

Fritz Wagner, Professor and Dean, College of Urban and Public Affairs, University of New Orleans, New Orleans, Louisiana.

Leah E. White, Doctoral Student, Department of Communication, Arizona State University, Tempe, Arizona.

Nancy Williams, Director, External Programs, GTE Telephone Operations, Irving, Texas.

Bert Winterbottom, Principal, LDR International, Inc., Columbia, Maryland.

Index